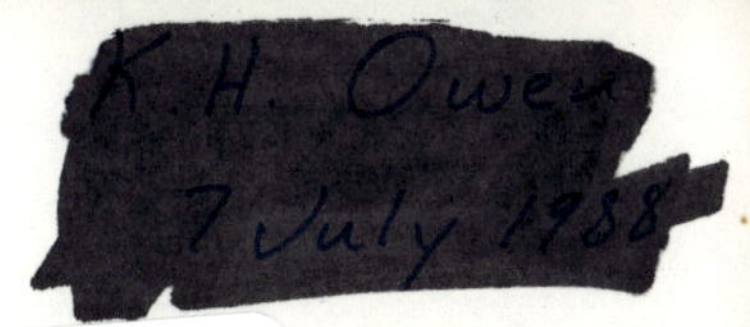

Advanced Assembly Language on the IBM PC

Also by Steven Holzner:

Creating Utilities with Assembly Language: 10 Best for the IBM PC & XT

Advanced Assembly Language on the IBM PC

Steven Holzner

A Brady Book
Published by Prentice Hall Press
New York, New York 10023

A Brady Book
Published by Prentice Hall Press
A Division of Simon & Schuster, Inc.
Gulf + Western Building
One Gulf + Western Plaza
New York, New York 10023

Manufactured in the United States of America

2 3 4 5 6 7 8 9 10

Library of Congress Cataloging-in-Publication Data

Holzner, Steven.
Advanced Assembly Language on the IBM PC.

"A Brady book."
Includes index.
1. IBM Personal Computer—Programming.
2. Assembler language (Computer program
language) I. Title.
QA76.8.I2594H646 1987 005.265 87—2382

ISBN 0-89303-633-1

Dedication

To Doug and Ellie

Contents

Limits of Liability and Disclaimer of Warranty

Trademarks

Foreword

In this book we assume that you already have a little bit of background. Perhaps you've picked up the basics of assembly language on your own, or perhaps you've read a book. In either case, we start at the level an introductory book might finish, taking for granted that you have a grasp of the essentials—and you want to learn more.

Introductory texts are good to get you started. But they are, after all, just the beginning. Introductory texts have no time for memory-resident code, no time for the 8087, macros, fast bit-by-bit graphics or interrupt handlers. Usually, this kind of knowledge takes a more advanced book.

Despite the popularity of assembly language on the PC, there have been no advanced assembler books published until recently. The only texts published have been introductory ones. Too often, these books are just dry catalogs of commands, more like dictionaries than learning aids. Reading them is like learning to fly by reading about plane construction.

There is no substitute for the real thing—seeing your code work. For that reason, this book will be as practical as possible, and as filled with examples as we can make it.

Also, many introductory texts skim over the system resources— the BIOS and DOS services—without going into detail. Since it is essential that an assembly language programmer know what the system resources offer, we will cover them fully. Appendix A is specially put aside as a reference section, listing all interrupts from 0 to FFH.

HOW THIS BOOK IS ORGANIZED

This book is organized functionally around the different parts of the machine—there are chapters on the disk drives, on the display, and so forth. This functional approach works better than simple catalogs of instructions, which leave people without the ability to connect what they have learned into a functioning whole. At the end of most chapters, there is a larger program that uses the concepts of the chapter in some application. These are intended to provide large-scale illustrations of the code in practice, and to supply working utilities.

Thoughout the book, we will use the IBM Macro Assembler Version 2.0 (very similar to the MicroSoft Assembler) and DOS 2+. If you have an earlier version of the Macro Assembler, all the code we write here will still work—except for the code written for the 8087 and SALUT (both new in Version 2.0). Also,

LIB.EXE, IBM's very useful library utility, is not provided in earlier versions. Using MASM 2.0 is not essential; the only real advances in Version 2.0 were the additions of 8087 instructions, SALUT, and improved error checking. If, however, you are using a version of DOS before 2.0, we strongly suggest you upgrade to a more current version.

Keep in mind that this is an advanced book and, for that reason, we will work at a pace a little faster than that of introductory books. Since our emphasis will be on writing working programs, we will start with the fundamental process of writing a program—where to use PROC, where to use ENDS, whether you need a stack or not, and so on. Many beginning texts never actually include programs you can simply type in, so this is our best starting point.

THE DISKETTE

This book comes with a diskette that contains both the code and executable files to match the example programs at the end of each chapter. The use of this diskette is recommended with this book, because each program corresponds to a particular chapter and topic. Rather than typing in the entire program yourself, it is much easier to simply use the diskette. You can order the diskette with the order form in this book. Appendix C covers the contents of the diskette.

Chapter 1

Writing a Program

INTRODUCTION

The first step toward seeing your code in action is being able to write programs. For that reason, this first chapter is devoted to a review of assembly language and a discussion of writing assembly language programs that work. Every piece of code you write will have to fit into a program of one sort or another to work at all, so this chapter will get us off the ground immediately. In addition, a number of concepts, such as segments, will be reviewed here to get us going.

THE FIRST PROGRAM

Let's start off with a program that you can simply type in and run. This program is a very simple one named PROTEC.ASM. It will change a file's attribute to Read-Only, which means that the file cannot be written to or deleted. The corresponding unprotect program, UNPROTEC.ASM, uses the same code except in the one line where the attribute is set. Both of these programs are small, and they are written to be made into .COM files. Assembling programs as .COM files rather than .EXE files makes them small and efficient in both code length and disk space.

The details, the instructions and their functions, of this program will become clear later in this chapter when we cover the **Program Segment Prefix** (PSP). What is important now is not the MOVs and INTs of PROTEC itself, but the way they are enclosed by the SEGMENT, PROC, ENDP, and ENDS statements. The one-line difference between PROTEC and UNPROTEC where different attributes (one to protect, zero to unprotect) are used is marked:

LISTING 1.1 PROTEC.ASM AND UNPROTEC.ASM

```
CODE_SEG            SEGMENT
          ASSUME    CS:CODE_SEG
          ORG       100H

PROTEC              PROC     NEAR
```

LISTING 1.1 CONTINUED

```
         MOV      DX,82H   ;Point DS:DX to filename
         MOV      DI,82H   ;Start looking in PSP
         MOV      AL,13    ;Look for carriage return
         MOV      CX,12    ;Scan up to 12 letters
REPNE    SCASB                         ;Find end of Input
         MOV      BYTE PTR [DI-1],0    ;Make string ASCIIZ
         MOV      AL,1     ;Function Code
       → MOV      CX,1     ;This is to protect
         MOV      AH,43H   ;Use Service 43H
         INT      21H      ; of INT 21H
         INT      20H      ;End the Program.
PROTEC            ENDP

CODE_SEG          ENDS
         END      PROTEC


------ UNPROTEC.ASM ------

CODE_SEG          SEGMENT
         ASSUME   CS:CODE_SEG
         ORG      100H

UNPROTEC          PROC     NEAR
         MOV      DX,82H   ;Point DS:DX to filename
         MOV      DI,82H   ;Start looking in PSP
         MOV      AL,13    ;Look for carriage return
         MOV      CX,12    ;Scan up to 12 letters
REPNE    SCASB                         ;Find end of Input
         MOV      BYTE PTR [DI-1],0    ;Make string ASCIIZ
         MOV      AL,1     ;Function Code
       → MOV      CX,0     ;This is to UNprotect.
         MOV      AH,43H   ;Use Service 43H
         INT      21H      ; of INT 21H
         INT      20H      ;End the Program.
UNPROTEC          ENDP

CODE_SEG          ENDS
         END      UNPROTEC
```

To enter PROTEC.ASM and UNPROTEC.ASM, type the code in with your word processor. (Don't type in the arrows.) In this case, name the two files PROTEC.ASM and UNPROTEC.ASM. To create PROTEC.COM, run PROTEC.ASM through these steps:

```
MASM    PROTEC;
LINK    PROTEC;
EXE2BIN PROTEC PROTEC.COM
```

The Macro assembler MASM will produce an object file named PROTEC.OBJ. The program LINK links this into an .EXE file, PROTEC.EXE. The linker will also produce a warning, indicating that PROTEC doesn't have a stack segment:

```
Warning: No STACK segment
```

.COM files don't need stack segments, however, so this warning is harmless. Even so, the linker still prints it out whenever it finds an .OBJ file without a stack segment. EXE2BIN (EXE to BINARY) converts PROTEC.EXE into PROTEC.COM. It is PROTEC.COM that we will run.

Running Our First Program

To protect a file named THISFILE.ASM from deletion or modification, all you have to do is type:

```
A>PROTEC  THISFILE.ASM
A>
```

THISFILE.ASM's attribute is now set as Read-Only, so that file cannot be deleted or overwritten. After creating UNPROTEC.COM, you can unprotect THISFILE.ASM with the corresponding command:

```
A>UNPROTEC THISFILE.ASM
A>
```

When the file is unprotected, you are free to delete or edit it again.

PROTEC uses DOS Interrupt 21H to set the protection of a file; since DOS does most of the work, we can keep our program small. Take a look at PROTEC.ASM and notice how everything is enclosed inside the segment CODE_SEG, and that the procedure itself is enclosed by the instructions PROTEC PROC NEAR and PROTEC ENDP.

MAKING .COM FILES

Except that it has no space for data, PROTEC is typical of .COM files. The most basic .COM file consists of one code segment enclosing one program. In Listing 1.2 there is a skeleton, or shell, of a .COM file, outlining its basic parts.

The program's name in this example is PROG_NAME. By looking at the skeleton, you can pick out the various parts of PROTEC. As we go on, this original shell will become more elaborate, and it will contain not only more procedures (PROG_NAME is the only one used here) but also different segments.

LISTING 1.2 A .COM FILE SHELL

```
CODE_SEG SEGMENT
         ASSUME CS:CODE_SEG,DS:CODE_SEG
         ORG 100H
ENTRY:   JMP PROG_NAME
         :
         Data here
         :
PROG_NAME PROC NEAR
         :
         :
         :
         Your program goes here
         :
         :
         :
INT 20H   ← Notice the Interrupt 20H used to finish the program
PROG_NAME ENDP
CODE_SEG ENDS
END ENTRY
```

Let's work through this skeleton line by line. The first statement is the start of the code segment in which the program will be placed, here named CODE_SEG:

```
→ CODE_SEG SEGMENT
           ASSUME CS:CODE_SEG,DS:CODE_SEG
           ORG 100H
    ENTRY: JMP PROG_NAME
           :
```

Segment Addresses

Everything we put into our programs will have to go into a segment of one sort or another, because our code is constrained by the architecture of the 8088. Addresses are always designated with two registers, such as CS:IP or DS:DX. To point to any address and fetch either data or code, two registers must always be set—a segment register and an offset register.

For that reason everything we do will be enclosed inside segments. The assembler will always know what segment we are referring to when we reference code or data this way.

ASSUME

When it's assembling our program, the assembler has no way of knowing how the segment registers will be set when the program runs. For example, if you wanted to look at the PC's internal clock at 0040:006C, your program would have to define a segment at 0040H and fill DS with that value. With SEGMENT, we were able to define a segment. With ASSUME, we will tell the assembler which of these defined segments will be pointed to by which segment registers. For this reason, you always have to provide a line like the next one in our .COM file shell:

```
CODE_SEG SEGMENT
       → ASSUME CS:CODE_SEG,DS:CODE_SEG
         ORG 100H
ENTRY:   JMP PROG_NAME
         :
```

This command is a **psuedo-OP**—a command to the assembler only. There are many pseudo-OPs available, but in this review we will only work with the ones necessary to write our .COM file. With this ASSUME, we are telling the assembler how CS and DS will be set. If we want to find the offset address of a label, the assembler will know that this address will be taken as an offset from the beginning of CODE_SEG.

The assembler relies on the ASSUME statements to be correct in generating code. Incorrect ASSUMES are one of the most common errors, yet often the most difficult to find.

Pseudo-OPs like ASSUME or SEGMENT produce no machine-executable code. They are only instructions to the assembler, telling it how certain registers will be set (ASSUME), where data will be placed (DB or DW), or where procedures start and end (PROC and ENDP). Macro instructions, which we will cover later, are also pseudo-Ops. 8088 instructions, like MOV CX,1, are different, because they do generate machine-executable code.

ORG 100H

The next line, ORG 100H, needs explanation as well:

```
CODE_SEG SEGMENT
         ASSUME CS:CODE_SEG,DS:CODE_SEG
       → ORG 100H
ENTRY:   JMP PROG_NAME
         :
```

This line is included in .COM files, but not in .EXE files. ORG tells the assembler where you are in a program—in particular, how IP is to be set.

ORG 100H tells the assembler we will now be assembling code that is to start 100H bytes into the program. If we use any labels, which will be translated into offsets, the assembler is to keep in mind that the beginning of our code is not location CS:0000 anymore, but location CS:0100. We do this in .COM files since we have to make room for the 256 byte (100H) Program Segment Prefix, the program's header that DOS provides. This prefix always starts at CS:0000. The executable code for all .COM files always starts just after the PSP, at CS:0100.

The Program Segment Prefix

When DOS loads your .COM file, say PROTEC.COM, into memory, it sets up a **program segment prefix**, or **PSP**, for it. A PSP is also set up for .EXE files, but with .COM files there is a special restriction: The PSP has to fit inside the one common segment. There is no such restriction with .EXE files, and we won't worry where the PSP is for them. All .COM files, however, must fit into one 64K space.

A typical .COM file in memory has a PSP from CS:0000 to CS:00FF, followed by the program at CS:0100. When the .COM file is loaded, all segment registers (CS, DS, ES, and SS) are set to the same common segment.

Even the stack, pointed to by SS:SP, has to be in the same segment. DOS sets up a stack for .COM files at the very end of the segment, and you should always take care not to overwrite this stack. In general, it is wise not to touch the last 256 bytes of the segment the .COM file has been given—addresses from CS:FF00 to CS:FFFF.

The PSP is 256 bytes long, and provides our program with as much help as DOS can give. This includes information about what was typed on the command line and other items. It is because of the restriction to one segment that our code will be placed after the PSP in memory. For this reason we put the pseudo-OP ORG 100H into the beginning of every .COM file.

The next command that the assembler sees after ORG 100H will be placed at CS:100H. This command is a jump:

```
CODE_SEG SEGMENT
          ASSUME CS:CODE_SEG,DS:CODE_SEG
          ORG 100H
→ ENTRY:  JMP PROG_NAME
          :
          :
          Data here
```

```
          :
PROG_NAME PROC NEAR
          :
          :
```

If we want to store data in our .COM file, we usually put it right at the beginning. The reason for this is that you should define your data labels before you reference them. Since .COM files always execute the instruction at 100H first, we make this instruction a jump over the data and go to the main procedure (JMP PROG_NAME). This way, the data is left undisturbed. When a .COM file is run, the 8088 will always be instructed to enter at CS:100H, and will always jump over the data to start the program:

```
   CODE_SEG SEGMENT
              ASSUME CS:CODE_SEG,DS:CODE_SEG
              ORG 100H
┌----ENTRY:   JMP PROG_NAME
|             :
|             The Data Area
|             :
└--→   PROG_NAME PROC NEAR
              :
```

Reserving space this way for our data is a little artificial, but it is convenient. It is the way .COM files are almost invariably written.

The Data

The assembler provides us with a number of ways of storing data, now that we've defined our data area. The data we want to supply our programs with can either be known ahead of time (like error messages or prompts that we want to type out), or not (like temporary storage for numbers our program is working on). Any space we set aside in memory can be given names so that we can reference those memory locations as variables in our program. The assembler converts those names into addresses when it assembles the program. Here are some examples of data storage, listed from the common to the more rare:

```
CODE_SEG SEGMENT
         ASSUME CS:CODE_SEG,DS:CODE_SEG
         ORG 100H
  ENTRY: JMP PROG_NAME
         APPLES  DB 3            ;One byte long, initialized to 3.
         ORANGES DB 5 DUP(0)     ;Five bytes, initialized to 0.
         STUFF   DB 1,2,3        ;Three bytes, set to 1,2,3 respectively.
         MESSAGE DB 'Disk full$' ;Ten bytes initialized with ASCII.
         ONEWORD DW ?            ;One word, not initialized.
         HRSINYR DW 24*365       ;This word set to the 8760 = 2238H.
```

```
          TWOWORD DW 2 DUP(ABCDH) ;Two words, both initialized to ABCDH.
          BIG     DD ?            ;A doubleword - can store addresses.
          BIGGER  DQ 'HI'         ;A QuadWord, two ASCII characters max.
          BIGGEST DT 'HO'         ;Ten bytes.
PROG_NAME PROC NEAR
          :
          :
          :
```

When .COM files are loaded into memory, they are loaded at the first available address that is a multiple of 16 bytes—a "paragraph" boundary in memory—by COMMMAND.COM. CS, DS, ES, and SS are all set to the same value. The assembler treats labels like APPLES and ORANGES as offsets from DS. Since DS is already set, we can just reference data labels defined in our data area like this:

```
CODE_SEG SEGMENT
          ASSUME CS:CODE_SEG,DS:CODE_SEG
          ORG 100H
  ENTRY:  JMP PROG_NAME
          APPLES  DB 3          ;One byte long, initialized to 3.
          ORANGES DB 5 DUP(0)   ;Five bytes, initialized to 0.
          :
PROG_NAME PROC NEAR
        → MOV     AX,APPLES
        → CMP     AX,ORANGES
        → MOV     ORANGES,AX
          :
```

If APPLES and ORANGES were in a different segment, we would have to set DS to that segment before referencing them.

We could print out the "Disk full" message using DOS' string printing service, service 9, of Interrupt 21H by first pointing DS:DX like this:

```
CODE_SEG SEGMENT
          ASSUME CS:CODE_SEG,DS:CODE_SEG
          ORG 100H
  ENTRY:  JMP PROG_NAME
          :
          MESSAGE DB 'Disk full$'
          :
  PROG_NAME PROC NEAR
        → LEA     DX,MESSAGE
        → MOV     AH,9
        → INT     21H
```

"Disk full" would appear on the screen (the '$' is used by service 9 as an end-of-string marker, telling it when the string ends). The command LEA DX, MESSAGE loads the effective address (the offset address) of MESSAGE into DX. Since we are working in a .COM file, DS is already set to the one and only segment.

When the assembler assembles the code, it will automatically store an address for the label MESSAGE. For example, if MESSAGE is three bytes into the program, LEA would find that MESSAGE is 103H bytes from DS:0000, and MESSAGE would be replaced with the address 103H. The code actually generated in the .OBJ file would look like this to the 8088:

```
LEA     DX,103H
MOV     AH,9
INT     21H
```

Besides bytes, of course, we can store words with DW, Define Word. The DD pseudo-OP, Define Doubleword, is less frequently used, but it is still often used to store two-word addresses.

The remaining two pseudo-OPs, Define Quadword (DQ) and Define Tenbytes (DT), are used primarily to store either large numbers or floating point notation. For example, with DQ you can store integers up to a whopping 18446744073709551615. Although you can store arbitrarily long ASCII codes byte by byte with an expression like:

```
MSG     DB      'Fatal Error! Look Out!'
```

it is worth noticing that the largest ASCII argument you can give to DW, DQ, or DT is two ASCII characters. DB "AB" will produce the ASCII code for "A" and then "B" in your code. DW "AB", however, will produce "B" first and then "A" in usual reverse order of low-byte, high-byte storage. (If you don't know what this means, it will be covered soon.) DQ "AB" will give you "B", then "A", then three words of zeros. DT "AB" will give "B", then "A", then eight bytes of zeros.

It is also worth noticing that although labels can be as long as you like, the assembler will only recognize the first 31 characters.

The Test Procedure in the .COM File

Let's continue down the .COM file shell with the procedure itself, which is the integral part of all .COM files.

```
  ENTRY:  JMP PROG_NAME
          :
          Data here
          :
→ PROG_NAME PROC NEAR
          :
          :
          :
          Program code goes here
          :
```

```
                :
                :
        INT 20H
PROG_NAME ENDP
```

The pseudo-OPs PROC and ENDP define a procedure.

In fact, PROC just defines a label, and the NEAR or FAR attribute associated with it can be associated with any label as well. The procedure TEST:

```
  CODE_SEG          SEGMENT
          ORG       100H
  START:  JMP       TEST
          (Data)
          :
→ TEST         PROC      NEAR
               MOV       AX,1
               INT       20H
  TEST         ENDP
  CODE_SEG          ENDS
        END       START
```

could have just as well been constructed using a NEAR label (that is, one with a colon after it). This code will generate the same .COM file:

```
     CODE_SEG          SEGMENT
             ORG       100H
     START:  JMP       TEST
             (Data)
             :
→ TEST:      MOV       AX,1
             INT       20H
     CODE_SEG          ENDS
             END       START
```

but using PROC and ENDP help keep order in large amounts of code.

In a .COM file, all procedures, including the main one, must be declared NEAR because a .COM file is limited to one segment. NEAR labels are intrasegment labels. A NEAR jump only uses the lower word of the label's address, the offset. In .EXE files, you can have FAR jumps because you can deal with multiple 64K areas, that is, multiple segments. In .EXE files, you could use the label TEST PROC FAR, and then call TEST from another segment (intersegment jumps). A FAR jump or call instruction uses both words of the destinations label's address.

Ending Your Program

Our procedure TEST ends with INT 20H, the way our .COM files will usually end. This interrupt passes control back to DOS. Another common way of ending procedures is with the command RET:

```
CODE_SEG            SEGMENT
         ORG        100H
START:   JMP        TEST
         (Data)
         :
TEST         PROC       NEAR
             MOV        AX,1
→            RET
TEST         ENDP
CODE_SEG            ENDS
         END        START
```

When .COM files are loaded, the stack pointer, SP, is set to the top of the available segment, and then a word of 0000 is pushed, leaving SP at FFFEH. When you have a RET at the end of a program, the word of zeros is popped off the stack and put into IP. Control is transferred to CS:IP (to CS:0000), the very first byte in the PSP. The first two bytes of every PSP, for any program, are always CDH 20H, machine code for INT 20H. RET at the end of .COM file therefore sends control back to the beginning of the PSP where an INT 20H is executed. This method is the same as including INT 20H at the end of your program.

In .EXE files, this word of zeros is not pushed onto the stack and, as we shall see, you have to put it on yourself at the beginning of each program.

Another way of ending programs that we will use is INT 27H, the terminate-but-stay-resident interrupt. Before finishing, we will load the address of the end of the program into DS:DX, and execute INT 27H. All the code from CS:0000 to the address DS:DX will then be held resident in memory by DOS. New programs that are to be run will be loaded in memory after the end of the resident program. In a very practical way, we will be able to modify DOS this way.

USING MORE THAN ONE PROCEDURE

Frequently, we will want to break massive, unwieldy sections of code up into more reasonable and manageable sections. For this purpose, high level languages like FORTRAN provide PROCEDUREs, SUBROUTINEs and FUNCTIONs, but in assembly language we only use another PROC. For instance, if we had a program that was to search all files in a given subdirectory for a particular string, it might look like this in outline:

```
  CODE_SEG         SEGMENT
          ORG      100H
  START:  JMP      TEST
          (Data)
          :
  FIND        PROC     NEAR
  NEW_FILE:
→             CALL     GET_FILE
              [-- Is the string we want in it? --]
              JE   YES
              JMP  NEW_FILE           ;No matches, get new file
  YES:        [-- Print file's name --]   ;Match! Print filename
              INT  20H
  FIND        ENDP

→ GET_FILE    PROC     NEAR
→                    [-- Find next file in the directory --]
→                    [-- Read it in --]
→                    RET
→ GET_FILE    ENDP

  CODE_SEG         ENDS
          END      START
```

Here we can safely put all the code to find a new file on the disk and read it into a subroutine named GET_FILE. Whenever we need a new file to search, we only need to call GET_FILE. When we do, control transfers to the first line in the subroutine GET_FILE. The entire subroutine is executed, and the RET instruction at the very end sends control back up to the line right after CALL GET_FILE in the procedure FIND.

Finishing the Code Segment

The last thing we'll do in Listing 1.2 is finish the code segment. The assembler is expecting to see everything inside some segment, and it must also be told when we are through with a given segment. To close a segment, we use the pseudo-OP SEGMENT's counterpart, ENDS, which means End Segment. In our case, it looks like this:

```
CODE_SEG SEGMENT
        ASSUME CS:CODE_SEG,DS:CODE_SEG
        ORG 100H
ENTRY:  JMP PROG_NAME
        :
```

```
          Data here
          :
PROG_NAME PROC NEAR
          :
          :
          :
          Your program goes here
          :
          :
          :
INT 20H ← Notice the Interrupt 20H used to finish the program
PROG_NAME ENDP
→ CODE_SEG ENDS
END ENTRY
```

In fact, however, you can still include labels outside segments. For example, the Disk Cache program we will include later stores the data from disk sectors at the end of the whole program—not in the Data area normally used—by using a label like this:

```
          :
          :
          Your program goes here
          :
          :
          :
INT 20H ← Notice the Interrupt 20H used to finish the program
PROG_NAME ENDP
CODE_SEG ENDS
→ DATA:
END ENTRY
```

This label can still be referred to by the program PROG_NAME. Using labels outside well-defined segments is a tricky business, however, and not usually done.

The END Pseudo-OP

The very last line, END ENTRY:

```
CODE_SEG SEGMENT
         ASSUME CS:CODE_SEG,DS:CODE_SEG
         ORG 100H
ENTRY:   JMP PROG_NAME
         :
         Data here
         :
PROG_NAME PROC NEAR
         :
         :
         :
         Your program goes here
         :
```

```
            :
            :
    INT 20H ← Notice the Interrupt 20H used to finish the program
    PROG_NAME ENDP
    CODE_SEG ENDS
  → END ENTRY
```

is the last pseudo-OP to the assembler that we will give. END tells the assembler to stop assembling, and the label ENTRY means that we want the 8088 to enter the program at the label ENTRY (at 100H). The entry point is the location in the program of the first instruction to be executed. There is only one entry point in any .COM or .EXE file. The location of a program's entry point is stored in the header of an .EXE file on disk, but in a .COM file, which has no header, it is always assumed to be 100H. In an .EXE file, you can set the entry point wherever you want it.

If you intend to make a file into a .COM file, you assemble and link it, and then pass it in the form of an .EXE file to EXE2BIN. If EXE2BIN does not find the specified entry point to be at 100H, it will give you the terse error message:

```
File cannot be converted.
```

which has given many programmers trouble. Using a line like END ENTRY and labeling the location at 100H as ENTRY solves the problem. When DOS enters at this point, it will immediately see the line:

```
ENTRY:   JMP PROG_NAME
```

As in most undertakings, now that you've seen it done there is little need to memorize the rules. If you want to write a .COM file, you can simply use the outline or shell.

This is one facet of programming that deserves stress throughout the book. Once you've got a working framework, it can be made into a foundation for other projects.

.EXE FILES VS .COM FILES

The other type of directly executable file that DOS supports is the .EXE file. Let's say a .COM file has been loaded at address AAAA:0000. When it runs, its code is limited to the region AAAA:0000 to AAAA:FFFF, or 64K memory bytes. .EXE files, on the other hand, can be large and can spread code and data over several segments.

All jumps or calls in .COM files only need to know the offset that they are to jump to—the segment address never changes. For this reason, a .COM file is ready to run right after the EXE2BIN stage.

In .EXE files, however, there can be calls from segment to segment, and so these FAR commands need additional information. In particular, FAR commands inside .EXE files need to know the full segment and offset addresses they are to call or jump to.

When DOS loads an .EXE file, it can be put almost anywhere in memory, at any segment address. Therefore, DOS must then **relocate** the code by fixing up all FAR commands to contain the proper segment addresses of their destinations. For that reason, a header is included at the beginning of every .EXE file. This header's length varies from file to file, but it is never less than the 28 bytes seen in Figure 1.1. After these 28 bytes, the addresses of FAR instructions that must be fixed up are stored.

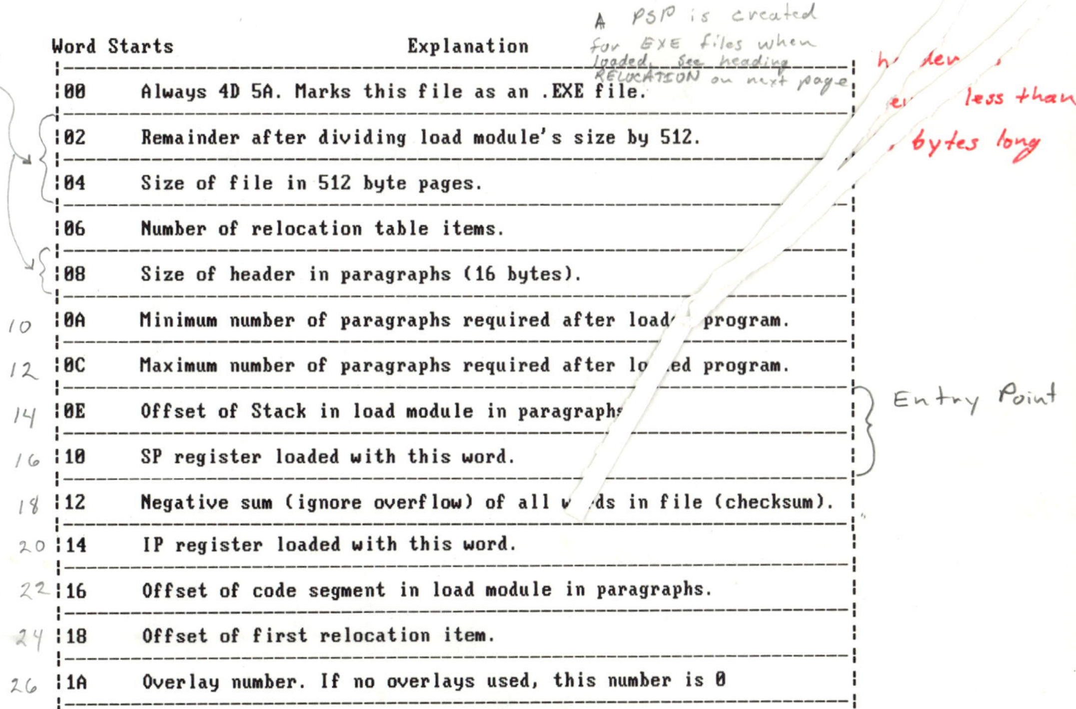

Word Starts	Explanation
00	Always 4D 5A. Marks this file as an .EXE file.
02	Remainder after dividing load module's size by 512.
04	Size of file in 512 byte pages.
06	Number of relocation table items.
08	Size of header in paragraphs (16 bytes).
0A	Minimum number of paragraphs required after loaded program.
0C	Maximum number of paragraphs required after loaded program.
0E	Offset of Stack in load module in paragraphs.
10	SP register loaded with this word.
12	Negative sum (ignore overflow) of all words in file (checksum).
14	IP register loaded with this word.
16	Offset of code segment in load module in paragraphs.
18	Offset of first relocation item.
1A	Overlay number. If no overlays used, this number is 0

Figure 1.1 .EXE File Header

In this book, we will never have occasion to develop files so large that they need to use the .EXE format. We will discuss .EXE files further later, but mostly we will use the much more convenient and common .COM files. .COM files are shorter, more compact, and can be made memory resident. They keep everything under control because only your code is there—no extras are added by DOS in a header. This is the level where you really have control of your PC. Nonetheless, sometimes using an .EXE file is unavoidable, so we'll review how they work, and what the header contains.

Relocation

Here's how the process of loading and relocating an .EXE file works: first, a Program Segment Prefix is built in the lowest available paragraph boundary. The first part of the .EXE file's header is read in and the size of the complete header is read from bytes 8–9. This size is stored in paragraphs, in units of 16 bytes, rounded up. A 33-byte header would have a three stored here (33/16, rounded up).

The size of the actual code that will run, the **load module**, is found from the difference of the total .EXE file size (calculated from bytes 2–5) and the header size (already found in bytes 8–9). A segment, called the **start segment**, is found in memory such that there will be enough space to take the load module. After the load module is loaded into memory,the **relocation table**—the addresses of commands in the load module that have to be modified—is examined.

For each command in the load module that needs to be fixed, there is a two-word address in the relocation table giving that command's location from the beginning of the load module. The command at that address is found, and the start segment is added to the address the command already contains. This process continues until the code is fully relocated and the program is ready to run. All the FAR jumps and calls are set up properly at this point.

That is how relocation works. Although it is simple enough, it is still a complication that we would like to avoid, so we will use .COM files wherever we can.

An .EXE File Shell

In Listing 1.3 there is an .EXE file shell. All the parts of this shell appear in almost all .EXE files.

LISTING 1.3 .EXE FILE SHELL

```
        DATA_SEG        SEGMENT
                :
                Your Data Goes Here
                :
        DATA_SEG        ENDS
```

LISTING 1.3 CONTINUED

```
        CODE_SEG            SEGMENT
                ASSUME      CS:CODE_SEG,SS:STACK
        PROG_NAME           PROC     FAR
                PUSH        DS
                XOR         AX,AX
                PUSH        AX
                MOV         AX,DATA_SEG
                MOV         DS,AX
                ASSUME         DS:DATA_SEG
                :
                The Program Goes Here
                :
                :
                RET
        PROG_NAME           ENDP
        CODE_SEG            ENDS

 STACK      SEGMENT PARA STACK 'STACK'
      DB      100 DUP(?)
 STACK      ENDS
        END      PROG_NAME
```

In .EXE files, we are not limited to one segment, so we do not have to fit the data in after a jump at ORG 100H. In fact, we don't need a special command at ORG 100H at all, since an .EXE file can set the entry point to be anywhere (the entry point is stored in bytes 14–17 of the header). END PROG_NAME at the end of the .ASM file would, for example, set the entry point to PROG_NAME. In .EXE files, we can have a special segment for the data alone, which we'll call DATA_SEG:

```
→ DATA_SEG          SEGMENT
          :
          Your Data Goes Here
          :
  DATA_SEG          ENDS

  CODE_SEG          SEGMENT
          ASSUME    CS:CODE_SEG,SS:STACK
  PROG_NAME         PROC     FAR
          PUSH      DS
          XOR       AX,AX
          PUSH      AX
          MOV       AX,DATA_SEG
```

All the data we will use in this program goes here, labeled as in .COM files, for example:

```
  DATA_SEG            SEGMENT
→           APPLES    DB       1
→           ORANGES   DB       5
  DATA_SEG            ENDS
```

In order to work directly with these numbers, however, we have to be sure that the Data Segment register (DS) is set correctly and points to DATA_SEG. This is one of the first things we will do in the code itself. It is always advisable to keep the data segment first, however, since the assembler should know the names of these labels before they are referenced in the program.

After the data segment comes the code segment:

```
  DATA_SEG            SEGMENT
            :
            Your Data Goes Here
            :
  DATA_SEG            ENDS

→ CODE_SEG            SEGMENT
            ASSUME    CS:CODE_SEG,SS:STACK
  PROG_NAME           PROC     FAR
            PUSH      DS
            XOR       AX,AX
            PUSH      AX
            MOV       AX,DATA_SEG
            MOV       DS,AX
            ASSUME       DS:DATA_SEG
            :
            The Program Goes Here
            :
```

When .COM files are loaded, all segment registers get set to the same value picked by the loader, COMMAND.COM. In .EXE files, the procedure is more complex. DS and ES are set to the segment of the PSP. Since you can place the stack anywhere you want, the stack segment's location in the load module is stored in the header (bytes E–11). SS and SP are loaded from this information, after the start segment is added to SS. Since the code and entry points are also up to you, CS and IP are loaded from values given in the header (bytes 14H–17H), after adding the start segment to CS. Therefore, the next line in our .EXE file shell is an ASSUME that looks like this:

```
  CODE_SEG            SEGMENT
→           ASSUME    CS:CODE_SEG,SS:STACK
  PROG_NAME           PROC     FAR
            PUSH      DS
            XOR       AX,AX
            PUSH      AX
            MOV       AX,DATA_SEG
```

```
MOV      DS,AX
ASSUME      DS:DATA_SEG
:
The Program Goes Here
:
```

We will need the segment address of the PSP, which is in DS right now, so we haven't used an ASSUME for DS yet. After setting CS and SS, we can start the procedure properly. Once again, we will use the name PROG_NAME for our program. The declaration of our main program is the same as in .COM files, except here the procedure must be declared FAR, just as in .COM files it must be NEAR:

```
CODE_SEG            SEGMENT
        ASSUME      CS:CODE_SEG,SS:STACK
PROG_NAME           PROC     FAR
        PUSH        DS
        XOR         AX,AX
        PUSH        AX
        MOV         AX,DATA_SEG
        MOV         DS,AX
        ASSUME         DS:DATA_SEG
        :
        The Program Goes Here
        :
```

The Stack in .EXE Files

In .COM files, the stack is all set up for you, and a word of zeroes is pushed already. When you return to DOS with RET, control can jump to CS:0000, where there is an INT 20H instruction waiting. A RET at the end of a FAR procedure will pop two words off the stack (at the end of a NEAR procedure, only one would be popped). In .EXE files you have to prime the stack yourself, customarily done with these commands:

```
CODE_SEG            SEGMENT
        ASSUME      CS:CODE_SEG,SS:STACK
PROG_NAME           PROC     FAR
        PUSH        DS
        XOR         AX,AX
        PUSH        AX
        MOV         AX,DATA_SEG
        MOV         DS,AX
        ASSUME         DS:DATA_SEG
        :
        The Program Goes Here
        :
```

Since DS contains the segment of the PSP, it is pushed first. Next, AX is set to zero with the fancy instruction XOR AX,AX. XOR is the exclusive-OR command; it works just like an OR command except that the result is zero when XORing two ones:

XOR	0	1
0	0	1
1	1	0

Whenever you XOR any number with itself, zeros always meet zeros and ones always meet ones, to give a net answer of zero. MOV AX,0 could have worked here as well, but professional programmers often use XOR since it is faster. After AX is zeroed, it too is pushed on the stack so that control will return to the first byte of the PSP, DS:0000.

DS is still set to the default value of the PSP, not to the DATA_SEG segment we have defined. To point DS properly, we use these commands:

```
CODE_SEG              SEGMENT
          ASSUME      CS:CODE_SEG,SS:STACK
PROG_NAME             PROC     FAR
          PUSH        DS
          XOR         AX,AX
          PUSH        AX
          MOV         AX,DATA_SEG
          MOV         DS,AX
          ASSUME         DS:DATA_SEG
          :
          The Program Goes Here
          :
```

following with an ASSUME DS:DATA_SEG to the assembler. After these commands, the program is written as usual, no differently than the ones we would write in a .COM file. The procedure PROG_NAME ends with a RET instruction and a PROG_NAME ENDP. The code segment also finishes with an ENDS:

```
CODE_SEG              SEGMENT
          ASSUME      CS:CODE_SEG,SS:STACK
PROG_NAME             PROC     FAR
          PUSH        DS
          XOR         AX,AX
          PUSH        AX
          MOV         AX,DATA_SEG
          MOV         DS,AX
          ASSUME         DS:DATA_SEG
          :
          The Program Goes Here
```

```
                    :
                    :
      →             RET
      → PROG_NAME          ENDP
      → CODE_SEG           ENDS
STACK        SEGMENT PARA STACK 'STACK'
     DB        100 DUP(?)
STACK        ENDS
       END        PROG_NAME
```

The final segment in our .EXE shell is the STACK segment. In .COM files, DOS sets up the stack for you, but in .EXE files you must do it yourself. Here we use these commands:

```
STACK        SEGMENT PARA STACK 'STACK' ←
     DB        100 DUP(?)               ←
STACK        ENDS                       ←
       END        PROG_NAME
```

The customary defining line of the stack segment deserves to be examined:

```
STACK        SEGMENT PARA STACK 'STACK'
```

Here we can see a few of the options available with the pseudo-OP SEGMENT. The label and the pseudo-OP SEGMENT we have already seen, but the additional instructions PARA STACK 'STACK' will take a little more explaining.

The command PARA is an **align-type specifier**. Other align-types are BYTE, WORD, and PAGE. PARA, the default align-type, simply specifies that this segment should start at an address that is a multiple of 16 (10H); in other words, at some paragraph boundary. The align-type BYTE means that the segment you are defining could start anywhere, WORD means that the segment should begin on a word boundary, and PAGE should start on a page boundary (256 bytes make up one page).

The next argument, STACK, indicates what type of segment you are defining. We will have more use for this argument, the **combine-type**, later. A combine-type of STACK is almost self-explanatory; it means that this segment is to be part of the stack of the run-time module. Another common combine-type is PUBLIC. If you define a segment to be public and then link the .OBJ file together with other .OBJ files containing PUBLIC segments, this segment will be concatenated to others of the same name. A third combine-type, COMMON, works very much like COMMON in FORTRAN. If you specify a COMMON combine-type, segments with the same name will be overlaid on top of each other. Many modules can have easy access to the same set of variables this way. Finally, if you use an argument of 'AT Address' such as:

```
DATA_SEG          SEGMENT AT 40H
```

you can define a segment starting at a specific address, such as 0040:0000 in this case.

AT AND .COM FILES

This way of defining a segment will be very important to us later because we will use this method frequently in our .COM files. If we want to enclose the BIOS data area at 0040:0000, we need only to define a segment around it. For example, in a .COM file, such a declaration may look like this:

```
→ DATA_SEG          SEGMENT AT 40H
          ORG       6CH
  TIMER_LOW         DW       ?          ;Clock low word
  TIMER_HIGH        DW       ?          ;Clock high word
  DATA_SEG          ENDS

  CODE_SEG          SEGMENT
          ASSUME    CS:CODE_SEG,DS:DATA_SEG
          ORG       100H
  ENTRY:  JUMP      PROGNAME
          :
  PROGNAME          PROC NEAR
          MOV       AX,DATA_SEG         ;Set up DS.
          MOV       DS,AX
          MOV       CX,TIMER_LOW
          :
          :
  CODE_SEG          ENDS
          END       ENTRY
```

Such a program would make a perfectly acceptable .COM file. At first it seems to break the .COM file's restriction to only one segment. But the prohibition was really only against the need to relocate code. If you know precisely where the bytes in memory that you want to work with are, the .COM file can be assembled with the full two-word addresses of those memory locations already in the code. In such cases, there is no need for relocation. We'll discuss this point more when we use it.

In other words, when the program references TIMER_LOW in the above .COM file shell, the assembler sees that DATA_SEG is defined at 40H, and that TIMER_LOW is at ORG 6CH, so it can substitute 0040:006CH for references to TIMER_LOW immediately. No relocation will be needed later. As soon as we know where the data we want to operate on is in memory, such as the PC's internal timer, the screen buffer, or the interrupt vector table, we only have to define a segment around it and .COM files can reach them, too.

The final argument in the STACK segment declaration of the .EXE file's skeleton is 'STACK':

```
STACK      SEGMENT PARA STACK 'STACK' ←
```

which is the class of the segment. We will not make explicit use of segment classes. A segment's class is an instruction to the linker, LINK.EXE, which will load all segments of the same class contiguously in the order in which they are encountered. We will not worry about linking multiple .OBJ files together until we reach Chapter 6.

After the stack segment, the .EXE file ends in the same way as .COM files end, with an END statement pointing to the entry point. Unlike .COM files, as we have said, .EXE files can be entered anywhere and so the line END PROG_NAME:

```
                    :
                    The Program Goes Here
                    :
                    :
                    RET
          PROG_NAME         ENDP
          CODE_SEG          ENDS

STACK      SEGMENT PARA STACK 'STACK'
     DB      100 DUP(?)
STACK     ENDS
       → END      PROG_NAME
```

does not have to point to an instruction at 100H. Since .COM files do not have the header that .EXE files do, it is assumed that .COM files will start right after the PSP in memory, at CS:100H.

THE PROGRAM SEGMENT PREFIX IN DETAIL

The Program Segment Prefix is one of the most useful things in assembly language programming. It is DOS' interface to your program. In both the file and disk handling of this book we will have something to say about the PSP.

A diagram of the PSP for any program is in Figure 1.2, and we will examine it in some detail. We will assume that this is a PSP for a .COM file,

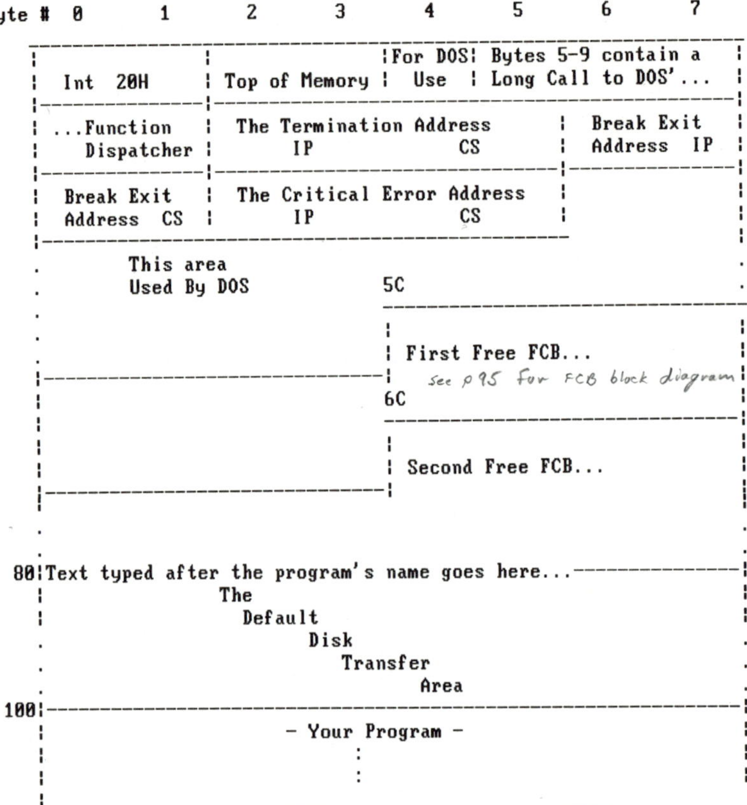

Figure 1.2 The Program Segment Prefix.

so that the PSP starts at CS:0000. Let's take the time to work through the PSP byte by byte.

Byte 0. As we have already seen, the first word of the PSP is CDH 20H, that is, the machine code for INT 20H. This command, at CS:0000, is usually the last command your program will execute.

Byte 2. The two bytes at locations CS:0002 and CS:0003 together form a word that gives you the location of the 'top of memory' in paragraphs; that is, the first segment not allocated to your program. A 2000H here would mean that the first available segment is 2000H, at address 2000:0000, or 128K. When a .COM file is loaded, it is allocated all available memory. The amount given to .EXE files depends on the minimum and maximum memory requirements, as given in the file's header. DOS keeps track of memory, and provides ways of allocating and deallocating sections of memory. If your program wants to load in other programs and run them, it must first make sure they will have adequate memory.

Bytes 5–9. These make up the stored machine code for a far jump to the DOS function dispatcher. This is the subroutine that dispatches your INT 21H call to various subprograms of that interrupt. DOS may make use of this call, but we will not. If you ever take the time to unassemble (using DEBUG) any portion of INT 21H, you will find several far jumps to this same address. The two bytes starting at CS:0006—part of the above five bytes—tells you the amount of free space left in the segment.

Byte 0AH. At CS:000A there is a two-word address, stored as IP:CS. This and all following addresses in the PSP are stored in the typical IBM PC memory fashion. Words are stored with their low bytes lower in memory, and high bytes higher. A pseudo-OP such as DW 1234H, therefore, leaves 34H 12H in memory, not 12H 34H.

The two words of an address are stored with the low word lower in memory (such as IP in CS:IP) and the higher word higher. An address such as the one for the DOS function dispatcher, F00D:FFF0, is stored as: F0 FF 0D F0. If you are not familiar with this reverse method of memory storage, it will take a little getting used to.

The two-word address at CS:000A is the Terminate Address. This is the address control will be returned to when the program is finished. Starting with DOS 2.0, programs can load in other programs and run them. When such a subprocess is done, control should return to the program that loaded it, not directly to DOS. By using this address, subprocesses can return to the calling process. In fact, you can change this address yourself and bypass DOS entirely when your program is done. This can lead to some interesting results in chaining programs together, if you are intrepid.

Byte 0EH. Following this address are two more addresses at locations CS:000E and CS:0012, also stored as IP:CS. The address at CS:000E is the Control Break Exit address. If you press a Ctrl-Break while your program is running, control will be sent to this address. If you want to add your own Ctrl-Break handler, you can change this address. You could, for example, add some diagnostics to your program that would be printed whenever a Ctrl-Break is typed.

Byte 12H. The address stored at CS:0012 is the Critical Error exit address. This error handler is supposed to intercept and inform you of hardware problems. Usually, this means disk problems. The familiar message: "Write Protect Error writing Drive A. Abort, Retry, Ignore?" comes from this error handler. If you want to handle errors yourself, you can change this address to point to part of your program's code. You will be able to tell what is wrong by the contents of the registers.

Byte 16H. The part of the PSP from CS:0016 to CS:005C is reserved for use by DOS. Most of this area is set to zero when your program is first loaded, ready to be used.

Byte 2CH. At CS:002C, you will find the segment address of the *environment string*. For example, if the bytes 08 09 appear here, then your environment string is at 0908:0000. The environment string tells you how the PC's environment has been set up.

For example, a copy of the last PROMPT (changing the PC's prompt from A›) or PATH commands are stored here. If you see a string like: PROMPT = tg in the environment string, you know that the prompt has been set up to display the time of day like this: 12:34:56›. PROMPT = pg will display the current directory. The default is PROMPT = ng.

The COMSPEC string is also part of the environment string. COMSPEC, the **command file specification**, tells DOS where to find the file COMMAND.COM if it should need to load it in again. A string such as 'COMSPEC=A:\' will appear there, and you can change it if you wish.

The environment string is not used by most programs at all, and IBM has not fully developed its potential. On machines where extensive configuring is possible, though, this string has more meaning.

Byte 50H. Also in the DOS reserved area, at CS:0050, are the bytes CD 21, or machine code for INT 21H. Just like the CD 20 stored at CS:0000, DOS can easily issue an INT 21H interrupt this way.

File Control Blocks

The real parts of interest for us in the PSP start at CS:005C. There are two default File Control Blocks, FCBs, provided by DOS for your program, one at CS:005C and another at CS:006C. A File Control Block is to DOS what a filename is to us. When a file is opened, the current position in it, its length, its name, its type, and so on are all kept in the FCB. Although DOS 2+ still supports the use of FCBs, using **file handles** is now the preferred method of file handling. This will be covered in more detail in Chapter 3.

Byte 5CH. DOS provides us with two free FCBs here in the PSP. If you type the name of any program with a file name following, such as 'MASM TEST.ASM', DOS loads MASM.EXE in and puts an unopened File Control Block for TEST.ASM at 5C in MASM's PSP. An unopened FCB consists only of the file's drive number and its name, as we'll see later.

Byte 6CH. If you have a program that can handle two files at once, such as 'EDIT FILE1.TXT FILE2.TXT', DOS sets up an FCB for FILE1.TXT at CS:005C, and one for FILE2.TXT at CS:006C. Opened file control blocks are longer than closed ones, however. When you open an FCB (open the file), it takes up 37 bytes, and the FCB at 5C overlaps the one at 6C, so the second one must be moved if you intend to use them both.

The Disk Transfer Area

Byte 80H. Half of the PSP, starting from CS:0080 and ending at CS:0100—80H or 128 bytes—makes up the **Disk Transfer Area** or DTA. This is a default DTA, set up for you by DOS. When you read from the disk or write to it, data is often moved to or from the DTA by the system programs. If you need more than 128 bytes, you can reset the DTA's address with a DOS interrupt (which we will do later).

Besides being a storage and work area for disk data, all the characters typed after the program's name (including the space) are loaded into the DTA so your program can read them. This way, the program can communicate with the person who uses it. For instance, if we typed: "MASM This is a test. This is ONLY a test.", the characters " This is a test. This is ONLY a test.‹cr›" (note the leading space) would appear in MASM's DTA, starting at offset 81H. The byte at 80H holds the number of characters typed.

Let's take another look at our earlier program PROTEC, which reads the file name we want to protect from the DTA:

```
CODE_SEG          SEGMENT
        ASSUME    CS:CODE_SEG
        ORG       100H
PROTEC            PROC     NEAR
        MOV       DX,82H   ;Point DS:DX to filename
        MOV       DI,82H   ;Start looking in PSP
        MOV       AL,13    ;Look for carriage return
        MOV       CX,12    ;Scan up to 12 letters
REPNE   SCASB                          ;Find end of Input
        MOV       BYTE PTR [DI-1],0    ;Make string ASCIIZ
        MOV       AL,1     ;Function Code
        MOV       CX,1     ;This is to protect
        MOV       AH,43H   ;Use Service 43H
        INT       21H      ; of INT 21H
        INT       20H      ;End the Program.
PROTEC            ENDP

CODE_SEG          ENDS
        END       PROTEC
```

PROTEC is a .COM file, so all the segment registers will be set to the same segment that holds the PSP. If you've typed 'PROTEC THIS.FIL', the characters ' THIS.FIL‹cr›' will appear in the DTA, where ‹cr› is an ASCII 13, 0DH.

Here is a DEBUG dump of PROTEC's DTA after the command 'PROTECzTHIS.FIL‹cr›' has been typed:

```
-D80
090F:0080  09 20 54 48 49 53 2E 46-49 4C 0D 00 00 00 00 00   . THIS.FIL......
090F:0090  00 00 00 00 00 00 00 00-00 00 00 00 00 00 00 00   ................
090F:00A0  00 00 00 00 00 00 00 00-00 00 00 00 00 00 00 00   ................
090F:00B0  00 00 00 00 00 00 00 00-00 00 00 00 00 00 00 00   ................
090F:00C0  00 00 00 00 00 00 00 00-00 00 00 00 00 00 00 00   ................
090F:00D0  00 00 00 00 00 00 00 00-00 00 00 00 00 00 00 00   ................
090F:00E0  00 00 00 00 00 00 00 00-00 00 00 00 00 00 00 00   ................
090F:00F0  00 00 00 00 00 00 00 00-00 00 00 00 00 00 00 00   ................
```

We have to find the name of the file to protect. In PROTEC's code, we point to the first letter of the filename, 'T', by pointing to offset 82H. 80H always holds the number of bytes typed, nine of them here, and 81H holds the space typed after 'PROTEC'. PROTEC then searches with the command REPNE SCASB for the carriage return character, 13, and puts a zero in place of it. If you are not familiar with string searches such as REPNE SCASB, we will cover it in a later chapter.

```
PROTEC          PROC    NEAR
        MOV     DX,82H  ;Point DS:DX to filename
        MOV     DI,82H  ;Start looking in PSP
        MOV     AL,13   ;Look for carriage return
        MOV     CX,12   ;Scan up to 12 letters
REPNE   SCASB                   ;Find end of Input
        MOV     BYTE PTR [DI-1],0   ;Make string ASCIIZ
        MOV     AL,1    ;Function Code
        MOV     CX,1    ;This is to protect
        MOV     AH,43H  ;Use Service 43H
        INT     21H     ; of INT 21H
        INT     20H     ;End the Program.
PROTEC          ENDP
```

Putting a zero byte after the file name makes the file name string into what is referred to as ASCIIZ (ASCII Zero) format. In this form we can pass the filename, 'THIS.FIL'0, directly to INT 21H, Service 43H, which changes the file's attributes. To select Service 43H, we place 43H into AH and issue an INT 21H command:

```
PROTEC          PROC    NEAR
        MOV     DX,82H  ;Point DS:DX to filename
        MOV     DI,82H  ;Start looking in PSP
        MOV     AL,13   ;Look for carriage return
        MOV     CX,12   ;Scan up to 12 letters
REPNE   SCASB           ;Find end of Input
```

```
        MOV     BYTE PTR [DI-1],0    ;Make string ASCIIZ
        MOV     AL,1    ;Function Code
        MOV     CX,1    ;This is to protect
        MOV     AH,43H  ;Use Service 43H
        INT     21H     ; of INT 21H
        INT     20H     ;End the Program.
PROTEC          ENDP
```

THE CODE IN .COM FILES

Our discussion of the DTA finishes the PSP. An experienced assembly language programmer frequently makes use of the resources in the PSP. Although IBM says that you are not supposed to work with any addresses in the PSP before 5CH, with care and practice, the whole PSP is available to you as an invaluable tool.

After the PSP is set up, the .COM file itself, the code, is loaded in memory. Since .COM files have no headers, the code in it is loaded verbatim. Finally, control is passed to CS:0100, and the program is on its own.

Now that the program, either .EXE or .COM, is fully loaded in memory, and we know what's available, we're all done with the general outlines of writing programs. But before we concentrate on what goes into programs, we will include a short chapter on an invaluable skill that we'll use later on—debugging them.

EXAMPLE PROGRAM

We've finished our chapter on writing and assembling programs. As mentioned in the Introduction, we will include a short sample program at the end of most chapters in this book. The reason for this is that the best way of learning, next to doing, is by seeing examples.

The sample program for this chapter is named LOCK. LOCK is a (medium) security file-scrambler that can be used to scramble files up to 62K in length. Its counterpart is UNLOCK, also provided. Except for two lines, they are the same program. The listing for LOCK is at the end of this chapter, and it provides us with a good-sized program that can be made into a working .COM file, as we worked through in this chapter. It makes use of the PSP, also discussed, to read in the file names it is to operate on.

LOCKing Files

The way to lock a file is to say LOCK FILE.EXT FILE.MIX, where FILE.MIX is the scrambled file that will be created. LOCK will ask you for a pass-phrase with which to scramble the file.

Please keep in mind that to unscramble the file (with the command UNLOCK FILE.MIX FILE.EXT), you have to provide the SAME pass-phrase. Also keep in mind that LOCK is only medium security (although you can scramble a scrambled file a second time too for extra security).

To use LOCK, just type in the code at the end of this chapter using a word processor. Create a file named LOCK.ASM, and then assemble, link, and convert it this way:

```
MASM LOCK;
LINK LOCK;
EXE2BIN LOCK LOCK.COM
```

Disregard the warning that the linker gives about a missing stack segment. To create UNLOCK.COM, copy LOCK.ASM to a new file, UNLOCK.ASM, and then change the two lines with rotate right commands (ROR) into rotate left commands (ROL) as indicated in the comments.

In the rest of the book, it is hoped that the reader will take the time to adapt the programs presented or develop his or her own since, finally, there is no better way of learning the material than plunging right in.

LISTING 1.4 THE PROGRAM LOCK

```
COMMENT*  Change ROR -> ROL in the TWO marked places to produce UNLOCK.ASM*
CODE_SEG        SEGMENT
        ASSUME  CS:CODE_SEG
        ORG     100H
HERE:   JMP     THERE
        COPY_RIGHT      DB      '(C)1985 Steven Holzner'
        PROMPT  DB      'Phrase: $'     ;All the messages & prompts
        DEFAULT DB      'FILE.LOC',0
        NOTSEEN DB      13,10,'File Not Found$'
        FULL:   DB      13,10,'Disk Full$'
        FILETWO DW      0               ;Address of 2nd File name
        FILEND  DW      0               ;End of read-in files in memory
THERE   PROC    NEAR                    ;Our procedure
        MOV     BX,81H                  ;Make the filenames into ASCIIZ
UP:     INC     BX                      ;Scan type-in for space, <cr>
        CMP     BYTE PTR [BX],' '       ;Space?
        JNE     NOSPACE
        MOV     BYTE PTR [BX],0         ;Put the Z in ASCIIZ
        MOV     FILETWO,BX
        INC     FILETWO                 ;Store filename starting location
NOSPACE:CMP     BYTE PTR [BX],13        ;If not a space, a <cr>?
        JNE     UP
        MOV     BYTE PTR [BX],0         ;If yes, replace with a 0
        CMP     FILETWO,0
```

LISTING 1.4 CONTINUED

```
        JNZ     OVER
        MOV     FILETWO,OFFSET DEFAULT;If no second file given, use default
OVER:   LEA     DX,PROMPT             ;Type out the prompt with string print
        MOV     AH,9
        INT     21H
        MOV     BX,80H+40H-2          ;Prepare 40H (64) buffer for key phrase
        MOV     BYTE PTR [BX],40H
        PUSH    BX                    ;Set up buffer address
        POP     DX
        MOV     AH,0AH                ;Buffered input
        INT     21H
        MOV     BX,80H+40H            ;Start of key phrase
        PUSH    BX
JUMP:   CMP     BYTE PTR [BX],13      ;Set up key phrase's ASCII values
        JE      READY                 ;Scan until <cr>
        OR      BYTE PTR [BX],1       ;Make it odd
        AND     BYTE PTR [BX],0FH     ;Use only lower four bits
        INC     BX
        JMP     JUMP                  ;Keep going until <cr>
READY:  POP     BX
        MOV     AX,3D00H              ;Open the file to encrypt
        MOV     DX,82H                ;Point to its name
        INT     21H
        JNC     OKFILE                ;Carry Flag → some problem, assume
        LEA     DX,NOTSEEN            ;  file doesn't exist, say so
        MOV     AH,9
        INT     21H
        JMP     OUT                   ;Exit

OKFILE: PUSH    BX              ;Store location in key phrase
        MOV     BX,AX                 ;Put handle into BX
        MOV     CX,62*1024      ;Ask for 62K bytes to be read from file
        LEA     DX,THEBOTTOM          ;And put at end of program
        MOV     AH,3FH                ;Read
        INT     21H
        ADD     AX,OFFSET THEBOTTOM   ;Actually read AX bytes
        MOV     FILEND,AX
        DEC     FILEND               ;Find how far the file extends in mem.
        MOV     AH,3EH                ;Close file, thank you very much.
        INT     21H
        POP     BX
        LEA     CX,THEBOTTOM         ;Save current location in file in CX

SCRMBLE:MOV     SI,CX                 ;Will scramble from [SI] to [DI]
        CMP     SI,FILEND             ;Past end?
        JAE     DONE                  ;If yes, exit
        MOV     DI,CX
        XOR     AX,AX
        MOV     AL,[BX]             ;How many to scramble? (from key phrase)
        ADD     DI,AX
        MOV     CX,DI
        INC     CX              ;Store new starting location for next time

        INC     BX             ;Also, get next character for next scramble
        CMP     BYTE PTR [BX],13      ;If at end of key phrase, wrap
        JNE     TWIST
        MOV     BX,80H+40H

TWIST:  CMP     DI,FILEND             ;Is DI past end?
        JBE     GRAB
```

LISTING 1.4 CONTINUED

```
        MOV     DI,FILEND                   ;If yes, only scramble to file end
        PUSH    DI
        SUB     DI,SI                       ;What about last byte?
        TEST    DI,1
        POP     DI
        JNZ     GRAB                        ;If left over, rotate it once
        ROR     BYTE PTR [DI],1             ;← ROL FOR UNLOCK!!!
        DEC     DI
        CMP     SI,DI
        JAE     DONE

GRAB:   MOV     DH,[SI]                     ;Get byte 1
        MOV     DL,[DI]                     ;Get byte 2
        PUSH    CX
        MOV     CL,[BX]                     ;Get number of times to rotate

        INC     BX                       ;Set up key phrase char for next time
        CMP     BYTE PTR [BX],13
        JNE     TWISTER
        MOV     BX,80H+40H
                                            ;Rotate the hybrid word
TWISTER:ROR     DX,CL                       ;← ROL FOR UNLOCK!!!
        POP     CX
        MOV     [SI],DH                     ;And replace the parts
        MOV     [DI],DL
        INC     SI                          ;Point to next part to scramble
        CMP     SI,DI                       ;Have SI and DI met yet?
        JE      SCRMBLE             ;If yes, move on to next part to scramble
        DEC     DI
        JMP     GRAB                        ;Go back until done
DONE:   MOV     AH,3CH                      ;Done
        MOV     CX,0                    ;Prepare to write out scrambled version
        MOV     DX,FILETWO
        INT     21H                         ;Create the file
        JC      ERROR
        MOV     BX,AX
        MOV     AH,40H
        LEA     DX,THEBOTTOM
        MOV     CX,FILEND                   ;File size to write
        SUB     CX,OFFSET THEBOTTOM
        INC     CX
        INT     21H                         ;Write it out
        CMP     AX,CX                    ;If error, (returned)AX .NE. (orig.)CX
        JE      CLOSE
ERROR:  LEA     DX,FULL                      ;Assume disk is full, say so, leave
        MOV     AH,9
        INT     21H
        JMP     OUT
CLOSE:  MOV     AH,3EH                      ;Otherwise, close the file and exit
        INT     21H
OUT:    INT     20H
THERE   ENDP
THEBOTTOM:                                  ;Read-in file starts here.
        CODE_SEG        ENDS
        END     HERE
```

Chapter 2

DEBUG.COM

INTRODUCTION

This short chapter is devoted to an essential utility used in assembly language programming, DEBUG. The program DEBUG.COM that comes on your DOS disk is one of the best utilities on it. DEBUG, or something like it, is invaluable to the assembly language programmer.

Although there are more advanced debuggers available, we cannot assume they are available to everyone in the same way that DEBUG is, so we'll only cover DEBUG here. This one program is more than satisfactory for our needs. DEBUG does more than debug programs. With it you have a disk editor, a memory probe, and you can even write full programs with the Assemble command. We will have a great deal of use for DEBUG throughout this book.

A DEBUG EXAMPLE

To begin our use of DEBUG, let's start with an example. Use a scratch disk, not a boot disk, and put it into drive B. Load a diskette with DEBUG on it into drive A. The first sector of every diskette contains a boot record. It is the job of this small (512-byte) program to read in IBMBIO.COM. This boot record is in the first sector of every diskette, so that if you boot with a non-system disk, you will get the message:

```
Non-System disk or disk error
Replace and strike any key when ready
```

Let's make a harmless change to this boot record message on the scratch disk, changing "Non-System disk" to "Not System disk". We will edit the machine-level code of the boot record itself. In order to do this, we will run DEBUG in drive A, and read in the first sector of the diskette in drive B (the scratch disk) with the command:

```
LCS:80 1 0 1
```

The LOAD Command

The DEBUG LOAD command is used to load files or sectors directly in from the disk. This command will load sectors from disk 1:

```
         |
         V
LCS:80 1 0 1
```

starting at relative sector 0 (the first sector on the disk) and read in one sector:

```
           | |
           V V
LCS:80 1 0 1
```

The data will be put at address CS:80. So far we have typed (DEBUG's prompt is the dash "-"):

```
A>DEBUG

-LCS:80 1 0 1
-
```

and DEBUG has read in the sector.

The Search Command

We have to find the "Non-System disk" message to change it. Here we can use the DEBUG search command, S (all 18 DEBUG commands are only one letter long). We will search from CS:80 to some high number, say CS:0FFF, for this message this way:

```
A>DEBUG

-LCS:80 1 0 1
-SCS:80 FFF 'Non-System'      ← The Search command.
08F7:0202                     ← DEBUG found a match at this address.
```

The Dump Command

If you had individual bytes to search for, say CDH 20H, you could search this way: SCS:80 FFF CD 20. Here we have turned up a match to our ASCII string at address 08F7:0202, so we dump memory starting at that location with the DUMP command, D:

```
A>DEBUG

-LCS:80 1 0 1
```

```
-SCS:80 FFF 'Non-System'
08F7:0202   ← DEBUG found a match at this address.
-D8F7:0202  ← So we will Dump it.
08F7:0202   4E 6F 6E 2D 53 79-73 74 65 6D 20 64 69 73          Non-System dis
08F7:0210   6B 20 6F 72 20 64 69 73-6B 20 65 72 72 6F 72 0D    k or disk error.
08F7:0220   0A 52 65 70 6C 61 63 65-20 61 6E 64 20 73 74 72    .Replace and str
08F7:0230   69 6B 65 20 61 6E 79 20-6B 65 79 20 77 68 65 6E    ike any key when
08F7:0240   20 72 65 61 64 79 0D 0A-00 0D 0A 44 69 73 6B 20     ready.....Disk
08F7:0250   42 6F 6F 74 20 66 61 69-6C 75 72 65 0D 0A 00 69    Boot failure...i
08F7:0260   62 6D 62 69 6F 20 20 63-6F 6D 30 69 62 6D 64 6F    bmbio  com0ibmdo
08F7:0270   73 20 20 63 6F 6D 30 00-00 00 00 00 00 00 55 AA    s  com0.......U*
08F7:0280   00 00                                              ..
```

We can see our message clearly in the ASCII translation portion of the screen on the right. The left-hand part of the display holds the hex values of each byte, 16 on a line, and the right hand section holds the corresponding ASCII.

The Edit Command

The letters we want to change in 'Non-System' start at 8F7:0204, so let's use DEBUG's EDIT command, E, to change them. Typing E8F7:0204 puts DEBUG into its edit mode:

```
-LCS:80 1 0 1
-SCS:80 FFF 'Non-System'
08F7:0202
-D8F7:0202
08F7:0202   4E 6F 6E 2D 53 79-73 74 65 6D 20 64 69 73          Non-System dis
08F7:0210   6B 20 6F 72 20 64 69 73-6B 20 65 72 72 6F 72 0D    k or disk error.
08F7:0220   0A 52 65 70 6C 61 63 65-20 61 6E 64 20 73 74 72    .Replace and str
08F7:0230   69 6B 65 20 61 6E 79 20-6B 65 79 20 77 68 65 6E    ike any key when
08F7:0240   20 72 65 61 64 79 0D 0A-00 0D 0A 44 69 73 6B 20     ready.....Disk
08F7:0250   42 6F 6F 74 20 66 61 69-6C 75 72 65 0D 0A 00 69    Boot failure...i
08F7:0260   62 6D 62 69 6F 20 20 63-6F 6D 30 69 62 6D 64 6F    bmbio  com0ibmdo
08F7:0270   73 20 20 63 6F 6D 30 00-00 00 00 00 00 00 55 AA    s  com0.......U*
08F7:0280   00 00                                              ..
-E8F7:0204            ← The Edit Command.
08F7:0204   6E._      ← DEBUG's response.
```

6E is the current Hex value of the byte at 8F7:0204. The cursor follows the period on the screen, prompting you to enter a new value for this memory location. 6EH is the ASCII value for 'n', and this is the character we want to change to a 't', or ASCII 74H. We can do this by simply typing a 74:

```
-E8F7:0204
08F7:0204   6E.74_
```

and then a space, which prompts the Edit command to put the next byte's value on the screen:

```
-E8F7:0204
08F7:0204  6E.74    2D._
```

2D is the ASCII value for the dash in 'Non-System', so we change that to a space, ASCII 20H, by typing 20, and then a carriage return which ends the Edit:

```
-E8F7:0204
08F7:0204  6E.74    2D.20<cr>
-_
```

If we had typed another space, DEBUG would have continued by typing out the next byte in memory and waiting for us to change it. To make sure we have edited the message correctly, we dump the same memory section again:

```
-E8F7:0204                                                         The new Message.
08F7:0204   6E.74    2D.20                                                    ||
-D8F7:0202 ← The Dump Command.                                                VV
08F7:0202   4E 6F 74 20 53 79-73 74 65 6D 20 64 69 73          Not System dis
08F7:0210   6B 20 6F 72 20 64 69 73-6B 20 65 72 72 6F 72 0D    k or disk error.
08F7:0220   0A 52 65 70 6C 61 63 65-20 61 6E 64 20 73 74 72    .Replace and str
08F7:0230   69 6B 65 20 61 6E 79 20-6B 65 79 20 77 68 65 6E    ike any key when
08F7:0240   20 72 65 61 64 79 0D 0A-00 0D 0A 44 69 73 6B 20     ready.....Disk
08F7:0250   42 6F 6F 74 20 66 61 69-6C 75 72 65 0D 0A 00 69    Boot failure...i
08F7:0260   62 6D 62 69 6F 20 20 63-6F 6D 30 69 62 6D 64 6F    bmbio  com0ibmdo
08F7:0270   73 20 20 63 6F 6D 30 00-00 00 00 00 00 00 55 AA    s  com0.......U*
08F7:0280   00 00                                              ..
```

and we see our new message is in place.

The Write Command

To write this back to the scratch diskette, we can use the same syntax as in the Load command, only this time using Write, and then we will Quit:

```
-LCS:80 1 0 1
-SCS:80 FFF 'Non-System'
08F7:0202   DEBUG found a match at this address.
       :
       :
-E8F7:0204
08F7:0204  6E.74   2D.20
-D8F7:0202
08F7:0202   4E 6F 74 20 53 79-73 74 65 6D 20 64 69 73          Not System dis
08F7:0210   6B 20 6F 72 20 64 69 73-6B 20 65 72 72 6F 72 0D    k or disk error.
08F7:0220   0A 52 65 70 6C 61 63 65-20 61 6E 64 20 73 74 72    .Replace and str
08F7:0230   69 6B 65 20 61 6E 79 20-6B 65 79 20 77 68 65 6E    ike any key when
08F7:0240   20 72 65 61 64 79 0D 0A-00 0D 0A 44 69 73 6B 20     ready.....Disk
08F7:0250   42 6F 6F 74 20 66 61 69-6C 75 72 65 0D 0A 00 69    Boot failure...i
08F7:0260   62 6D 62 69 6F 20 20 63-6F 6D 30 69 62 6D 64 6F    bmbio  com0ibmdo
```

```
08F7:0270  73 20 20 63 6F 6D 30 00-00 00 00 00 00 00 55 AA   s  com0.......U*
08F7:0280  00 00                                               ..
-WCS:80 1 0 1 ← Write the sector back to the diskette.
-Q
```

and the same sector, relative sector 0, is written out again.

To test the new boot record, try booting from it in the A drive. We get the new message:

```
Not System disk or disk error
Replace and strike any key when ready
```

This points out some of DEBUG's power. With it, you have a tool that can deal directly with assembled code and change it as you wish.

DEBUGGING FILES

With DEBUG you can change code, as well as data, after it's been assembled. For instance, our example program PROTEC.COM differs from UNPROTEC.COM in only one line:

```
CODE_SEG        SEGMENT
        ASSUME  CS:CODE_SEG
        ORG     100H

PROTEC          PROC     NEAR
        MOV     DX,82H   ;Point DS:DX to filename
        MOV     DI,82H   ;Start looking in PSP
        MOV     AL,13    ;Look for carriage return
        MOV     CX,12    ;Scan up to 12 letters
REPNE   SCASB                        ;Find end of Input
        MOV     BYTE PTR [DI-1],0    ;Make string ASCIIZ
        MOV     AL,1     ;Function Code
     →  MOV     CX,1     ;This is to protect
        MOV     AH,43H   ;Use Service 43H
        INT     21H      ; of INT 21H
        INT     20H      ;End the Program.
PROTEC          ENDP

CODE_SEG        ENDS
        END     PROTEC
```

In UNPROTEC, this line is MOV CX,0. Let's see if we can change PROTEC.COM to UNPROTEC.COM directly. Again, it's safer to try this on a scratch disk that has DEBUG on it. We will start with the command:

```
A>DEBUG PROTEC.COM FILE.EXT
```

When you are debugging files, it is best to keep the debugging environment as close to usual operating conditions as possible. When you normally use PROTEC, you would supply some file name to protect, say a file named FILE.EXT.

To see what would happen in that case, and to allow you to trace through the program as it would actually work, DEBUG allows you to enter file names or arguments after the program's name. DEBUG enters them in the program's PSP as they would normally appear. In DEBUG, we can dump the area from CS:5C to CS:7C to look at the default (unopened) File Control Block (FCB) that DOS provides for FILE.EXT at 5C:

```
-D5C 7C
090B:005C  00 46 49 4C                                         .FIL
090B:0060  45 20 20 20 20 45 58 54-00 00 00 00 00 20 20 20   E    EXT.....
090B:0070  20 20 20 20 20 20 20 20-00 00 00 00 00                    .....
```

The first byte in the FCB is the drive number, and here 1 stands for A, 2 for B and so on. Since we did not specify a drive number for FILE.EXT, a zero (for default drive) is placed here. Next comes the file's name, which takes up eight places with extra padded spaces, and then its three-place extension, EXT.

The Register Command

When a program such as PROTEC.COM is loaded by DEBUG, the register pair BX:CX is set to the file's size in bytes. For example, if you loaded COMMAND.COM, which is 17792, or 4580H, bytes long, BX would contain 0000 and CX would contain 4580H. The size loaded in BX:CX is the **load module's size**. If you want to find the size of an .EXE file's header, just subtract BX:CX from the file size in the directory. Our file PROTEC.COM is 28, or 1CH, bytes long, and we can examine the contents of the CX register with the Register, or R, command like this:

```
-D5C 7C
090B:005C  00 46 49 4C                                         .FIL
090B:0060  45 20 20 20 20 45 58 54-00 00 00 00 00 20 20 20   E    EXT.....
090B:0070  20 20 20 20 20 20 20 20-00 00 00 00 00                    .....
-RCX          ←
CX 001C       ←
:_            ←
```

The cursor is to the right of the colon prompt. You can change the value in the CX register by typing in a new hex number here. A carriage return keeps the old value intact. As we expected, the file's length, recorded in CX, is 1CH.

The Name Command

Since we're now about to work directly with the code of PROTEC.COM, we should change the file's name at once to avoid writing out a new version of PROTEC.COM by mistake. DEBUG has the Name, N, command for this purpose, and we immediately change the file's name that we are debugging to UNPROTEC.COM:

```
-D5C 7C
090B:005C  00 46 49 4C                                         .FIL
090B:0060  45 20 20 20 20 45 58 54-00 00 00 00 20 20 20   E     EXT.....
090B:0070  20 20 20 20 20 20 20 20-00 00 00 00                        .....
-RCX
CX 001C
:
-NUNPROTEC.COM  ←
-_
```

The Unassemble Command

Let's take a look at the code we have in memory with the Unassemble, U, command. Since .COM files are set up with entry points at CS:100H, that is where DEBUG will begin if we ask it to execute the program. To unassemble the program's code, we type U100 (the U command assumes the use of the Code Segment unless otherwise specified):

```
-D5C 7C
090B:005C  00 46 49 4C                                         .FIL
090B:0060  45 20 20 20 20 45 58 54-00 00 00 00 20 20 20   E     EXT.....
090B:0070  20 20 20 20 20 20 20 20-00 00 00 00                        .....
-RCX
CX 001C
:
-NUNPROTEC.COM
  -U100               ← Unassemble, starting at CS:100.
  090B:0100 BA8200         MOV     DX,0082
  090B:0103 BF8200         MOV     DI,0082
  090B:0106 B00D           MOV     AL,0D
  090B:0108 B90C00         MOV     CX,000C
  090B:010B F2             REPNZ
  090B:010C AE             SCASB
  090B:010D C645FF00       MOV     BYTE PTR [DI-01],00
  090B:0111 B001           MOV     AL,01
  090B:0113 B90100         MOV     CX,0001
  090B:0116 B443           MOV     AH,43
  090B:0118 CD21           INT     21
```

```
090B:011A CD20          INT     20
090B:011C 0000          ADD     [BX+SI],AL
090B:011E 0000          ADD     [BX+SI],AL
```

Here we can see the 28 bytes (CS:100 to CS:11C) of PROTEC.COM. None of the pseudo-OPs like SEGMENT, PROC, or ORG appear here, just the actual assembly language commands. The machine code for each instruction appears next to its address, and the unassembled instructions appear on the right.

Notice at the very end of this unassembly that the U command 'unassembled' some extra zeros in memory at the end of the program, assuming that they, too, were code. The command U100 alone unassembles 32 bytes, but we could change that range with commands such as U100 110, for example, which unassembles the bytes from CS:100 to CS:110.

In particular, the line we want, MOV CX,1, starts at CS:113:

```
090B:0111 B001          MOV     AL,01
090B:0113 B90100        MOV     CX,0001  ← We will change this line.
090B:0116 B443          MOV     AH,43
```

This is the line we want to change to MOV CX,0 before we write the file out as UNPROTEC.COM.

The Assemble Command

In order to replace the machine level command, B9 01 00, we first have to find what to replace it with—we need the corresponding machine code for MOV CX,0. For such purposes DEBUG provides an Assemble command, A. Starting at any address, we can assemble our own code immediately. We can use the 128 bytes of the default DTA, starting at CS:80H, as a scratch area. Whatever trial instructions we put there will not harm our program. The command for this is A80, and DEBUG prompts us with:

```
-A80
090B:0080 _
```

The cursor is a prompt to type in an assembler command. Here we type in MOV CX,0‹cr› and then another ‹cr› to stop assembling:

```
-A80
090B:0080 MOV CX,0<cr>      ← Command typed by you.
090B:0083 <cr>
-_
```

To find the machine code for this instruction, we will Unassemble the same code, now at CS:80:

```
-U80
090B:0080 B90000        MOV     CX,0000     ;Our assembled command.
090B:0083 50            PUSH    AX          ;Meaningless bytes in
090B:0084 52            PUSH    DX          ;memory.
          :
          :
```

and we can see that the machine code is B9 00 00, the same length as the command we are replacing. We could replace MOV CX,1 with Edit as we did in the first example. But since both commands assemble to three bytes, we can simply use the Assemble command to write over what is already there at CS:113:

```
-NUNPROTEC.COM
-U100
090B:0100 BA8200        MOV     DX,0082
090B:0103 BF8200        MOV     DI,0082
090B:0106 B00D          MOV     AL,0D
090B:0108 B90C00        MOV     CX,000C
090B:010B F2            REPNZ
090B:010C AE            SCASB
090B:010D C645FF00      MOV     BYTE PTR [DI-01],00
090B:0111 B001          MOV     AL,01
090B:0113 B90100        MOV     CX,0001
090B:0116 B443          MOV     AH,43
090B:0118 CD21          INT     21
090B:011A CD20          INT     20
090B:011C 0000          ADD     [BX+SI],AL
090B:011E 0000          ADD     [BX+SI],AL
-A113                   ← Replace the command at 113.
090B:0113 MOV CX,0<cr>
090B:0116 <cr>          ← Type a carriage return here to stop assembling.
-_
```

We should check our work by once again Unassembling the entire program:

```
-A113
090B:0113 MOV CX,0
090B:0116
-U100           ← Unassemble the new program with U.
090B:0100 BA8200        MOV     DX,0082
090B:0103 BF8200        MOV     DI,0082
090B:0106 B00D          MOV     AL,0D
090B:0108 B90C00        MOV     CX,000C
090B:010B F2            REPNZ
090B:010C AE            SCASB
090B:010D C645FF00      MOV     BYTE PTR [DI-01],00
090B:0111 B001          MOV     AL,01
090B:0113 B90000        MOV     CX,0000   ← This is correct for UNPROTEC.
090B:0116 B443          MOV     AH,43
090B:0118 CD21          INT     21
090B:011A CD20          INT     20
090B:011C 0000          ADD     [BX+SI],AL
090B:011E 0000          ADD     [BX+SI],AL
```

and we can see that MOV CX,1 has been changed to MOV CX,0.

To write out the renamed and debugged file, the W (Write) command can be used without any arguments. It writes a file with the name as set by the Name command, and the number of bytes it writes is the number stored in the register pair BX:CX. Since we have not changed either value, BX still holds 0 and CX still holds 1CH; we only need to type W and then quit with Q:

```
-A113
090B:0113 MOV CX,0
090B:0116
-U100
090B:0100 BA8200          MOV     DX,0082
090B:0103 BF8200          MOV     DI,0082
090B:0106 B00D            MOV     AL,0D
090B:0108 B90C00          MOV     CX,000C
090B:010B F2              REPNZ
090B:010C AE              SCASB
090B:010D C645FF00        MOV     BYTE PTR [DI-01],00
090B:0111 B001            MOV     AL,01
090B:0113 B90000          MOV     CX,0000
090B:0116 B443            MOV     AH,43
090B:0118 CD21            INT     21
090B:011A CD20            INT     20
090B:011C 0000            ADD     [BX+SI],AL
090B:011E 0000            ADD     [BX+SI],AL
-W
Writing 001C bytes  ← DEBUG's message
-Q
```

and we've produced a new file, UNPROTEC.COM. This technique, that of patching an existing program, is very powerful, but should always be used with caution.

OTHER DEBUG COMMANDS

Our practice sessions have made use of many of DEBUG's commands, but certainly not all of them. In Figure 2.1 there is a complete list of commands, along with an example for each showing how it is used.

Many commands use ranges of memory locations to either search through or move. There are two ways to use such commands—either by giving the beginning and ending addresses or by using the L, Length, parameter and listing how many bytes the range holds. For example, these two are the same search command:

```
S100 FFFF 'Non-System'
SCS:100 LFF00 'Non-System'
```

Command	Name	Uses	What it does
A	Assemble	A100	Allows you to type in instructions at CS:100 (DOS 2+ only)
C	Compare	C100 109 400	Compare the bytes at DS:100-109 to DS:400-409
		C100L10 400	Compare 10 bytes from DS:100 to ones at DS:400
D	Dump	DCS:100 110	Dumps bytes CS:100-110 (D alone dumps 128)
		DCS:100	Dumps 128 bytes starting at CS:100
E	Enter	ECS:100 12 10	Enter two bytes 12H and 10H starting at CS:100
		ECS:100	Start entering bytes at CS:100
F	Fill	F80L3 0	Fills 3 bytes starting at DS:80 with 0
		F80 82 0	Same thing
G	Go	G400	Run program from current location until CS:400
		G400 500	Stops at either CS:400 or CS:500
H	Hex	H E 1	Calculates both E+1 (=0FH) and E-1 (=0DH)
I	Input	I60	Reads a byte from the keyboard port 60H
L	Load	L	Loads the file whose FCB is at CS:5C
		LDS:80 1 5 7	Loads 7 sectors starting at 5 from B: to DS:80
M	Move	M100 102 300	Moves bytes DS:100-102 to 300-302
		M100L3 300	Same thing
N	Name	NDORMAT.COM	Names the file
O	Output	OAA 10	10H is output to port AA
Q	Quit	Q	Quit, Exit, Fin and Stop
R	Register	R	Displays the contents of all registers
		RCX	Displays CX and allows you to modify it
S	Search	S100 FFFF 'Y'	Searches DS:100 to DS:FFFF for 'Y'
		S100LFF00 'Y'	Searches FF00 bytes from DS:100 for 'Y'
T	Trace	T	Executes the current line
		T5	Executes 5 lines
U	Unassemble	U100	Unassembles 32 bytes (Default)
		U100 110	Unassembles CS:100 to CS:110
		U100L9	Unassembles 9 bytes from CS:100
W	Write	W	Load BX:CX with file size, writes out file
		W80 1 5 7	Writes 7 sectors (first is 5) on B: from CS:80

Figure 2.1 DEBUG Commands

The Trace and Register Commands

Trace and **Register** are among the most frequently used DEBUG commands. With Trace, you can execute single lines of programs one by one. With the Register command, R, you can either load a register with a new value or examine all registers at once. R displays the next line of code to be executed as well.

For example, let's debug PROTEC.COM once again. We will look at the program with Unassemble, use R to get our bearings, and then Trace through the first command, MOV DX,82:

```
A>DEBUG PROTEC.COM
-U100
090B:0100 BA8200        MOV     DX,0082
090B:0103 BF8200        MOV     DI,0082
090B:0106 B00D          MOV     AL,0D
090B:0108 B90C00        MOV     CX,000C
090B:010B F2            REPNZ
090B:010C AE            SCASB
090B:010D C645FF00      MOV     BYTE PTR [DI-01],00
090B:0111 B001          MOV     AL,01
090B:0113 B90100        MOV     CX,0001
090B:0116 B443          MOV     AH,43
090B:0118 CD21          INT     21
090B:011A CD20          INT     20
090B:011C F6FF          IDIV    BH
090B:011E 76C2          JBE     00E2
```

The Register command gives us our current CS:IP location, the next command to execute, and displays the contents of the registers as well:

```
-R
AX=0000  BX=0000  CX=001C  DX=0000  SP=FFFE  BP=0000  SI=0000  DI=0000
DS=090B  ES=090B  SS=090B  CS=090B  IP=0100   NV UP DI PL NZ NA PO NC
090B:0100 BA8200        MOV     DX,0082
```

DEBUG is set to execute the command at CS:100, MOV DX,82H. We can trace through this command with T:

```
-T
                    DX is now loaded with 82H.
                                |
                                V
AX=0000  BX=0000  CX=001C  DX=0082  SP=FFFE  BP=0000  SI=0000  DI=0000
DS=090B  ES=090B  SS=090B  CS=090B  IP=0103   NV UP DI PL NZ NA PO NC
090B:0103 BF8200        MOV     DI,0082
```

Let's look at the next command about to be executed:

```
-R
AX=0000  BX=0000  CX=001C  DX=0082  SP=FFFE  BP=0000  SI=0000  DI=0000
DS=090B  ES=090B  SS=090B  CS=090B  IP=0103   NV UP DI PL NZ NA PO NC
090B:0103 BF8200        MOV     DI,0082  ← Now pointing to the next command.
```

A command such as T3 will execute the next three lines of code. You can use this to skip already proofed sections of code, or you can skip over them by directly changing the CS:IP (which point to the instruction about to be executed) with the commands RCS or RIP.

The Hex Command

Because not many people are proficient with hex arithmetic, DEBUG has a **Hex** command that does both addition and subtraction at the same time:

```
-H10 10
0020  0000
```

10H + 10H = 20H and 10H − 10H = 0H. Unfortunately, Hex does not convert from decimal to Hex, which is often essential, especially when working with ASCII bytes.

The Input and Output Commands

The **Input** and **Output** commands can directly input or output data on the I/O bus of the PC. We will not have very much to do with the I/O bus, but most of the hardware (which is run by controllers of some kind) is controlled by it. For example, we could turn the speaker on, examine the state of the video controller, or reset the disk controller this way.

The Go Command

Go is something like Trace. With it you can run your code, or parts of it, in memory. If you type, for example, G103, the program you are debugging is executed until CS:103H is reached. If you just enter G, the program itself runs.

Go works by putting a breakpoint, INT 3, into your code, and taking over when you hit that breakpoint. It is not always possible to put an INT 3 into the code—the code in ROM, for example, cannot be changed. Even so, we can still give the Go command a try by running a few routines in ROM.

For instance, we can run the subroutine in ROM BIOS that produces the beep you hear whenever there is an error or the machine boots. If you have a ROM-BIOS dated 10/27/82, the beep routine is at F000:E603. You can check the date of your ROM-BIOS by dumping the memory location at FFFF:0000. The date is stored shortly after this point.

```
                                                                      |
                                                                      |
-DFFFF:0000                                                           V
FFFF:0000  EA 5B E0 00 F0 31 30 2F-32 37 2F 38 32 FF FF 77   j[.p10/27/82..w
FFFF:0010  72 30 E3 00 47 01 70 00-C3 E2 00 F0 47 01 70 00   r0c.G.p.Cb.pG.p.
FFFF:0020  47 01 70 00 54 FF 00 F0-47 FF 00 F0 47 FF 00 F0   G.p.T..pG..pG..p
FFFF:0030  A5 FE 00 F0 87 E9 00 F0-DD E6 00 F0 DD E6 00 F0   %~.p.i.p]f.p]f.p
FFFF:0040  DD E6 00 F0 DD E6 00 F0-57 EF 00 F0 47 01 70 00   ]f.p]f.pWo.pG.p.
FFFF:0050  65 F0 00 F0 4D F8 00 F0-41 F8 00 F0 59 EC 00 F0   ep.pMx.pAx.pYl.p
FFFF:0060  39 E7 00 F0 59 F8 00 F0-2E E8 00 F0 D2 EF 00 F0   9g.pYx.p.h.pRo.p
FFFF:0070  00 00 00 F6 F2 E6 00 F0-6E FE 00 F0 40 01 70 00   ...vrf.pn~.p@.p.
```

The duration of the beep is set by the value in the BX register. A long beep uses a value of 6; a short beep, a value of 1. If we want to execute the beep routine at F000:E603, we have to load CS and IP correctly, using the Register command:

```
-RCS
CS 08F7
:F000
-RIP
IP 0100
:E603               ← Get ready to start executing at F000:E603.
-RBX                ← Let's set BX to 1 for a short beep.
BX 0000
:1
```

Let's take a look at the beep subroutine itself:

```
-R  ← R will tell us the contents of the registers.
AX=0000  BX=0001  CX=0000  DX=0000  SP=FFEE  BP=0000  SI=0000  DI=0000
DS=08F7  ES=08F7  SS=08F7  CS=F000  IP=E603   NV UP DI PL NZ NA PO NC
F000:E603 B0B6          MOV     AL,B6
-U  ← U will unassemble part of the beep subroutine.
F000:E603 B0B6          MOV     AL,B6
F000:E605 E643          OUT     43,AL
F000:E607 B83305        MOV     AX,0533
F000:E60A E642          OUT     42,AL
F000:E60C 8AC4          MOV     AL,AH
F000:E60E E642          OUT     42,AL
F000:E610 E461          IN      AL,61
F000:E612 8AE0          MOV     AH,AL
F000:E614 0C03          OR      AL,03
F000:E616 E661          OUT     61,AL
F000:E618 2BC9          SUB     CX,CX
F000:E61A E2FE          LOOP    E61A
F000:E61C FECB          DEC     BL
F000:E61E 75FA          JNZ     E61A
F000:E620 8AC4          MOV     AL,AH
F000:E622 E661          OUT     61,AL
-G
```

You can see a number of OUT commands sending information out over the I/O bus to the speaker at port 42H. After we type G the PC will beep.

The location FFFF:0000 is interesting for another reason besides the date. This is the address of the first command executed after the machine is booted. If we Unassemble the code starting at FFFF:0000:

```
-UFFFF:0000
FFFF:0000 EA5BE000F0     JMP     F000:E05B
FFFF:0005 3130           XOR     [BX+SI],SI
FFFF:0007 2F             DAS
FFFF:0008 3237           XOR     DH,[BX]
FFFF:000A 2F             DAS
FFFF:000B 3832           CMP     [BP+SI],DH
FFFF:000D FFFF           ???     DI
FFFF:000F 7772           JA      0083
FFFF:0011 30E3           XOR     BL,AH
FFFF:0013 004701         ADD     [BX+01],AL
FFFF:0016 7000           JO      0018
FFFF:0018 C3             RET
FFFF:0019 E200           LOOP    001B
FFFF:001B F0             LOCK
FFFF:001C 47             INC     DI
FFFF:001D 017000         ADD     [BX+SI+00],SI
```

we can see the first command executed is a jump. If you want to, you can work through the code at F000:E05B (a test routine that tests the 8088, followed by the memory checks and then reading in the boot record). You can even execute this boot program directly. This gives you an unusual way of warm-booting, by loading CS and IP with the address of this jump (F000:E05B in this version of ROM) and typing Go. The machine will reboot just as if you had typed Ctrl-Alt-Del.

If you boot up without a diskette, ROM BASIC appears on the screen. What actually happens is that an Interrupt 18H, ROM BASIC, is executed. We can execute the same interrupt from DEBUG and start ROM BASIC ourselves.

To do this, we need to find the address of the code for INT 18H. We can find this address in the Interrupt Vector Table. This address will be stored at 0000:4x18H, or 0000:0060H. (Recall that there are four bytes, two words, stored for each interrupt vector in the interrupt vector table, and that the table starts at 0000:0000.) With the D command we can simply dump the Interrupt Vector Table, starting at 0000:0060:

```
-D0000:0060
           |  |  |  |
           V  V  V  V
0000:0060  00 00 00 F6 F2 E6 00 F0-6E FE 00 F0 40 01 70 00   ...vrf.pn~.p@.p.
0000:0070  53 FF 00 F0 A4 F0 00 F0-22 05 00 00 00 00 00 F0   S..p$p.p"......p
0000:0080  07 0B E3 00 38 01 0A 06-42 02 53 06 70 02 53 06   ..c.8...B.S.p.S.
0000:0090  E2 04 3A 05 E0 13 E3 00-2E 14 E3 00 13 27 E3 00   b.:..c...c..'c.
0000:00A0  13 0B E3 00 2E 01 70 00-00 00 00 00 00 00 00 00   ..c...p.........
0000:00B0  00 00 00 00 00 00 00 00-6D 03 3A 05 00 00 00 00   ........m.:.....
0000:00C0  EA 14 0B E3 00 00 00 00-00 00 00 00 00 00 00 00   j..c............
0000:00D0  00 00 00 00 00 00 00 00-00 00 00 00 00 00 00 00   ................
```

The first four bytes, 00 00 00 F6, make up the address F600:0000—stored in the typical PC fashion—IP followed by CS, both with their bytes reversed. If you load CS with F600 and IP with 0000, then type G, ROM BASIC will take over and clear the screen with its own startup message.

The Compare Command

With **Compare**, you can easily spot differences in certain sections of memory. With a command such as C000 80 100, the memory locations from CS:0000 to CS:80 will be compared with the locations at CS:100 to CS:180. This command is usually of use *only* to the proficient DEBUG operator.

The Move Command

Often, if you have to insert some new code into a program, the patch will not be the same length as the part it is replacing. For that reason there is a **Move** command, which lets you move sections of code so new sections can be put in or bad sections removed.

The Fill Command

The **Fill** command is a time-saving command. If you want to fill a certain range of memory with a certain value—zero, for example—Fill will repeat a value list that you've given it until the memory range is filled up.

Chapter 3

Keyboard Handling

INTRODUCTION

As mentioned in the Foreword, the first part of this book is divided into sections that correspond to the various subsections of the PC. For example, there is a chapter covering the disks, a chapter covering the screen, and a chapter covering files. In each chapter we'll go through all the ways to work with each subsystem, which usually means we'll cover BIOS and DOS services first and then develop our own strategies later in the chapter.

Since you already know most of the 8088 commands, there are very few we will cover. The important next step is application. A beginning text will cover 8088 assembly language command by command; it is up to the advanced level books to explore the system resources, such as the BIOS and DOS services, in detail.

A thorough knowledge of the system services is essential to the assembly language programmer. Introductory books usually cover only the rudimentary services, but in this book we will cover the full range of what BIOS and DOS have to offer, including the most advanced services.

Chapter 3 is all about the ways that programs can accept keyboard input. We'll start with the usual methods, using the INT 21H or **BIOS services**. Afterward, we'll continue to the more advanced, in-depth method of using a memory-resident program to read from the keyboard buffer directly: intercepting keystrokes as they are typed. This latter method is the way many professional packages work, including keyboard macro packages.

In this chapter, we will review only the BIOS and DOS interrupts that have to do with accepting keyboard input. For more systematic coverage of the BIOS and DOS interrupts, or for reference, see Appendix A on page 311, which lists all the PC interrupts from 0 to FFH.

Table 3.1 DOS' Keyboard Input Services

INT 21H Service	Will Wait	^Break Seen	Will Echo
1	X	X	X
6			
7	X		
8	X	X	

DOS INTERRUPT SERVICES

INT 21H Service 1—Character Input with Echo

Input	Output
AH = 1	AL = ASCII code of struck key Does Echo on screen

Checks for ^C or ^Break

This is the most basic, beginning level method of reading in keystrokes. There are four DOS services that deal explicitly with character input: Services 1, 6, 7, and 8. For a comparison between them, see Table 3.1. To call Service 1, you simply load a one into the AH register—selecting Service 1—and use an INT 21H command, like this:

```
MOV     AH,1
INT     21H
```

The PC will wait until a key is struck (or read one key from what was typed ahead) and return the struck key's ASCII code in AL.

If AL returns 00, then a special key, requiring an "extended ASCII code" was struck. If this happens, you must issue another INT 21H Service 1 call. This time AL will contain the second byte of the extended ASCII code of the struck key. For the moment, however, we are not anticipating the use of any function keys or any other keys that need extended ASCII codes, so we will put off their description until we cover BIOS INT 16H.

The SMALL.COM Program Using DEBUG

Here's a short example that can readily be typed in with DEBUG. All this program, SMALL.COM, does is to read keystrokes, convert lower case ASCII into upper case ASCII, then type the character back. To type the character back, we use INT 21H Service 2, covered in Chapter 4. This service types out the ASCII code in the DL register, so we have to load it properly.

```
A>DEBUG

-NSMALL.COM        ← Call this file SMALL.COM
-A100              ← And start it at 100H
08F7:0100 MOV AH,1         ← Select INT 21H service 1
08F7:0102 INT 21H          ← Read the typed in character
08F7:0104 ADD AL,20        ← Add 20H = ASCII 'A' - ASCII 'a'
08F7:0106 MOV AH,2         ← Now use service 2 of INT 21H
08F7:0108 MOV DL,AL        ← And set up the DL register for it
```

```
08F7:010A INT 21H         ← Print out the small character
08F7:010C JMP 100         ← And jump back to the beginning
08F7:010E INT 20H         ← This INT 20H is only for form's sake.
08F7:0110
```

There are one or two points that should be made here. Whenever you work with DEBUG, it will assume all numbers you give it are in Hex. For example, to convert the byte ASCII 'A' (ASCII 65) into the small letter ASCII 'a' (ASCII 97), we have to add 32 (97 − 65), or 20H. In DEBUG we type this in this way:

```
08F7:0104 ADD AL,20       ← Add 20H = ASCII 'A' - ASCII 'a'
```

DEBUG always assumes that we are using Hex notation. Further, we can't use labels in DEBUG, since DEBUG is not really a full assembler. DEBUG assembles the lines we give it line by line, however, so we can see the addresses we want to jump to. After we read in one capital letter and type back the small version, we want to jump up to the top of the program and start all over again. To do this we will use a JMP command which sends us back to the beginning of the program, CS:100, this way:

```
08F7:010C JMP 100         ← And jump back to the beginning
```

After typing our program in, let's check what we've written with the U command:

```
-U
08F7:0100 B401        MOV     AH,01
08F7:0102 CD21        INT     21
08F7:0104 0420        ADD     AL,20
08F7:0106 B402        MOV     AH,02
08F7:0108 88C2        MOV     DL,AL
08F7:010A CD21        INT     21
08F7:010C EBF2        JMP     0100
08F7:010E CD20        INT     20
08F7:0110 F62B        IMUL    BYTE PTR [BP+DI]
08F7:0112 06          PUSH    ES
08F7:0113 96          XCHG    SI,AX
08F7:0114 F63B        IDIV    BYTE PTR [BP+DI]
08F7:0116 46          INC     SI
08F7:0117 C27310      RET     1073
08F7:011A C646C800    MOV     BYTE PTR [BP-38],00
08F7:011E 8946C2      MOV     [BP-3E],AX
```

We can see that our program takes up 16 bytes, from CS:100 to CS:10F. To write it out as a functioning .COM file, we load CX with 16 (=10H) and use the W command:

```
-RCX
CX 0000
:10
-
-W
Writing 0010 bytes
-Q
```

To make sure our file got written, we do a directory search:

```
A>DIR SMALL.COM

Volume in drive A is DEVEL
Directory of  A:\

SMALL     COM       16   2-24-86    8:43p          ← 16 Bytes
        1 File(s)     63488 bytes free
```

and then run it. After you type SMALL, SMALL will be loaded and run, but it will provide you with no prompt. Any capital letters you type, however, will appear on the screen with the corresponding small letter next to them:

```
A>SMALL
AaBbCcDdEeFf
```

We've made no provision for quitting SMALL.COM; it would happily accept volumes of capital letters and convert them into lower case for you. Fortunately, however, this DOS keyboard input interrupt service checks for ^C or ^Break, and so you can type either to quit.

INT 21H Service 6—Read Key without Wait

Input	Output
AH = 6	
DL = FF →	AL holds character if one ready.
DL < FF →	Type ASCII code in DL on screen.
	Does NOT Echo on screen.

NOTE: Does not check for ^C or ^Break.

This service is the Direct Console I/O service. Service 6 does not wait for a character to be typed. If you load DL with FFH and call Service 6 (load AH with 6 and issue an INT 21H instruction), AL will return the character that was typed, if one was typed, and the zero flag will not be set.

On the other hand, if no character is in the keyboard buffer, the zero flag will be set, and no character will be returned in AL. Like all the other DOS keyboard services, if the typed key has an extended ASCII code, AL will first return 00 and you must call service 6 again to get the second byte of the extended code.

If you load a character's ASCII code (not FF) into DL and call Service 6, that character's ASCII code will be printed out, making this a particularly versatile Service. This Service, however, does not check for ^C or ^Break.

The REPEATER.COM Program

Let's write a quick example using this Service called REPEATER.COM. REPEATER's job will be to read whatever character has been typed in and type it back out until a new character is typed. Service 6 is the only DOS keyboard service that returns characters and yet does NOT wait for you to type something in. If nothing was typed in, we want to keep typing out what we have been typing. Here is our brief program. Notice that since there is only one procedure, we did not even use the PROC and ENDP pseudo-OPs:

```
CODE_SEG        SEGMENT

         ASSUME  CS:CODE_SEG
         ORG     100H
START:   MOV     AH,6           ;We'll only use Service 6 here.
TOP:     MOV     DL,0FFH        ;Read a character in.
         INT     21H            ;With INT 21H
         JZ      TYPEOUT        ;If there was NO character, type out old one.
         MOV     CL,AL          ;Store new character
         CMP     AL,'E'         ;Was it an 'E'?
         JE      FINISH         ;Yes, jump to the end of the program.
TYPEOUT: MOV     DL,CL          ;Type out the stored character
         INT     21H            ;Again with service 6
         JMP     TOP            ;And begin again.
FINISH:  INT     20H            ;Finish up here and exit.

CODE_SEG        ENDS
        END     START
```

Also, because Service 6 does not check for the ^C or ^Break characters, we check to see if the typed character was an 'E' (for End). If so, we jump to the end of the program and quit. Service 6 does NOT echo to the screen.

This service is different from Service 1 because it does not wait for you to type a character before returning, does not check for ^C or ^Break, and can even type characters out itself if you set DL properly.

INT 21H Service 7—Read Key with Wait.

Input	Output
AH = 7	AL = ASCII code of struck key NO Echo on screen.

NOTE: Does NOT Check for ^C or ^Break

This DOS service is very much like Service 1, except that it does not echo characters on the screen and does NOT check for ^C or ^Break. Table 3.1 compares Service 7 to the other character-handling services.

This service, too, has its uses. If for any reason you do not want what your type to appear on the screen (in the middle of a game, for example, or as a password), then you might want to use it. Since it does not check for ^C or ^Break, we can even write a little program called HOLD.COM that will not allow anyone to use your PC until they type in a three-letter password ("DOS"). HOLD.COM is immune to ^C or ^Break, but it will not stand up against a reboot.

The HOLD.COM Program

If you run HOLD, the PC will simply wait until the three-letter password, "DOS" is typed:

```
CODE_SEG            SEGMENT

          ASSUME   CS:CODE_SEG
          ORG      100H
START:    MOV      AH,7             ;Here we will use service 7.
          INT      21H              ;Of INT 21H.
          CMP      AL,'D'           ;Was the typed letter a D?
          JNE      START            ;No, start over.
          INT      21H              ;Yes, get next letter.
          CMP      AL,'O'           ;Was this letter an O?
          JNE      START            ;No, start over.
          INT      21H              ;Get last letter.
          CMP      AL,'S'           ;An 'S'?
          JNE      START            ;Nope, start over.
FINISH:   INT      20H              ;Yes, finish up and exit.

CODE_SEG            ENDS
         END        START
```

INT 21H Service 8—Read Key Without Echo

Input	Output
AH = 8	AL = ASCII code of struck key. Does NOT echo the typed key.

NOTE: Checks for ^C or ^Break

This service is the same as 1, except that it does not echo the typed key on the screen. The only difference between this service and Service 7 is that Service 7 doesn't check for ^C or ^Break. If you want to use passwords, but also want to include ^C or ^Break checking, this is the service to use.

INT 21H Service 0AH—String Input

Input	Output
AH = 0AH	Buffer at DS:DX filled.
[DS:DX]=Length of buffer	Echo the typed keys.

NOTE: Checks for ^C or ^Break

Service 0AH was written to take buffered keyboard input. For the first time, we will have to deal with more than one key at a time, so we will cover the 8088's string-handling commands in the following section.

Many parts of DOS itself use this service. To use Service 0AH, we have to point DS:DX at an area in memory to be filled with keyboard input. The first byte of that area, the byte at location DS:DX, has to hold the (non-zero) number of bytes that the buffer can hold. If your buffer can hold 16 bytes, you would put 10H in the first byte.

Whatever is typed is written in the buffer, starting at the third byte. The rubout key works as it should when you are typing, and mistakes that are erased never reach the final buffer. (If you have to load input buffers and make manual provisions for the rubout key, it can be very difficult.) The buffer will keep storing characters until the next to last byte is reached. If you try to type any more characters, besides a carriage return, the PC will beep with the familiar type-ahead-full beep. Please note that the buffer length stored in the first byte is the actual number of bytes the buffer can take, which excludes the first two bytes at DS:DX and DS:DX+1. When you type a carriage return, input is ended.

When control returns from INT 21H, the second byte in the buffer will hold the number of characters typed, and the last character will be an ASCII 0DH, a carriage return. For example, if we typed 'Testing...', our buffer would end up like this:

```
DS:DX points here.
  |    Number of bytes typed.
  |    |
  V    V   'T' 'e' 's' 't' 'i' 'n' 'g' '.' '.' '.'
 10   0A   54  65  73  74  69  6E  67  2E  2E  2E  0D  00  00  00  00  00
           |<------------------------ 16 Bytes ------------------------>|
```

THE 8088'S STRING COMMANDS

There are many ways that assembly language excels in string handling jobs, most notably in string searches or comparisons. Since we will use these string commands—MOVS, CMPS, SCAS, LODS, and STOS—later, and since many introductory books do not cover them at all, they deserve our attention here.

The string commands are so important to the 8088 that the SI and DI registers have been set aside for them. String operations assume that as you move data, it moves from the address ES:[SI] to DS:[DI]. SI stands for Source Index, and DI for Destination Index. The string commands increment or decrement these indices automatically.

MOVS, MOVSB, MOVSW, and REP

MOVS, or Move String, is the most elementary of string operations. All you must do is point DS:SI at the source string and ES:DI at the destination area and execute MOVS. To copy a string that is 20 bytes long from POINT_A to POINT_B, you could do it like this:

```
            DATA_SEG        SEGMENT
            POINT_A DB 'This is ONLY a test.'
            POINT_B DB 20 DUP(?)
            DATA_SEG        ENDS

            CODE_SEG        SEGMENT
;Copy string of 20 bytes from POINT_A to POINT_B
            PUSH    DS              ;First set up ES (See below).
            POP     ES
            ASSUME  ES:DATA_SEG     ;Tell the Assembler.
            LEA     SI,POINT_A
            LEA     DI,POINT_B
            CLD                     ;Make sure we increment.
            MOV     CX,20D          ;Put 20 Decimal into loop counter.
    AGAIN:  MOVS    POINT_B,POINT_A     ←
            LOOP    AGAIN
                    :
                    :
```

One or two lines above should be discussed. Since ES may theoretically be set to any value, and the strings we want to use are in the DATA_SEG segment, we first set up ES to point to DATA_SEG with these commands:

```
PUSH    DS              ;First set up ES (See below).
POP     ES
ASSUME  ES:DATA_SEG     ;Tell the Assembler
```

These lines are shorthand for a process that usually takes longer. Since segment registers cannot be loaded directly into each other, they usually must go through some all-purpose register (like this: MOV AX,DS MOV ES,AX). The stack is a way around that, and it is commonly used since each PUSH or POP assembles into only one byte of machine code.

The command **CLD**, or Clear Direction Flag, is an important (but often neglected) part of this type of code:

```
;Copy string of 20 bytes from POINT_A to POINT_B
            PUSH    DS              ;First set up ES (See below).
            POP     ES
            ASSUME  ES:DATA_SEG     ;Tell the Assembler.
            LEA     SI,POINT_A
            LEA     DI,POINT_B
            CLD                     ;Make sure we increment.
            MOV     CX,20D          ;Put 20 Decimal into loop counter.
    AGAIN:  MOVS    POINT_B,POINT_A
            LOOP    AGAIN
```

As soon as the MOVS command is executed, both SI and DI are automatically incremented. If you had used CLD's complement, STD (Set Direction Flag), both DI and SI would be decremented every time you use MOVS.

The **MOVS** command itself also deserves comment. When you move data, the 8088 must know whether you intend to move bytes or words, since words are stored with their bytes in reverse order. When you use an instruction such as MOVS POINT_B,POINT_A, the assembler can check the declaration of both POINT_A and POINT_B. Since both have been declared with DB, the assembler knows that you intend to move one byte at a time. Instead of assembling this command into MOVS, the command is actually assembled into MOVSB, Move String Byte. Similarly, if you had declared POINT_A and POINT_B with DW, the Assembler would have used MOVSW in the final code.

The string commands come with a built-in loop command as well; REP, for repeat. The same code as above could have been done this way:

```
;Copy string of 20 bytes from POINT_A to POINT_B
            PUSH    DS              ;First set up ES (See below).
            POP     ES
            ASSUME  ES:DATA_SEG     ;Tell the Assembler
            LEA     SI,POINT_A
            LEA     DI,POINT_B
            CLD                     ;Make sure we increment.
            MOV     CX,20D          ;Put 20 Decimal into loop counter.
        REP MOVS    POINT_B,POINT_A
```

REP is a prefix for string commands that turns them into one-line loops. Like LOOP, REP decrements the CX counter until it is zero.

We could have used the command **MOVSB** in this case. For instance, this code is also equivalent to that above. (Note that MOVSB and MOVSW take no operands, but you must set up SI and DI:)

```
;Copy string of 20 bytes from POINT_A to POINT_B
            PUSH    DS              ;First set up ES (See below).
            POP     ES
            ASSUME  ES:DATA_SEG     ;Tell the Assembler
            LEA     SI,POINT_A
```

```
        LEA     DI,POINT_B
        CLD                         ;Make sure we increment.
        MOV     CX,20D              ;Put 20 Decimal into loop counter.
    REP MOVSB
```

CMPS, CMPSB, CMPSW, REPE, and REPNE

CMPS also works with two strings at a time, like MOVS. A normal CMP is done comparing the bytes (or words) at DS:SI and ES:DI, the flags are set, and then SI and DI are incremented (or decremented, depending on the direction flag). For example, let's say we want to find where the differences in TRAVELOG_A and TRAVELOG_B are. Here's how they've been set up in the data segement:

```
DATA_SEG        SEGMENT
TRAVELOG_A      DB 'I went to Ireland$'
TRAVELOG_B      DB 'I went to Iceland$'
DATA_SEG        ENDS
```

and here's how we would find the first non-matching byte:

```
DATA_SEG          SEGMENT
TRAVELOG_A        DB 'I went to Ireland$'
TRAVELOG_B        DB 'I went to Iceland$'
DATA_SEG          ENDS

CODE_SEG          SEGMENT
;Find first NON-matching byte in the two strings
        PUSH      DS
        POP       ES
        ASSUME    ES:DATA_SEG
        LEA       DI,TRAVELOG_A
        LEA       SI,TRAVELOG_B
        CLD
        MOV       CX,18
   REPE CMPS      TRAVELOG_A,TRAVELOG_B    ;Repeat WHILE Equal
        JNE       MIS_MATCH
 MATCH: MOV       AX,1
                  :
                  :
 MIS_MATCH:
```

With this code we can search through the first 18 bytes of the strings. REPE CMPS compares the two strings, TRAVELOG_A and TRAVELOG_B, until two characters do NOT match. REPE means repeat WHILE EQUAL. When two characters do not match, the flags are set to indicate that the elements being compared were not equal: we can take advantage of that with a JNE MIS_MATCH.

```
        MOV     CX,18
   REPE CMPS    TRAVELOG_A,TRAVELOG_B    ;Repeat WHILE Equal
     →  JNE     MIS_MATCH
 MATCH: MOV     AX,1
```

If the branch to MIS_MATCH is taken, there was a mismatch in the strings. (DI and SI are incremented after all comparisons, however, so the address of the non-matching bytes would be DS:SI − 1 and ES:DI − 1 when you reached the label MIS_MATCH.) If the two strings matched completely, CX would be 0, the flags would be set so that the JNE is not taken, and control would continue with the next line:

```
          MOV     CX,18
     REPE CMPS    TRAVELOG_A,TRAVELOG_B    ;Repeat WHILE Equal
          JNE     MIS_MATCH
 → MATCH: MOV     AX,1
```

This section of code finds when the first byte of two strings, STRING_A and STRING_B, DO match:

```
 ;Find first MATCHING byte in the two strings
        PUSH     DS
        POP      ES
        ASSUME   ES:DATA_SEG
        LEA      DI,STRING_A
        LEA      SI,STRING_B
        CLD
        MOV      CX,500
 → REPNE CMPSB             ;Repeat While NOT Equal
        JE       SAME_BYTE
  DIFFERENT:
        MOV      AX,1
```

Here we are using **CMPSB**, which takes no operands, and using **REPNE**, repeat while NOT equal. In this example, only the first 500 bytes would be compared for a match. The command **CMPSW** is just the same as CMPSB, except that it compares full words at a time.

SCAS, SCASB, and SCASW

These commands are similar to CMPS, but instead of comparing two strings, **scan string** commands compare a byte in AL or a word in AX to a string. Here's an example that accepts input with INT 21H service 0AH and tells you the position of the first character 'a' in the string. This program, FIND_a, will type out the position of 'a' in a string, starting with position 0. For example, 'abcde' would yield an answer of 0. FIND_a is a simple program, and it can only handle input strings of up to 10 bytes including the carriage return (since it has to return a single digit answer). Here it is:

```
CODE_SEG         SEGMENT
         ASSUME  CS:CODE_SEG
         ORG     100H                       ;Make this a COM file.
START:   JMP     FIND_a
         STRING  DB      10,11 DUP(0)       ;Buffer, starting with 10 in 1st byte.
FIND_a   PROC    NEAR
         MOV     AH,0AH                     ;Select Service 0AH.
         MOV     DX,OFFSET STRING           ;Set up DS:DX.
         INT     21H
         CLD                                ;Make sure DI increments.
         MOV     AL,'a'                     ;Scan for 'a' by putting it in AL.
         MOV     DI,OFFSET STRING+2         ;Point to beginning of string.
         MOV     CX,10                      ;Scan up to 10 letters.
REPNE    SCASB          ← Repeat while NOT equal, Scan byte.
         JNE     OUT                        ;If no match, just exit.
         MOV     AH,2                       ;A match was found, print <cr><lf>
         MOV     DL,13                      ;<cr>
         INT     21H
         MOV     DL,10                      ;<lf>
         INT     21H
         DEC     DI                         ;Point to matching byte.
         MOV     DX,DI                      ;We want to print ASCII value of DI.
         SUB     DX,OFFSET STRING+2         ;Subtract offset of beginning of string.
         ADD     DL,'0'                     ;Add beginning of numerals in ASCII.
         INT     21H                        ;And type out answer.
 OUT:    INT     20H      ;End the Program.
 FIND_a  ENDP
 CODE_SEG         ENDS
         END     START
```

In FIND_a.ASM, we use the command REPNE SCASB, one of the most common string commands, to locate a byte, 'a', in the typed-in string. If we had been looking for an entire word, say 'apple', instead of just 'a', a typical method would be to search for the first character, 'a' with REPNE SCASB and then to follow it with a CMPSB command to check whether the characters following 'a' are 'pple'.

A few things are worth noticing in this example. One is that we set up our keyboard input buffer using DB wisely, initializing the first byte to hold 10, our buffer length:

```
CODE_SEG         SEGMENT
         ASSUME  CS:CODE_SEG
         ORG     100H                       ;Make this a COM file.
START:   JMP     FIND_a
       → STRING  DB      10,11 DUP(0)       ;Buffer, starting with 10 in 1st byte.
FIND_a   PROC    NEAR
                 :
```

Another new thing is our use of the OFFSET pseudo-OP, which loads a label's offset from the beginning of the segment into a register. In the code, we reference the beginning of the input string with the address STRING+2:

```
                 :
        MOV      AL,'a'                   ;Scan for 'a' by putting it in AL.
      → MOV      DI,OFFSET STRING+2       ;Point to beginning of string.
        MOV      CX,10                    ;Scan up to 10 letters.
REPNE   SCASB          ← Repeat while NOT equal, Scan byte.
        JNE      OUT                      ;If no match, just exit.
        MOV      AH,2                     ;A match was found, print <cr><lf>
```

If we had wanted to, we could have set up the data area this way:

```
         ASSUME  CS:CODE_SEG
         ORG     100H                     ;Make this a .COM file.
START:   JMP     FIND_a
       → BUFFER  DB      10,0
       → STRING  DB      10 DUP(0)
FIND_a   PROC    NEAR
                 :
```

This would have still given us an unbroken string in memory of 12 bytes, the first one set to 10, the rest to zero. But we then could have referenced the beginning of the input string directly with the label 'STRING' and could have simply said MOV DI,OFFSET STRING.

To use REPNE SCASB, we loaded the counter, CX, with 10. This means that if no match is found in 10 repetitions, control will pass on to the next instruction. If a match is found, control will also pass on to the next command (since REPNE means Repeat While NOT Equal), so we have to distinguish between the two.

SCASB is just like CMP in setting the flags, so if we found a match, the flags will be set as though a CMP between two equal items had just been done. If no match is found, the flags will have been set as though a CMP had been done between unequal items. In this case, we want to quit, so we test the result of our scan with JNE OUT, testing the last comparison done in REPNE SCASB:

```
                 :
        MOV      AL,'a'                   ;Scan for 'a' by putting it in AL.
        MOV      DI,OFFSET STRING+2       ;Point to beginning of string.
      → MOV      CX,10                    ;Scan up to 10 letters.
REPNE   SCASB          ← Repeat while NOT equal, Scan byte.
      → JNE      OUT                      ;If no match, just exit.
        MOV      AH,2                     ;A match was found, print <cr><lf>
```

If a match is found, we want to print its position in the string out (beginning with 0). We first send a carriage return (ASCII 13) line-feed (ASCII 10) pair using the DOS printing service, number 2. We first print a ‹cr›, then a ‹lf›, and finally find the position of the 'a'. (Recall that the REPNE SCASB left ES:DI pointing at the byte following the match, so it has to be decremented first.)

```
                  :
REPNE   SCASB          ← Repeat while NOT equal, Scan byte.
        JNE     OUT                     ;If no match, just exit.
        MOV     AH,2                    ;A match was found, print <cr><lf>
        MOV     DL,13                   ;<cr>
        INT     21H
        MOV     DL,10                   ;<lf>
        INT     21H
      → DEC     DI                      ;Point to matching byte.
      → MOV     DX,DI                   ;We want to print ASCII value of DI.
      → SUB     DX,OFFSET STRING+2      ;Subtract offset of beginning of string.
      → ADD     DL,'0'                  ;Add beginning of numerals in ASCII.
        INT     21H                     ;And type out answer.
```

LODS and STOS

The last two string commands of the 8088 are the Load String (**LODS**) and **Store String** (STOS) commands. The purpose of LODS is to load strings byte by byte from DS:[SI] into AL. STOS stores them byte by byte into ES:[DI]. After each move, DI or SI is incremented. These commands both provide quick, easy access to string manipulation and handling.

As with all string commands, even if you use an instruction like:

```
START:  JMP      LOOK
        STRING1  DB       'Apple of my eye.'
LOOK    PROC     NEAR
        LEA      SI,STRING1
      → LODS     STRING1
```

it will actually be put into the code as LODSB, without any operands. In fact, the only reason that you have to include the name of the string STRING1 in the command above is so the assembler can check the attribute of STRING1 (it is BYTE) and make sure it will use LODSB instead of LODSW.

The assembler assembles STOS into STOSB or STOSW. STOS is an excellent command to use if you want to store a string and, at the same time, check for a particular character. Since each character in the string being stored moves through AL, you can check it before storing it. With STOSB, you can move byte after byte from AL into memory.

This finishes our survey of the 8088's string commands, although you should keep in mind that they are an important part of the ability of assembly language to deal with large quantities of data rapidly. We will have more use for them later in the book, but now we will continue with the available keyboard input services that DOS provides.

DOS KEYBOARD INPUT SERVICES

INT 21H Service 0BH—Check Keyboard Buffer

Input	Output
AH = 0BH	AL = FF → Character ready. AL = 00 → Nothing to read in.

NOTE: ^Break is checked for

This DOS service in unique. Without actually reading a character, you can check and see if something has been typed. Its use is simple: All you do is load AH with 0BH and issue an INT 21H command. If a ^Break has been typed, the program is interrupted. If not, control returns from INT 21H and you can look at the contents of AL to see if there is a key or keys to be read in. If AL is FF, all bits set, there is something to be read in with one of the keyboard services. If not, AL is 0.

The utilty of this service is that with it you can use Services 1, 7, 8, or A without the usual wait. If you want to pick up characters and echo them on the screen, for example, you could use Service 1, but only if you don't mind waiting until there is something there to read. On the other hand, with Service B, you can check and see if some key is waiting to be read from the keyboard buffer. Use Service 1 if there is a key waiting.

INT 21H Service 0CH—Clear Keyboard Buffer and Execute Service

Input	Output
AH = 0CH AL = Keyboard function #	Standard output from the selected service.

NOTE: ^Break is checked for

DOS Service 0CH clears the keyboard buffer and then will invoke a keyboard service (1, 6, 7, 8, or 0AH). You will have to wait until a key is typed because the first thing it does is erase keys typed ahead in the keyboard buffer.

The use of this service is specialized, but when it is called for, it is necessary. In particular, when crucial choices have to be made, it is important that typed-ahead bytes in the keyboard buffer not be interpreted as responses. When you type DEL *.*, for example, a prompt always comes up asking 'Are you sure (y/n)?'. Before this message is typed, the keyboard buffer is cleared to take care of incorrect responses. The same thing is true for the disk error message: 'Error reading Drive:B Abort, Retry or Ignore?'. FORMAT.COM also clears the keyboard buffer before asking 'Format another (y/n)?'

After the keyboard buffer is cleared, the number in AL is read and that DOS Service is executed. For example, if we had put a 0AH there, we would first have cleared the keyboard buffer and then executed DOS Service 0AH, buffered input, just as if we had put 0AH into AH.

BIOS INTERRUPTS

We've completed the DOS interrupts dealing with the keyboard. There are still a number of BIOS interrupts to work through, however. In general, DOS provides services with more error checking and options, while BIOS provides the sturdy, low-level services DOS is built on.

BIOS INT 16H

Input	Output
AH = 0	AH=Scan Code AL=ASCII code
AH = 1	Zero Flag=1 → buffer empty
	Zero Flag=0 → AH=Scan Code
	AL=ASCII Code
AH = 2	AL=Keyboard Status byte.

BIOS is the really low-level worker of the PC. A complete listing, which is a novelty for IBM, of BIOS is given in the *Technical Reference Manual*, and is highly recommended for any assembly language programmer.

An essential difference for us between BIOS and DOS is that the BIOS interrupts are **re-enterable**. What this means is that if some program is executing a BIOS interrupt, another program can start to execute the **same** interrupt before the first program is done. This is not the case for DOS. What this really means is that memory-resident programs, like the ones we will develop, can use BIOS interrupts but *not* DOS interrupts or service calls.

For example, if a program is in the middle of executing a BIOS interrupt when a memory-resident program takes control and tries to execute the same interrupt, there would be no problem. With DOS interrupts, however, this is a disaster—the machine is likely to crash. We will have more to say about this difference when it becomes important in what we are doing.

The BIOS keyboard interrupt, INT 16H, is one of the fundamental interrupts of the PC. In fact, it can often return information that is too low-level for our applications, because besides returning the ASCII value of a typed key, it will also return the character's **scan code**.

Keyboard Scan Codes

For each of the 83 (53H) keys on the PC's keyboard, there is a code called a **scan code**. This is the code the microprocessor in the keyboard sends to the PC when a key is typed. All the scan codes are listed in the *Technical Reference Manual*. Also, this BASIC program:

```
10      FOR I=1 TO 10:KEY I,"":NEXT I
20      DEF SEG = &H40
30      FKEY$=INKEY$:IF FKEY$="" GOTO 30
40      TAIL=PEEK(26):TAIL=TAIL-2:IF TAIL < 30 THEN TAIL = 60
50      CODE1=PEEK(TAIL):CODE2=PEEK(TAIL+1)
60      PRINT HEX$(CODE1) SPC(1) HEX$(CODE2) SPC(2);:GOTO 20:END
```

will read any key's scan and ASCII code directly from the keyboard buffer and print them out in Hex, ASCII code, and then scan code. The "A" key has an ASCII code of 41H and a scan code of 1EH. The "S" key, right next to it, has an ASCII code of 53H and a scan code of 1FH.

Extended ASCII Codes

IBM found that there are more keys on their keyboard than there is space in ASCII to represent them, especially when you take into account Alt, Num Lock, and Control combinations. For instance, the F1 key leaves an ASCII code of zero in the keyboard buffer and a scan code of 3BH. All keys leave two bytes in the keyboard buffer—an ASCII code and a scan code—but some keys' ASCII codes are zero. Those keys are represented by an extended ASCII code. When one of the DOS keyboard Services returns a zero in the AL register, the key that was pushed has no normal ASCII code, and you must reissue the same service call again to get a new number into AL, the extended ASCII code. This code is the same as the scan code of the typed key for Extended ASCII values of 3–53H. There are no scan codes greater than 53H.

Extended ASCII codes greater than 53H have to do with Shift, Control, or Alt states of the function or cursor keys, and all these Extended ASCII codes may be found in tables in the *Technical Reference Manual*, by using the above BASIC program, or in the BASIC manual that comes with the PC.

INT 16H Service 0—Read Key

BIOS INT 16H can return to your program both the scan and ASCII code of a typed character. If you set AH to 0 before issuing an INT 16H command, INT 16H waits for a key to be typed if there are none waiting, and then returns the key's scan code in AH and its ASCII code in AL. If AL is 0, the key is an extended ASCII key, and the extended ASCII code is in AH.

INT 16H Service 1—Examine Keyboard and Read

If you set AH=1, INT 16H examines the keyboard for you without altering it. If the Zero Flag is 1 on return, the buffer is empty and there is no key to be read. If the Zero Flag is 1, AX is set just as it would be in INT 16H Service 0, that is, AH contains the scan code and AL contains the ASCII code.

INT 16H Service 2—Read Status Byte

Finally, setting AH to 2 before issuing an INT 16H returns the keyboard status byte in AL. This keyboard status byte is read directly from the **BIOS data area** at 40:00. This area also contains the keyboard buffer. There is an immense amount of information in the BIOS Data Area; a listing of its contents can be found in Table 3.2.

Table 3.2 BIOS Data Area

Address(es)	Contents
40:0000–40:0006	Addresses of RS 232 adapters 1–4
40:0008–40:000E	Addresses of printer adapters 1–4
40:0010	Equipment Flag (returned by Int 11H)
40:0012	Manufacturer's test mark
40:0013	Motherboard memory (in Kbytes)
40:0015	I/O channel memory
40:0017	The Keyboard Flags (see below)
40:0019	Numbers input with Alt key
40:001A	Location of Keyboard Buffer Head
40:001C	Location of Keyboard Buffer Tail
40:001E–40:003D	Keyboard buffer
40:003E	Status of Diskette Seek
40:003F	Status of Diskette Motor
40:0040	Timeout of Diskette Motor
40:0041	Status of Diskette
40:0042–40:0048	Status Bytes of Diskette Controller (the NEC)
40:0049	Display Mode (see the section on Clock)

Table 3.2 BIOS Data Area continued

Address(es)	Contents
40:004A	Number of columns (40 or 80)
40:004C	Length of Video Regen. Buffer
40:004E	Starting Address in Regen. Buffer
40:0050–40:005E	Positions of cursors on screen pages 1–8
40:0060	Mode of the Cursor
40:0062	Active Page Number
40:0063	Address of current display adapter

We should examine the two bytes that begin at 40:0017 because they are often useful to assembly language programmers (it is the byte at 40:17 that INT 16H Service 2 returns in AL). Table 3.3 is a breakdown of 40:17 and 40:18 bit by bit, starting with bit 0.

Table 3.3 The BIOS Words 40:17 and 40:18

Bit	State	Byte at 40:0017	Byte at 40:0018
0	Right Shift	1 -> Key is pressed	
1	Left Shift	1 -> Key is pressed	
2	Cntrl Shift	1 -> Key is pressed	
3		1 ->Alt Shift Pressed	1 ->^Num Lock On
4	Scroll_Lock	1 -> On	1 -> Key is pressed
5	Num-Lock	1 -> On	1 -> Key is pressed
6	Caps-Lock	1 -> On	1 -> Key is pressed
7	Insert	1 -> On	1 -> Key is pressed

Any program that can get into these bytes can change the keyboard state of the PC, since the scan codes that come in from the keyboard are interpreted with the aid of this byte. We can write, in DEBUG, a small program named TURNCAPS.COM that simply turns on the CapsLock state of the PC by ORing 40H, or 01000000B, with the status byte at 40:17. Using DEBUG we can write TURNCAPS.COM:

```
A> DEBUG
   NTURNCAPS.COM
   A100
   MOV AX,40
   MOV DS,AX
   MOV BX,17
   OR BYTE PTR [BX],40
   INT 20
   <CR>
```

```
RCX
D
W
Q
```

This program can be run from your AUTOEXEC.BAT file to turn on capital letters when you boot.

THE KEYBOARD BUFFER

Now we can pass into the real depth of keyboard handling on the PC: the keyboard buffer and INT 9. When you strike a key on the PC's keyboard, a complex sequence of events occurs. The keyboard is a peripheral like any other, the disk or speaker, for example. As such, it communicates with the 8088 through an I/O port. The keyboard itself is complex enough to have its own microprocessor on board, an Intel 8048, which is a true microprocessor in its own right. When you press one of the PC's keys, the 8048 generates a code depending on the key's position on the keyboard. This, as we've mentioned, is the key's scan code.

This byte-long code is then stored in a register, and the 8048 generates an Interrupt 9. This interrupt works as discussed: An address is found at the correct interrupt vector, 0000:0024 (9 × 4 = 36 = 24H) and the code there (stored in ROM) is run. If your program has turned interrupts off with a CLI command:

```
     MOV      DX,48A9H ;Find I/O address
   → CLI               ;Don't let in interrupts now.
 REP STOSB             ;Move the data
```

then INT 9 cannot take place and typed keys are ignored. If interrupts are enabled, however, the byte scan code waiting to be read in is read through its own port, port 60H. If it were not for this one line in BIOS, IN AL, 60H, the PC would be a useless machine.

Let's take a brief look, with DEBUG, at the beginning of the keyboard interrupt, Interrupt 9, in ROM BIOS. First, we must find the address at which its Service routine begins, so we dump the interrupt vector at 0000:0024:

```
              |  |  |  |
-D0:24        V  V  V  V
0000:0024    87 E9 00 F0-DD E6 00 F0 DD E6 00 F0              .i.p]f.p]f.p
0000:0030    DD E6 00 F0 DD E6 00 F0-57 EF 00 F0 47 01 70 00  ]f.p]f.pWo.pG.p.
0000:0040    65 F0 00 F0 4D F8 00 F0-41 F8 00 F0 59 EC 00 F0  ep.pMx.pAx.pYl.p
0000:0050    39 E7 00 F0 59 F8 00 F0-2E E8 00 F0 D2 EF 00 F0  9g.pYx.p.h.pRo.p
0000:0060    00 00 00 F6 F2 E6 00 F0-6E FE 00 F0 40 01 70 00  ...vrf.pn~.p@.p.
```

```
0000:0070  53 FF 00 F0 A4 F0 00 F0-22 05 00 00 00 00 00 F0   S..P$P.P"......P
0000:0080  07 0B E3 00 80 01 3A 05-42 02 06 06 70 02 06 06   ..C....:.B...P...
0000:0090  E2 04 3A 05 E0 13 E3 00-2E 14 E3 00 13 27 E3 00   b.:..C...C..'C.
0000:00A0  13 0B E3 00                                       ..C.
```

These bytes, 87 E9 00 F0, give us the address F000:E987, so we unassemble that address:

```
-UF000:E987
F000:E987 FB            STI
F000:E988 50            PUSH    AX    ← Store all registers
F000:E989 53            PUSH    BX
F000:E98A 51            PUSH    CX
F000:E98B 52            PUSH    DX
F000:E98C 56            PUSH    SI
F000:E98D 57            PUSH    DI
F000:E98E 1E            PUSH    DS
F000:E98F 06            PUSH    ES
F000:E990 FC            CLD
F000:E991 E8AA15        CALL    FF3E
F000:E994 E460          IN      AL,60  ← Read in the character.
F000:E996 50            PUSH    AX
F000:E997 E461          IN      AL,61  ← Read keyboard control port.
F000:E999 8AE0          MOV     AH,AL
F000:E99B 0C80          OR      AL,80
F000:E99D E661          OUT     61,AL  ← Reset keyboard for next character.
F000:E99F 86E0          XCHG    AL,AH
F000:E9A1 E661          OUT     61,AL
F000:E9A3 58            POP     AX
F000:E9A4 8AE0          MOV     AH,AL
F000:E9A6 3CFF          CMP     AL,FF  ← FF means the 8048's buffer is full.
-Q
```

Right before us is the actual line used to read in keyboard characters.

The number read in this way is then compared with a lookup table, the **scan code table**, at address F000:E896, and ASCII values are found for those characters that have them. Some controlling characters get no farther than INT 9 and do not leave any mark in the keyboard buffer at all. For example, although keys like Shift, Alt, and Control produce INT 9's (all keys do), they just modify what comes in next. BIOS keeps track of which one of these are active by checking the keyboard status byte at 40:0017.

After a key's ASCII code is found, it is put together with the key's scan code into the keyboard buffer. For each key that leaves anything in the buffer, two bytes appear.

Circular Buffers

The keyboard buffer itself is a set of 16 words in memory in the BIOS data area. These bytes are set up to be what is called a **circular buffer**. Since the reading and writing operations from and to this buffer are independent, circular buffering allows you to put in and take out keys easily. At any given time, one of these 16 words, called the "head", is the position that the next character will be read from. Another, the "tail", is the position that the next character can be written to. When keys are typed in, the tail advances. When you read one, the head advances. When either comes to the end of their sixteen-word range, they wrap around to the beginning again. A good model for this circular buffer is a ring of sixteen words, with the head forever chasing the tail. Two more bytes in the BIOS data area hold the current addresses of the head and the tail.

When everything is read, the head catches up with the tail; the two are at the same address, and the buffer is empty. Conversely, if the tail wraps around and comes up from behind the head, the buffer is full.

With DEBUG, we should be able to take a direct look at the keyboard buffer at 40:1E. In particular, we can examine it with the Dump command. Let's fill the buffer with A's and then examine it. To avoid having to type D0040:001E, which would fill the buffer up, let's do a Dump of 128 bytes before 40:1E so we only have to type D ‹cr› since Dump takes up just where it stopped. Here's how it looks:

```
-D0:39E         ← 128 Bytes before the Keyboard buffer
0000:039E  00 00                                              ..
0000:03A0  00 00 00 00 00 00 00 00-00 00 00 00 00 00 00 00   ................
0000:03B0  00 00 00 00 00 00 00 00-00 00 00 00 00 00 00 00   ................
0000:03C0  00 00 00 00 E5 FE 00 F0-E5 FE E5 FE 00 F0 FF FF   ....e~.pe~e~.p..
0000:03D0  5D EF FF FF 40 00 3A EF-00 F0 06 00 00 00 01 00   ]o..@.:o.p......
0000:03E0  40 00 6F EC 00 00 43 E6-80 00 02 00 00 00 01 00   @.ol..Cf........
0000:03F0  00 7C 21 E7 00 F0 46 F2-04 00 CF E5 00 F0 97 F2   .|!g.pFr..Oe.p.r
0000:0400  00 00 00 00 00 00 00 00-BC 03 00 00 00 00 00 00   ........<.......
0000:0410  BD 40 00 00 01 C0 00 40-00 00 38 00 38 00         =@...@.@..8.8.
-AAAAAAAAAAAAAAAA            ← Fill the buffer with "A"
     ^ Error                 ← Which DEBUG naturally thinks is an error.
-D                           ← And now examine it.
0000:041E  41 1E                                              A.
0000:0420  41 1E 41 1E 41 1E 41 1E-41 1E 41 1E 41 1E 41 1E   A.A.A.A.A.A.A.A.
0000:0430  41 1E 41 1E 41 1E 41 1E-0D 1C 44 20 0D 1C 03 80   A.A.A.A...D ....
0000:0440  3A 00 04 00 00 0D 01 03-02 07 50 00 00 40 00 00   %.........P..@..
0000:0450  00 18 00 00 00 00 00 00-00 00 00 00 00 00 00 00   ................
0000:0460  07 06 00 B4 03 29 30 E6-0A 00 00 00 98 4D 11 00   ...4.)0f.....M..
0000:0470  00 00 FF FF 00 00 00 00-14 14 14 14 01 01 01 01   ................
0000:0480  1E 00 3E 00 00 00 00 00-00 00 00 00 00 00 00 00   ..>.............
0000:0490  00 00 00 00 00 00 00 00-00 00 00 00 00 00         ..............
-Q
```

If you look at the ASCII part of the display you'll see our typed As. Each A is stored as a 41H (its ASCII code) and a 1E (its scan code). At the end of the last A the carriage return we typed (AAAAAAAAAAAAAAAA‹cr›) is stored as 0D (=ASCII 13) 1C (its scan code). Finally, you can see our D‹cr› command. This last ‹cr› leaves us at the top of the buffer. The next key typed would be wrapped around, and stored at the beginning at 40:1E.

It is worth noting that although there are 16 words in the keyboard buffer, the buffer can only take 15 keystrokes before it is filled and you get beeped.

The reason for this is that the tail word is where the next character will go. Let's assume the tail is right behind the head, and that there are 15 characters in the buffer. If the buffer took one more keystroke, the tail would advance and overlap the head. But an overlapping head and tail is the signal for an empty buffer. Since there is no way to distinguish a 16-character filled buffer and an empty buffer, BIOS allows a maximum of 15 characters.

In addition, when you type a key, the 8048 in the keyboard generates a scan code from 1 to 83. When you release the key, a second scan code is generated (and another INT 9 is issued). This second scan code is the same as the original value plus 128. This is the IBM PC's signal that you have released the key. If it doesn't see this signal about 1/2 second after receiving the original scan code, it will start to generate repeating characters (typematic). If you are writing code that will intercept the keyboard interrupt, INT 9, it is important to know about this second call made after a key has been released. For this second call, though, the position of the head and tail do not change, so your program will be able to tell that no new characters were added.

Intercepting INT 9

It is possible to intercept INT 9 before BIOS gets to it. If you do so, it is left to you to interpret the scan code that comes in and readjust the keyboard port correctly. Usually, it is much easier to let BIOS interpret the scan codes and put the character into the keyboard buffer before working on it. After all, the scan code table that BIOS uses is large and it is hard to see a reason for duplicating all the keyboard handling code.

Since we have now seen the fundamentals behind the keyboard buffer, we should put it to work by introducing some code that intercepts the keyboard buffer interrupt. Such code is usually memory-resident, and is used by programs that can pop up on your screen—calculators, notepads, or whatever—at any time. All they do is to watch the keyboard buffer continually for a certain set of trigger keys; when they see them, they take over. Furthermore, some programs, such as keyboard macros and the program included at the end of this chapter, KEEPER, have the ability to fill the keyboard buffers themselves.

When you run KEEPER, it attaches itself to DOS through a method we will learn about very shortly. When installed, it watches all the commands you type. Normally, DOS allows you to recall the last command typed with the F3 key, but KEEPER allows you to recall the last ten commands. When you are at monitor level, working with DOS, press a trigger key (that you've previously selected) and a window will appear on the screen. By using the up and down cursor keys, you can select a command that had been typed a while ago. When you press the trigger key again, the window disappears and the command you selected is typed to DOS just as if you had typed it yourself. We will spend a little time going over the pertinent parts of KEEPER, not the whole program, because it is important to see the ideas we've covered applied in code. First, though, comes the idea of memory-resident programs.

A MEMORY-RESIDENT .COM FILE SHELL

Only .COM files can be made memory-resident. .EXE files are not such self-contained packages; they must have their own stack segments and they can be loaded into high memory, so DOS will not allow you to make one memory-resident. .COM files do not have their own stack segments, relying instead on DOS to provide one.

When a .COM file is made memory-resident, the stack that DOS supplies, usually at the top of the segment, isn't used anymore. Instead, a memory-resident program will use DOS's own internal stack. This means that when programming and testing memory-resident code, it is easy to crash the machine if you destroy the stack. In fact, that is the most common bug you'll have to worry about when developing such programs.

On the other hand, the advantages are many. You can change the way DOS works, from deleting files to changing subdirectories, from flashing notepads on the screen to handling critical disk errors. Memory-resident packages provide some of the most amazing programs you can write. Needless to say, this is a skill that only the assembly language programmer can use.

.COM Files with a Second Segment

We mentioned in Chapter 1 that the code in .COM files needs to be restricted to 64K or under. Also, the data need not be restricted to that range; if you know the location of what you want, its address can be included directly in the machine code without the need for relocation.

Our memory-resident .COM file shell begins with a new segment, INTERRUPTS. Here it is:

LISTING 3.1 THE MEMORY-RESIDENT .COM FILE SHELL

```
INTERRUPTS SEGMENT AT 0H
        ORG (INTERRUPT #) × 4
        OLD_INT_VECTOR LABEL DWORD
INTERRUPTS ENDS
```

LISTING 3.1 CONTINUED

```
CODE_SEG SEGMENT
         ASSUME CS:CODE_SEG
         ORG 100H
ENTRY:   JMP BOOSTER
         :
         OLD_INTERRUPT DD ?
         Data Section
         :
THE_PROG PROC NEAR
         :
         PUSHF
         CALL OLD_INTERRUPT
         :
         :
         Program that stays in memory goes here.
         :
         :
         :
         IRET
THE_PROG ENDP

BOOSTER  PROC NEAR
         :
         :
         Initialization Code here
         :
         ASSUME DS:INTERRUPTS
         MOV AX,INTERRUPTS
         MOV DS,AX
         MOV AX, OLD_INT_VECTOR
         MOV OLD_INTERRUPT,AX
         MOV AX, OLD_INT_VECTOR[2]
         MOV OLD_INTERRUPT[2],AX
         :
         MOV     OLD_INT_VECTOR,OFFSET THE_PROG
         MOV     OLD_INT_VECTOR[2],CS
         :
         MOV     DX,OFFSET BOOSTER
         INT     27H
BOOSTER ENDP

CODE_SEG ENDS
END ENTRY
```

The new segment, INTERRUPTS, encloses the Interrupt Vector Table starting at the bottom of memory, 0000:0000:

```
INTERRUPTS SEGMENT AT 0H
        ORG (INTERRUPT #) × 4
        OLD_INT_VECTOR LABEL DWORD
INTERRUPTS ENDS
```

We are assuming that this memory-resident .COM file will be used to intercept interrupts. This means that when the interrupt is called (INT 16H, for example) control will come to our memory-resident program instead. This way, you can watch the parameters being passed to the interrupt and decide if you should take action.

If your program does not intercept an interrupt, then you must provide some alternate method of activating it. If you just put the code in memory and attach it after DOS, there is no reason that it would ever get run. For our purposes, we will assume that we are always channeling an interrupt through our memory-resident program. Therefore, the first thing we must do when loading the program into memory is rechannel the interrupt's address vector so that control will come to it instead of the interrupt.

Interrupts

The idea behind interrupts is a good one. When IBM buys an 8088 and installs it, it must be connected to all the hardware before you have a computer. Doing this is a difficult task. If we were to read through INT 21H, Service 1, we would find an immense amount of code. To allow companies to tailor the 8088 to the machine it will be in, Intel added interrupt commands. This way, the programmer does not have to include immense amounts of code every time he or she wants to read a character; instead, all he or she has to do is issue an INT 21H instruction. Since DOS versions vary in length, the interrupt service routines are at different memory locations in different versions. For this reason, the Interrupt Vector Table is written in RAM, rather than ROM, and it is filled every time you boot. What we are going to do is refill a particular interrupt vector with our own address. For each interrupt, there are four bytes in the vector table (two address words). To point to the one we've selected to replace, use an ORG pseudo-OP, and the new LABEL pseudo-OP:

```
INTERRUPTS SEGMENT AT 0H
     → ORG (INTERRUPT #) × 4
     → OLD_INT_VECTOR LABEL DWORD
INTERRUPTS ENDS
```

ORG points us to the right interrupt vector; that is, to the address of the interrupt's service routine. To reference this address, we will label it. We could use either a pseudo-OP like DD (Define Doubleword) or, as we have done, LABEL. Here we give the interrupt vector the name OLD_INT_VECTOR.

The Booster

When you run a standard memory-resident program for the first time, a special initialization section of the program is run. This part is called **the booster**, because it is jettisoned after the memory-resident part is installed. The booster's job is to do whatever initialization needs to be done for the memory-resident part (such as telling it if there is a graphics monitor in place), rechannel the interrupt through the memory-resident part, and then attach it to DOS.

As usual, whenever a .COM file is run, control enters at 100H. Since we want to run the booster program first, we have a JMP command there, like this one:

```
INTERRUPTS SEGMENT AT 0H
        ORG (INTERRUPT #) × 4
        OLD_INT_VECTOR LABEL DWORD
INTERRUPTS ENDS

CODE_SEG SEGMENT
        ASSUME CS:CODE_SEG
        ORG 100H
ENTRY:  JMP BOOSTER
        :
        OLD_INTERRUPT DD ?
```

At the end of the program is the BOOSTER, written to refill the interrupt vector like this:

```
BOOSTER PROC NEAR
        :
        :
        Initialization Code here
        :
        ASSUME DS:INTERRUPTS
        MOV AX,INTERRUPTS
        MOV DS,AX
        MOV AX, OLD_INT_VECTOR
        MOV OLD_INTERRUPT,AX
        MOV AX, OLD_INT_VECTOR[2]
        MOV OLD_INTERRUPT[2],AX
        :
        MOV     OLD_INT_VECTOR,OFFSET THE_PROG
        MOV     OLD_INT_VECTOR[2],CS
        :
        MOV     DX,OFFSET BOOSTER
```

```
        INT     27H
BOOSTER ENDP

CODE_SEG ENDS
END ENTRY
```

We run this part of the code to store the old interrupt vector first:

```
→ ASSUME DS:INTERRUPTS
→ MOV AX,INTERRUPTS
→ MOV DS,AX
  MOV AX, OLD_INT_VECTOR
  MOV OLD_INTERRUPT,AX
  MOV AX, OLD_INT_VECTOR[2]
  MOV OLD_INTERRUPT[2],AX
```

The first three lines set DS to point at the segment INTERRUPTS. The next four lines:

```
→ MOV AX, OLD_INT_VECTOR
→ MOV OLD_INTERRUPT,AX
→ MOV AX, OLD_INT_VECTOR[2]
→ MOV OLD_INTERRUPT[2],AX
```

load the words of the interrupt vector from the table,

```
INTERRUPTS SEGMENT AT 0H
        ORG (INTERRUPT #) × 4
      → OLD_INT_VECTOR LABEL DWORD
INTERRUPTS ENDS

CODE_SEG SEGMENT
        ASSUME CS:CODE_SEG
        ORG 100H
ENTRY:  JMP BOOSTER
        :
        OLD_INTERRUPT DD ?
        Data Section
```

into our data area right after the JMP at ORG 100H:

```
INTERRUPTS SEGMENT AT 0H
        ORG (INTERRUPT #) × 4
        OLD_INT_VECTOR LABEL DWORD
INTERRUPTS ENDS

CODE_SEG SEGMENT
        ASSUME CS:CODE_SEG
```

```
         ORG 100H
ENTRY:   JMP BOOSTER
         :
       → OLD_INTERRUPT DD ? Data Section
```

We want to store the old interrupt's address because, in most cases, we will want to call it ourselves. For example, when we intercept INT 9, we will let BIOS do the work of interpreting the byte read from Port 60H itself. Only after the interrupt, but before control returns to the interrupted program, will we examine and possibly change what was typed.

Next in the booster, we load the address of our program, THE_PROG, into the interrupt vector, IP and then CS, with these lines:

```
CODE_SEG SEGMENT
         ASSUME CS:CODE_SEG
         ORG 100H
ENTRY:   JMP BOOSTER
         :
         OLD_INTERRUPT DD ?
         Data Section
         :
→ THE_PROG PROC NEAR
         :
         Program that stays in memory goes here.
         :
BOOSTER  PROC    NEAR
         :
         ASSUME DS:INTERRUPTS
         MOV AX,INTERRUPTS
         MOV DS,AX
         MOV AX, OLD_INT_VECTOR
         MOV OLD_INTERRUPT,AX
         MOV AX, OLD_INT_VECTOR[2]
         MOV OLD_INTERRUPT[2],AX
         :
       → MOV     OLD_INT_VECTOR,OFFSET THE_PROG
       → MOV     OLD_INT_VECTOR[2],CS
         :
         MOV     DX,OFFSET BOOSTER
         INT     27H
BOOSTER ENDP
```

We have now readjusted the interrupt to point directly at our program in memory. The interrupt vector table has been "fixed." Our last step is to install the memory-resident part, but not the booster part that follows it, in memory. The whole .COM file was loaded right after DOS in memory. Now we will point to the end of the memory-resident part (the beginning of the procedure BOOSTER), and make it memory resident. The next time DOS loads a program in, it will load it after this address, so our code will remain undamaged. Attaching code in memory is done with INT 27H. We set DS:DX to the new address at which DOS may load programs, and simply issue an INT 27H, which ends the .COM file:

```
            :
            ASSUME DS:INTERRUPTS
            MOV AX,INTERRUPTS
            MOV DS,AX
            MOV AX, OLD_INT_VECTOR
            MOV OLD_INTERRUPT,AX
            MOV AX, OLD_INT_VECTOR[2]
            MOV OLD_INTERRUPT[2],AX
            :
            MOV     OLD_INT_VECTOR,OFFSET THE_PROG
            MOV     OLD_INT_VECTOR[2],CS
            :
          → MOV     DX,OFFSET BOOSTER
          → INT     27H
BOOSTER ENDP
```

All that is left now in memory is our interrupt intercepter. When an intercepted interrupt is issued, the address found in the interrupt vector table points to the address we have loaded into it, the address of THE_PROG:

```
CODE_SEG SEGMENT
            ASSUME CS:CODE_SEG
            ORG 100H
ENTRY:      JMP BOOSTER
            :
            OLD_INTERRUPT DD ?
            Data Section
            :
→ THE_PROG PROC NEAR
            :
            PUSHF
            CALL OLD_INTERRUPT
            :
            :
            Program that stays in memory goes here.
            :
            :
            :
            IRET
THE_PROG ENDP
```

Usually, the first thing in THE_PROG is a series of PUSHes. We will be making use of the registers—AX, BX, and so forth—in THE_PROG. At the same time, we want to make sure that we return to the interrupted program in the same condition we left it, so that it may continue without problem. To make sure our new interrupt doesn't change the registers, our first step is to store the ones we will use:

```
THE_PROG            PROC      NEAR
        → PUSH     AX
        → PUSH     BX
        → PUSH     CX
          PUSHF
          CALL OLD_INTERRUPT
                    :
```

The next step, usually, is to call the old interrupt so that it can perform its task:

```
THE_PROG            PROC      NEAR
          PUSH     AX
          PUSH     BX
          PUSH     CX
        → PUSHF
        → CALL OLD_INTERRUPT
                    :
```

For example, we want the keyboard Interrupt to put the scan and ASCII codes of the typed character into the keyboard buffer before we take a look at them. Sometimes, though, you may want to rewrite the entire interrupt. At other times, you may want to select which service calls you intercept. To do this, you can test the AH register before making this call.

Please note, however, that these commands, PUSHF and CALL OLD_INTERRUPT, will not work with INT 21H. For some mysterious, internal reason, you will get a stream of errors if you try to intercept INT 21H this way. One solution is to intercept INT 21H, do whatever you wish to do, and then use the command JMP OLD_INTERRUPT. For example, if you wanted to not allow certain files to be opened, you could intercept INT 21H and test AH. If the file opening service was not called for, you could JMP to OLD_INTERRUPT. If it was called, you could examine the file name requested and either JMP OLD_INTERRUPT or not, depending on whether or not the file asked for was protected.

IRET

Following the PUSHF and CALL OLD_INTERRUPT commands is the body of the memory-resident code. At this point, for example, KEEPER examines the head and tail of the keyboard buffer and sees which key has just been typed. If it is the trigger key, KEEPER takes over by displaying it on the screen. If not, KEEPER just exits by jumping to the end of the program, where the instruction IRET is:

```
CODE_SEG SEGMENT
         ASSUME CS:CODE_SEG
         ORG 100H
ENTRY:   JMP BOOSTER
         :
         OLD_INTERRUPT DD ?
         Data Section
         :
THE_PROG PROC NEAR
         :
         PUSHF
         CALL OLD_INTERRUPT
         :
         :
         Program that stays in memory goes here.
         :
         :
         :
         IRET
THE_PROG ENDP
```

IRET is the special RET command used at the end of interrupt service routines. We had to use PUSHF before calling OLD_INTERRUPT because a normal INT command first pushes the flags onto the stack, then it pushes CS and then IP. The flags are pushed so that the state of the 8088 is preserved as perfectly as possible. If, for example, a clock-tick interrupt (Interrupt 8), executed 18.2 times per second in the PC, interrupted your program and changed the flags, the result would be chaos. IRET returns from an Interrupt, making sure that first IP is loaded from the stack, then CS, and then the flags.

That's it for memory-resident code. If you want to, you could look at the code for KEEPER.ASM at the end of the chapter and pick out the features we have been covering—the booster, how the interrupt vector is reset, PUSHF CALL OLD_INTERRUPT, IRET, and so forth. There is still a part of KEEPER that we have not covered yet, and that is in-depth manipulations of the keyboard buffer.

USING THE KEYBOARD BUFFER IN CODE

Let's say we have a program named TEST that is supposed to intercept keystrokes. It would have a segment INTERRUPTS like this:

```
INTERRUPTS      SEGMENT AT 0H   ;This is where the keyboard interrupt
    ORG         9H*4            ;holds the address of its service routine
KEYBOARD_INT    LABEL   DWORD
INTERRUPTS      ENDS
```

and we would have to enclose the keyboard buffer itself in a segment called, say, ROM_BIOS_DATA:

```
ROM_BIOS_DATA   SEGMENT AT 40H  ;BIOS statuses held here, also keyboard buffer
        ORG     1AH
        HEAD DW      ?                  ;Unread chars go from Head to Tail
        TAIL DW      ?
      → BUFFER       DW      16 DUP (?)         ;The buffer itself
        BUFFER_END   LABEL   WORD
ROM_BIOS_DATA   ENDS
```

Next would come the CODE_SEG. The first command, at ORG 100H, is a JMP command to TEST's booster, LOAD_TEST, at the end of the program. Next, in the data area, the booster has stored INT 9's old address in OLD_KEYBOARD_INT:

```
CODE_SEG        SEGMENT
        ASSUME  CS:CODE_SEG
        ORG     100H                ;ORG = 100H to make this into a .COM file
FIRST:  JMP     LOAD_TEST           ;First time through jump to initialize routine
                :
      → OLD_KEYBOARD_INT            DD      ?       ;Location of old kbd interrupt
                :
TEST    PROC    NEAR                ;The keyboard interrupt will now come here.
        ASSUME  CS:CODE_SEG
        PUSH    AX                  ;Save the used registers for good form
        PUSH    BX
        PUSH    CX
                :
```

The booster points INT 9 at the address of the procedure TEST. The first thing done in TEST is to push all registers we will use. Just before the IRET at the end, all the registers are popped.

Since INT 9 was called, there must be a key waiting to be read in at Port 60H, so we call INT 9 ourselves:

```
CODE_SEG        SEGMENT
        ASSUME  CS:CODE_SEG
        ORG     100H                ;ORG = 100H to make this into a .COM file
FIRST:  JMP     LOAD_TEST           ;First time through jump to initialize routine
                :
        OLD_KEYBOARD_INT            DD      ?       ;Location of old kbd interrupt
                :
TEST    PROC    NEAR                ;The keyboard interrupt will now come here.
        ASSUME  CS:CODE_SEG
        PUSH    AX                  ;Save the used registers for good form
        PUSH    BX
        PUSH    CX
        PUSH    DX
        PUSH    DI
        PUSH    SI
        PUSH    DS
        PUSH    ES
      → PUSHF                       ;First, call old keyboard interrupt.
      → CALL    OLD_KEYBOARD_INT
```

```
        ASSUME  DS:ROM_BIOS_DATA        ;Examine the char just put in.
        MOV     BX,ROM_BIOS_DATA
        MOV     DS,BX
                :
```

We point DS to ROM_BIOS_DATA so we may read keys from the buffer easily with the indirect, [BX], mode of addressing. Our first real move is to check whether or not the keyboard interrupt has deleted the struck key or put it into the buffer. For that we check the values of the head and tail, labeled HEAD and TAIL in ROM_BIOS_DATA, this way:

```
CODE_SEG        SEGMENT
        ASSUME  CS:CODE_SEG
        ORG     100H            ;ORG = 100H to make this into a .COM file
FIRST:  JMP     LOAD_TEST       ;First time through jump to initialize routine
                :
        OLD_KEYBOARD_INT        DD      ?       ;Location of old kbd interrupt
                :
TEST    PROC    NEAR            ;The keyboard interrupt will now come here.
        ASSUME  CS:CODE_SEG
        PUSH    AX              ;Save the used registers for good form
        PUSH    BX
        PUSH    CX
        PUSH    DX
        PUSH    DI
        PUSH    SI
        PUSH    DS
        PUSH    ES
        PUSHF                   ;First, call old keyboard interrupt.
        CALL    OLD_KEYBOARD_INT

        ASSUME  DS:ROM_BIOS_DATA        ;Examine the char just put in.
        MOV     BX,ROM_BIOS_DATA
        MOV     DS,BX
      → MOV     BX,TAIL                 ;Point to current tail.
      → CMP     BX,HEAD                 ;If at head, kbd int has deleted char.
      → JE      OUT                     ;So leave.
        SUB     BX,2                    ;Point to just read in character.
```

Reading the Character

If nothing was typed, HEAD equals TAIL, so we jump to the end of the program, labeled OUT. If HEAD was not equal to TAIL, there is a character to be read, and it is positioned right behind the current position of TAIL. We subtract two from the tail's position, in BX, and then check if we have undershot the buffer. If so, we wrap around to the top:

```
CODE_SEG        SEGMENT
        ASSUME  CS:CODE_SEG
        ORG     100H            ;ORG = 100H to make this into a .COM file
FIRST:  JMP     LOAD_TEST       ;First time through jump to initialize routine
                :
        OLD_KEYBOARD_INT        DD      ?       ;Location of old kbd interrupt
                :
TEST    PROC    NEAR            ;The keyboard interrupt will now come here.
```

```
        ASSUME  CS:CODE_SEG
        PUSH    AX                ;Save the used registers for good form
        PUSH    BX
        PUSH    CX
        PUSH    DX
        PUSH    DI
        PUSH    SI
        PUSH    DS
        PUSH    ES
        PUSHF                     ;First, call old keyboard interrupt.
        CALL    OLD_KEYBOARD_INT

        ASSUME  DS:ROM_BIOS_DATA         ;Examine the char just put in.
        MOV     BX,ROM_BIOS_DATA
        MOV     DS,BX
        MOV     BX,TAIL                  ;Point to current tail.
        CMP     BX,HEAD                  ;If at head, kbd int has deleted char.
        JE      OUT                      ;So leave.
      → SUB     BX,2                     ;Point to just read in character.
      → CMP     BX,OFFSET BUFFER         ;Did we undershoot buffer?
      → JAE     NO_WRAP                  ;Nope.
      → MOV     BX,OFFSET BUFFER_END     ;Yes_move to buffer top.
      → SUB     BX,2                     ;And point to character.
NO_WRAP:MOV     DX,[BX]                  ;Char in DX now.
        CMP     DX,310EH                 ;Is the char a Cntrl-N?.
```

Our last step is to move [BX] into the DX register. DX now holds the key that the INT 9 was issued for. In particular, DL holds the ASCII code of the typed key and DH holds the scan code. We can compare DX to a string of test values to determine what action to take. For instance, in our example, we start by comparing DX to the value it would hold if the typed key was a ^N. (Recall that the scan and ASCII codes of keys can be found with the small BASIC program earlier in this chapter, or in the BASIC manual.)

If the key is some control character, say ^N, we might first wish to remove the ^N from the buffer. That way, when we are finished, whatever program is running won't find a leftover ^N to read. To remove this key, all we have to do is to move the tail, labeled TAIL, back two bytes. If it undershoots the beginning of the buffer, then we must wrap around to the top. This is done in KEEPER.

When the INT 9 interception routine is done, it finishes with an IRET and control goes back to the program it interrupted. In this way, you can type some control character while editing, have some operation performed, and then return smoothly to where you were in your editing job.

THE PROGRAM KEEPER.COM

The only thing yet to be covered in this chapter are a few details concerning the use of KEEPER. The use of KEEPER is intended to be simple. All you have to do is to type in the (admittedly long) listing, run it through MASM, LINK, and EXE2BIN. To install KEEPER, just run KEEPER.COM.

When it's installed, you can use it when you are at DOS level. For example, if you want to recall the command before last, just hit ^N and KEEPER will open a window on the screen. Move the cursor (the blinking line) up to the command you want to recall, and type ^N again. This second ^N both turns off the window and types the command directly to DOS by putting characters into the keyboard buffer.

If you'd prefer some trigger key besides ^N, this is the line you have to change in KEEPER:

```
CMP      DX,310EH                    ;Is the char a Cntrl-N?.
```

This line compares the typed-in key, in DX, to 310EH. 31H is ^N's scan code, and 0EH its ASCII code. To change this to a key of your choosing, you can run the short BASIC program listed earlier in this chapter to find your preferred key's scan and ASCII codes.

How KEEPER Works

The way KEEPER works is simple: It always watches what you type, storing all strings terminated with a ‹cr› ‹lf› in a buffer. When you type the trigger character, KEEPER notices that too and puts its window on the screen (this kind of screen manipulation will be covered in detail in a later chapter). By watching the cursor keys, it moves the blinking cursor up and down in the window. When you type the trigger key again, KEEPER knows the line it's supposed to type in. It types the characters in by using the timer interrupt—KEEPER fills the keyboard buffer with as many characters as it can and then checks 18.2 times a second if the buffer can hold any new ones. To the eye, the process looks quite continuous.

LISTING 3.2 KEEPER.ASM

```
VECTORS SEGMENT AT 0H              ;Set up segment to intercept Interrupts
        ORG     9H*4               ;The keyboard Interrupt
KEYBOARD_INT     LABEL   DWORD
        ORG     1CH*4              ;Timer Interrupt
TIMER_VECTOR      LABEL   DWORD
VECTORS ENDS

SCREEN  SEGMENT AT 0B000H          ;A dummy segment to use as the
SCREEN  ENDS                       ;Extra Segment

ROM_BIOS_DATA   SEGMENT AT 40H  ;BIOS statuses held here, also keyboard buffer

        ORG     1AH
        HEAD DW       ?                 ;Unread chars go from Head to Tail
        TAIL DW       ?
```

LISTING 3.2 CONTINUED

```
        BUFFER       DW     16 DUP (?)         ;The buffer itself
        BUFFER_END   LABEL  WORD

ROM_BIOS_DATA   ENDS

CODE_SEG        SEGMENT
        ASSUME  CS:CODE_SEG
        ORG     100H            ;ORG = 100H to make this into a .COM file
FIRST:  JMP     LOAD_KEEPER         ;First time through

        COPY_RIGHT       DB     '(C)1985 S.HOLZNER' ;Ascii autograph
        PAD              DB     20*102 DUP(0)       ;Memory storage for pad
        PAD_CURSOR       DW     9*102               ;Current position in pad
        ATTRIBUTE        DB     112             ;Pad Attribute_reverse video
        LINE_ATTRIBUTE   DB     240             ;Flashing Rev video
        OLD_ATTRIBUTE    DB     7               ;Original screen attrib: normal
        PAD_OFFSET       DW     0               ;Chooses 1st 250 bytes or 2nd
        FIRST_POSITION   DW     ?               ;Position of 1st char on screen
        TRIGGER_FLAG     DW     0               ;Trigger on or off
        FULL_FLAG        DB     0               ;Buffer Full Flag
        LINE             DW     9               ;Line number, 0-9
        SCREEN_SEG_OFFSET       DW      0       ;0 for mono, 8000H for graphics
        IO_CHAR          DW     ?               ;Holds addr of Put or Get_Char
        STATUS_PORT      DW     ?               ;Video controller status port
        OLD_KEYBOARD_INT        DD      ?       ;Location of old kbd interrupt
        FINISHED_FLAG           DB      1       ;If not finished,f buffer
        COMMAND_INDEX           DW      1       ;Stores positior timer)
        ROM_TIMER               DD      1       ;The Timer interrupt's address
        OLD_HEAD         DW     0

KEEPER   PROC    NEAR            ;The keyboard interrupt will now come here.
        ASSUME  CS:CODE_SEG
        PUSH    AX              ;Save the used registers for good form
        PUSH    BX
        PUSH    CX
        PUSH    DX
        PUSH    DI
        PUSH    SI
        PUSH    DS
        PUSH    ES
        PUSHF                           ;First, call old keyboard interrupt
        CALL    OLD_KEYBOARD_INT
        ASSUME  DS:ROM_BIOS_DATA        ;Examine the char just put in
        MOV     BX,ROM_BIOS_DATA
        MOV     DS,BX
        MOV     BX,TAIL                 ;Point to current tail
        CMP     BX,HEAD                 ;If at head, kbd int has deleted char
        JE      BYE                     ;So leave
        MOV     DX,HEAD
        SUB     DX,2                    ;Point to just read in character
        CMP     DX,OFFSET BUFFER        ;Did we undershoot buffer?
        JAE     NOWRAP                  ;Nope
        MOV     DX,OFFSET BUFFER_END    ;Yes--move to buffer top
        SUB     DX,2                    ;Compare two bytes back from head
NOWRAP: CMP     DX,TAIL                 ;If it's the tail, buffer is full
        JNE     NOTFULL                 ;We're OK, jump to NotFull
        CMP     FULL_FLAG,1             ;Check if keyboard buffer full
        JE      BYE                     ;Yep, leave
        MOV     FULL_FLAG,1             ;Oops, full, set flag and take
        JMP     CHK                     ; this last character
```

LISTING 3.2 CONTINUED

```
NOTFULL:MOV     FULL_FLAG,0             ;Always reset Full_Flag when buff clears
CHK:    CMP     TRIGGER_FLAG,0          ;Is the window on (triggered?)
        JNE     SUBT                    ;Yep, keep going
        MOV     DX,OLD_HEAD             ;Check position of buffer head
        CMP     DX,HEAD
        JNE     CONT
        MOV     OLD_HEAD,0
BYE:    JMP     OUT
CONT:   MOV     DX,HEAD
        MOV     OLD_HEAD,DX
SUBT:   SUB     BX,2                    ;Point to just read in character
        CMP     BX,OFFSET BUFFER        ;Did we undershoot buffer?
        JAE     NO_WRAP                 ;Nope
        MOV     BX,OFFSET BUFFER_END    ;Yes--move to buffer top
        SUB     BX,2                    ;
NO_WRAP:MOV     DX,[BX]                 ;Char in DX now
        ;------ CHAR IN DX NOW -------
        CMP     FINISHED_FLAG,0
        JE      IN
        CMP     DX,310EH                ;Default trigger is a ^N here.
        JNE     NOT_TRIGGER             ;No
        MOV     TAIL,BX
        NOT     TRIGGER_FLAG            ;Switch Modes
        CMP     TRIGGER_FLAG,0          ;Trigger off?
        JNE     TRIGGER_ON              ;No, only other choice is on
TRIGGER_OFF:
        MOV     OLD_HEAD,0              ;Reset old head
        MOV     AH,OLD_ATTRIBUTE        ;Get ready to restore screen
        MOV     ATTRIBUTE,AH            ;Pad and blinking line set to orig.
        MOV     LINE_ATTRIBUTE,AH       ; values
        MOV     PAD_OFFSET,10*102       ;Point to 2nd half of pad
        LEA     AX,PUT_CHAR             ;Make IO call Put_Char as it scans
        MOV     IO_CHAR,AX              ;over all locations in pad on screen
        CALL    IO                      ;Restore screen
        CMP     LINE,9                  ;Was the window turned off without
        JE      IN                      ; using up-down keys? If so, exit
        MOV     AX,LINE                 ;No, there is a line to stuff in
        MOV     CL,102                  ; keyboard buffer
        MUL     CL                      ;Find its location in Pad
        MOV     COMMAND_INDEX,AX        ;And send to Put
        CALL    PUT                     ;Which will do actual stuffing
IN:     JMP     OUT                     ;Done
TRIGGER_ON:                             ;Window just turned on
        MOV     LINE,9                  ;Set blinking line to bottom
        MOV     PAD_OFFSET,10*102       ;Point to screen storage part of pad
        LEA     AX,GET_CHAR             ;Make IO use Get_char so current screen
        MOV     IO_CHAR,AX              ;is stored
        CALL    IO                      ;Store Screen
        CALL    DISPLAY                 ;And put up the pad
        JMP     OUT                     ;Done here.
NOT_TRIGGER:
        TEST    TRIGGER_FLAG,1          ;Is Trigger on?
        JZ      RUBOUT_TEST
        MOV     TAIL,BX                 ;Yes, delete this char from buffer
UP:     CMP     DX,4800H                ;An Up cursor key?
        JNE     DOWN                    ;No, try Down
        DEC     LINE                    ;Move blinker up one line
        CMP     LINE,0                  ;At top? If so, reset
        JGE     NOT_TOP
        MOV     LINE,9
```

LISTING 3.2 CONTINUED

```
NOT_TOP:CALL    DISPLAY                 ;Display result
        JMP     OUT                     ;And leave
DOWN:   CMP     DX,5000H                ;Perhaps Down cusor key pushed
        JNE     IN                      ;If not, ignore key
        INC     LINE                    ;If so, move down one
        CMP     LINE,9                  ;If at bottom, wrap to top
        JLE     NOT_BOT
        MOV     LINE,0
NOT_BOT:CALL    DISPLAY                 ;Show results
        JMP     OUT                     ;And exit
RUBOUT_TEST:
        CMP     DX,0E08H                ;Is it a Rubout?
        JNE     CHAR_TEST               ;No--try carriage return-line feed
        MOV     BX,PAD_CURSOR           ;Yes--get current pad location
        CMP     BX,9*102                ;Are we at beginning of last line?
        JLE     NEVER_MIND              ;Yes--can't rubout past beginning
        SUB     PAD_CURSOR,2            ;No, rubout this char
        MOV     PAD[BX-2],20H           ;Move a space in instead (3920H)
        MOV     PAD[BX-1],39H
NEVER_MIND:
        JMP     OUT                     ;Done here.
CHAR_TEST:
        CMP     DL,13                   ;Is this a carriage return?
        JE      PLUG                    ;If yes, plug this line into Pad
        CMP     DL,32                   ;If this char < ASCII 32, delete line
        JGE     PLUG
        MOV     PAD_CURSOR,9*102        ;Clear the current line
        MOV     CX,51
        MOV     BX,9*102
CLEAR:  MOV     WORD PTR PAD[BX],0
        ADD     BX,2
        LOOP    CLEAR
        JMP     OUT                     ;And exit

PLUG:   MOV     BX,PAD_CURSOR           ;Get current pad location
        CMP     BX,10*102-2             ;Are we past the end of the pad?
        JGE     CRLF_TEST               ;Yes--throw away char
        MOV     WORD PTR PAD[BX],DX     ;No--move ASCII code into pad
        ADD     PAD_CURSOR,2            ;Increment pad location
CRLF_TEST:
        CMP     DX,1C0DH                ;Is it a carriage return-line feed?
        JNE     OUT                     ;No--put it in the pad
        CALL    CRLF                    ;Yes--move everything up in pad
OUT:    POP     ES                      ;Having done Pushes, here are the Pops
        POP     DS
        POP     SI
        POP     DI
        POP     DX
        POP     CX
        POP     BX
        POP     AX
        IRET                    ;An interrupt needs an IRET
KEEPER   ENDP

DISPLAY PROC    NEAR                    ;Puts the whole pad on the screen
        PUSH    AX
        MOV     ATTRIBUTE,112           ;Use reverse video
        MOV     LINE_ATTRIBUTE,240
        MOV     PAD_OFFSET,0            ;Use 1st 250 bytes of pad memory
        LEA     AX,PUT_CHAR             ;Make IO use Put-Char so it does
```

LISTING 3.2 CONTINUED

```
        MOV     IO_CHAR,AX
        CALL    IO                      ;Put result on screen
        POP     AX
        RET                             ;Leave
DISPLAY ENDP

CRLF    PROC    NEAR                    ;This handles carriage returns
        PUSH    BX                      ;Push everything conceivable
        PUSH    CX
        PUSH    DI
        PUSH    SI
        PUSH    DS
        PUSH    ES
        ASSUME  DS:CODE_SEG             ;Set DS to Code_Seg here
        PUSH    CS
        POP     DS
        ASSUME  ES:CODE_SEG             ;And ES too
        PUSH    DS
        POP     ES
        LEA     DI,PAD                  ;Get ready to move contents of Pad
        MOV     SI,DI                   ; up one line
        ADD     SI,102                  ;DI-top line, SI-one below top line
        MOV     CX,9*51
        MOV     BX,PAD_CURSOR           ;But first finish line with a 0
        CMP     BX,9*102+2              ; as a flag letting Put know line is
        JE      POPS                    ; done.
        MOV     WORD PTR PAD[BX],0
REP     MOVSW                           ;Move up Pad contents
        MOV     CX,51                   ;Now fill the last line with spaces
        MOV     AX,3920H
REP     STOSW                           ;Using Stosw
POPS:   MOV     PAD_CURSOR,9*102        ;And finally reset Cursor to beginning
        POP     ES                      ; of the last line again.
        POP     DS
        POP     SI
        POP     DI
        POP     CX
        POP     BX
DONE:   RET                             ;And out.
CRLF    ENDP

GET_CHAR        PROC    NEAR    ;Gets a char from screen and advances position
        ASSUME  ES:SCREEN,DS:ROM_BIOS_DATA
        PUSH    DX
        MOV     SI,2            ;Loop twice, once for char, once for attribute
        MOV     DX,STATUS_PORT  ;Get ready to read video controller status
G_WAIT_LOW:                     ;Start waiting for a new horizontal scan -
        IN      AL,DX           ;Make sure the video controller scan status
        TEST    AL,1            ;is low
        JNZ     G_WAIT_LOW
G_WAIT_HIGH:                    ;After port has gone low, it must go high
        IN      AL,DX           ;before it is safe to read directly from
        TEST    AL,1            ;the screen buffer in memory
        JZ      G_WAIT_HIGH
        MOV     AH,ES:[DI]      ;Do the move from the screen, one byte at a time
        INC     DI              ;Move to next screen location
        DEC     SI              ;Decrement loop counter
        CMP     SI,0            ;Are we done?
        JE      LEAVE           ;Yes
        MOV     PAD[BX],AH      ;No--put char we got into the pad
```

LISTING 3.2 CONTINUED

```
        JMP     G_WAIT_LOW      ;Do it again
LEAVE:  MOV     OLD_ATTRIBUTE,AH
        ADD     BX,2
        POP     DX
        RET
GET_CHAR        ENDP

PUT_CHAR        PROC    NEAR    ;Puts one char on screen and advances position
        PUSH    DX
        MOV     AH,PAD[BX]      ;Get the char to be put onto the screen
        CMP     AH,32
        JAE     GO
        MOV     AH,32
GO:     MOV     SI,2            ;Loop twice, once for char, once for attribute
        MOV     DX,STATUS_PORT  ;Get ready to read video controller status
P_WAIT_LOW:                     ;Start waiting for a new horizontal scan -
        IN      AL,DX           ;Make sure the video controller scan status
        TEST    AL,1            ;is low
        JNZ     P_WAIT_LOW
P_WAIT_HIGH:                    ;After port has gone low, it must go high
        IN      AL,DX           ;before it is safe to write directly to
        TEST    AL,1            ;the screen buffer in memory
        JZ      P_WAIT_HIGH
        MOV     ES:[DI],AH      ;Move to screen, one byte at a time
        MOV     AH,ATTRIBUTE    ;Load attribute byte for second pass
        INC     DI              ;Point to next screen position
        DEC     SI              ;Decrement loop counter
        JNZ     P_WAIT_LOW      ;If not zero, do it one more time
        ADD     BX,2
        POP     DX
        RET                     ;Exeunt
PUT_CHAR        ENDP

IO      PROC    NEAR            ;This scans over all screen positions of the pad
        ASSUME  ES:SCREEN       ;Use screen as extra segment
        MOV     BX,SCREEN
        MOV     ES,BX

        PUSH    DS
        MOV     BX,ROM_BIOS_DATA
        MOV     DS,BX
        MOV     BX,4AH
        MOV     BX,DS:[BX]
        SUB     BX,51
        ADD     BX,BX
        MOV     FIRST_POSITION,BX
        POP     DS

        MOV     DI,SCREEN_SEG_OFFSET    ;DI will be pointer to screen postion
        ADD     DI,FIRST_POSITION       ;Add width of screen minus pad width
        MOV     BX,PAD_OFFSET           ;BX will be pad location pointer
        MOV     CX,10                   ;There will be 10 lines

LINE_LOOP:
        PUSH    WORD PTR ATTRIBUTE
        PUSH    CX                      ;Figure out whether this is blinking
        NEG     CX                      ; line and if so, temporarily change
        ADD     CX,10                   ; display attribute
        CMP     CX,LINE
        JNE     NOLINE
```

LISTING 3.2 CONTINUED

```
        MOV     CL,LINE_ATTRIBUTE
        MOV     ATTRIBUTE,CL
NOLINE: POP     CX
        MOV     DX,51                       ;And 51 spaces across
CHAR_LOOP:
        CALL    IO_CHAR                     ;Call Put-Char or Get-Char
        DEC     DX                          ;Decrement character loop counter
        JNZ     CHAR_LOOP                   ;If not zero, scan over next character
        ADD     DI,FIRST_POSITION           ;Add width of screen minus pad width

        POP     WORD PTR ATTRIBUTE
        LOOP    LINE_LOOP                   ;And now go back to do next line
        RET                                 ;Finished
IO      ENDP

PUT  PROC    NEAR    ;Here it is.
        ASSUME  DS:ROM_BIOS_DATA          ;Free DS
        PUSH    DS                        ;Save all used registers
        PUSH    SI
        PUSH    DI
        PUSH    DX
        PUSH    CX
        PUSH    BX
        PUSH    AX
        MOV     AX,ROM_BIOS_DATA            ;Just to make sure
        MOV     DS,AX                       ;Set DS correctly
FIN:    MOV     FINISHED_FLAG,1             ;Assume we'll finish
        MOV     BX,TAIL                     ;Prepare to move to buffer's tail
        MOV     SI,COMMAND_INDEX            ;Get our source index

STUFF:  MOV     AX,WORD PTR PAD[SI]
        ADD     SI,2                        ;Point to the command's next character
        CMP     AX,0                        ;Is it a zero? (End of command)
        JE      NO_NEW_CHARACTERS           ;Yes, leave with Finished_Flag=1
        MOV     DX,BX                       ;Find position in buffer from BX
        ADD     DX,2                        ;Move to next position for this word
        CMP     DX,OFFSET BUFFER_END ;Are we past the end?
        JL      NO_WRAP2                    ;No, don't wrap
        MOV     DX,OFFSET BUFFER            ;Wrap
NO_WRAP2:
        CMP     DX,HEAD                     ;Buffer full but not yet done?
        JE      BUFFER_FULL                 ;Time to leave, set Finished_Flag=0.
        ADD     COMMAND_INDEX,2             ;Move to next word in command
        MOV     [BX],AX                     ;Put it into the buffer right here.
        ADD     BX,2                        ;Point to next space in buffer
        CMP     BX,OFFSET BUFFER_END ;Wrap here?
        JL      NO_WRAP3                    ;No, readjust buffer tail
        MOV     BX,OFFSET BUFFER            ;Yes, wrap
NO_WRAP3:
        MOV     TAIL,BX                     ;Reset buffer tail
        JMP     STUFF                       ;Back to stuff in another character.
BUFFER_FULL:                                ;If buffer is full, let timer take over
        MOV     FINISHED_FLAG,0             ; by setting Finished_Flag to 0.
NO_NEW_CHARACTERS:
        POP     AX                          ;Restore everything before departure.
        POP     BX
        POP     CX
        POP     DX
        POP     DI
        POP     SI
```

LISTING 3.2 CONTINUED

```
        POP     DS
        STI
        RET
PUT  ENDP

        ASSUME  DS:CODE_SEG
INTERCEPT_TIMER   PROC    NEAR          ;This completes filling the buffer
        PUSHF                           ;Store used flags
        PUSH    DS                      ;Save DS since we'll change it
        PUSH    CS                      ;Put current value of CS into DS
        POP     DS
        CALL    ROM_TIMER               ;Make obligatory call
        PUSHF
        CMP     FINISHED_FLAG,1         ;Do we have to do anything?
        JE      OUT1                     ;No, leave
        CLI                             ;Yes, start by clearing interrupts
        PUSH    DS                      ;Save these.
        PUSH    SI
        PUSH    DX
        PUSH    BX
        PUSH    AX
        ASSUME  DS:ROM_BIOS_DATA        ;Point to the keyboard buffer again.
        MOV     AX,ROM_BIOS_DATA
        MOV     DS,AX
        MOV     BX,TAIL                 ;Prepare to put characters in at tail
        MOV     FINISHED_FLAG,1         ;Assume we'll finish
        MOV     SI,COMMAND_INDEX        ;Find where we left ourselves

STUFF2: MOV     AX,WORD PTR PAD[SI]     ;The same stuff loop as above.
        ADD     SI,2                    ;Point to next command character.
        CMP     AX,0                    ;Is it zero? (end of command)
        JNE     OVER                    ;No, continue.
        JMP     NO_NEW_CHARACTERS2      ;Yes, leave with Finished_Flag=1
OVER:   MOV     DX,BX                   ;Find position in buffer from BX
        ADD     DX,2                    ;Move to next position for this word
        CMP     DX,OFFSET BUFFER_END    ;Are we past the end?
        JL      NO_WRAP4                ;No, don't wrap
        MOV     DX,OFFSET BUFFER        ;Do the Wrap rap.
NO_WRAP4:
        CMP     DX,HEAD                 ;Buffer full but not yet done?
        JE      BUFFER_FULL2            ;Time to leave, come back later.
        ADD     COMMAND_INDEX,2         ;Point to next word of command.
        MOV     [BX],AX                 ;Put into buffer
        ADD     BX,2                    ;Point to next space in buffer
        CMP     BX,OFFSET BUFFER_END    ;Wrap here?
        JL      NO_WRAP5                ;No, readjust buffer tail
        MOV     BX,OFFSET BUFFER        ;Yes, wrap
NO_WRAP5:
        MOV     TAIL,BX                 ;Reset buffer tail
        JMP     STUFF2                  ;Back to stuff in another character
BUFFER_FULL2:
        MOV     FINISHED_FLAG,0         ;Set flag to not-done-yet.
NO_NEW_CHARACTERS2:
        POP     AX                      ;Restore these.
        POP     BX
        POP     DX
        POP     SI
        POP     DS
OUT1:   POPF                            ;And Exit.
        POP     DS
```

LISTING 3.2 CONTINUED

```
        IRET                            ;With customary IRET
INTERCEPT_TIMER   ENDP

LOAD_KEEPER         PROC    NEAR    ;This procedure intializes everything
        ASSUME  DS:VECTORS   ;The data segment will be the Interrupt area
        MOV     AX,VECTORS
        MOV     DS,AX

        MOV     AX,KEYBOARD_INT           ;Get the old interrupt service routine
        MOV     OLD_KEYBOARD_INT,AX       ;address and put it into our location
        MOV     AX,KEYBOARD_INT[2]        ;OLD_KEYBOARD_INT so we can call it.
        MOV     OLD_KEYBOARD_INT[2],AX

        MOV     KEYBOARD_INT,OFFSET KEEPER  ;Now load the address of our notepad
        MOV     KEYBOARD_INT[2],CS          ;routine into the keyboard interrupt

        MOV     AX,TIMER_VECTOR           ;Now same for timer
        MOV     ROM_TIMER,AX
        MOV     AX,TIMER_VECTOR[2]
        MOV     ROM_TIMER[2],AX

        MOV     TIMER_VECTOR,OFFSET INTERCEPT_TIMER
        MOV     TIMER_VECTOR[2],CS        ;And intercept that too.

        ASSUME  DS:ROM_BIOS_DATA
        MOV     AX,ROM_BIOS_DATA
        MOV     DS,AX
        MOV     BX,OFFSET BUFFER     ;Clear the keyboard buffer.
        MOV     HEAD,BX
        MOV     TAIL,BX
        MOV     AH,15                     ;Ask for service 15 of INT 10H
        INT     10H                       ;This tells us how display is set up
        MOV     STATUS_PORT,03BAH          ;Assume this is a monochrome display
        TEST    AL,4                      ;Is it?
        JNZ     EXIT                      ;Yes - jump out
        MOV     SCREEN_SEG_OFFSET,8000H ;No - set up for graphics display
        MOV     STATUS_PORT,03DAH

EXIT:   MOV     DX,OFFSET LOAD_KEEPER       ;Set up everything but LOAD_PAD to
        INT     27H                       ;stay and attach itself to DOS
LOAD_KEEPER         ENDP

        CODE_SEG        ENDS

        END     FIRST   ;END "FIRST" so 8088 will go to FIRST first.
```

Chapter 4

File Handling

INTRODUCTION

In this chapter we are going to cover an essential topic rarely covered in beginning assembly language books—handling files. For the most part, we can do little by ourselves here without an enormous investment of time, so we will work our way through the DOS services that handle files. We will work with FCBs, DOS' old reliable file handling method, and the somewhat more modern file handles used in DOS 2+ and 3+.

In general, file handles will be easier and more natural for the assembly language programmer to use. Using handles you can specify subdirectories (which you cannot with File Control Blocks), and you can specify just how many bytes to read in, a very welcome relief from the FCB method of current records, blocks, and record sizes. To get the two straight, let's work our way through an FCB right away.

A FILE CONTROL BLOCK

FCBs are supported under all versions of DOS, and were the only available option under DOS 1.1. We can get a quick look at an FCB with DEBUG. DOS gives you two default FCBs in the PSP whenever you load a program. Since we need a program to DEBUG, let's use DEBUG itself, and then type it a third time to get it into the PSP:

```
A>DEBUG DEBUG.COM DEBUG.COM
```

The FCB that is made is 37 (25H) bytes long, and starts at CS:5CH (the second one, if required, starts at 6CH). Let's take a look at it:

```
-D5C L 25
090B:005C   00 44 45 42                                          .DEB
090B:0060   55 47 20 20 20 43 4F 4D-00 00 00 00 00 20 20 20   UG   COM.....
090B:0070   20 20 20 20 20 20 20 20-00 00 00 00 00 00 00 00           ........
090B:0080   0A
```

This unopened FCB is mostly spaces (ASCII 20H). The only bytes filled in are the first byte, which holds the drive number (0 since we didn't specify a drive), followed by the file's name (eight letters for the name itself, padded with spaces to fill it out, and three letters for the extension). If we had said DEBUG DEBUG.COM A:DEBUG.COM, the first byte would have held 1 for drive A (and 2 for B, and so on).

Since we're debugging DEBUG anyway, we can take a quick look at the beginning of its code, just to see what it looks like, by unassembling it:

```
-U100
090B:0100 B430          MOV     AH,30
090B:0102 CD21          INT     21
090B:0104 86E0          XCHG    AL,AH
090B:0106 3D0002        CMP     AX,0200
090B:0109 7309          JNB     0114
090B:010B BA772B        MOV     DX,2B77
090B:010E B409          MOV     AH,09
090B:0110 CD21          INT     21
090B:0112 CD20          INT     20
090B:0114 B451          MOV     AH,51
090B:0116 CD21          INT     21
090B:0118 891E5D2B      MOV     [2B5D],BX
090B:011C BCE22A        MOV     SP,2AE2
090B:011F A2E92C        MOV     [2CE9],AL
```

The first thing done is to request an INT 21H Service, Service 30H, which checks the DOS number. If the DOS version is 1, the message at CS:2B77 is displayed. It is easy to guess what this message is:

```
-D2B77
090B:2B77                       49-6E 63 6F 72 72 65 63 74           Incorrect
090B:2B80  20 44 4F 53 20 76 65 72-73 69 6F 6E 0D 0A 24 0D    DOS version..$.
090B:2B90  0A 50 72 6F 67 72 61 6D-20 74 65 72 6D 69 6E 61   .Program termina
090B:2BA0  74 65 64 20 6E 6F 72 6D-61 6C 6C 79 0D 0A 24 49   ted normally..$I
090B:2BB0  6E 76 61 6C 69 64 20 64-72 69 76 65 20 73 70 65   nvalid drive spe
090B:2BC0  63 69 66 69 63 61 74 69-6F 6E 0D 0A 24 46 69 6C   cification..$Fil
090B:2BD0  65 20 6E 6F 74 20 66 6F-75 6E 64 0D 0A 24 4E 6F   e not found..$No
090B:2BE0  20 72 6F 6F 6D 20 69 6E-20 64 69 73 6B 20 64 69    room in disk di
090B:2BF0  72 65 63 74 6F 72 79                              rectory
-Q
```

Opened FCBs

An opened FCB is more complicated than an unopened one. If you point DS:DX at 5CH in the PSP and request Service 0FH of INT 21H, the FCB will be opened. For DEBUG.COM, the opened FCB will look like Figure 4.1.

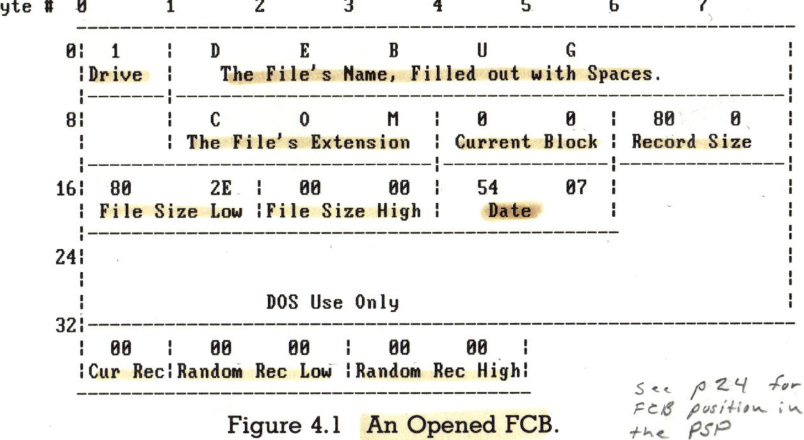

Figure 4.1 An Opened FCB.

The record size, file size, drive, and date areas are filled in. We can read the file's size as 2E80H, or 11904 bytes. The record size (the amount of data taken from or put into the DTA at one time) is set to the default of 128 bytes (the size of the default DTA).

Whenever you issue a write using FCBs, this field tells DOS how many bytes to read or write. If you do not like this small size, it is up to your program to directly change it by overwriting this value in the FCB.

This is how a typical FCB looks and works. We'll use the various parts of an FCB later; it is worth noticing now, however, that the only parts of an FCB that your program is routinely expected to change (if you want to) are the record size field, and the current record and block fields.

The date is 0754H. Dates are stored as:

$$512 \times (\text{year} - 1980) + 32 \times (\text{month}) + (\text{day}).$$

and from this we can figure out that 0754H (1876D) means the file was created 10/20/83.

Extended FCBs

You may have noticed that there is no space in this FCB for either the file's creation time or its attribute. You can add the attribute by using an **extended FCB**. An extended FCB looks the same as an FCB, except there are an additional seven bytes added to the beginning—a byte of FFH, five bytes of zeros, and the attribute byte. For example, to create or search for a file with attribute 1 (read-only), you would start your FCB out this way: FF 00 00 00 00 00 01, and follow it with a normal FCB. Table 4.1 shows the possible attributes you can give a file.

Table 4.1 File Attributes

Attribute	Meaning
0	Normal, plain file.
1	Read-Only. Cannot be opened for reading or writing.
2	Hidden File. This attribute means directory searches will not find this file.
4	System File. Same attribute as IBMBIO.COM or IBMDOS.COM has.
8	Volume Label. The eleven letters of the file's name and extension are actually the disk's label.
10H	Subdirectory. This file name names a subdirectory.
20H	Archive. This bit is checked by the program BACKUP to see if the file has been rewritten since last being backed up.

If you use an extended FCB with the DOS services, you can specify a file's attribute while creating it or searching for it.

The other information—current record, current block, and random record—needs more explanation. There are two ways of using files in the FCB method, sequentially and randomly. Each has to be understood before we can progress on to the DOS functions.

SEQUENTIAL AND RANDOM FILES

Data is stored in files in **records**. To read record 517 in **sequential files**, you have to read 516 records first, sequentially, before coming to the one you want. In **random files** you can randomly access whichever record you want. Sequential files need a marker between records (in the PC this is almost always a ‹cr› ‹lf› pair), but because each record is so clearly marked, sequential files can have records with different sizes.

If you use the sequential reading and writing services of DOS, you don't need to worry about what these markers are at all, since DOS will take care of that for you when it reads and writes.

Random files need to have the same size records. Filling records like this is easily done if you set them up using DW and DB:

```
RECORD    LABEL    BYTE
INDEX     DW       ?
NAME      DB       20 DUP(?)
DATE      DB       20 DUP(?)
```

or if you use STRUC and set up a structure named RECORD. FCB operations always read and write from and to the DTA, so make sure you set up your records there. (We will cover how to move the DTA where you want it later in this chapter.)

Sequential Reading and Writing

If you choose the sequential services, you have to set the current block and current record fields of the FCB (File Handles will prove much easier). DOS cuts all files into **blocks** of 128 records. Therefore, the current record field can vary only from 0 to 127. The block number, also starting at 0, can be larger. Figure 4.2 shows the fields you have to fill for sequential reading and writing.

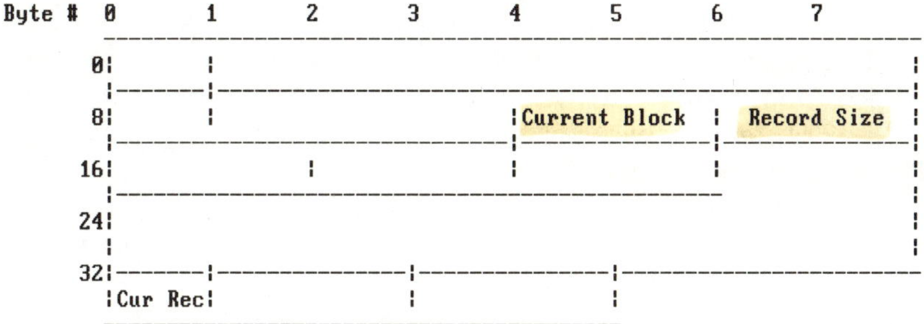

Figure 4.2 Sequential Reading and Writing.

For example, to read record 517 (= 4 × 128 + 5) you would put 4 in the current block field and 5 in the current record field.

Random Reading and Writing

On the other hand, random reading and writing depend only on the random record field. You must figure out what number your record is in the file, given the record size, and put that into the random record field. If you want to read record 517, you don't have to break it up into blocks and current records; you just put 517 in the Random Record Low field, as shown in Figure 4.3.

The big difference between the random and sequential DOS services is that the sequential services will automatically increment the current record and

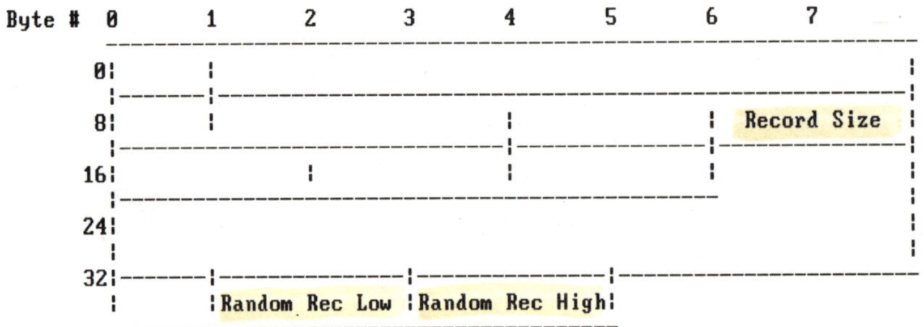

Figure 4.3 Random Reading and Writing.

current block fields for you, but you must set the random record fields by yourself if you want to use them.

Keep in mind that space is allocated for intervening records in a file even if you don't write to them. For example, if you write random records 1 and then 5, records 2–4 (and, thus, 3*(record length) bytes) will be included in your file, and they will be made up of whatever was on the disk before you wrote at all.

Using records and blocks may be fine for BASIC, but it hinders full use of files. Fortunately, IBM realized that assembly language programmers can cut files up into blocks on their own if they want to, so the file handle method doesn't deal with records at all. If you want to divide your file up into records of, say, 1,024 bytes, you just ask for 1,024 bytes each time you read. The file handle method is much easier than the FCB method.

With records and blocks, even as simple an operation as copying a file was made difficult. If you had a file of 1,025 bytes, and had a record size of 1,024, for example, you would need two reads and two writes. But the two records you wrote would leave you with a 2,048-byte file, and the last 1,023 bytes would be made up of whatever bytes were left in the DTA after the first write.

FILE HANDLES

Starting with DOS 2+, IBM introduced **file handles**. They operate essentially like FCBs, except that all the fields of the FCB are hidden inside DOS. All you need to keep track of a file is its file handle, a 16-bit word that you can move around from register to register. Whenever you want to refer to that file, you can move its file handle into whatever register the INT 21H service requires, usually BX.

File handles 0–4 are already predefined, so the lowest handle a file can get is 5. Table 4.2 shows how 0–4 are set aside.

Table 4.2 File Handles 0–4

Handle Number	Assigned Meaning
0	Standard Input Device (usually keyboard)
1	Standard Output Device (usually screen)
2	Standard Error Output Device
3	Standard Auxiliary Device (AUX)
4	Standard Printer Device (PRN)

This means you can treat any of these devices as a file. For example, if you wrote to Device 1 by loading BX with 1 and calling INT 21H Service 40H, whatever you wrote would appear on the screen (DS:DX points to the data to write, CX the number of bytes to write. We'll cover this service further on). Many new DOS programs do write this way so that output can be easily redirected into a file. On the other hand, you could read from Device 0, the keyboard.

To open a file and get a file handle for it, you can use either INT 21H Services 3CH (create a file) or 3DH (open a file). All that is required is an ASCII string that ends with a 0 (a real zero, not an ASCII '0'), for example:

```
SOURCE   DB 'B:\SUB1\FILE.EXT',0
         :
LEA      DX,SOURCE
MOV      AH,3DH
INT      21H
JC       ERROR
```

The file's handle is returned in BX. To write to this file, or read from it, you can place the same file handle in BX and call one of the various reading or writing services. Notice that file handles can use pathnames, but FCBs cannot.

The DOS Error Return Table

There are a variety of errors such calls can have. Here, for reference, is the **Error Return Table** often referred to in DOS literature. If there is an error condition, the carry flag will always be set and you can test it with JC. The error will be returned in AL if the carry flag is set. Interestingly, the only thing DOS does *not* treat as an error when you are using file handles is a full disk; the carry flag is not set. Instead, you must check the number of bytes you told it to write against the number it actually wrote. This will also be covered later. The DOS error return table is in Table 4.3.

Table 4.3 DOS Error Return Table

Error Number	Error
AL=1	Function number not valid.
2	File was not found.
3	Invalid path.
4	Too many files open at the same time.
5	Access is denied. (See Access Codes later.)
6	The file handle was invalid.
7	Memory control blocks were destroyed.
8	Not enough memory.
9	Memory block address was invalid.
10	Environment string was invalid.
11	Format invalid.
12	Access code invalid.
13	Data invalid.
15	An invalid drive was specified.
16	Attempt made to remove current directory.
17	Not same device.
18	No more files found.

FILE SERVICES FOR FCBS

The FCB services were introduced in DOS 1.0, so their services were assigned lower numbers than the file handle services. They have utility primarily for three reasons: DOS provides you with quick and easy default FCBs in the PSP; they are valuable if you want to try to include backward compatibilty in your programs; and if you really want to break your file up into current blocks and records, the FCBs are better suited for it than file handles.

INT 21H Service 0FH—Open Pre-Existing File

Input	Output
DS:DX points to an FCB	AL=0 → Success
AH=0FH	AL=FF → Failure

This is the most basic of file services, and it is used to open an **existing** file. It will NOT create a file for you. If you want to create a file using FCBs, use Service 16H. In our earlier example, we could have pointed DS:DX at CS:5C, where our default FCB for DEBUG.COM was, and opened it with this service. As soon as you do so, the drive number is filled in, the record length is set to a default 128 (80H) bytes, and the size and date are set according to the directory entry, as we have seen.

Before you can do anything with a file name except delete it or search for directory matches to it, which only need unopened FCBs, you must open an FCB for it. If you actually want to do anything with the file *after* you've opened it, you must set the record size and current record or random record fields in the FCB first.

INT 21H Service 10H—Close File

Input	Output
DS:DX points to an FCB	AL=0 → Success
AH=10H	AL=FF → Failure

This service is the obvious counterpart of service 0FH, Open file. Needless to say, you cannot exit a program without closing all your files and expect to keep all their data intact.

DOS has a maximum number of files you can have open at any time (the default is 8, unless you have a line like FILES=20 in CONFIG.SYS), so it is worthwhile to close files when you are finished with them.

This service really only reads what's in the FCB (in particular, the file's size) and writes it out to the directory. Its primary function is to give the file a nonzero size. Usually DOS keeps track of the file's size, but if you want to, you can change it just before closing the file. If you've copied one file into another, for example, and don't want the target file to end up with a length that is some multiple of the record length, you can read the original file's length from *its* FCB and write that in the target file's size field.

INT 21H Service 11H—Search for First Matching File

Input	Output
DS:DX points to an unopened FCB	AL=FF → Failure
AH=11H	AL=0 → Success
	DTA holds FCB for match.

This service is extremely useful, and it is the one DOS uses itself to search the disk for files. All you have to do is point DS:DX at an unopened FCB and call this service. The FCB can have '?'s for wildcards, but not '*'. (File handle services can use '*', however.) If you wanted to search for *.BAS, for example, you would have to fill in the FCB with the file name ???????? and the extension with BAS. Note that ????????.BAS will match any length file name, from BASEBALL.BAS to A.BAS.

If there is a match, an unopened FCB for the matching file on the disk will be put in the DTA, starting at CS:80. You can use this FCB to open, write to, or delete files, just as you would any other FCB.

To find the *next* matching file, however, you have to use not Service 11H, but Service 12H, one of DOS's peculiarities.

INT 21H Service 12H—Search for Next Matching File

Input	Output
DS:DX points to an unopened FCB	AL=FF → Failure
AH=12H	AL=0 → Success
	DTA holds FCB for match.

This service takes over after Service 11H. After you have found the first match using Service 11H, DOS fills part of the reserved areas in the FCB. Service 12H uses that information and finds the next match in the directory. Typically, if you are going to loop over files in the directory, you would use Service 11H before entering the loop, and Service 12H from then on. DELETER is a small program that assembles into a towering 24 bytes and just deletes all files that match what it is given. For example, if you typed DELETER *.BAS, it would delete all .BAS files in the current directory.

The Program DELETER.COM

DELETER uses the next DOS service, Service 13H, to delete files by pointing at the FCB that Service 11H or 12H generated in the DTA. In itself, it doesn't do anything DOS doesn't already do, but you can easily modify such a program to type out a prompt using the found file's name (from the new FCB at CS:80) while it is looping over files. For instance, you could have it type: "Delete BASEBALL.BAS (Y/N)?" and have it take a one-character reply.

LISTING 4.1 DELETER.ASM

```
CODE_SEG SEGMENT
         ASSUME CS:CODE_SEG,DS:CODE_SEG
         ORG    100H
ENTRY:   MOV    AH,11H
LOOK:    MOV    DX,5CH
         INT    21H
         CMP    AL,0FFH             ;Match Found?
         JE     OUT
```

LISTING 4.1 CONTINUED

```
            MOV     DX,80H              ;Delete Found File.
            MOV     AH,13H
            INT     21H
            MOV     AH,12H              ;Search for next Match.
            JMP     LOOK
 OUT:       INT     20H                 ;Exit here.
 CODE_SEG   ENDS
            END     ENTRY
```

INT 21H Service 13H—Deletes Files

Input	Output
DS:DX points to an unopened FCB	AL=FF → Failure
AH=13H	AL=0 → Success

This is a very useful file-deleting service. As you can see from the previous example, it is easily invoked. All you have to do is to point DS:DX at an unopened FCB and call this service. Probably the easiest thing to do with files in DOS is to delete them.

INT 21H Service 14H—Sequential Read

Input	Output
DS:DX points to an opened FCB.	Requested Record put in DTA.
AH=14H	AL=0 Success.
Current Block & Record Set in FCB.	1 End of File, no data in record.
	2 DTA Segment too small for record.
	3 End of File, record padded with zeros.
	Record Address Incremented.

This is where we begin real file operations. Service 14H gives you a sequential read of one record from an opened file. As is usual with sequential operations, you have to set the current block field (bytes 0CH–0DH in the FCB) and the current record field from 0–127 (byte 1FH). Also, as usual, the data read from the file is dumped in the DTA. If you changed the record length from the default 128 bytes to, 4,096 bytes, you would get 4K of data in the DTA.

As with most sequential file operations, the record address is incremented. This means that if the current record is 127, the next record will be 0 and the current block will be incremented.

Once again, unless your file is rigidly segmented into controlled records, you will find file handles easier to use. If you do store your data in specific records, however, you might want to set up the DTA in a way that will assist you in reading your read-in data. As mentioned, this can be done with DB and DW or with STRUC. In particular, it is suggested that you change the location of the DTA first to wherever you want it using DOS Service 1AH, covered later in this section.

INT 21H Service 15H—Sequential Write

Input	Output
DS:DX points to an opened FCB.	One record read from DTA and written.
AH=15H	AL=0 Success.
Current block & record set in FCB.	1 Disk full.
	2 DTA Segment too small for record.
	Record Address Incremented.

This is the counterpart of Service 14H. Here, one record is written from the DTA (always used in FCB operations) to an open file, and the record address is incremented, as is standard for sequential file handling. It is worth noticing that if you use a record size significantly smaller than one sector (512 bytes), DOS will buffer what you are writing and only write it out when there is sufficient data to write, or when you end the program. (This is one of the details that INT 20H or INT 27H take care of for you).

There are three types of returns from this service: AL=0, which means the transfer was successful; AL=1, which means the target disk was full; and AL=2, which means the record to be written extended over segment boundaries (it could not all be reached without changing DS, which DOS services will not do).

After you have opened a file and written to it, all that remains is closing it (Service 10H).

INT 21H Service 16H—Create File

Input	Output
DS:DX points to an unopened FCB.	AL=0 Success.
AH=16H	=FF Directory Full.

This service is the counterpart of Service 0FH—it creates files rather than opening them. Normally, if you want to work with a file using sequential FCB access, you would open it up using Service 0FH. On the other hand, Service 16H creates a file from scratch. If a file already exists with the name given in the (unopened) FCB you supply, it will be opened and set to zero length. If there is no identical file already in the directory, a directory entry is opened for this file.

If there is no space left in the directory (if you have used over 112 files in the root directory of a floppy, 224 in a 1.2M floppy, or 512 on a hard disk), AL will return FF, and you must free some space in the directory.

If you wish, you can give this file an attribute, such as hidden, by using an extended FCB (see the discussion of FCBs at the beginning of this chapter).

INT 21H Service 17H—Rename File

Input	Output
DS:DX points to a MODIFIED FCB. AH=17H	AL=0 Success. =FF Failure.

NOTE: Modified FCB → Second file name starts 6 bytes after the end of the first file name, at DS:DX+17.

This is the way that DOS renames files. You can use wildcards with this service (keep in mind that you must use '?'s in FCBs, and not '*'s). All files that match the file name you supply will be renamed, unless a file so named already exists.

To use this service, set up an unopened FCB for the file(s) you want to rename. If you wanted to rename all *.BAS files to *.BAK, you would set up an unopened FCB for ????????.BAS. To rename them to *.BAK, you must add *another* file name in the middle of the FCB, starting at DS:DX+17. In this case, you would put ????????.BAK there and then call this Service.

INT 21H Service 1AH—Set the DTA Location

Input	Output
DS:DX points to new DTA address. AH=1AH	None.

DOS does an excellent job of getting you started when running programs by supplying default FCBs and a default DTA. Even so, its efforts are a compromise between convenience and memory usage. The default DTA, and the default record size in FCBs, are both only 128 bytes. This may satisfy the users of BASIC, but assembly language programmers usually want more speed and size. For that reason, DOS allows you to change the record size in an FCB. To accommodate a bigger record size, you can change the location of the Disk

Transfer Area for more space with this service. One suggested location for your new DTA is the end of your program in memory.

When DOS loads a .COM file in, it gives it all of the memory to work with. (This is not always true for .EXE files, which have maximum and minimum memory requests in the .EXE file header.) This means that the space from the end of your program to the top of the CS segment is open for you to use. BUT, you must be careful not to overwrite the stack that DOS supplies at the top of every .COM file's segment, so write data in the new DTA accordingly.

THE PROGRAM PAGER.ASM

Now that we've covered opening and closing, and reading and writing, sequential files, we are ready for an example that puts all these concepts together. PAGER.ASM is our example here. PAGER is nothing extraordinary when it comes to utility; it just reads in a text file and prints it out on the screen, 20 lines at a time. After 20 lines are printed, it waits until you press a key (any key) and then continues.

You can invoke PAGER by typing PAGER FILE.EXT. PAGER uses the default FCB set up for FILE.EXT to open the file (Service 0FH). It changes the record length at 5CH+14 to 1024 from 128, moves the DTA to the end of the code and then reads in the first 1K of the text file. If the read failed, it quits. If the read was a success, PAGER prints out the first 20 lines (it counts the number of ‹lf›s it has typed out).

If less than 1,024 bytes were read in because the end of file was reached, DOS fills the rest of the record with zeros. In this case, AL returns 3 from the reading service (Service 14H). PAGER handles this by examining the bytes that are printed. When it finds the zeros in the DTA, it quits, assuming that the end of file has been reached.

After PAGER has printed 20 lines, it waits for a character to be typed (which will be read with Service 7) and then continues. After the file has been completely printed, it closes the file (Service 10H) and quits. Even though PAGER includes only minimal error checking, it is still a pretty long program for what it does (it makes a 94-byte .COM file). Dealing with files is always a little complex because of the number of specific, separate actions you must undertake (opening, reading, writing, closing, and so on).

LISTING 4.2 PAGER.ASM

```
CODE_SEG SEGMENT
        ASSUME CS:CODE_SEG,DS:CODE_SEG
        ORG    100H
```

LISTING 4.2 CONTINUED

```
ENTRY:    LEA    DX,DATA              ;Set up the DTA FIRST.
          MOV    AH,1AH
          INT    21H
          MOV    DX,5CH               ;Now OPEN the file.
          MOV    AH,0FH
          INT    21H
          MOV    BX,5CH+14            ;Set record size in FCB to 1024.
          MOV    [BX],1024
          MOV    CX,0
LOOPER:   MOV    AH,14H               ;Do the read of one record at a time.
          MOV    DX,5CH
          INT    21H
          CMP    AL,0                 ;Success?
          JE     READ_OK
          CMP    AL,3                 ;Partial Success?
          JE     READ_OK
          JMP    OUT                  ;Failure, exit.
READ_OK:  LEA    BX,DATA              ;Point [BX] at DTA to print data out.
PRINT:    MOV    DL,[BX]              ;Get character from DTA.
          CMP    DL,0                 ;Record filled out with 0s? Exit.
          JE     OUT
          MOV    AH,2                 ;Print one character at a time.
          INT    21H
          INC    BX
          CMP    BX,OFFSET DATA+1024       ;Need more data?
          JE     LOOPER
          CMP    DL,10                ;Look for <lf> of <cr><lf> pair.
          JNE    PRINT
          INC    CX                   ;CX records number of <cr><lf>s.
          CMP    CX,20                ;20 lines printed?
          JB     PRINT
          MOV    CX,0                 ;Reset <cr><lf> counter.
          MOV    AH,7                 ;Wait for character to be typed.
          INT    21H
          JMP    PRINT
OUT:      MOV    AH,10H
          MOV    DX,5CH               ;CLOSE the file at the end.
          INT    21H
          INT    20H
DATA:                                 ;We will store our data here.
CODE_SEG         ENDS
          END    ENTRY
```

One more line of Pager should be covered:

```
          INT    21H
          INC    BX
          CMP    BX,OFFSET DATA+1024       ;Need more data?
          JE     LOOPER
          CMP    DL,10                ;Look for <lf> of <cr><lf> pair.
          JNE    PRINT
```

Pager loops over all the data in the DTA, reading it with the indirect form [BX]. To check if we need more data, we can examine BX and see whether it is past the end of the buffer. At its minimum, BX will hold the beginning offset address of DATA, not 0. We should therefore compare BX to OFFSET DATA+1024 to see if we have to read in another record from the file.

RANDOM FILE USE IN DOS INTERRUPTS

We are now through with the sequential handling of FCB-controlled files, and will turn next to the Random access handling that DOS services support.

INT 21H Service 21H—Random Read

Input	Output
DS:DX points to an opened FCB.	AL=00 Success.
Set FCB's random record field	=01 end of file, no more data.
at DS:DX+33 and DS:DX+35	=02 not enough space in DTA segment.
AH=21H	=03 end of file, partial record padded with zeros.

To write into the DTA from a random record, you must set the random record field in an opened FCB. DS:DX+33 (33 decimal) holds the low word of the random record number, and DS:DX+35 the high word. For instance, if you were keeping track of coats in a store with a vast inventory, and you wanted to adjust the price of coat number 65537, you would want record number 65536 (since the first record is record 0). Since 65536 = 10000H, you would put 0000 in the FCB's random record low word at DS:DX+33 and 0001 at DS:DX+35.

When you request the read, the current block and current record fields are set by DOS for you. Random access is appropriate if you have something that you want to keep track of that can be divided nicely into records.

INT 21H Service 22H—Random Write

Input	Output
DS:DX points to an opened FCB.	AL=00 Success.
Set FCB's random record field	=01 Disk is full.
at DS:DX+33 and DS:DX+35	=02 not enough space in DTA segment.
AH=21H	

This is Service 21H's complement. To use it, you must fill the DTA with the record you want to write. In addition, you must set the random record field in the FCB. DOS will set the current block and current record fields itself.

The only danger here is in setting the random record field. When you write to the disk, you are overwriting something. If your record field is set incorrectly, you may overwrite previously-written data. Furthermore, if your record number is set to some value far above the number of records you really want to write, DOS will obligingly extend your file—writing your record at the end of it—and include whatever was in the intervening disk space in your file.

Sequential Versus Random Services

As with all random access reads and writes, you have to set the random record field yourself. Also, keep in mind that when you are done, DOS does not automatically increment the record number as it does when you are working with sequential services.

INT 21H Service 23H—File Size

Input	Output
DS:DX points to an unopened FCB. AH=23H	AL=00 Success. =FF No file found that matched FCB. Random Record Field set to file length in records, rounded up.

This is a very useful service that the file handle services lack. If you want a file's size, you can find it without opening the file. All you need is an unopened FCB. Point DS:DX at the FCB and DOS will search the current directory for a match to the file name. If there is no match to the file name you give, AL will return FFH. If there is a match, the random record fields of the FCB will be set to the total length of the file in records (rounded up). A file that is 256 bytes long will thus return 2 in the random record field if the record size (at DS:DX+14) is 128. If the file is 257 bytes long, the same call will return a 3 (=257/128 rounded up) in the random record field. If you want the file's size in bytes, set the record length to 1 byte.

INT 21H Service 24H—Set Random Record Field

Input	Output
DS:DX points to an opened FCB. AH=24H	Random record field set to match current record and current block.

This is a service call that DOS itself uses in dealing with FCBs. It makes the transition between sequential file handling and random access file handling easier. If you set the current record and current block fields correctly, this Service will set the random record field. Since it is usually easier to calculate the random record number than the current record and current block (1 block = 128 records), this Service is of little real service.

INT 21H Service 27H—Random Block Read

Input	Output
DS:DX points to an opened FCB. Set FCB's random record field at DS:DX+33 and DS:DX+35 AH=27H	AL=00 Success. =01 end of file, no more data. =02 not enough space in DTA segment. =03 end of file, partial record padded with zeros. CX=Number of records read. Random record fields set to access next record.

With Service 27H, you can read in as many random records as you have space for. This and the next service are random access services that DO update the random record field. When this service call is done, the random record field is set to the number of the NEXT, unread record. To read in blocks of records, one after another, you just have to repeatedly call this service.

Incrementing the random record number, though, is the only thing that makes this call exceptional. If you wanted to, you could simply adjust the record size to some large number of records and read them all at once. For example, if your records were 128 bytes long, you could adjust the record size temporarily to 512 and read in four records in your own "block read."

INT 21H Service 28H—Random Block Write

Input	Output
DS:DX points to an opened FCB. Set FCB's random record field at DS:DX+33 and DS:DX+35 CX=number of records to write. AH=28H	AL=00 Success. =01 Disk is full. =02 not enough space in DTA segment. Random record fields set to access next record.

NOTE: CX=0 File set to the size indicated by the Random Record field

With this service, you can write blocks of random records to disk. If you store many records in the DTA, you can set CX to the number of records and then write them all at once.

The two differences between this and the last service are that if AL returns 1 here it means that the disk is full—not an end of file. If you set CX to 0 when you call this service, the file will be set to the length given by the random record field (even if the file has to be truncated or enlarged). If enlarged, whatever junk that is in free sectors on the disk will be included in your file.

FILE HANDLE SERVICES

The more modern and efficient method of file handling is to use file handles. It is recommended that whenever you want to work with files that you use handles and not FCBs, especially if your files are in subdirectories, which FCBs can't use. File handle services use ASCIIZ strings. (As we have already seen, these are strings of ASCII characters that end with a 0.) If there is an error while using these services, the carry flag will be set, and AL will contain an error code that you can look up in the error return table. For instance, if you wanted to create a file, you could try something like this:

```
MOV     AH,3CH
INT     21H
JC      ERROR    ;Do error analysis - check AL
MOV     AH,3EH   ;No error if you reach here.
```

and check the error code in AL at the label ERROR.

INT 21H Service 3CH—Create a File

Input	Output
DS:DX points to ASCIIZ file name.	No Carry → AX=File Handle.
CX=Attribute of File.	Carry → AL=3 Path not found.
AH=3CH	=4 Too many files open.
	=5 Dir. full, or previous read-only file exists.

With this service we can create files. If you supply an ASCIIZ string including pathname and drive like this:

```
FILENAME DB 'C:\LOW\LOWER\UNDER.TXT',0
```

and point DS:DX at it (LEA DX,FILENAME), this service will create UNDER.TXT in C:\LOW\LOWER. If such a file already existed, it is set to zero length, so caution is best here. If that file already existed and was marked Read-Only, though, you will get an error (AL=5). You can supply the file's attribute at the same time you create it by loading the correct code into CX. Those codes are shown in Table 4.1.

If everything goes smoothly, a 16-bit file handle will be returned in AX. This word is the key to the file from now on. Whenever you need to access the file, you can refer to it by loading this word into some required register (typically BX) before making a service call.

INT 21H Service 3DH—Open a File

Input	Access Codes	Output
DS:DX points to ASCIIZ file name.	AL=0 File Opened for Reading.	No Carry → AX=File Handle.
AL=Access Code.	AL=1 File Opened for Writing.	Carry → AL=Error Code
AH=3DH	AL=2 File Opened for Reading and Writing.	(Check Error Table).

This service is the way the file handle services deal with already existing files. You don't have to specify if you are opening a file for sequential or random access. Nor do you have to specify a record size. All you have to do is give an ASCIIZ string with the drive, path name, and file name of the file to be opened.

In addition, you must specify an **access code** in AL. This code, which can be 0, 1, or 2, specifies how you want to work with the file. If you specify 0, the file is opened only for reading; 1 for writing; and 2 for both. This is done so that files don't inadvertently get written over. Experience has shown that the access codes are not a perfect safeguard, however, so don't rely on them alone.

The file handle is returned in AX. If the carry flag is set, there has been some error, and you have to decode the error code in AL by examining the error code table covered earlier in this chapter.

The Read/Write Pointer

If you want to read in the file you have just opened and copy it to another file, the process is simple. Select a number of bytes to read (usually as many as you can fit into your DTA) and read them in. If the file was less than this length, DOS tells you how many bytes were actually read in. You can copy data in blocks just by reading from the first file and then writing out to the next one. DOS keeps track of your place in both files as you read and write.

It is more common, however, that you will want to set your position in your file yourself. For example, if you had set up your file in terms of random records, you would want to position yourself correctly before requesting a read. DOS keeps track of your position in the file through a **read/write pointer**. For example, if you had a file that was 3K long, and you were reading in 1K sections at a time, Figure 4.4. shows the Read/Write Pointer would be positioned just before and after a read.

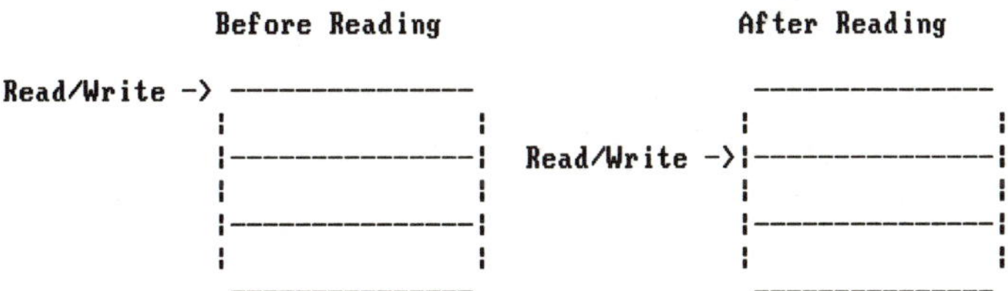

Figure 4.4 The Read/Write Pointer.

Service 3DH, which opens files, sets the read/write pointer right at the beginning. If you want to reset this pointer to some other position and move around inside the file, you will have to use Service 42H, which we will work through later.

INT 21H Service 3EH—Close a File Handle

Input	Output
BX holds a valid file handle. AH=3EH	Carry → AL=6 → Invalid Handle.

Having just learned how to open files, this service lets you close them. It is one of the simplest file-handling services there is. To use it, load the file handle of the file to be closed into BX, and 3EH into AH. Upon return, if there was an error, the carry flag will be set. The only error this service returns is AL=6, Invalid File Handle.

INT 21H Service 3FH—Read from File or Device

Input	Output
DS:DX = Data Buffer Address. CX=Number of bytes to read. BX=File Handle. AH=3FH	No Carry→ AX=Number of bytes read. Carry→ AL=5 Access Denied. AL=6 Invalid Handle.

This service illustrates the difference between file handle and FCB file handling. It reads from files not in terms of records, but in terms of bytes—a method that seems much more intuitive to the assembly language programmer. If you want to read in 1,747 bytes, you simply put 1747 into CX. Service 3FH will read in the 1,747 bytes and put them in memory, starting at the location given by DS:DX (NOT the DTA).

If the carry flag is not set, AX will hold the number of bytes actually read. Since DOS cannot read past the end of the file, this number may not be the same as the number you requested in CX. If not, you can assume that you have reached the end of the file.

If the carry flag has been set, there has been an error and AL holds either 5 ("Access denied"), which should mean the file was opened with an access code that forbids reading, but is really a catch-all error) or 6 (Invalid Handle).

To read in a particular random record of 256 bytes from a file, position the Read/Write pointer to the record's beginning and then request this service to read in 256 bytes.

INT 21H Service 40H—Write to File or Device

Input	Output
DS:DX = Data Buffer Address.	No Carry→ AX=Number of bytes written.
CX=Number of bytes to write.	Carry→ AL=5 Access Denied.
BX=File Handle.	AL=6 Invalid Handle.
AH=40H	

NOTE: Full disk is NOT considered an error. Check the number of bytes you wanted to write (CX) against the number actually written (returned in AX). If they do not match, the disk is probably full.

Here is the file handle all-purpose write service. Its use is much like the reading service, 3FH, with the expected variations. You must load CX with the number of bytes to write, not read. AX returns the number of bytes actually written. If this is not the same as the number you requested (in CX), then the disk is most likely full. For some reason, IBM does *not* treat this as an error, and instead you must check these quantites against each other instead of relying on the carry flag.

DOS uses this service itself for a great number of things, since it can use the preset file handles for the standard input and output devices. Using this service makes redirection of input or output very easy (you can see that all that needs to be changed is the file handle to switch from printing to the screen to writing to a file).

Note, though, that if you use the keyboard as an input "file", you will get no more than one line at a time. Even if you request 1,024 bytes to be read, you will not get more than 80.

THE PROGRAM PRNT.ASM

We now have file handle basics sufficiently in mind to work through an example. This example is PRNT.ASM, a program that can be made into a .COM file. PRNT is a simple program, of no great utility; it is only supposed to serve as an example of file handle file control.

PRNT will print out text files on your printer and will add carriage returns so you don't print over the page-break. Specifically, each page of standard printer paper is 66 lines long. PRNT will print out three blank lines at the top of each page, 60 lines of text, then three blank lines at the bottom.

All PRNT does is watch for carriage return-line feeds when it is printing out the file. When it has seen enough of them, it adds the required <cr><lf>s for the space between pages. You can easily modify this program to indent text by printing, say, five spaces after each <lf> is found.

LISTING 4.3 PRINT.ASM

```
CODE_SEG SEGMENT
        ASSUME  CS:CODE_SEG,DS:CODE_SEG
        ORG     100H
ENTRY:  JMP     PRNT                    ;The Data Area is Next.
CRS             DB      0               ;Number of <cr><lf>s seen.
BYTES_READ      DW      0               ;How many bytes actually read from the file.
COUNTER         DW      0               ;Counts how many bytes we've printed.
CRLF            DB      13,10           ;To print out <cr><lf> ourselves.
FILE_HANDLE     DW      ?               ;Store the file handle here.
PRNT:   MOV     BX,80H                  ;First, make the filename at 80H into ASCIIZ.
        MOV     AL,[BX]                 ;Find number of bytes typed from 80H.
        ADD     BL,AL                   ;Add to BX (already 80H).
        INC     BX                      ;And point to LAST character (<cr>).
        MOV     BYTE PTR [BX],0         ;Add the Z in ASCIIZ.
        MOV     AX,3D00H                ;Select Service 3DH, Access code 00 (in AL).
        MOV     DX,82H                  ;Point to beginning of filename.
        INT     21H                     ;OPEN IT.
        JC      OUT                     ;If error, quit.
        MOV     FILE_HANDLE,AX          ;Save file handle in FILE_HANDLE.
        MOV     DI,3                    ;Prepare to type out 3 <cr><lf>s to start
        CALL    PRINT_CRS               ; first page properly.
READ:   MOV     BX,FILE_HANDLE          ;Put file handle in BX, ready to read.
        LEA     DX,DATA                 ;Point DS:DX at buffer at end of program.
        MOV     CX,1024                 ;Read in 1024 byte blocks.
        MOV     AH,3FH                  ;With Service 3FH.
        INT     21H                     ;DO THE READ.
        JC      OUT                     ;Leave if there was a problem.
        MOV     BYTES_READ,AX           ;Store the number of bytes read (for eof check).
```

LISTING 4.3 CONTINUED

```
        MOV     COUNTER,AX        ;Also here to type out the same number.
        LEA     SI,DATA           ;Point both SI (to check for <lf>) and
        LEA     DX,DATA           ; DX (to pass byte to print to DOS) at DATA.
        MOV     BX,4              ;STANDARD PRINTER FILE HANDLE.
TOP:    MOV     CX,1              ;Get ready to print out ONE byte.
        MOV     AH,40H            ;Select the output service.
        INT     21H               ;PRINT OUT ONE BYTE.
        CMP     BYTE PTR [SI],10          ;Was the just-printed byte a <lf>?
        JNE     CHECK             ;No, check if we have to read in more data.
        INC     CRS               ;Yes, increment the number of <cr><lf>s seen.
        CMP     CRS,60            ;Are we at 60 yet?
        JNE     CHECK             ;No, check if we have to read in more data.
        MOV     CRS,0             ;Yes, reset <cr><lf> counter.
        MOV     DI,6              ;And print 6 <cr><lf>s ourselves.
        CALL    PRINT_CRS         ;With this subroutine.
CHECK:  INC     SI                ;Increment [SI] to point to next byte.
        INC     DX                ;Same for DS:DX.
        DEC     COUNTER           ;But DEC number of bytes actually read in.
        JNZ     TOP               ;If more left to print, keep printing.
        CMP     BYTES_READ,1024           ;Need more data-had we reached eof?
        JE      READ              ;No, read in full 1024 last time-read more.
        MOV     BX,FILE_HANDLE    ;Get ready to close the file.
        MOV     AH,3EH            ;With Service 3EH.
        INT     21H               ;CLOSE THE FILE.
OUT:    INT     20H               ;And Exit.

PRINT_CRS       PROC    NEAR      ;Small subroutine to print <cr><lf>s.
        PUSH    DX                ;Save DX because we will use it.
GO:     MOV     BX,4              ;Select printer handle.
        MOV     CX,2              ;And print 2 bytes (<cr>,<lf>).
        LEA     DX,CRLF           ;Point DS:DX to our bytes.
        MOV     AH,40H            ;Select Service 40H.
        INT     21H               ;And PRINT <cr><lf>.
        DEC     DI                ;Have we printed all we need to?
        JNZ     GO                ;No, print another.
        POP     DX                ;Yes, restore DX,
        RET                       ;And return.
PRINT_CRS       ENDP              ;End of procedure.
DATA:                             ;Put our read-in data from the file here.
CODE_SEG        ENDS              ;End of CODE_SEG.
        END     ENTRY             ;Set up for a COM file.
```

The first thing you might notice is the (relatively) large number of variables in the data area—CRS, BYTES_READ, COUNTER, etc. This is an inevitable result of using file handles. The file handle services, lacking FCBs, usually tie up all the registers. For example, to read, you need to specify the file handle in BX, the number of bytes to read in CX, the location of the buffer in DS:DX, and then set AH to 3FH (and even AL is used to return errors). With File Control Blocks the process uses fewer registers: You point to an open FCB, the record size is read from it, and data is put into the DTA.

The first thing we will do is assume that you've invoked PRNT by typing something like: PRNT HAMLET.TWO. PRNT will search for a file name in the unformatted data area at 80H in the PSP. Once it finds it, it will put a 0 byte right after it and make it into an ASCIIZ string directly:

```
CODE_SEG SEGMENT
        ASSUME  CS:CODE_SEG,DS:CODE_SEG
        ORG     100H
ENTRY:  JMP     PRNT                ;The Data Area is Next.
CRS             DB      0           ;Number of <cr><lf>s seen.
BYTES_READ      DW      0           ;How many bytes actually read from the file.
COUNTER         DW      0           ;Counts how many bytes we've printed.
CRLF            DB      13,10       ;To print out <cr><lf> ourselves.
FILE_HANDLE     DW      ?           ;Store the file handle here.
PRNT:   MOV     BX,80H ←           ;First, make the filename at 80H into ASCIIZ.
→       MOV     AL,[BX]             ;Find number of bytes typed from 80H.
→       ADD     BL,AL               ;Add to BX (already 80H).
→       INC     BX                  ;And point to LAST character (<cr>).
→       MOV     BYTE PTR [BX],0     ;Add the Z in ASCIIZ.
        MOV     AX,3D00H            ;Select Service 3DH, Access code 00 (in AL).
        MOV     DX,82H              ;Point to beginning of filename.
        INT     21H                 ;OPEN IT.
```

We have to open the file with Service 3DH, and select an access code (we'll use 0 for because we only want to read the file). We have to point DX at 82H (because 80H holds the number of bytes typed and 81H holds the space in the string "PRNT HAMLET.TWO‹cr›"):

```
        ORG     100H
ENTRY:  JMP     PRNT                ;The Data Area is Next.
CRS             DB      0           ;Number of <cr><lf>s seen.
BYTES_READ      DW      0           ;How many bytes actually read from the file.
COUNTER         DW      0           ;Counts how many bytes we've printed.
CRLF            DB      13,10       ;To print out <cr><lf> ourselves.
FILE_HANDLE     DW      ?           ;Store the file handle here.
PRNT:   MOV     BX,80H              ;First, make the filename at 80H into ASCIIZ.
        MOV     AL,[BX]             ;Find number of bytes typed from 80H.
        ADD     BL,AL               ;Add to BX (already 80H).
        INC     BX                  ;And point to LAST character (<cr>).
        MOV     BYTE PTR [BX],0     ;Add the Z in ASCIIZ.
        MOV     AX,3D00H            ;Select Service 3DH, Access code 00 (in AL).
        MOV     DX,82H              ;Point to beginning of filename.
        INT     21H                 ;OPEN IT.
```

If there was an error opening the file, we will just exit without any fancy error messages since this is only a demonstration program. If there is no error opening the file, our first action is to print three carriage returns on the printer, starting the first page of output. We will use a subroutine named PRINT_CRS, which we will not review here. (It is a very simple subroutine that you can examine in the code, and it simply sends ‹cr›‹lf› pairs to the printer handle.)

Reading From the File

Now that our file is open, we can read from it. We'll use a "record size" of 1024, and read in 1K at a time. The opening service returned the file's handle in AX, so we store it in the memory location labelled FILE_HANDLE. To read, we will use a buffer at the end of the program—we just put a label DATA:

there (see the listing of PRNT.ASM) and can read in the first 1,024 bytes into it with Service 3FH:

```
        ORG     100H
ENTRY:  JMP     PRNT               ;The Data Area is Next.
CRS             DB      0          ;Number of <cr><lf>s seen.
BYTES_READ      DW      0          ;How many bytes actually read from the file.
COUNTER         DW      0          ;Counts how many bytes we've printed.
CRLF            DB      13,10      ;To print out <cr><lf> ourselves.
FILE_HANDLE     DW      ?          ;Store the file handle here.
PRNT:   MOV     BX,80H             ;First, make the filename at 80H into ASCIIZ.
        MOV     AL,[BX]            ;Find number of bytes typed from 80H.
        ADD     BL,AL              ;Add to BX (already 80H).
        INC     BX                 ;And point to LAST character (<cr>).
        MOV     BYTE PTR [BX],0    ;Add the Z in ASCIIZ.
        MOV     AX,3D00H           ;Select Service 3DH, Access code 00 (in AL).
        MOV     DX,82H             ;Point to beginning of filename.
        INT     21H                ;OPEN IT.
        JC      OUT                ;If error, quit.
   →    MOV     FILE_HANDLE,AX     ;Save file handle in FILE_HANDLE.
   →    MOV     DI,3               ;Prepare to type out 3 <cr><lf>s to start
   →    CALL    PRINT_CRS          ; first page properly.
READ:   MOV     BX,FILE_HANDLE     ;Put file handle in BX, ready to read.
   →    LEA     DX,DATA            ;Point DS:DX at buffer at end of program.
   →    MOV     CX,1024            ;Read in 1024 byte blocks.
   →    MOV     AH,3FH             ;With Service 3FH.
        INT     21H                ;DO THE READ.
        JC      OUT                ;Leave if there was a problem.
        MOV     BYTES_READ,AX      ;Store the number of bytes read (for eof check).
        MOV     COUNTER,AX         ;Also here to type out the same number.
        LEA     SI,DATA            ;Point both SI (to check for <lf>) and
        LEA     DX,DATA            ; DX (to pass byte to print to DOS) at DATA.
        MOV     BX,4               ;STANDARD PRINTER FILE HANDLE.
```

If there is an error, we will just jump to the end of the program, the label OUT. If there is no error, a number of bytes are read (not necessarily the number we asked for) and put into our buffer starting at DS:DX. We will store the number of bytes read (returned in AX) in BYTES_READ. When we are considering reading in another section of the file, we will check BYTES_READ to see if it is 1024. If not, DOS supplied us with as many bytes as it could; we will assume that we have reached the end of the file and there are no more bytes to read.

This is dangerous by itself. What if the file is some exact multiple of 1K? For these files, we will loop again and attempt to read past the end of file. In that case, the carry flag will be set and control will simply exit as before.

Printing Out the Data

Now that there are data in memory, we can begin printing them out. Since we are going to print out all the bytes we read, we store the number of bytes read also in COUNTER, which will be decremented as we print. Each time we print a byte, we will have to check to see if it corresponds to a line feed. PRNT keeps track of the ‹lf› (ASCII 10) in ‹cr›‹lf› pairs. Since printing is relatively slow, we can afford to check every byte as we print it. We will instruct DOS (Service 40H) to only print one byte at a time. We also will keep incrementing DX so that DS:DX points to the next byte to type and compare that byte to ‹lf›:

```
        ORG     100H
ENTRY:  JMP     PRNT                ;The Data Area is Next.
CRS             DB      0           ;Number of <cr><lf>s seen.
BYTES_READ      DW      0           ;How many bytes actually read from the file.
COUNTER         DW      0           ;Counts how many bytes we've printed.
CRLF            DB      13,10       ;To print out <cr><lf> ourselves.
FILE_HANDLE     DW      ?           ;Store the file handle here.
PRNT:   MOV     BX,80H              ;First, make the filename at 80H into ASCIIZ.
        MOV     AL,[BX]             ;Find number of bytes typed from 80H.
                :
                :
READ:
: ......MOV     CX,1                ;Get ready to print out ONE byte.
:       LEA     DX,DATA             ;Point DS:DX at buffer at end of program.
:       MOV     CX,1024             ;Read in 1024 byte blocks.
:       MOV     AH,3FH              ;With Service 3FH.
:       INT     21H                 ;DO THE READ.
:       JC      OUT                 ;Leave if there was a problem.
:       MOV     BYTES_READ,AX       ;Store the number of bytes read (for eof check).
:       MOV     COUNTER,AX          ;Also here to type out the same number.
:       LEA     SI,DATA             ;Point both SI (to check for <lf>) and
:       LEA     DX,DATA             ; DX (to pass byte to print to DOS) at DATA.
:       MOV     BX,4                ;STANDARD PRINTER FILE HANDLE.
TOP:
: ......MOV     CX,1                ;Get ready to print out ONE byte.
: :     MOV     AH,40H              ;Select the output service.
: :     INT     21H                 ;PRINT OUT ONE BYTE.
: :     CMP     BYTE PTR [SI],10            ;Was the just-printed byte a <lf>?
: :     JNE     CHECK               ;No, check if we have to read in more data.
: :     INC     CRS                 ;Yes, increment the number of <cr><lf>s seen.
: :     CMP     CRS,60              ;Are we at 60 yet?
: :     JNE     CHECK               ;No, check if we have to read in more data.
: :     MOV     CRS,0               ;Yes, reset <cr><lf> counter.
: :     MOV     DI,6                ;And print 6 <cr><lf>s ourselves.
: :     CALL    PRINT_CRS           ;With this subroutine.
CHECK:  INC     SI                  ;Increment [SI] to point to next byte.
: :     INC     DX                  ;Same for DS:DX.
: :     DEC     COUNTER             ;But DEC number of bytes actually read in.
: :.....JNZ     TOP                 ;If more left to print, keep printing.
:       CMP     BYTES_READ,1024             ;Need more data-had we reached eof?
:.......JE      READ                ;No, read in full 1024 last time-read more.
```

We are ready for the loop that prints out the bytes we have read in. To print, we load BX with four, the standard printer handle, and that is all that is required to set up the printer. We loop over the data in the printing loop TOP. CX is loaded with one to print only one byte at a time, and after we print it we check to see if it was a ‹lf›. If it was, we increment the number of ‹cr›‹lf›s seen, which we store in CRS. If that number has reached 60, we print six ‹cr›‹lf›s to cover the space between the pages and reset CRS:

```
        ORG     100H
ENTRY:  JMP     PRNT                ;The Data Area is Next.
CRS             DB      0           ;Number of <cr><lf>s seen.
BYTES_READ      DW      0           ;How many bytes actually read from the file.
COUNTER         DW      0           ;Counts how many bytes we've printed.
CRLF            DB      13,10       ;To print out <cr><lf> ourselves.
FILE_HANDLE     DW      ?           ;Store the file handle here.
PRNT:   MOV     BX,80H              ;First, make the filename at 80H into ASCIIZ.
        MOV     AL,[BX]             ;Find number of bytes typed from 80H.
                :
                :
READ:
........MOV     BX,FILE_HANDLE      ;Put file handle in BX, ready to read.
:       LEA     DX,DATA             ;Point DS:DX at buffer at end of program.
:       MOV     CX,1024             ;Read in 1024 byte blocks.
:       MOV     AH,3FH              ;With Service 3FH.
:       INT     21H                 ;DO THE READ.
:       JC      OUT                 ;Leave if there was a problem.
:       MOV     BYTES_READ,AX       ;Store the number of bytes read (for eof check).
:       MOV     COUNTER,AX          ;Also here to type out the same number.
:       LEA     SI,DATA             ;Point both SI (to check for <lf>) and
:       LEA     DX,DATA             ; DX (to pass byte to print to DOS) at DATA.
:       MOV     BX,4                ;STANDARD PRINTER FILE HANDLE.
TOP:
: ...   MOV     CX,1                ;Get ready to print out ONE byte.
: :     MOV     AH,40H              ;Select the output service.
: :     INT     21H                 ;PRINT OUT ONE BYTE.
: :     CMP     BYTE PTR [SI],10        ;Was the just-printed byte a <lf>?
: :     JNE     CHECK               ;No, check if we have to read in more data.
: :     INC     CRS                 ;Yes, increment the number of <cr><lf>s seen.
: :     CMP     CRS,60              ;Are we at 60 yet?
: :     JNE     CHECK               ;No, check if we have to read in more data.
: :     MOV     CRS,0               ;Yes, reset <cr><lf> counter.
: :     MOV     DI,6                ;And print 6 <cr><lf>s ourselves.
: :     CALL    PRINT_CRS           ;With this subroutine.
CHECK:  INC     SI                  ;Increment [SI] to point to next byte.
: :     INC     DX                  ;Same for DS:DX.
: :     DEC     COUNTER             ;But DEC number of bytes actually read in.
: :.....JNZ     TOP                 ;If more left to print, keep printing.
:       CMP     BYTES_READ,1024         ;Need more data-had we reached eof?
:.......JE      READ                ;No, read in full 1024 last time-read more.
```

The last thing we must do is check if there are any more bytes to print. To do this, we decrement COUNTER, which originally held the number of bytes read every time we loop. If this doesn't leave 0, we jump back up to the printing loop, TOP, to print out another byte. If decrementing COUNTER does leave 0, though, we check BYTES_READ to see if we got the full 1,024 bytes we asked for in the last read. If we did, we assume there is more data in the file and loop back up to the outer loop READ to read in 1,024 more. If BYTES_READ is *not* 0, we assume we have reached the end of file and so exit, which concludes PRNT:

```
READ:
:       LEA     DX,DATA             ;Point DS:DX at buffer at end of program.
:       MOV     CX,1024             ;Read in 1024 byte blocks.
:       MOV     AH,3FH              ;With Service 3FH.
:       INT     21H                 ;DO THE READ.
:       JC      OUT                 ;Leave if there was a problem.
```

```
:       MOV     BYTES_READ,AX    ;Store the number of bytes read (for eof check).
:       MOV     COUNTER,AX       ;Also here to type out the same number.
:       LEA     SI,DATA          ;Point both SI (to check for <lf>) and
:       LEA     DX,DATA          ; DX (to pass byte to print to DOS) at DATA.
:       MOV     BX,4             ;STANDARD PRINTER FILE HANDLE.
TOP:
: ......MOV     CX,1             ;Get ready to print out ONE byte.
: :     MOV     AH,40H           ;Select the output service.
: :     INT     21H              ;PRINT OUT ONE BYTE.
: :     CMP     BYTE PTR [SI],10         ;Was the just-printed byte a <lf>?
: :     JNE     CHECK            ;No, check if we have to read in more data.
: :     INC     CRS              ;Yes, increment the number of <cr><lf>s seen.
: :     CMP     CRS,60           ;Are we at 60 yet?
: :     JNE     CHECK            ;No, check if we have to read in more data.
: :     MOV     CRS,0            ;Yes, reset <cr><lf> counter.
: :     MOV     DI,6             ;And print 6 <cr><lf>s ourselves.
: :     CALL    PRINT_CRS        ;With this subroutine.
CHECK:  INC     SI               ;Increment [SI] to point to next byte.
: :     INC     DX               ;Same for DS:DX.
: :     DEC     COUNTER          ;But DEC number of bytes actually read in.
: :.....JNZ     TOP              ;If more left to print, keep printing.
:       CMP     BYTES_READ,1024          ;Need more data-had we reached eof?
:....   JE      READ             ;No, read in full 1024 last time-read more.
        MOV     BX,FILE_HANDLE   ;Get ready to close the file.
        MOV     AH,3EH           ;With Service 3EH.
        INT     21H              ;CLOSE THE FILE.
OUT:    INT     20H              ;And Exit.
```

MORE FILE HANDLE SERVICES

INT 21H Service 41H—Delete a File

Input	Output
DS:DX = ASCIIZ filename.	No Carry→ Success.
AH=41H	Carry→ AL=2 File Not Found.
	AL=5 Access Denied.

NOTE: No wildcards allowed in file name.

This service corresponds to Service 13H for FCBs: with it it is as easy, if not easier, to delete files. All you need to delete a file is its name. If the file cannot be deleted, the carry flag will be set when control returns, and AL will have an error code in it.

It is worth noticing that no wildcards are allowed in the file's name. In other words, you can only delete one file at a time. If you want to delete files that match strings like "C:\CELLAR*.EXT" or "A:\SUB\SUB2\I?ELAND.MAP" (strings can be a maximum of 63 characters), you must first search for directory matches to these names with Services 4EH and 4FH. A ?, such as in

I?ELAND.MAP, matches one character, and so I?ELAND.MAP will match either IRELAND.MAP or ICELAND.MAP.

INT 21H Service 42H—Move Read/Write Pointer

Input	Output
BX=File Handle	No Carry→DX:AX=New Location of Pointer.
CX:DX=Desired offset.	Carry→AL=1 Illegal Function Number.
AH=42H	AL=6 Invalid Handle.
AL=Method Values:	
AL=0	Read/write pointer moved to CX:DX from the start of the file.
AL=1	Pointer incremented CX:DX bytes.
AL=2	Pointer moved to end-of-file plus offset (CX:DX).

The read/write pointer is your active position in the file. With FCB file handling, DOS takes care of this for you after you have set the record sizes, the current record, and the current block. With file handles, you can skip around the file at will.

For instance, if your file was made up of 100-byte records, and you wished to access record number N, all you need do is select the appropriate "method", here AL=0 (see the above list), and use code something like this:

```
MOV     AL,0
MOV     AH,42H
MOV     BX,FILE_HANDLE
MOV     CX,0                ;Assuming 100xN < 63335.
MOV     DX,100xN
INT     21H
```

This is also the way you can find a file's size. "Method" 2 (AL=2) can extend the read/write pointer beyond the end of the file, and thus extend the file. If you use Method 2 and load CX:DX with 0000:0000, the read/write pointer will be positioned at the end of the file. When control returns from INT 21H, and if there was no error, DX:AX will hold the new distance of the read/write pointer from the beginning of the file. In this case, that is the file's length. Let's give this a try with DEBUG and find the length of COMMAND.COM, which is 17792 (4580H) bytes long:

```
A>DEBUG COMMAND.COM
-D80 8E          ← First, make COMMAND.COM an ASCIIZ string.
090B:0080  00 0D 43 4F 4D 4D 41 4E-44 2E 43 4F 4D 0D 33      ..COMMAND.COM.3
-E8D
090B:008D  0D.00
-A100            ← Now assemble our program.
```

```
090B:0100 MOV   DX,82
090B:0103 MOV   AX,3D00             ← Open COMMAND.COM
090B:0106 INT   21H
090B:0108 MOV   BX,AX               ← Load BX with the file handle.
090B:010A MOV   CX,0
090B:010D MOV   DX,0
090B:0110 MOV   AX,4202             ← Request Service 42H, Method 2 (in AL).
090B:0113 INT   21H
090B:0115 INT   20H
090B:0117
-U100                               ← Take a look at the program.
090B:0100 BA8200        MOV     DX,0082
090B:0103 B8003D        MOV     AX,3D00
090B:0106 CD21          INT     21
090B:0108 89C3          MOV     BX,AX
090B:010A B90000        MOV     CX,0000
090B:010D BA0000        MOV     DX,0000
090B:0110 B80242        MOV     AX,4202
090B:0113 CD21          INT     21
090B:0115 CD20          INT     20
090B:0117 0000          ADD     [BX+SI],AL
090B:0119 0000          ADD     [BX+SI],AL
090B:011B 0000          ADD     [BX+SI],AL
090B:011D 0000          ADD     [BX+SI],AL
090B:011F 0000          ADD     [BX+SI],AL
-G115           ← And run it. The length returns in DX:AX.

AX=4580  BX=0005  CX=0000  DX=0000  SP=FFFE  BP=0000  SI=0000  DI=0000
DS=090B  ES=090B  SS=090B  CS=090B  IP=0115   NV UP DI PL NZ NA PO NC
090B:0115 CD20          INT     20
-Q
```

The correct length of 4580H bytes is returned.

INT 21H Service 43H—Change File's Attribute

Input	Output
DS:DX = ASCIIZ Filestring.	No Carry→Success.
AL=1→ File attrib. changed. CX holds new attribute.	Carry→AL=2 File Not Found.
AL=0→File's current attribute returned in CX.	AL=3 Path Not Found.
AH=43H	AL=5 Access Denied.
	If AL was 0, CX returns the attribute.

Ever since DOS 2+, you have had the option of setting a file's attribute, and this is the service that does it. The list of the possible attributes a file can have (to be loaded in CX before the call is made) is in Table 4.1.

The program at the end of this chapter, DIREX.ASM, uses Service 43H to help in managing your directory. To use DIREX, you type DIREX or DIREX C:\UNDER, and all the files in the requested directory are put on the screen. You can then mark files at will (see the instructions at the end of this chapter), and change the protection of many files all at once. (DIREX also deletes files or copies them en masse to another directory.)

For a little extra security, you can make files "hidden" by giving them an attribute of 2. All they are hidden from, though, are directory searches. Attribute 4 is saved for system files like the two needed to boot up, IBMDOS.COM and IBMBIO.COM, that are on all boot disks but can't be seen because of this protection.

An attribute of 10H is used for file names that are actually subdirectories.

INT 21H Service 45H—Duplicate a File Handle

Input	Output
BX=File handle to duplicate.	No Carry→AX=New, duplicated handle.
AH=45H	Carry→AL=4 Too many files open.
	AL=6 Invalid Handle.

In case you ever want to refer to a file with more than one handle, this service will duplicate the file handle for you. If you move around using one handle, the other handle's read/write pointer is moved, too.

INT 21H Service 46H—Force Duplication of a File Handle

Input	Output
BX=File handle to duplicate.	No Carry→Handles refer to same "stream"
CX=Second file handle.	Carry→AL=6 Invalid handle.
AH=46H	

With this service you can redirect output. For example, let's assume the output of one of your programs normally goes to the screen. If you want to redirect output from the screen to a file instead, all you need to do is put 1 in CX (the handle to be superseded), and the file handle of the file that will now take output in BX. This service will make handle CX (= 1, the screen, in this example) point to the file in BX (= the file). The DOS manuals say that CX now refers to the same "stream" of data as BX. If you now write to handle 1, output goes to your file instead, since that "stream" has been redirected. When the program finishes, handle 1 will be reset to the screen again.

Of course, this is all done much easier by simply choosing the right file handle when it comes time to output data. Your program can select 1, 2, or whatever it wants. If you are locked into using 1, or some particular handle, however, this service can point it to other places. Table 4.4 shows the meanings for the handles.

Table 4.4 Handles

Input	Output
Handle 0 Standard Input.	Input can be redirected.
Handle 1 Standard Output.	Output can be redirected.
Handle 2 Standard Error Output.	Output CANNOT be redirected.

If you try to redirect the output of a handle that cannot be redirected, such as the standard error output device, handle 2, this service will show no error—but your program will crash if it tries to write to that handle.

INT 21H Service 4EH—Find First Matching File

Input	Output
DS:DX→ASCIIZ filestring.	Carry→AL=2 No match found.
CX=Attribute to match.	AL=18 No more files.
AH=4EH	No Carry→DTA filled as follows:
	21 Bytes=reserved.
	1 Byte=found attribute.
	2 Bytes=file's time.
	2 Bytes=file's date.
	2 Bytes=low word of size.
	2 Bytes=high word of size.
	13 Bytes=name and extension of found file in ASCIIZ form (NO pathname).

This service is the counterpart of FCB Service 11H. You can point DS:DX at an ASCIIZ file string including drive letters, pathnames, and wildcards, and find matches in the directory. You set CX with the attribute you want to match.

If there is a carry when control returns from INT 21H, the service ran out of files to find. The error return will be 18 (12H), No More Files. (Although IBM says you can get error 2, File Not Found, I have only seen error 18 from this service.)

If a file is found, the DTA is filled with a sort of FCB. This is a rare use by the file handle services of the DTA. Forty-three bytes are returned, including the file's size, date, and time. This information can be seen in Table 4.5.

Table 4.5 DTA Information from DOS Service 4EH

DTA: Fills As Follows

21 Bytes are reserved.
1 Byte for found attribute.
2 Bytes for file's time.
2 Bytes for file's date.
2 Bytes for low word of size.
2 Bytes for high word of size.
13 Bytes name and extension of found file in ASCIIZ form (NO pathname).

This return is a little awkward. The matching file name that we were looking for is placed near the end in an ASCIIZ string, not at the beginning. Nor is it prefaced with a pathname, so even if you had searched some other directory by pointing DS:DX to an ASCIIZ filestring like "C:\DOWN\HERE*.*"0, you would only get file names like "BASEBALL.BAT" in return, not "C:\DOWN\HERE\BASEBALL.BAT"0. If you want to open C:\DOWN\HERE\BASEBALL.BAT, though, you still have to supply the full name in an ASCII filestring—"C:\DOWN\HERE\BASEBALL.BAT"0. This means that you have to construct the full file name yourself by adding pathname to file name, which is often inconvenient.

INT 21H Service 4FH—Find Next Matching File

Input	Output
Use Service 4EH BEFORE 4FH. AH=4FH	Carry→AL=18 No More Files. No Carry→DTA filled as follows: 21 Bytes=reserved. 1 Byte=found attribute. 2 Bytes=file's time. 2 Bytes=file's date. 2 Bytes=low word of size. 2 Bytes=high word of size. 13 Bytes=name and extension of found file in ASCIIZ form (NO pathname).

This service finds all subsequent directory matches to a file name after the first match has been found. The input required by this service is the 21 bytes that DOS reserved in the DTA when Service 4EH was called. You must call Service 4EH to find the first matching file before calling this service.

As with FCB Services 11H and 12H, the usual pattern is that you start a search with Service 4EH and then enter a loop where Service 4FH is called repeatedly. If no more files are found, the carry flag is set and the error returned in AL is 18, No More Files. If there is no carry, this service returns data in the same way Service 4EH does.

INT 21H Service 56H—Rename File

Input	Output
DS:DX=ASCIIZ filestring to be renamed.	No Carry→Success.
ES:DI=ASCIIZ filestring that holds the new name.	Carry→ AL=3 Path not found.
AH=56H	AL=5 Access denied.
	AL=17 Not same device.

NOTE: File CANNOT be renamed to another drive.

To use this service, set up two ASCIIZ filestrings (you can use wildcards) at DS:DX and ES:DI. The string at DS:DX is the original name and the one at ES:DI is the new name.

This is how DOS renames files after they have been created. This service will not copy files for you, although it will move them from subdirectory to subdirectory (not between disks). If you try to rename the file name to an existing file's name, you will get a carry and AL will be 5, Access Denied. If you try to copy to a different disk, you will get error 17, Not Same Device.

This service changes the file's directory entry. If you are leaving the file in the same subdirectory, DOS will simply change the file's name in its directory entry. If you are moving from one subdirectory to another, DOS will just delete the file's entry in the current subdirectory, open the file that represents the new subdirectory, and put the file's directory entry in there. (We will learn more about subdirectories and how they work soon.) For this reason, the file itself is never even opened, and so it cannot be copied to a new disk.

INT 21H Service 57H—Get or Set a File's Date and Time

Input	Output
BX=File Handle.	
AL=0→Get Date & Time	No Carry: CX returns Time. DX returns Date.
AL=1→Set Time to CX Set Date to DX.	File's date and time set.
	Carry→AL=1 Invalid Function Number. =6 Invalid Handle.

The time and date of a file are stored like this:

Time = 2048 × Hours + 32 × Minutes + Seconds/2

Date = 512 × (Year − 1980) + 32 × Month + Day

You can change a file's date and time with this service, but the file must already be opened because it requires a file handle to use this service.

Pass the file handle in BX as usual, and load AL with either 0 or 1. AL=0 means you will get the time and date returned in CX and DX respectively. AL=1 means the file's time and date will be set to the values in CX and DX respectively.

SUBDIRECTORIES

Although it is appropriate to say a little about the way subdirectories work we will for the most part wait until the chapter on disk handling, where we will take a subdirectory apart with DEBUG.

Subdirectories were introduced in DOS 2+. Since DOS has only a fixed amount of space in the main directory for directory entries, there was little expansion that could be done there. Instead, the 11 letters of a directory entry usually given to the file's name can now hold the name of a subdirectory. In fact, the subdirectory *is* a file.

Subdirectory Files

If you have a subdirectory named TEST, there is a file named TEST on your disk. TEST is made up entirely of 32-byte directory entries for each of the files in that subdirectory. (It also holds the two entries that appear as '.' and '..' in a directory listing. These entries orient the subdirectory by keeping track of its root directory and by allocating space for the file TEST itself in that root directory.)

The file TEST has an entry in the root directory, and it is given a length of 0. Despite that, it takes up space in the File Allocation Table (or FAT), which maps what files are stored in what sectors on the disk. Each of the files in the subdirectory TEST uses some of the space the file TEST has been given in the FAT.

This becomes rather complex on an assembly language level. It is usually far easier to use the DOS services to change subdirectories than to work directly with the files like TEST (since you first would have to change its attribute and then its length to be able to even read it in). On the other hand, sometimes it is unavoidable to work on this level. We will find ourselves in the middle of the FAT, for example, in the chapter on disk handling.

THE PROGRAM DIREX.COM

The program at the end of this chapter is named DIREX. DIREX is a directory manager. If you run it (type DIREX), it will put all the names of the files in the current subdirectory on the screen. You can move the highlighted cursor around with the cursor arrows.

DIREX lets you work with many files at once. You can copy, delete, protect (make Read-Only), or unprotect all marked files at the same time. To mark a file, position the cursor over that file and push the space bar. When you move away from the file, its name stays highlighted. To unmark a file, position the cursor over a highlighted name and push the space bar again.

The line at the bottom of the screen lists the commands. To delete all the marked files, type D. DIREX will ask for confirmation that you really do want to delete all the marked files before deleting them. If you want to protect them all, so they may not be deleted or written over, type P. To unprotect them, type U. If you wish to change subdirectories, type N (for New directory), and supply the new directory's pathname when DIREX prompts you. To quit, type Q.

How DIREX Works

DIREX uses practically all the file-handle services we've covered. To begin, it searches through the subdirectory with DOS services to find all the file names available. After you select which ones you want to work on by marking them, other DOS file services are used. If you want to copy files, the opening, reading, writing, and closing services are used. If you want to delete files, that service is used; the same for protecting and unprotecting. DIREX also uses the subdirectory-changing service if you want to change subdirectories. The most complex part of DIREX, however, doesn't have to do with these services at all, but in reading what you have to type: changing lowercase to uppercase, adding omitted backslashes for pathnames, and so on, take up a lot of room in almost any program where there are many possible commands to give.

LISTING 4.4 DIREX.ASM

```
        TARGET EQU 0D8H
        SOURCE EQU 0B0H
CODE_SEG        SEGMENT
        ASSUME  CS:CODE_SEG,DS:CODE_SEG,ES:CODE_SEG
        ORG     100H
START:  JMP     DIREX
        PROMPT DB 'D=Delete P=Protect U=Unprotect C=Copy <Space>=Mark'
               DB ' N=New Dir Q=Quit$'
        COPY_PROMPT      DB      'Pathname to copy marked files to: $'
        NEW_DIR_PROMPT   DB      'New Directory: $'
        FULL_MSG         DB      '*        TARGET DISK FULL!           *$'
        DEL_MSG          DB      'Delete Marked Files (Y/N)? $'
        COPY_FLAG        DB      0        ;Set for Coping.
        DISP_FLAG        DB      0
        FULL_FLAG        DB      0        ;Disk Full?
        SOURCE_HANDLE    DW      0        ;To keep track of the Source files.
        TARGET_HANDLE    DW      0        ;Ditto for targets.
        SOURCE_PATH_END  DW      ?        ;Where we are.
        TARGET_PATH_END  DW      ?        ;Where we are going to be.
        BYTES_READ       DW      ?        ;For copying.
        BYTES_ASKED      DW      ?        ;Also for copying.
        MARKED  DB       ?                ;Is this file marked?
        ATTRIB  DB       ?                ;For the display.
        WILDCARDS        DB      '*.*',0
        CURSOR_X         DB      ?        ;Position of cursor.
        CURSOR_Y         DB      ?
        TEMPX            DB      ?        ;Storage for cursor positions.
        TEMPY            DB      ?

DIREX   PROC    NEAR
        CALL    DISPLAY                   ;Put filenames on screen.
        MOV     SI,SOURCE_PATH_END
        CALL    GET_FILE_NAME
TOPPER: MOV     ATTRIB,70H                ;Reverse Video.
        CALL    COLOR
TOP:    MOV     AH,0                      ;Read typed key.
        INT     16H

SPACE:  CMP     AL,20H                    ;Was typed character a space?
        JNE     RIGHT                     ;No--check right arrow.
        MOV     AH,8                      ;Yes, get end character from screen.
        MOV     BX,0
        ADD     CURSOR_X,12
        CALL    SET_CURSOR
        INT     10H
        CMP     AL,0FFH                   ;Marked?
        JE      OPP                       ;Yes.
        MOV     AL,0FFH                   ;No, mark it now.
        JMP     PPO
OPP:    MOV     AL,0
PPO:    MOV     AH,10
        MOV     CX,1
        INT     10H
        SUB     CURSOR_X,12               ;Move to beginning of filename.
        CALL    SET_CURSOR
        JMP     TOP                       ;Get next typed key.
RIGHT:  CMP     AH,4DH                    ;Was right arrow typed?
        JNE     LEFT                      ;No, check left arrow.
        MOV     ATTRIB,7                  ;Yes, set attribute for screen.
        CALL    COLOR                     ;Color out file name.
```

LISTING 4.4 CONTINUED

```
         CALL     INC_CURSOR                ;Move to next file name.
         MOV      ATTRIB,70H                ;Color in file name.
         CALL     COLOR
         JMP      TOP                       ;Read in next char.

LEFT:    CMP      AH,4BH                    ;Left arrow typed?
         JNE      UP                        ;No--check up key.
         MOV      DL,CURSOR_X               ;Get ready to move back.
         MOV      DH,CURSOR_Y
         MOV      ATTRIB,7                  ;Reset color of current file name.
         CALL     COLOR                     ;Color it out.
         SUB      DL,13                     ;Move back.
         JNC      OK                        ;Past edge of screen?
         MOV      DL,5*13                   ;Yes, wrap.
         SUB      DH,1                      ; and go up one line.
         JNC      OK
         MOV      DL,CURSOR_X
         MOV      DH,CURSOR_Y
OK:      MOV      CURSOR_X,DL
         MOV      CURSOR_Y,DH
         CALL     SET_CURSOR                ;Set current file name in rev. video.
         MOV      ATTRIB,70H
         CALL     COLOR
         JMP      TOP                       ;And wait for next command.

UP:      CMP      AH,48H                    ;Up arrow typed?
         JNE      DOWN                      ;No--check down arrow.
         MOV      DL,CURSOR_X               ;Prepare to move down.
         MOV      DH,CURSOR_Y
         MOV      ATTRIB,7
         CALL     COLOR                     ;Color out current file name.
         SUB      DH,1
         JNC      NOTTOP                    ;Can we move down?
         ADD      DH,1                      ;Yes.
NOTTOP:  MOV      CURSOR_X,DL
         MOV      CURSOR_Y,DH
         CALL     SET_CURSOR                ;Get ready to color current name in.
         MOV      ATTRIB,70H                ;Do it.
         CALL     COLOR
         JMP      TOP                       ;Get next command.

DOWN:    CMP      AH,50H                    ;Was this a down arrow typed?
         JNE      LETTERS                   ;No--check if it was a letter.
         MOV      ATTRIB,7                  ;Color out current file name.
         CALL     COLOR
         INC      CURSOR_Y
         CALL     SET_CURSOR                ;Are we pointing to a
         MOV      SI,SOURCE_PATH_END        ; valid file name?
         CALL     GET_FILE_NAME
         CMP      BYTE PTR DS:[SI],' '
         JA       GO
NOGO:    DEC      CURSOR_Y                  ;No, do not move down.
         CALL     SET_CURSOR
GO:      MOV      ATTRIB,70H                ;Yes, color in current file name.
         CALL     COLOR
         JMP      TOP                       ;Wait for next command.

LETTERS:CMP       AL,'Z'          ;Convert to lower case.
         JL       GOL
         SUB      AL,'a'-'A'
```

LISTING 4.4 CONTINUED

```
GOL:    CMP     AL,'Q'          ;Are we supposed to quit?
        JNE     DEL             ;No, check deleting.
        JMP     OUT1            ;Yes, quit.
DEL:    CMP     AL,'D'          ;Delete?
        JE      OKD             ;Yes, do the delete.
        JMP     PRO             ;No, check protecting.
OKD:    MOV     ATTRIB,7        ;To delete.
        CALL    COLOR           ;Color out current file name.
        MOV     CURSOR_X,0      ;Get ready to put
        MOV     CURSOR_Y,24     ; the deleting message at bottom
        CALL    SET_CURSOR      ; of the screen.
        MOV     AH,9
        MOV     CX,80
        MOV     AL,' '
        MOV     BX,7
        INT     10H
        MOV     CURSOR_X,0
        MOV     CURSOR_Y,24
        CALL    SET_CURSOR
        MOV     AH,9
        MOV     DX,OFFSET DEL_MSG       ;Type out deleting message.
        INT     21H
        MOV     AH,1
        INT     21H
        CMP     AL,'Z'                  ;Capitalize response.
        JL      CHECKY
        SUB     AL,'a'-'A'
CHECKY: CMP     AL,'Y'                  ;Should we delete?
        JE      GODEL                   ;Yes!
        CALL    DSPLAY2                 ;No, redisplay screen (wiping off
        MOV     ATTRIB,70H              ; delete message).
        CALL    COLOR
        JMP     TOP
GODEL:  MOV     CURSOR_X,0              ;Begin the delete.
        MOV     CURSOR_Y,0              ;Start checking file by file.
        CALL    SET_CURSOR
LOOPD:  CALL    GET_MARKED_FILE         ;Get next marked file.
        MOV     DX,SOURCE               ;Get full name.
        MOV     AH,41H                  ;Do the delete.
        INT     21H
        CALL    INC_CURSOR              ;Move on to next file name.
        CMP     DX,0FFH                 ;At end?
        JE      FIND                    ;Yes, leave.
        CMP     CX,0FFH                 ;More to delete?
        JNE     LOOPD
FIND:   CALL    DSPLAY2                 ;Move cursor to top left
        MOV     ATTRIB,70H              ; and redisplay.
        CALL    COLOR
        JMP     TOP
PRO:    CMP     AL,'P'                  ;Here we will protect a file.
        JNE     UNPRO                   ;If not, jump to unprotect.
        MOV     ATTRIB,7                ;Color out current file name if poss.
        CALL    COLOR
        MOV     CURSOR_X,0
        MOV     CURSOR_Y,0
        CALL    SET_CURSOR
LOOPP:  CALL    GET_MARKED_FILE         ;Loop over files to protect.
        MOV     DX,SOURCE               ;Set up full name.
        MOV     AH,43H                  ;Protect the file.
        MOV     AL,01
```

LISTING 4.4 CONTINUED

```
        MOV     CX,1
        INT     21H
        CALL    INC_CURSOR              ;Move on to next one.
        CMP     DX,0FFH                 ;Can we?
        JE      FINP                    ;No.
        CMP     CX,0FFH
        JNE     LOOPP                   ;Yes.
FINP:   CALL    DSPLAY2                 ;Done_redisplay.
        MOV     ATTRIB,70H              ;Move cursor to top left.
        CALL    COLOR
        JMP     TOP                     ;Get next command.
UNPRO:  CMP     AL,'U'                  ;Are we supposed to unprotect?
        JNE     COPY                    ;No, try copy.
        MOV     ATTRIB,7                ;Color out current file name.
        CALL    COLOR
        MOV     CURSOR_X,0
        MOV     CURSOR_Y,0
        CALL    SET_CURSOR
LOOPU:  CALL    GET_MARKED_FILE         ;Loop over files to unprotect.
        MOV     DX,SOURCE
        MOV     AH,43H
        MOV     AL,01                   ;And unprotect them.
        MOV     CX,0
        INT     21H
        CALL    INC_CURSOR              ;Move on to next one.
        CMP     DX,0FFH                 ;Done?
        JE      FINU                    ;Yes.
        CMP     CX,0FFH
        JNE     LOOPU                   ;No.
FINU:   CALL    DSPLAY2                 ;All finished. Redisplay.
        MOV     ATTRIB,70H
        CALL    COLOR
        JMP     TOP                     ;Wait for next command.

COPY:   CMP     AL,'C'                  ;Are we supposed to copy?
        JE      GOC                     ;Yes.
        JMP     NEW_DIR                 ;No--try directory change.
GOC:    MOV     FULL_FLAG,0             ;Let's copy!
        MOV     ATTRIB,7                ;Color out current file name.
        CALL    COLOR
        MOV     CURSOR_X,0
        MOV     CURSOR_Y,24
        CALL    SET_CURSOR              ;Get pathname to copy marked
        MOV     AH,9                    ; files to.
        MOV     CX,80
        MOV     AL,' '
        MOV     BX,7
        INT     10H
        MOV     CURSOR_X,0
        MOV     CURSOR_Y,24
        CALL    SET_CURSOR
        MOV     AH,9
        MOV     DX,OFFSET COPY_PROMPT   ;Put that name in TARGET.
        INT     21H
        MOV     AH,0AH
        MOV     BX,TARGET-2
        MOV     DX,TARGET-2
        MOV     BYTE PTR [BX],32        ;Add a space.
        INT     21H
```

LISTING 4.4 CONTINUED

```
        MOV     SI,TARGET
TRANS:  CMP     BYTE PTR [SI],13        ;Check for final slash on pathname.
        JE      SLASH2
        INC     SI                      ;Add it if it's missing.
        JMP     TRANS
SLASH2: CMP     BYTE PTR [SI-1],'\'
        JE      FILER2
        MOV     BYTE PTR [SI],'\'
        INC     SI
FILER2: MOV     TARGET_PATH_END,SI      ;All set to copy.
        MOV     ATTRIB,7
        CALL    COLOR                   ;Color out current file name.
        MOV     CURSOR_X,0
        MOV     CURSOR_Y,0
        CALL    SET_CURSOR
LOOPC:  MOV     COPY_FLAG,1             ;Set copy flag for GET_MARKED_FILE.
        CALL    GET_MARKED_FILE         ;Find file to copy.
        MOV     COPY_FLAG,0             ;Reset Copy flag.
        CMP     CX,0FFH                 ;Find any?
        JNE     OPEN                    ;Yes, open it.
        JMP     FINC                    ;No, finished with copy.
OPEN:   MOV     DX,SOURCE               ;Open the source file.
        MOV     AX,3D00H
        INT     21H
        JC      BOTC                    ;If error, quit.
        MOV     SOURCE_HANDLE,AX        ;Store source handle.
        MOV     DX,TARGET               ;Create Target.
        MOV     AH,3CH
        MOV     CX,0
        INT     21H
        JC      BOTC                    ;If problem, assume disk full, quit.
        MOV     TARGET_HANDLE,AX        ;Store target handle.
STUFF:  MOV     DX,OFFSET DATA
        MOV     CX,62*1024              ;Work in 62K chunks.
        MOV     AH,3FH
        MOV     BX,SOURCE_HANDLE        ;Read from source.
        INT     21H
        MOV     BYTES_READ,AX           ;How much did we get?
        MOV     CX,AX                   ;No. bytes read.
        MOV     BYTES_ASKED,CX
        MOV     AH,40H                  ;Write to target.
        MOV     BX,TARGET_HANDLE
        MOV     DX,OFFSET DATA          ;From DATA area.
        INT     21H
        CMP     AX,BYTES_ASKED          ;Did we write everything?
        JNE     FULL                    ;No, assume disk full.
        CMP     BYTES_READ,62*1024      ;More to read?
        JE      STUFF                   ;Yes.
        JMP     BOTC                    ;No.
FULL:   MOV     CURSOR_X,0              ;Disk is full.
        MOV     CURSOR_Y,24             ;Reset display and quit.
        CALL    SET_CURSOR
        LEA     DX,FULL_MSG
        MOV     AH,9                    ;Type out full message.
        INT     21H
        MOV     FULL_FLAG,1
        MOV     CURSOR_X,0
        MOV     CURSOR_Y,0
        CALL    SET_CURSOR
BOTC:   MOV     AH,3EH                  ;Done. Close all files.
```

LISTING 4.4 CONTINUED

```
        MOV     BX,SOURCE_HANDLE
        INT     21H                     ;Close Source.
        MOV     AH,3EH
        MOV     BX,TARGET_HANDLE        ;Close Target.
        INT     21H
        CMP     FULL_FLAG,1
        JNE     NOTFULL
        MOV     DX,TARGET
        MOV     AH,41H
        INT     21H
        JMP     TOPPER                  ;Go back to beginning.
NOTFULL:CALL    INC_CURSOR
        CMP     DX,0FFH
        JE      FINC
        JMP     LOOPC                   ;Copy another file.

FINC:   CALL    DSPLAY2                 ;Done with copy.
        MOV     ATTRIB,70H              ;Set cursor on.
        CALL    COLOR
        JMP     TOP                     ;Wait for next command.

NEW_DIR:CMP     AL,'N'                  ;Change directory?
        JE      GON                     ;Yes.
        JMP     TOP                     ;No--ignore command. Wait for next.
GON:    MOV     ATTRIB,7                ;Color out current file name.
        CALL    COLOR
        MOV     CURSOR_X,0
        MOV     CURSOR_Y,24
        CALL    SET_CURSOR              ;Ask for new directory.
        MOV     AH,9
        MOV     CX,80
        MOV     AL,' '
        MOV     BX,7
        INT     10H
        MOV     CURSOR_X,0
        MOV     CURSOR_Y,24
        CALL    SET_CURSOR
        MOV     AH,9
        MOV     DX,OFFSET NEW_DIR_PROMPT
        INT     21H                     ;And now change subdirectories.
        MOV     AH,0AH
        MOV     BX,80H
        MOV     DX,80H
        MOV     BYTE PTR [BX],32        ;Blank out new dir message.
        INT     21H
        JMP     DIREX

OUT:    INT     20H                     ;Grand Exit.
DIREX   ENDP

GET_MARKED_FILE PROC    NEAR            ;Find marked files from screen.
                                        ;CX=FF → no more to be found.
BEGI:   MOV     AH,8
        ADD     CURSOR_X,12
        CALL    SET_CURSOR
        MOV     BX,0                    ;Check last byte of file name on screen.
        INT     10H
        SUB     CURSOR_X,12
        CALL    SET_CURSOR
        CMP     AL,0FFH                 ;If it is FF, the file is marked.
```

LISTING 4.4 CONTINUED

```
        JE      FINI
        CALL    INC_CURSOR
        CMP     DX,0FFH
        JNE     BEGI
        MOV     CX,0FFH                 ;NO MORE to be found!
        JMP     OUTER
FINI:   MOV     CX,0
        MOV     SI,SOURCE_PATH_END
        CALL    GET_FILE_NAME
        CMP     COPY_FLAG,1             ;Set up SI?
        JNE     OUTER
        MOV     SI,TARGET_PATH_END      ;Yes for copying.
        CALL    GET_FILE_NAME
OUTER:  RET
GET_MARKED_FILE ENDP

GET_FILE_NAME   PROC    NEAR            ;Gets file name from screen.
        ;Call with DS:SI as address to put name at.
        PUSH    CX
        PUSH    SI
        PUSH    WORD PTR CURSOR_X       ;Store cursor.
        MOV     AH,8
        MOV     BX,0
        MOV     CX,12                   ;12 Letters in name.
LOOPB:  MOV     AH,8
        INT     10H                     ;Get a letter.
        INC     CURSOR_X
        CALL    SET_CURSOR
        MOV     DS:[SI],AL              ;Move it to DS:SI.
        INC     SI                      ;Move on to next character.
        LOOP    LOOPB
        MOV     BYTE PTR DS:[SI],0      ;Make it ASCIIZ.
        POP     WORD PTR CURSOR_X
        POP     SI
        CALL    SET_CURSOR              ;Reset cursor.
        POP     CX
        RET                             ;And return.
GET_FILE_NAME   ENDP

COLOR   PROC    NEAR                    ;Set color of file name.
        PUSH    CX                      ;If marked, leave rev. video.
        PUSH    WORD PTR CURSOR_X       ;Save cursor.
        MOV     CX,12                   ;12 characters in file name.
        CMP     ATTRIB,7                ;Should we color out?
        JNE     HERE                    ;No.
        MOV     AH,8
        ADD     CURSOR_X,12             ;Yes.
        CALL    SET_CURSOR              ;Check if we should.
        MOV     BX,0
        INT     10H
        SUB     CURSOR_X,12
        CALL    SET_CURSOR
        CMP     AL,0FFH                 ;Is file marked?
        JE      FINE                    ;Yes, don't color out.
HERE:   MOV     BX,0
        MOV     AH,8            ;Change attribute character by character.
        INT     10H
        PUSH    CX
        MOV     CX,1
        MOV     BL,ATTRIB
```

LISTING 4.4 CONTINUED

```
        MOV     AH,9
        INT     10H
        POP     CX
        INC     CURSOR_X
        CALL    SET_CURSOR
        LOOP    HERE
FINE:   POP     WORD PTR CURSOR_X       ;Restore cursor.
        CALL    SET_CURSOR
        POP     CX
        RET
COLOR   ENDP

DISPLAY PROC    NEAR                    ;Puts up main display on screen.
        MOV     DI,SOURCE               ;Get source subdirectory.
        MOV     SI,82H
        MOV     SOURCE_PATH_END,SOURCE
        MOV     BX,80H
        CMP     BYTE PTR [BX],0
        JE      FILER
TRANS2: CMP     BYTE PTR [SI],13        ;Check for the slash at the end of it.
        JE      SLASH
        MOVSB
        JMP     TRANS2                  ;If it's not there, add it.
SLASH:  CMP     BYTE PTR [DI-1],'\'
        JE      FILER
        MOV     BYTE PTR [DI],'\'
        INC     DI
FILER:  MOV     SOURCE_PATH_END,DI      ;Get ready to find file name.
DSPLAY2:MOV     CX,25                   ;Short version--don't check source.
        MOV     CURSOR_X,0
        MOV     CURSOR_Y,0              ;Set cursor to top left.
        CALL    SET_CURSOR
WIPE:   PUSH    CX                      ;Clear the screen.
        CALL    SET_CURSOR
        MOV     CX,80
        MOV     AH,9
        MOV     BX,7
        MOV     AL,0
        INT     10H
        POP     CX
        INC     CURSOR_Y
        LOOP    WIPE
        MOV     CURSOR_X,6      ;Put up command line.
        MOV     CURSOR_Y,24
        CALL    SET_CURSOR
        MOV     AH,9
        MOV     DX,OFFSET PROMPT
        INT     21H
        MOV     CURSOR_X,0
        MOV     CURSOR_Y,0
        CALL    SET_CURSOR      ;Get ready to search.
        MOV     AH,4EH
        MOV     CX,4
        MOV     DI,SOURCE_PATH_END      ;Add the *.* at the end of the path.
        MOV     SI,OFFSET WILDCARDS
REP     MOVSB
        MOV     DX,SOURCE
        INT     21H                     ;Search for first match to wildcards.
        JC      ENDER                   ;If done, exit.
        MOV     DX,0
```

LISTING 4.4 CONTINUED

```
        MOV     AH,2
        INT     10H
        CALL    PRINT                   ;Print file name on screen.
        MOV     CX,120                  ;Max of 120 files.
LOOPER: MOV     AH,4FH
        INT     21H                     ;Find next match.
        JC      ENDER                   ;If no match, exit.
        MOV     DISP_FLAG,0FFH          ;Set DISP_FLAG for INC_CURSOR.
        CALL    INC_CURSOR
        MOV     DISP_FLAG,0
        CALL    PRINT
        MOV     DX,OFFSET WILDCARDS
        LOOP    LOOPER                  ;Look for next file name.
ENDER:  MOV     CURSOR_X,0              ;Set cursor up at top left.
        MOV     CURSOR_Y,0
        CALL    SET_CURSOR
        RET                             ;And exit.
DISPLAY ENDP

INC_CURSOR      PROC    NEAR    ;Move cursor to next file.
        PUSH    CX              ;Success→DX=0.
        MOV     DL,CURSOR_X
        MOV     DH,CURSOR_Y
        MOV     TEMPX,DL        ;Store cursor.
        MOV     TEMPY,DH
        ADD     DL,13           ;End of screen?
        CMP     DL,75
        JL      FIN
        MOV     DL,0
        INC     DH
FIN:    MOV     CURSOR_X,DL
        MOV     CURSOR_Y,DH
        MOV     DX,0                    ;Return OK signal.
        CALL    SET_CURSOR
        CMP     DISP_FLAG,0             ;Is this a DISPLAY?
        JNE     SET
        MOV     SI,SOURCE_PATH_END      ;Yes, is the next character a space?
        CALL    GET_FILE_NAME
        CMP     BYTE PTR DS:[SI],' '
        JA      SET                     ;No.
        SUB     CURSOR_X,13
        CMP     CURSOR_X,0
        JG      LEAV
        MOV     DL,TEMPX                ;If we can, update cursor.
        MOV     CURSOR_X,DL             ;If not, restore it.
        MOV     DH,TEMPY
        MOV     CURSOR_Y,DH
LEAV:   CALL    SET_CURSOR
        MOV     DX,0FFH
SET:    POP     CX                      ;Restore CX.
        RET                             ;And exit.
INC_CURSOR      ENDP

SET_CURSOR      PROC    NEAR            ;Position the cursor.
        PUSH    AX
        MOV     DL,CURSOR_X
        MOV     DH,CURSOR_Y             ;Use INT 10H.
        MOV     AH,2
        INT     10H
```

LISTING 4.4 CONTINUED

```
        POP     AX
        RET                             ;Finish.
SET_CURSOR      ENDP

PRINT   PROC    NEAR                    ;Print file names.
        PUSH    CX
        MOV     DX,80H+30               ;Check at CS:80H+30.
        MOV     BX,DX
        MOV     CX,13                   ;Search 13 chars for end of file name.
LOOPA:  CMP     BYTE PTR [BX],0         ;Find end of file name.
        JE      FOUND
        INC     BX
        LOOP    LOOPA
FOUND:  MOV     BYTE PTR DS:[BX+1],'$'  ;Use string print.
        MOV     AH,9                    ;Print out file name.
        INT     21H
        POP     CX
        RET                     ;Finish.
PRINT   ENDP
DATA:                           ;Store data for copies starting here.
CODE_SEG        ENDS
        END     START
```

Chapter 5
Screen Handling

INTRODUCTION

This is the chapter on screen output—the ways to see the results of our programs. In it, we will examine all the ways that characters can be written on the screen, how to the manipulate the cursor, how to read characters from the screen, how fast line graphics work, and how to use windows. To begin, let's immediately start working in the screen buffer itself.

THE SCREEN BUFFER

For each character on the screen, there are two bytes stored in memory. The first byte stored is the IBM ASCII code of the character. The second byte is a special attribute byte that displays *how* the character will be displayed. We have used the term IBM ASCII here because standard ASCII is really only a 7-bit code, defining only 128 characters ($128=2^7$). IBM adds another 128 characters that you may have seen on the screen, such as parts of boxes (ASCII 179–218), Greek letters (ASCII 224–238), and umlauted or European characters (ASCII 128–168). To see an ASCII code at DOS level, type Alt and the ASCII number (while holding down the Alt key). If you put the PC in high-resolution graphics mode (graphics monitors only) you can redesign the top 128 ASCII characters yourself and have the PC print them out. This is something we'll do later in this chapter.

Attributes

Table 5.1 shows the attributes you can use in graphics monitors bit by bit.

Table 5.1 Character Attributes

Bit Value	Color Generated
1	Blue Foreground
2	Green Foreground
4	Red Foreground
8	High Intensity
16	Blue Background
32	Green Background
64	Red Background
128	Blinking

To form the attribute byte you want, add the bit values. For example, to get a normal setting of white on black, you would turn all the foreground colors (the letter itself) on this way: 1 + 2 + 4 = 7. All the background colors are off, so they are set to 0. This value of 7 is the normal startup screen attribute value. If you wanted to make that high intensity, you would add 8 to give 15 = 0FH. If you wanted blinking reverse video in white, set all the background colors on, and add 128 to make it blink: 16 + 32 + 64 + 128 = 240 = 0F0H.

On monochrome screens you can't use the individual colors, but you can use the normal screen (7), high intensity (0FH), blinking normal (87H), blinking reverse video (F0H), and underlined, which graphics monitors don't have. To turn on underlining, use a blue foreground (making an attribute of 1). You can also have intense underlining (attribute of 9).

A character's ASCII and attribute bytes are stored in the screen buffer. This buffer, therefore, carries two bytes per character. There are 25 lines × 80 columns = 2,000 positions on the screen, so the screen buffer requires 4,000 bytes of memory (about 4K) to display a single page. In monochrome monitors, this memory starts at B000:0000, and in graphics monitors at B800:0000. We can reach either of these directly with DEBUG, of course. Give this a try on a monochrome screen (if you have a Graphics screen, use EB800:0220):

```
A>CLS
A>DEBUG
-EB000:0220
B000:0220  20.47   07.F0   20.4F   07.F0   20.4F   07.F0   20.44   07.F0
B000:0228  20.20   07.F0   20.57   07.F0   20.4F   07.F0   20.52   07.F0
B000:0230  20.4B   07.F0   20.<cr>
-Q
```

This will put a message into the screen buffer using DEBUG's Edit command. The CLS command clears the screen, and all you need type to DEBUG is EB000:0220‹cr› and the prompt 20.__ will come up. If you type 47‹space›F0‹space›4F‹space› and so forth, DEBUG will wrap around to the next line automatically when you run out of space on one line. At the end, after the last F0, type a ‹cr›. The message should be on the screen in blinking letters.

We can see the values that were in the screen buffer before we edited them: ASCII 20, a space (what the CLS command put there), and an attribute of 7 (the normal screen attribute).

Graphics Monitors in Graphics Mode

The graphics monitor, when it is doing pixel-by-pixel graphics, requires 16K instead of 4K. This memory is always available on the graphics card, and since it is enough to make up four full screens of text, IBM allows you to use **pages** in the graphics monitor when dealing with text. Normally, all pages are copies of each other, and page 0 is displayed. With BIOS, though, you can skip between pages and selectively write to particular pages. You can, of course, directly write to the memory part of any page also. In 80 column × 25 line mode there are four pages at 4K intervals, numbered 0–3, and in 40 × 25 mode there are eight pages, numbered 0–7. (Monochrome monitors only have one page, page 0.)

THE BIOS AND DOS SERVICES

BIOS and DOS provide you with a number of ways of reaching the screen and manipulating the cursor. They provide rudimentary graphics (i.e., putting ONE dot on the screen for you), and can let you change screen modes. We can do all these things ourselves, of course, just by manipulating memory locations. On the other hand, there are a lot of details that these services take care of that we'd often rather not worry about. For example, these services can take care of automatic carriage returns for you. For most applications, it is much easier to use these services than to write everything yourself, and for this reason we will cover the system resources before striking out on our own. Since this book is intended to be more advanced than introductory texts, we are going to list the full range of BIOS services, something that is often glossed over or only selectively covered. To become a competent assembly language programmer, it is important that you know what is available. The system interrupt that all graphics services in the PC are built on is BIOS INT 10H. Even DOS uses it to provide its own services.

BIOS INT 10H

BIOS INT 10H is mammoth. Because it is so big, we will take one service at a time. The services are called the same way as in DOS INT 21H, by loading an appropriate number into AH.

BIOS INT 10H Service 0—Set Screen Mode

Input	Output	
AH=0	Screen Set to:	
AL=0	40 × 25 B&W	Graphics Screen
1	40 × 25 Color	Graphics Screen
2	80 × 25 B&W	Graphics Screen
3	80 × 25 Color	Graphics Screen
4	320 × 200 Color	Graphics Screen
5	320 × 200 B&W	Graphics Screen
6	640 × 200 Color	Graphics Screen
7	80 × 25 Monochrome	Monochrome Screen

With this service you can change the "mode" of a graphics monitor. B&W above means Black and White on graphics screens—it does not refer to the monochrome screen. Black and white, of course, usually means black and green, and is used for single-color graphics monitors.

You can change the screen to a variety of modes, 40 × 25, 80 × 25, the graphics modes of medium resolution (320 × 200 pixels) and high resolution (640 × 200). When we redesign the top 128 characters of ASCII, for example, we will have to put the PC in high resolution graphics mode to see them.

BIOS INT 10H Service 1—Set Cursor Type

Input	Output
AH = 1	New Cursor
CH = Cursor Start Line	
CL = Cursor End Line	

This service gives you some control over the cursor. You cannot stop it from blinking (since it is set in hardware), but you can redesign it, or even eliminate it. The cursor on a monochrome monitor is 14 lines tall, and is eight lines tall on a graphics monitor.

Imagine we wanted to change the cursor on a monochrome monitor. The top line is 0 and the bottom line is 13 (0DH). CH holds the starting line of the new cursor, and CL the line at which it will end. If you wanted the cursor to use only the bottom two lines available, you would set CH to 0CH and CL to 0DH. If you just wanted to use one line at the bottom, you could set both CH and CL to 0DH. Here's how to do it with DEBUG:

```
-A100
08F7:0100 MOV    AH,1
08F7:0102 MOV    CH,0D
08F7:0104 MOV    CL,0D
08F7:0106 INT    10H
08F7:0108 INT    20H
08F7:010A
-U100 10A
08F7:0100 B401          MOV     AH,01
08F7:0102 B50D          MOV     CH,0D
08F7:0104 B10D          MOV     CL,0D
08F7:0106 CD10          INT     10
08F7:0108 CD20          INT     20
-G
```

The cursor can wrap around as well, and if you wanted to use the top and bottom lines *only*, you could set the start line (CH) at 0DH and the end line (in CL) at 00:

```
 -A102
08F7:0102 MOV    CH,0D
08F7:0104 MOV    CL,00
08F7:0106 INT    10H
08F7:0108 INT    20H
-G
-Q
```

To turn the cursor off entirely, set both values to something beyond the available range, such at 0FH.

BIOS INT 10H Service 2—Set Cursor Position

Input	Output
DH,DL = Row, Column BH = Page Number AH=2	Cursor position changed.

NOTE: DH,DL = 0,0 = Upper Left

This service is able to change the cursor's position on the screen. Cursor manipulations are best left to the system services, because it's usually easier. With this service, you can position the cursor wherever you wish on the screen, then print out characters. If you want to update some part of the screen over on the right, for example, just move the cursor there and go. With Service 8 you can read the characters that are already on the screen after you have moved the cursor in place. For graphics monitors, you can move the cursor on a particular page by putting the page number (0–3 for 80 × 25 mode and 0–7 for 40 × 25 mode) in BH.

BIOS INT 10H Service 3—Find Cursor Position

Input	Output
BH=Page Number	DH,DL=Row, Column of Cursor.
AH=3	CH,CL=Cursor Mode currently Set.

With this service you can locate the position of the cursor on the screen. Since you can maintain different cursor positions for each page of screen memory, you have to supply the graphics page number (0 for monchrome and when in graphics mode). The location of the cursor will be returned in DH and DL as row and column number.

This service also returns the "mode" of the cursor in CH and CL. This simply specifies the type of cursor—CH and CL will be set as they would be for a call to INT 10H Service 1, Set Cursor Type. From this information you can reset the cursor type if you wish. For example, you could eliminate the cursor altogether and replace it by typing out every timer tic, or some ASCII character such as an arrow or an angle bracket.

BIOS INT 10H Service 4—Read Light Pen Position

Input	Output
AH=4	AH=0→Light pen switch not down. AL=1→DH,DL=Row, Column of Light Pen position. CH Raster line (Vertical) 0-199 BX Pixel Column (Horizontal) 0-319,639

Light pens watch the scan line on monitors, and from internal timing checks they can tell where they are on the screen. This is the only support IBM offers for pens, except for the PEN commands in BASIC. Light pens can certainly be useful, but we won't use them here. Despite their ease of use, very little light-pen software has been developed.

BIOS INT 10H Service 5—Set Active Display Page

Input	Output
AL=0-7 (Screen Modes 0,1) 0-3 (Screen modes 2,3) AH=5	Active Page Changed.

NOTE: Different pages available in alphanumeric modes only (Graphics Adapters)

This is the way to shuttle back and forth between the various pages in text mode for graphics monitors. If you look at the types of modes possible in Service 0, you'll see that extra memory is only available in modes 0–1 (40 × 25 alphanumeric in graphics adapters) and modes 2–3 (80 × 25). The first range gives you eight pages (0–7) to work with and the second range gives four pages (0–3).

The PC is not the most capable screen-handling computer available. If you want to improve your screen-handling, and if you have a graphics screen to work with, you can work by setting up screens in memory and, when the time comes, change the active page immediately. Of course this only works in alphanumeric modes since when you are doing graphics on the graphics monitor only one page (page 0) is available.

BIOS INT 10H Service 6—Scroll Active Page Up

Input

AL=#Lines blanked at bottom (0→Blank whole area).
CH,CL=Upper Left Row,Column of area to scroll.
DH,DL=Lower Right Row,Column of area to scroll.
BH=Attribute used on blank line.
AH=6

This service is useful for scrolling windows on the screen, or selectively clearing part of the screen. For example, you could write a notepad program that scrolled only its own window on the screen. Select the window you want to scroll by loading the values of the window's corners in CH,CL (Row, Column) and DH,DL as shown in Figure 5.1.

If your notepad is reverse video, or any other attribute, you can preserve that attribute when you scroll the window by putting the attribute in BH before the call.

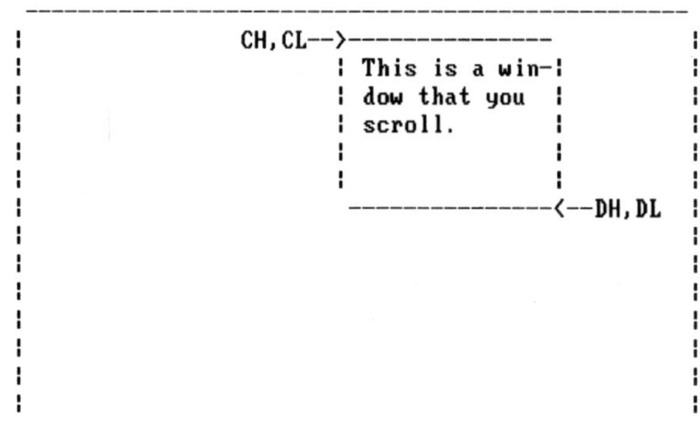

Figure 5.1 A Window on the Screen.

SCROLL.ASM

Let's give this service a try with a small program, SCROLL.ASM. SCROLL will scroll a window on the screen when invoked. Fill the screen up with some output (do a "DIR", for example) and give SCROLL.COM a try:

```
CODE_SEG SEGMENT
        ASSUME  CS:CODE_SEG
ENTRY:  ORG     100H
        MOV     AH,6            ←Service 6.
        MOV     CH,5            ←Window dimensions.
        MOV     CL,0
        MOV     DH,15
        MOV     DL,15
        MOV     AL,1            ←Number of lines to scroll.
        MOV     BH,7            ←Attribute of 7.
        INT     10H
        INT     20H
CODE_SEG ENDS
        END     ENTRY
```

Running SCROLL.COM makes a unique display since only parts of the screen scroll—an interesting show to watch.

If you had wanted to blank that portion of the screen, you could have filled AL with 0 instead of 1. Although this will blank the selected part of the screen, this same thing is usually done much more quickly by loading memory in the screen buffer directly, as we will see.

BIOS INT 10H Service 7—Scroll Active Page Down

Input

AL=#Lines blanked at bottom (0→Blank whole area).
CH,CL=Upper Left Row,Column of area to scroll.
DH,DL=Lower Right Row,Column of area to scroll.
BH=Attribute used on blank line.
AH=7

This is the corresponding downward scroll. Between these two, you can manage quite a bit of screen-handling. DOS uses these services to scroll the screen up itself. If you want to change the way the screen scrolls (for example, if you wanted to add a permanent status line at the bottom), you may want to intercept this service.

BIOS INT 10H Service 8—Read Attribute and Character at Cursor Position

Input	**Output**
BH = Page Number	AL=Character read (ASCII).
AH=8	AH=Attribute of character (Alphanumerics only).

This service is very useful in letting you read from the screen. It is used extensively in last chapter's DIREX. DIREX begins by displaying all the file names in a directory on the screen. It actually uses the screen buffer as storage for the file names that it is working on. After you have selected the files you want to delete, DIREX reads them directly from the screen buffer.

If you are using a graphics monitor in alphanumeric mode, you can select which page you want to work on by loading BH. Otherwise, everything is all set for you since the cursor is already in place. AL returns the one byte ASCII code, and AH returns the one-byte attribute of the character.

BIOS INT 10H Service 9—Write Attribute and Character at Cursor Position

Input

BH=Page Number
BL→Alpha Modes=Attribute
    Graphics Modes=Color
CX=Count of characters to write
AL=IBM ASCII code.
AH=9

This is how BIOS writes on the screen. In fact, this is how DOS writes to the screen, since DOS uses the BIOS interrupts. With this service you can select which page you write on (on graphics monitors). To write to the screen at the current cursor position, just put the character's ASCII code into AL and call this service.

In graphics modes, the screen can still print characters just as before (although the cursor is turned off), but the whole video buffer is used to store the graphics image, which means you cannot select different pages. Furthermore, in graphics modes, only the first 128 ASCII characters are defined; it is up to you to define the others in a table. This table must be made memory resident, and an interrupt vector must be pointed at it. This vector is made up of the double word at 0000:007C.

Designing Your Own Characters with Service 9

If we ask the PC to display a character with an ASCII number above 128 with Service 9 while we are in graphics mode, it looks for the table of character definitions we've supplied it with. As soon as it arrives at our table, the PC must find it coded in the form it can use. For high-resolution graphics this is actually fairly easy. Each character is given its own 8 X 8 grid of dots on the screen in which to be defined. (This gives it just enough dots so that 80 characters can fit comfortably into one row across the screen and 25 up and down.)

Each position, or dot, can be either on or off on the screen, just as a bit can be either 1 or 0. Our character becomes eight rows of eight bits each. Eight bits naturally becomes one byte, so the character becomes eight bytes, one on top of the other. To turn a dot in some row of some character on, just make its matching position in that byte a one, as shown in Figure 5.2.

```
Column Number 76543210
              ----------
            0 |X       |     Byte 0 = 128
            1 | X      |     Byte 1 = 64
            2 |  X     |     Byte 2 = 32
            3 |   X    |     Byte 3 = 16
            4 |    X   |     Byte 4 = 8
            5 |     X  |     Byte 5 = 4
            6 |      X |     Byte 6 = 2
            7 |XXXXXXXX|     Byte 7 = 255
              ----------
```

Figure 5.2 Bit Positions in a Character.

For the odd character above, the leftmost bit in the top row is the only one on, so that byte (byte 0 of the character) becomes 128. The next byte is 64, and so on down to the bottom row (byte 7), which is completely lit, giving it a value of 255. The next character (ASCII 129) will start at byte 8 in our table. The table is therefore nothing more than 128 characters, one after the other, with 8 bytes each or 1,024 bytes in total.

After you've made up your 1024 byte table, you can load them in memory with a small .ASM file like this (put the 1K table in TABLE in the data area):

```
VECTORS  SEGMENT AT 0H
        ORG      07CH
TABLE_INT_LOW    LABEL    WORD
        ORG      07EH
TABLE_INT_HIGH   LABEL    WORD
VECTORS  ENDS

CODE_SEG SEGMENT
        ASSUME CS:CODE_SEG,DS:VECTORS
        ORG      100H
ENTRY:  JMP BOOSTER
        TABLE    DB 1024 DUP(0)   ;←Put character definitions here.
BOOSTER:MOV      AX,0
        MOV      DS,AX
        MOV      TABLE_INT_LOW, OFFSET TABLE
        PUSH     CS
        POP      TABLE_INT_HIGH
        LEA      DX,BOOSTER
        INT      27H
CODE_SEG ENDS
        END      ENTRY
```

To actually use these characters now that you've produced them, you have to get the PC into high-resolution graphics mode and print out the high characters using BIOS Service 9, or a BASIC command like this: PRINT CHR$(128), which prints the ASCII character 128 from BASIC.

Changing the Color of Your Screen with Service 9

With INT 10H Service 9, you can write multiple copies of the character you are printing. You can even write a screenful in one Interrupt call (except in graphics modes, where this service will not skip to the next line automatically). Here is a program to set the screen (alphanumeric modes only) to whatever attribute you want by typing out 4000 spaces, each with the attribute required (see the attributes in Table 5.1):

```
CODE_SEG SEGMENT
         ASSUME CS:CODE_SEG,DS:CODE_SEG
         ORG      100H
ENTRY:   MOV      AH,2     ← Position cursor at (0,0).
         MOV      BH,0
         MOV      DX,0
         INT      10H
         MOV      AH,9
         MOV      CX,4000  ← Write 80 columns × 25 lines.
         MOV      BH,0
```

```
          MOV     AL,' '
          MOV     BL,7    ← Put desired attribute here.
          INT     10H
          INT     20H
CODE_SEG ENDS
          END     ENTRY
```

In the graphics mode, BL will hold the color of the character to be printed, not its attribute. We will see how this is done in the graphics section that follows shortly.

BIOS INT 10H Service A—Write Character ONLY at Cursor Position

Input	Output
BH=Page Number CX=Count of characters to write. AL=IBM ASCII code. AH=0AH	Character written on screen at Cursor Position.

This service is the same as Service 9 except that it does not write the character's attribute. If someone has set their screen to a particular, preferred attribute, for example, it is usually best not to change it, and this service does not.

GRAPHICS

After these services comes the PC's graphics services. Before covering the system services for graphics, it is essential to review how graphics work in the PC. A few pages will be devoted to this review.

The PC is not really a good graphics machine. Some modern microcomputers can do a lot of graphics in hardware, even faster than in assembly language. Animation can even be done in their hardware. The PC is a different story. There are three "modes" of resolution in the PC—low, medium, and high. The number of pixels (which stands for picture element) up and down (in the Y direction) is always the same—200. The number in the across direction (the X direction) varies from 160 (low resolution), through 320 (medium resolution) to 640 (high resolution).

You can only display the maximum number of colors available, 16, in low-resolution mode. However, there is *no* support in the PC's software, BIOS or DOS, for low resolution. The graphics video controller can be put in low-resolution mode, though, so if you want to take the time, you can provide support yourself. As it is, we will concentrate here only on medium- and high-resolution graphics.

In medium-resolution graphics you can display four colors at any pixel, and in high-resolution only two (on and off). Even the four colors of medium resolution are an illusion, because you are free to pick only one of the four; the other three (colors 1,2, and 3) can only be chosen by picking one of two palettes.

Table 5.2 holds the possible 16 colors along with their **color values**, the values you use when drawing with pixels.

Table 5.2 Color Values

Color Value	Color
0	Black (off)
1	Blue
2	Green
3	Cyan (Green+Blue)
4	Red
5	Magenta (Red+Blue)
6	Brown
7	White
8	Black
9	Light Blue
10	Light Green
11	Light Cyan
12	Light Red
13	Light Magenta
14	Yellow
15	Light White

As you will see shortly, you choose one color of the 16 above with INT 10H, Service 11, and this color then makes up color 0 whenever you put pixels on the screen. At the same time, you choose from the two palettes: green, red, yellow, or cyan, magenta, white. The palette colors then make up colors 1, 2, and 3. When you turn a pixel on the screen on, you specify which color—0, 1, 2, or 3—to make it.

THE SCREEN BUFFER IN GRAPHICS MODE

In high-resolution mode, 640x200 pixels, you can choose only on or off, 0 or 1. The PC only needs to save one bit per pixel in this case. Since there are 200 lines down (on graphics monitors characters are 8 scan lines high, and 8 × 25 lines = 200) and 640 lines across, there are 640 × 200 = 128,000 bits needed. This makes 16,000 bytes, rounded up in the PC's graphics video buffer to 16K.

In medium resolution, 320x200, we can specify one of four colors for each pixel, so we need two bits to hold the possible values for each pixel. Since there are only half as many pixels (320 across vs 640 across), we still use the same size video buffer, 16K.

In high-resolution mode it seems natural that if you wanted to turn the pixel on at location (0,0), the top left corner of the screen, you would set the first bit in the video buffer to 1. That is actually how it works. To turn the next pixel in the top row (row 0) on, you would set the next bit to 1, and so forth to the end of the first line on the screen, the first 640 pixels (numbers 0–639).

It also seems natural that if you wanted to turn on the first pixel of the second row (row 1), you would set bit 640 in the video buffer to 1, since the first line goes from 0 to 639. Unfortunately, that is not how it works.

Graphics Buffer Memory Blocks

IBM decided to separate the graphics video buffer into two blocks of 8K each. The first block, starting at location B800:0000, holds the EVEN scan lines on the screen; the second block, starting at B800:2000, holds the ODD scan lines. This is done because the video controller scans over all the even lines on the screen first, and then does all the odd ones. To facilitate its operation, IBM gives it the bits in the order needed. This is an added complication for any program; now it has to split up its image between two blocks in memory. In practice this is not very hard if you have a subroutine to put pixels on the screen that keeps track of which block they go into, or if you use INT 10H, Service 12.

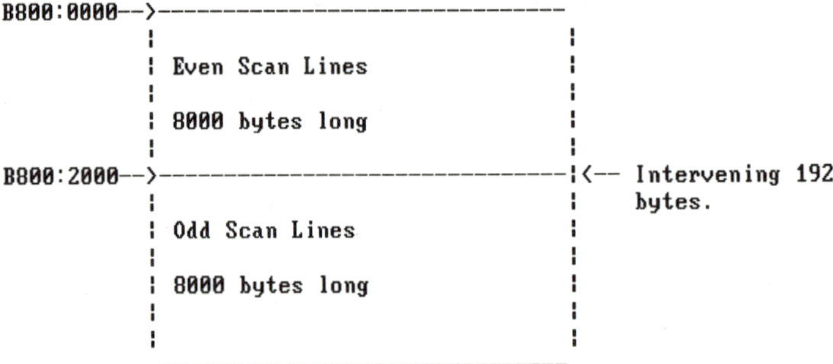

Figure 5.3 Graphics Video Buffer.

The scheme in medium resolution is similar, but here there can be four colors, not just two. Four colors demand two bits, so every two bits in the screen buffer can be grouped together into one pixel. Since there are only one-half as many pixels on a line, but twice as many bits per pixel, there are the same number of memory bits corresponding to each screen line, 640.

The Program PUT_PIXEL

Here's a small program, PUT_PIXEL, that will turn high-resolution pixels on:

LISTING 5.1 PUT_PIXEL

```
PUT_PIXEL       PROC    NEAR
        ;SUPPLY DX=ROW,CX=COLUMN. ASSUMES ES=B800H and screen in High
        ; Resolution mode (Use BIOS INT 10H Service 0).
        XOR     BX,BX
        SHR     DX,1
        JNC     CALC
        ADD     BX,8*1024
CALC:   MOV     AX,DX               ;GET 80*DX
        SHL     DX,1
        SHL     DX,1
        ADD     DX,AX
        MOV     AX,CX
        MOV     CL,4
        SHL     DX,CL               ;DX NOW MULTIPLIED BY 80 (16*5)
        ADD     BX,DX               ;ADD TO INDEX
        MOV     DX,AX
        AND     DX,7                ;GET X3 INTO DX
        MOV     CL,3
        SHR     AX,CL               ;CX/8
        ADD     BX,AX               ;FIND BYTE ALONG ROW
        NEG     DL
        ADD     DL,7
        MOV     CL,DL               ;GET BIT TO TURN ON
        MOV     AL,1
        SHL     AL,CL
        OR      ES:[BX],AL
        RET
PUT_PIXEL       ENDP
```

PUT_PIXEL is about three times as fast as the equivalent BIOS service call. If you ever want to work in graphics on the PC, you should know how to address individual pixels on the screen; for that reason we'll work through PUT_PIXEL in a little detail.

The first job of PUT_PIXEL is to determine whether the pixel is to be put in an even or odd row. The pixel's coordinates are given to PUT_PIXEL in DX (= row, 0–199) and CX (= column, 0–639). We have to check if DX is odd or even. The first 8K of the screen buffer holds lines 0,2,4,6,8, etc.; the second 8K holds lines 1,3,5,7,9 and so forth as shown in Table 5.3.

Table 5.3 Even and Odd Scan Lines

Screen Row #	1st or 2nd 8K	Line inside 8K Block
0	1	0
1	2	0
2	1	1
3	2	1
4	1	2

For each even line across the screen, there is a row of 640 bits in the first 8K block, and for each odd line, a row of 640 bits in the second 8K block. To find which line of 640 bits a particular pixel is in, just divide the row number by two and disregard the remainder (see the above table). This is the same as shifting to the right. Since we have to check the low bit of DX (the block number) anyway, we can shift that bit into the carry bit and do this with JNC:

```
PUT_PIXEL          PROC     NEAR
          ;SUPPLY  DX=ROW,CX=COLUMN.  ASSUMES ES=B800H
          XOR      BX,BX
        → SHR      DX,1
        → JNC      CALC
        → ADD      BX,8*1024
CALC:     MOV      AX,DX                  ;GET 80*DX        ←
```

DS:[BX] will be used to point to the byte in the screen buffer we have to change. If the pixel is in an odd row, we just add 8K to BX so it points to the second 8K block.

These commands both check which block the pixel is in and set DX to that pixel's row of 640 bits. To find what offset from the beginning of the 8K block that makes in bytes, we have to multiply the number in DX by 640 bits/8 bits per byte = 80 bytes per row on the screen. Multiplying DX by 80 will give us the byte offset of the pixel's line from the beginning of its block.

The 8088 has a multiply command, of course, but it is very slow. We should try to avoid using it when speed is of the essence, as it is in graphics. To multiply by 80, we could just multiply by 5 and then by 16, or—even better—we could multiply DX by 4, add DX to it again to make five times, and then multiply by 16. Multiplying by powers of two, of course, is done by shifting to the left. The 8088 can shift registers to the left like this:

```
          SHL      DX,1
or
          MOV      CL,3
          SHL      DX,CL
```

Here's our multiplication by 80:

```
PUT_PIXEL       PROC    NEAR
        ;SUPPLY DX=ROW,CX=COLUMN. ASSUMES ES=B800H and screen in High
        ; Resolution mode (Use BIOS INT 10H Service 0).
        XOR     BX,BX
        SHR     DX,1
        JNC     CALC
        ADD     BX,8*1024
CALC:   MOV     AX,DX  ←        ;GET 80*DX
        SHL     DX,1   ←
        SHL     DX,1   ←
        ADD     DX,AX  ←
        MOV     AX,CX  ←
        MOV     CL,4   ←
        SHL     DX,CL  ←        ;DX NOW MULTIPLIED BY 80 (16*5)
        ADD     BX,DX             ;ADD TO INDEX
```

DX now holds the byte offset, inside the 8K block, of the line in which our pixel lies. What we've done so far is shown in Figure 5.4.

```
DX=Row Number on Screen.
Low Bit(DX) --> 8K Block Number
SHR DX,1=Row Number in its 8K Block.
(SHR DX,1)x80=Offset of correct line in 8K Block.
```

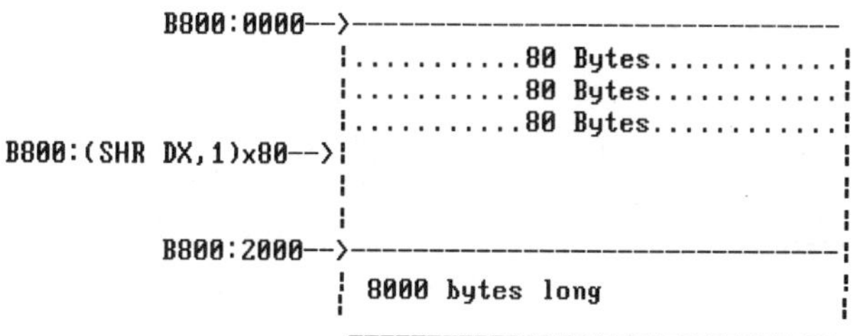

Figure 5.4 How PUT_PIXEL Works.

To point to the correct line that holds the pixel we want to change with [BX], we add (SHR DX,1) × 80 to BX. Once we're in the right row, we still have to find which byte to work on, and that depends on the column required, 0-639. Since each of these 640 places is a bit, to find the correct byte we have to divide CX by 8 and add that to BX. This process is shown in Figure 5.5.

```
PUT_PIXEL       PROC    NEAR
        ;SUPPLY DX=ROW,CX=COLUMN. ASSUMES ES=B800H and screen in High
        ; Resolution mode (Use BIOS INT 10H Service 0).
        XOR     BX,BX
        SHR     DX,1
        JNC     CALC
        ADD     BX,8*1024
CALC:   MOV     AX,DX           ;GET 80*DX
        SHL     DX,1
        SHL     DX,1
        ADD     DX,AX
```

```
          MOV     AX,CX
          MOV     CL,4
          SHL     DX,CL          ;DX NOW MULTIPLIED BY 80 (16*5)
          ADD     BX,DX          ;ADD TO INDEX
       →  MOV     DX,AX
          AND     DX,7           ;GET X3 INTO DX
       →  MOV     CL,3
       →  SHR     AX,CL          ;CX/8
       →  ADD     BX,AX          ;FIND BYTE ALONG ROW
```

```
                B800:0000-->------------------------------
                            |...........80 Bytes............|
                            |...........80 Bytes............|
                            |...........80 Bytes............|
    B800:(SHR DX,1)x80-->|.....................[CX/8]    |
                            |                               |
                            |                               |
                B800:2000-->--------------------------------|
                            |                               |
                            |                               |
                            |                               |
                            | 8000 bytes long               |
                            |                               |
                            |                               |
                             -------------------------------
```

Figure 5.5 Screen Buffer Location.

At the same time, we have to calculate which bit in that byte to turn on. If CX (which can range from 0 to 639) was 0, we would want to turn on the left-most bit of the 0th byte of that line, bit 7. In general, the bit we want to turn on is 7 – (CX Mod 8), where CX Mod 8 is the remainder of dividing CX by 8. CX Mod 8 is just AND CX,7, so we end up with these instructions:

```
PUT_PIXEL        PROC     NEAR
        ;SUPPLY DX=ROW,CX=COLUMN. ASSUMES ES=B800H and screen in High
        ; Resolution mode (Use BIOS INT 10H Service 0).
        XOR     BX,BX
        SHR     DX,1
        JNC     CALC
        ADD     BX,8*1024
CALC:   MOV     AX,DX          ;GET 80*DX
        SHL     DX,1
        SHL     DX,1
        ADD     DX,AX
        MOV     AX,CX
        MOV     CL,4
        SHL     DX,CL          ;DX NOW MULTIPLIED BY 80 (16*5)
        ADD     BX,DX          ;ADD TO INDEX
        MOV     DX,AX
      → AND     DX,7           ;GET X3 INTO DX
        MOV     CL,3
        SHR     AX,CL          ;CX/8
        ADD     BX,AX          ;FIND BYTE ALONG ROW
      → NEG     DL
```

```
        → ADD       DL,7
        → MOV       CL,DL           ;GET BIT TO TURN ON
          MOV       AL,1
          SHL       AL,CL
          OR        ES:[BX],AL
          RET
PUT_PIXEL           ENDP
```

At the end, we put a 1 into AL and shift it DL (=7 − AND(CL,7)) times, then OR the result with whatever byte is in the screen buffer at location [BX]. And that, finally, turns the pixel on. It's pretty clear that working with graphics directly in the PC is not a job that's especially easy. With the rudimentary graphics offerings of BIOS, that is disappointing. Let's examine those BIOS graphics services ourselves.

BIOS GRAPHICS SERVICES

BIOS INT 10H Service 11—Set Color Palette

Input

BH=Palette Color ID
BL BH=0→BL=Background Color
BH=1→BL=Palette Number
(0=Green/Red/Yellow)
(1=Cyan/Magenta/White)
AH=11

NOTE: You can set border colors in 640x200 mode: see below.

This service takes a little bit of explaining, but with it you select both the one color (of 16) that you are allowed to choose, and the one palette (of two possible) that you will use.

Selecting the Background Color

For 320x200 modes, where the PC can support colors, you put either 0 or 1 into BH. If you set BH to 0, then BIOS expects BL to hold the color that will be assigned to **color value** 0. The palette will make up colors 1–3, and we will select the palette later by setting BH to 1.

It is important to realize that selecting color 0 is really selecting the background color. Whichever of the 16 available colors you select for color value 0 (you can choose from colors 0–15 as given previously) will then appear on the screen as the background. From then on, whenever you put a pixel with color value 0, it will appear the same color as the background.

Selecting the Palette

If BH=1, then BIOS assumes you are selecting the palette. To choose the Green/Red/Yellow palette, put a 0 in BL. To choose Cyan/Magenta/White, put a 1 in BL.

If you choose Green/Red/Yellow, then every time you write a pixel, you can select what color it will be by supplying a 1 for green, 2 for red, and 3 for yellow (these values are referred to as the color values of that palette). Keep in mind that only one palette can be valid at any one time. Whenever you change the palette, all the pixels on the screen with values 1, 2, or 3, will change, too.

For 640x200 modes, on the other hand, there are only two colors, on and off, and you don't have to select palettes.

BIOS INT 10H Service 12—Write Dot

Input

DX=Row Number (0–199). [0,0] is upper left.
CX=Column Number (0–319,639).
AL=Color Value (0–3).
AH=12

NOTE: If bit 7 of AL is 1, the color value is XORed with the current value of the dot.

Here is just about the only low-level support given to graphics on the PC: a pixel-writer. All you can do with this service is turn on or off individual pixels; it does take care of separating which block of 8K (even or odd) the pixel belongs in the screen buffer for you. But if you can do that, you can write your own little program that is much faster, like PUT_PIXEL (although PUT_PIXEL only works for high-resolution graphics, 640x200).

Like PUT_PIXEL, you load DX with the row number (0-199) and CX with the column number (0-319, 639—medium, high resolution). AL is loaded with a color value. For high-resolution graphics, a 0 will turn the pixel off, and a 1 will turn it on. For medium-resolution graphics, 320x200, the color values can range from 0–3, and are set by Service 11.

Line Drawing

What if you wanted to do more? What if, say, you wanted to draw a line on the screen? You can make many figures just by connecting lines, yet there is no

BIOS or DOS support for it. If you wrote such a program yourself, how long would it be? One answer (for high-resolution graphics only) is in Listing 5.2.

LISTING 5.2 LINE.ASM

```
SCREEN    SEGMENT AT 0B800H
SCREEN    ENDS

CODE_SEG SEGMENT
          ORG      100H
          ASSUME   CS:CODE_SEG,DS:CODE_SEG,ES:SCREEN
ENTRY:    JMP      LINE
          X1       DW      0       ;Draw a line from (X1,Y1) to (X2,Y2).
          X2       DW      639
          Y1       DW      0
          Y2       DW      199
          INCX     DW      0
          INCY     DW      0
          NUMBER   DW      0
LINE      PROC     NEAR
          ;NOTE: X1,X2,Y1,Y2 DESTROYED BY THIS PROGRAM!
          MOV      AX,SCREEN
          MOV      ES,AX
          MOV      AX,6
          INT      10H
          MOV      INCX,32            ;2**5
          MOV      INCY,128           ;2**7
          MOV      AX,X2
          SUB      AX,X1              ;X range IN AX
          MOV      CX,AX
          JNC      CHECK_Y
          NEG      AX
          NEG      INCX
CHECK_Y:MOV        BX,Y2
          SUB      BX,Y1              ;Y range in BX
          MOV      DX,BX
          JNC      COMP_XY
          NEG      INCY
          NEG      BX
COMP_XY:CMP        AX,BX
          JG       XBIGGER
          MOV      NUMBER,BX          ;Y range bigger.
          MOV      DX,0               ;We want INCX here = CX/!BX!.
          CMP      CX,0               ;INCX = XRANGE/!YRANGE!
          JG       XPOS
          NOT      DX                 ;Sign extend for IDIV of DX:AX
XPOS:     MOV      AX,CX
          CMP      AX,0
          JNE      DIVX
          MOV      INCX,0
          JMP      SHORT   DRAW
DIVX:     MOV      CL,5
          SAL      AX,CL
          IDIV     BX
          MOV      INCX,AX
```

LISTING 5.2 CONTINUED

```
        JMP     SHORT   DRAW
XBIGGER:MOV     NUMBER,AX
        MOV     BX,AX           ;Get in same position as before.
        MOV     CX,DX           ;We want INCY here = DX/!AX!.
        MOV     DX,0            ;Now INCY = CX/!BX! again.
        CMP     CX,0            ;YRANGE/!XRANGE! = INCY
        JG      YPOS
        NOT     DX
YPOS:   MOV     AX,CX
        CMP     AX,0
        JNE     DIVY
        MOV     INCY,0
        JMP     SHORT   DRAW
DIVY:   MOV     CL,7
        SAL     AX,CL
        IDIV    BX
        MOV     INCY,AX
DRAW:   MOV     DI,NUMBER
        MOV     CL,5
        SAL     X1,CL
        MOV     CL,7
        SAL     Y1,CL           ;X1,Y1,INCX,INCY all set.
        MOV     SI,INCX
        MOV     BP,INCY
LOOPER: MOV     BX,X1
        MOV     CL,5
        SAR     BX,CL
        MOV     DX,Y1
        MOV     CL,7
        SHR     DX,CL
        MOV     CX,BX           ;DX=ROW,CX=COLUMN now.
        CALL    PUT_PIXEL
        ADD     X1,SI           ;DI=INCX
        ADD     Y1,BP           ;BP=INCY
        DEC     DI
        JNZ     LOOPER
        RET
LINE    ENDP

PUT_PIXEL       PROC    NEAR
        ;SUPPLY DX=ROW,CX=COLUMN. ASSUMES ES=B800H
        XOR     BX,BX
        SHR     DX,1
        JNC     CALC
        ADD     BX,8*1024
CALC:   MOV     AX,DX           ;GET 80*DX
        SHL     DX,1
        SHL     DX,1
        ADD     DX,AX
        MOV     AX,CX
        MOV     CL,4
        SHL     DX,CL           ;DX now multiplied by 80 (16*5)
        ADD     BX,DX           ;Add to index.
```

LISTING 5.2 CONTINUED

```
        MOV     DX,AX
        AND     DX,7            ;Get X3 into DX.
        MOV     CL,3
        SHR     AX,CL           ;CX/8
        ADD     BX,AX           ;Find byte along row.
        NEG     DL
        ADD     DL,7
        MOV     CL,DL           ;Get bit to turn on.
        MOV     AL,1
        SHL     AL,CL
        OR      ES:[BX],AL
        RET
PUT_PIXEL       ENDP
CODE_SEG        ENDS
        END     ENTRY
```

This program, LINE.ASM, is quite long, and it calls PUT_PIXEL. All you must do is load the coordinates (X goes from 0 to 639 and Y from 0 to 199) in the memory locations (X1,Y1) and (X2,Y2), and LINE will draw a line between them on the screen.

You can get an idea of just how poorly the 8088 handles mathematics just by looking at the length of the program. All LINE.ASM really does is figure out the slope of the line and call PUT_PIXEL, but it takes a long time to do it in integer mathematics (partly because such slopes can be negative).

The idea is simple. There are two points we want to draw on the screen, and the distances between them are as shown in Figure 5.6.

```
                 X Range = 24 Pixels.
              .........................(X2,Y2)
              .
              .
Y Range = 6 Pixels.
              .
              .
           (X1,Y1)
```

Figure 5.6 Pixel Ranges

The number of pixels we have to draw on the diagonal line connecting (X1,Y1) to (X2,Y2) will be the greater of the two numbers above, to make sure there are no gaps in the line. In other words, each pixel in the example shown will have a different X value, but it may have the same Y value, so we will have to write a total of 24 pixels, the number in the X direction.

At the same time we write these 24 pixels, we will have to go up 6 pixels in the Y direction, or one-fourth pixel for each pixel we draw. Drawing the line then is easy: for every pixel we draw, we increment one pixel in the X direction and one-fourth pixel in Y. Then all we have to do is to draw 24 pixels and we're done.

Unfortunately, the PC only works in integer arithmetic, so we will have trouble keeping track of the quarter pixel we are supposed to add to the Y value each time. Registers hold whole numbers only from 0 to 65,535, certainly not one-fourth. The solution for this problem is the standard technique used whenever we want to preserve accuracy in integer arithmetic, and that is to multiply all operands involved by a certain multiplier. This is a technique used time and time again on the PC, so it is a good one to cover in a little depth.

In our example, we have to supply the row number (0–199) in DX, and the column number (0–639) in CX. Let's say we multiply the value in DX by 2^7. Since DX can only be as large as 199, and we have a full word in DX to work with, it seems we could multiply by 2^8 and preserve even more accuracy. In fact, though, the lines we want to fit may have negative slopes. This means we may add a small negative amount each time we put a new pixel on the screen, so we have to leave one bit undisturbed for the leading sign bit (which we'll learn all about in chapter 7). The number in CX we multiply by 2^5. In these terms, the one-fourth pixel we add each time to the Y coordinate becomes $1/4x2^7$, or 32. In LINE.ASM, both the values in the words labeled X1 and Y1 are multiplied, by 32 and 128, respectively.

In general, LINE figures out how much to add in the X direction every time it turns a pixel on, multiplies by 32, and stores that in INCX. The Y increment is multiplied by 128 and stored in INCY. LINE.ASM then loops over all the pixels it has to draw and keeps adding INCX to X1 and INCY to Y1 to form new X and Y values. Before giving these new X and Y values to PUT_PIXEL, we divide again by 32 and 128, which is easily done by shifting.

All in all, though, this shifting is an easy way to keep a little accuracy in integer arithmetic, and a similar idea is used for all floating point calculations computers do, as we'll see when we work with exponents in the 8087.

BIOS INT 10H Service 13—Read Dot

Input	Output
DX=Row Number CX=Column Number AH=13	AL=Dot Read (Color Value).

NOTE: [0,0] is upper left.

This is the necessary complement to Service 12. If, after putting what you want on the screen, you forget what is there, or to check how someone else set it so that you can restore it later, this service works well. Although you can read all pixels on the screen this way in order to save them in memory, it might not be such a good idea unless you have a free 16K available.

BIOS INT 10H Service 14—Teletype Write to Active Page

<u>Input</u>

AL=IBM ASCII code.
BL=Foreground Color
(Graphics mode).
AH=14

This is called "Teletype Write" because this service is different from INT 10H Services 9 and 10, which also print characters. This service will advance the cursor after typing the character, which neither Service 9 or 10 will do. In addition, it handles the cursor correctly at the edge of the screen if you keep typing past the end of the line. You can specify a number of times to repeat the typed character with Services 9 and 10, but you cannot type past the end of line with either of them. The default page is used here, so if you need to switch between pages, use INT 10H Service 5 to select the active page first.

It is also worth noticing that if you type out nonalphanumeric ASCII codes between 0 and 32, you will get a symbol when using the BIOS printing services (like the suits of cards, or up and down arrows), but the same characters won't print out in the DOS services. For example, BIOS interprets ASCII 9 as a little ring and prints that on the screen, while the DOS interrupts interpret ASCII 9 as the standard tab (see the ASCII table in the BASIC manual for example), and tabs to the right by the correct number of spaces.

BIOS INT 10H Service 15—Return Video State

Input	Output
AH=15	AH=Number of alphanumeric columns on screen. AL=Current mode (See INT 10H Service 0). BH=Active display page.

This, the last of the INT 10H services, is the perfect complement for the first, Service 0 (set video mode). The only input demanded here is that AH=15. AH will return the number of columns (40 or 80) that the screen is set to, AL will return the video mode (values 0–7). For an explanation of what these modes correspond to, see the description of Service 0. Finally, BH returns the current active page being used (alphanumeric modes only).

THE DOS SCREEN-HANDLING SERVICES

DOS screen handling is less complete than the BIOS services. In fact, there are only four: DOS INT 21H Services 2, 6, 9, and 40H. Please bear in mind that while INT 10H services CAN be used by memory resident programs, the DOS services usually CANNOT, because DOS is not re-enterable.

DOS INT 21H Service 2—Character Output

Input

DL=IBM ASCII character
AH=2

This is the simplest of the DOS screen output services to use. All it does is to print one character and advance the cursor. This service will also pay attention to screen control; if you type out an ASCII 9, for example, it will tab the cursor over as it should rather than printing out the little ring symbol of ASCII 9 as the BIOS services do. This DOS service uses both BIOS INT 10H Services 10 (write character only at cursor position) and 14 (teletype output).

To print any character, just put its ASCII code into DL, set AH to 2, and use an INT 21H instruction.

DOS INT 21H Service 6—Console I/O

Input

DL=IBM ASCII code (NOT FF).
AH=6

We saw this service before when we discussed input. This DOS service also will print to the standard output device, just as Service 2 will. Load the character to be printed in DL, but do not use 0FFH, because Service 6 will then return an input character from the keyboard.

DOS INT 21H Service 9—String Print

Input

DS:DX point to a string
 that ends in '$'.
AH=9

This is a very popular DOS service. If you just point DS:DX at any string of bytes, Service 9 will print them all out until it reaches a '$' (ASCII code 24H). Many of DOS' own programs use this service to print out messages. For example, we can DEBUG DEBUG to find:

```
A>DEBUG DEBUG.COM

-D2C16
090B:2C16  24 44-69 73 6B 24 57 72 69 74                    $Disk$Writ
090B:2C20  65 20 70 72 6F 74 65 63-74 24 20 65 72 72 6F 72  e protect$ error
090B:2C30  20 72 65 61 64 69 6E 67-20 64 72 69 76 65 20 41   reading drive A
090B:2C40  0D 0A 24 72 65 61 64 77-72 69 74 49 6E 73 75 66  ..$readwritInsuf
090B:2C50  66 69 63 69 65 6E 74 20-6D 65 6D 6F 72 79 0D 0A  ficient memory..
090B:2C60  24 5E 20 45 72 72 6F 72-0D 8A 20 88 45 72 72 6F  $^ Error.. .Erro
090B:2C70  72 20 69 6E 20 45 58 45-20 6F 72 20 48 45 58 20  r in EXE or HEX
090B:2C80  66 69 6C 65 0D 0A 24 45-58 45 20 61 6E 64 20 48  file..$EXE and H
090B:2C90  45 58 20 66 69 6C                                EX fil
-Q
```

We get a number of messages, all ending with the characteristic '$'. Here is an example of the way such messages are set up:

```
ERROR   DB 'There has been an error.$'
MESSAGE DB 'Please get an adult.$'
           :
LEA        DX,ERROR
MOV        AH,9
INT        21H
```

The most common problem in using this service is to forget the '$' at the end of the message; if you do, DOS will keep printing, typing out quantities of nonsense bytes until it hits a byte that is 24H (ASCII '$') by accident, and stops. With this service you could print out an entire file after you've got it in memory just by putting a '$' at the end.

DOS INT 21H Service 40H—Device Write

Input	Output
BX=File Handle (=1 for screen). CX=Number of bytes to print. DS:DX=Address of data to print. AH=40H	AX=Number of bytes actually printed.

We've seen this service before when we wrote to files using file handles. Since file handle 1 stands for the screen, this service can write to the screen easily and so should be included here. In fact, a good number of new DOS programs use this as their primary output service, directing data to the screen whenever desirable. The advantage of this service is that output can be redirected just by changing the file handles or forcing a file handle duplication. Another advantage is that you don't have to end your output with a '$', but need only to load CX with the number of bytes to print. One of the disadvantages is that, as usual with file handle services, it requires the use of all four general-purpose registers.

DIRECT SCREEN BUFFER MANIPULATION

Now we come to a level more advanced than using BIOS or DOS services—working directly with the video buffer itself. Although we've already seen how PUT_PIXEL works, we have yet to really work with the screen buffer in alphanumeric mode.

There is much room for the assembly language expert to work in here. For instance, such programs could be made memory-resident, and, when required, could flash notepads onto the screen. Or they could pop calculators (provided you were willing to simulate floating point operations on the 8088), menus, screen blankers to prevent burnout (see below), screen clocks, screen savers to save a screen for later reference (see PHOTO.ASM at the end of this chapter), and so on.

The screen buffer is 4,000 bytes long, and it is given 4K in memory. The 80×25 = 2,000 characters on the screen are stored here. Each character, as we saw in the beginning of this chapter, is given two bytes The first one is the IBM ASCII code, and the second byte is the attribute, or display, byte, as shown in Figure 5.7.

[Note: 07 is the "normal" attribute: white on black]

Figure 5.7 Screen Buffer to Screen.

In monochrome monitors, the screen buffer begins at B000:0000, and in graphics monitors (both color and black & white) at B800:0000. The graphics monitor, because of its extra memory, is divided into four pages in 80x25 mode and eight pages in 40x25 mode. We will only discuss the active page (which can be found with BIOS INT 10H Service 15), and 80x25 mode.

The Program BLANK.ASM

As an example to show what you can do using this screen buffer, here's a sample program that has some utility. This program, BLANK.COM, will blank the screen on your PC if you don't type anything for about three minutes (actually 3,000 timer counts, or 3000/18.2 = 165 seconds). Although it does not erase the cursor, you can easily add that to the program by using BIOS INT 10H Services 1 and 3 (set and read cursor mode). Keep in mind that you can use BIOS Interrupts, but not DOS ones in a memory-resident program.

The program itself is simple, and assembles to only 227 bytes (although it takes up an additional 4,000 bytes in memory to store the screen when it is running). Every time there is a clock interrupt on the PC, 18.2 times a second, a counter (COUNT, below) is incremented. If this count reaches 3,000, the contents of the screen buffer are stored in memory (starting at location STORAGE at the end of the program) and blanks are moved into the screen with STOSW.

As soon as you type a character, or even any key, an INT 9 interrupt is generated. As soon as it is, COUNT is set to 0 and, if the screen is off, it is turned back on. BLANK.ASM can be seen in Listing 5.3.

LISTING 5.3 BLANK.ASM

```
SCREEN   SEGMENT AT 0B000H
SCREEN   ENDS

VECTORS SEGMENT AT 0H
        ORG      9H*4
KEYBOARD_INT_VECTOR      LABEL    WORD
        ORG      1CH*4
TIMER_VECTOR       LABEL    WORD
VECTORS ENDS

CODE_SEG         SEGMENT
        ASSUME   CS:CODE_SEG
        ORG      100H
BEGIN:  JMP      INIT_VECTORS
SCREEN_OFFSET    DW       0
COUNT            DW       0
SCREEN_OFF       DB       0
KEYBOARD_INT LABEL   DWORD
ROM_KEYBOARD     DW 2 DUP(0)
TIMER_INT LABEL   DWORD
ROM_TIMER        DW 2 DUP(0)

INTERCEPT_KEYBOARD_INT  PROC    NEAR
        ASSUME  CS:CODE_SEG,DS:CODE_SEG,ES:SCREEN
        PUSHF                              ;Push all used registers.
        PUSH    ES
        PUSH    DS
```

LISTING 5.3 CONTINUED

```
        PUSH    SI
        PUSH    DI
        PUSH    CX
        PUSH    CS
        POP     DS
        MOV     COUNT,0                 ;Reset the count that turns off screen.
        CMP     SCREEN_OFF,0FFH         ;Screen off?
        JNE     JUMP
        MOV     CX,SCREEN               ;Screen is off, turn it on.
        MOV     ES,CX
        MOV     DI,SCREEN_OFFSET        ;ES:DI points at screen, DS:SI at
        LEA     SI,STORAGE              ; STORAGE.
        MOV     CX,2000                 ;Move 2000 words back to the screen.
        CLD                             ;Make sure DI and SI are incremented.
REP     MOVSW                           ;Move to screen.
        NOT     SCREEN_OFF              ;Reset SCREEN_OFF flag back to 0.
JUMP:   POP     CX                      ;Now jump to Keyboard Interrupt.
        POP     DI
        POP     SI
        POP     DS
        POP     ES
        POPF
        JMP     CS:KEYBOARD_INT
INTERCEPT_KEYBOARD_INT  ENDP

        ASSUME  DS:CODE_SEG,ES:CODE_SEG
INTERCEPT_TIMER   PROC    NEAR          ;Check here if it's time to
        PUSHF                           ; turn off screen yet.
        PUSH    ES
        PUSH    DS
        PUSH    SI
        PUSH    DI
        PUSH    CX
        PUSH    AX
        PUSH    CS
        POP     DS
        INC     COUNT                   ;Reached about 3 minutes?
        CMP     COUNT,3000
        JNE     JUMP2                   ;No, jump out.
        NOT     SCREEN_OFF              ;Yes, set SCREEN_OFF flag.
        PUSH    CS
        POP     ES                      ;Set ES:DI to point to storage.
        LEA     DI,STORAGE
        MOV     CX,SCREEN
        ASSUME  DS:SCREEN               ;Set DS:SI to point to screen.
        MOV     DS,CX
        MOV     SI,SCREEN_OFFSET
        CLD                             ;Make sure SI, DI increment.
        MOV     CX,2000                 ;Store 2000 words = 4000 bytes.
REP     MOVSW                           ;Screen now stored.
        ASSUME  ES:SCREEN
        PUSH    DS                      ;Now fill with blanks, attrib. 7.
        POP     ES
        MOV     CX,2000
        MOV     AX,700H
        MOV     DI,SCREEN_OFFSET        ;Fill ES:DI.
REP     STOSW                           ;With STOSB.
JUMP2:  POP     AX                      ;Pop used registers.
        POP     CX
        POP     DI
```

LISTING 5.3 CONTINUED

```
        POP     SI
        POP     DS
        POP     ES
        POPF
        JMP     CS:TIMER_INT       ;Use CS:TIMER_INT, not TIMER_INT since DS
INTERCEPT_TIMER   ENDP             ; has been restored to value when interrupted.

INIT_VECTORS    PROC    NEAR
        ASSUME  DS:VECTORS
        PUSH    DS                 ;Point Keyboard Int and Timer Int to our prog.
        MOV     AX,VECTORS
        MOV     DS,AX
        CLI
        MOV     AX,KEYBOARD_INT_VECTOR  ;Keyboard Interrupt first.
        MOV     ROM_KEYBOARD,AX
        MOV     AX,KEYBOARD_INT_VECTOR[2]
        MOV     ROM_KEYBOARD[2],AX
        MOV     KEYBOARD_INT_VECTOR,OFFSET INTERCEPT_KEYBOARD_INT
        MOV     KEYBOARD_INT_VECTOR[2],CS
        MOV     AX,TIMER_VECTOR         ;Now Timer Int.
        MOV     ROM_TIMER,AX
        MOV     AX,TIMER_VECTOR[2]
        MOV     ROM_TIMER[2],AX
        MOV     TIMER_VECTOR,OFFSET INTERCEPT_TIMER
        MOV     TIMER_VECTOR[2],CS
        STI
        ASSUME  DS:CODE_SEG             ;Check screen type.
        PUSH    CS
        POP     DS
        MOV     AH,15
        INT     10H
        CMP     AL,7
        JE      FIN                     ;If monochrome, screen at B000:0000.
        MOV     SCREEN_OFFSET,8000H     ;If graphics, screen at B800:0000.
FIN:    LEA     DX,STORAGE
        ADD     DX,4000          ;Make Storage 4000 Bytes = 2000 Words.
        INT     27H
INIT_VECTORS    ENDP
STORAGE:                ;Put STORAGE here so COM file doesn't have to include
CODE_SEG        ENDS    ; 4000 empty bytes.
        END     BEGIN
```

Even though it looks large, it is mostly booster program and PUSHes and POPs. An outline might look like this:

```
        ORG     100H
BEGIN:  JMP     INIT_VECTORS

INTERCEPT_KEYBOARD_INT  PROC    NEAR
:                       :
:       Move 0 into COUNT.
:                       :
:       If SCREEN_OFF = 0FFH, Screen is off, turn it on by restoring it
:               from STORAGE. Set SCREEN_OFF to 0.
:                       :
:       JMP     CS:KEYBOARD_INT
INTERCEPT_KEYBOARD_INT  ENDP

INTERCEPT_TIMER   PROC    NEAR
```

```
:               :
:       Add 1 to COUNT
:               :
:       If COUNT = 3000, Reset COUNT to 0, store the screen, blank it,
:               and set SCREEN_OFF to 0FFH.
:               :
:       JMP     CS:TIMER_INT
INTERCEPT_TIMER    ENDP

INIT_VECTORS    PROC    NEAR
:               :
:       Point the TIMER and KEYBOARD interrupts to go through the above
:               two programs.
:               :
:       Add 4000 to the address of STORAGE and become memory-resident.
:               :
:       INT     27H
INIT_VECTORS    ENDP
STORAGE:
```

How BLANK.ASM Works

When DOS enters BLANK.COM for the first time, it will see the command at 100H:

```
BEGIN:  JMP     INIT_VECTORS
```

and jump to INIT_VECTORS. INIT_VECTORS changes the address vectors of INTs 9 (Keyboard) and 1CH (Timer) so that they point to our programs INTERCEPT_KEYBOARD_INT and INTERCEPT_TIMER. In addition, INIT_VECTORS decides if a graphics screen or monochrome screen is in use with BIOS INT 10H Service 15. If this service returns AL=7, a monochrome screen is used and the screen buffer is at B000:0000:

```
        → MOV   AH,15
        → INT   10H
        → CMP   AL,7
        → JE    FIN                     ;If monochrome, screen at B000:0000.
        → MOV   SCREEN_OFFSET,8000H     ;If graphics, screen at B800:0000.
FIN:      LEA   DX,STORAGE
          ADD   DX,4000         ;Make Storage 4000 Bytes = 2000 Words.
          INT   27H
INIT_VECTORS    ENDP
STORAGE:                ;Put STORAGE here so COM file doesn't have to include
```

If AL is not 7, then we assume a graphics screen is being used and the screen buffer starts at B800:0000. In order to point to the screen, we have set up a dummy segment SCREEN at the beginning of the program:

```
SCREEN  SEGMENT AT 0B000H
SCREEN  ENDS
```

It would be inconvenient if we had to use a different segment depending on which monitor the PC had (but we could do it that way). Instead, we can see that B800:0000 is the same address as B000:8000, and we can use a variable SCREEN_OFFSET in the data area:

```
CODE_SEG            SEGMENT
         ASSUME     CS:CODE_SEG
         ORG        100H
BEGIN:   JMP        INIT_VECTORS
SCREEN_OFFSET       DW      0
COUNT               DW      0
SCREEN_OFF          DB      0
KEYBOARD_INT LABEL    DWORD
ROM_KEYBOARD        DW 2 DUP(0)
TIMER_INT LABEL    DWORD
ROM_TIMER           DW 2 DUP(0)
```

This variable is zero for monochrome monitors and is set to 8000H for graphics monitors. The address of the screen buffer will always just be B000:SCREEN_OFFSET. INIT_VECTORS fills SCREEN_OFFSET for us (note that in this example we are assuming page 0 is the active one).

At the end of INIT_VECTORS is the label STORAGE, which is the starting address for the screen data. To become memory-resident, we must provide INT 27H with an address, DS:DX, below which everything will stay in memory undisturbed. To become memory-resident, INIT_VECTORS takes the address of STORAGE, puts it into DX, and simply adds 4,000 bytes (2,000 words) before calling INT 27H. This will give us enough room to store the screen in.

```
FIN:     LEA     DX,STORAGE
         ADD     DX,4000         ;Make Storage 4000 Bytes = 2000 Words.
         INT     27H
INIT_VECTORS     ENDP
STORAGE:                 ;Put STORAGE here so COM file doesn't have to include
CODE_SEG         ENDS    ; 4000 empty bytes.
         END     BEGIN
```

It is important to realize that in a memory-resident program, the only registers you can be certain of when you get control are CS and IP (because they were loaded from the interrupt vector that INIT_VECTORS set). All other registers will be just as they were when the program that is running in the foreground was interrupted. In particular, since labels like COUNT are really stored as offsets from DS, you must set DS before you access them. Therefore, the first thing we will do is to set DS to CS (and include an ASSUME so the assembler knows what we've done).

A timer interrupt is executed 18.2 times a second, no matter what program is running (unless it explicitly turns off interrupts with a CLI command). Therefore, 18.2 times a second, the PC will execute INTERCEPT_TIMER. Every time it does, the variable COUNT is incremented. Each time we increment COUNT, we check to see if it has reached 3000 yet; if about three minutes have passed since the last keystroke (which sets COUNT to 0):

```
ASSUME  DS:CODE_SEG,ES:CODE_SEG ←
INTERCEPT_TIMER    PROC     NEAR          ;Check here if it's time to
        PUSHF                             ; turn off screen yet.
        PUSH     ES
        PUSH     DS
        PUSH     SI
        PUSH     DI
        PUSH     CX
        PUSH     AX
      → PUSH     CS                       ;Set up DS!
      → POP      DS
      → INC      COUNT                    ;Reached about 3 minutes?
      → CMP      COUNT,3000
      → JNE      JUMP2                    ;No, jump out.
        NOT      SCREEN_OFF               ;Yes, set SCREEN_OFF flag.
                 :
```

If COUNT is equal to 3000, we do not take the jump to JUMP2, which would exit the program. Instead, we store what is on the screen. We also toggle the SCREEN_OFF flag from 0 to FFH with NOT SCREEN_OFF (a value of FFH means that the screen is off). This way, INTERCEPT_KEYBOARD_INT will know when the screen is off and so whether it needs to be restored whan a key is typed.

To move the screen into storage, we will set up DS:SI to point to the screen, and ES:DI to point at STORAGE. To do the actual storing, we use MOVSW (note the use of SCREEN_OFFSET, which holds either 0 or 8000H):

```
        ASSUME   DS:CODE_SEG,ES:CODE_SEG
INTERCEPT_TIMER    PROC     NEAR          ;Check here if it's time to
        PUSHF                                   ; turn off screen yet.
        PUSH     ES
        PUSH     DS
        PUSH     SI
        PUSH     DI
        PUSH     CX
        PUSH     AX
        PUSH     CS               ;Set up DS!
        POP      DS
        INC      COUNT                    ;Reached about 3 minutes?
        CMP      COUNT,3000
        JNE      JUMP2                    ;No, jump out.
      → NOT      SCREEN_OFF               ;Yes, set SCREEN_OFF flag.
      → PUSH     CS
      → POP      ES                       ;Set ES:DI to point to storage.
      → LEA      DI,STORAGE
      → MOV      CX,SCREEN
      → ASSUME   DS:SCREEN                ;Set DS:SI to point to screen.
      → MOV      DS,CX
      → MOV      SI,SCREEN_OFFSET
      → CLD                               ;Make sure SI, DI increment.
```

```
        → MOV     CX,2000                    ;Store 2000 words = 4000 bytes.
REP       MOVSW ←                            ;Screen now stored.
          :
          :
```

The screen is now safe, so we can fill it with blanks using STOSW (BLANK.COM uses ASCII nulls, 0, and an attribute of 7). STOSW and MOVSW are used because they are faster than STOSB and MOVSB, which can only move bytes at a time. To use STOSW, which stores the word in AX, we have to load AX and point ES:DI to the screen:

```
        ASSUME  DS:CODE_SEG,ES:CODE_SEG
INTERCEPT_TIMER   PROC    NEAR          ;Check here if it's time to
        PUSHF                           ; turn off screen yet.
        PUSH    ES
        PUSH    DS
        PUSH    SI
        PUSH    DI
        PUSH    CX
        PUSH    AX
        PUSH    CS              ;Set up DS!
        POP     DS
        INC     COUNT                   ;Reached about 3 minutes?
        CMP     COUNT,3000
        JNE     JUMP2                   ;No, jump out.
        NOT     SCREEN_OFF              ;Yes, set SCREEN_OFF flag.
        PUSH    CS
        POP     ES                      ;Set ES:DI to point to storage.
        LEA     DI,STORAGE
        MOV     CX,SCREEN
        ASSUME  DS:SCREEN               ;Set DS:SI to point to screen.
        MOV     DS,CX
        MOV     SI,SCREEN_OFFSET
        CLD                             ;Make sure SI, DI increment.
        MOV     CX,2000                 ;Store 2000 words = 4000 bytes.
REP     MOVSW                           ;Screen now stored.
        ASSUME  ES:SCREEN
      → PUSH    DS                      ;Now fill with blanks, attrib. 7.
      → POP     ES
      → MOV     CX,2000
      → MOV     AX,700H         ;Bytes stored in memory in reverse order,
                                ; so put attribute byte first.
      → MOV     DI,SCREEN_OFFSET        ;Fill ES:DI.
REP     STOSW ←                         ;With STOSB.
JUMP2:  POP     AX                      ;Pop used registers.
        POP     CX
        POP     DI
        POP     SI
        POP     DS
        POP     ES
        POPF
        JMP     CS:TIMER_INT    ;Use CS:TIMER_INT, not TIMER_INT since DS
INTERCEPT_TIMER   ENDP          ; has been restored to value when interrupted.
```

One line in INTERCEPT_TIMER deserves further comment:

```
JMP      CS:TIMER_INT     ;Use CS:TIMER_INT, not TIMER_
INT since DS
```

We've done what we wanted to: We've stored the screen and signaled to our keyboard intercept that it's off. We now want to let the timer interrupt continue to do what it normally would, so we jump to the original interrupt vector, now stored in TIMER_INT. TIMER_INT is not a label for a line of code, but rather a double word label that holds the original interrupt vector that we want to jump to. This JMP is an indirect jump to the contents of TIMER_INT:

```
CODE_SEG          SEGMENT
        ASSUME    CS:CODE_SEG
        ORG       100H
BEGIN:  JMP       INIT_VECTORS
SCREEN_OFFSET     DW      0
COUNT             DW      0
SCREEN_OFF        DB      0
KEYBOARD_INT LABEL   DWORD
ROM_KEYBOARD      DW 2 DUP(0)
TIMER_INT LABEL   DWORD
ROM_TIMER         DW 2 DUP(0)
```

INTERCEPT_KEYBOARD

INTERCEPT_KEYBOARD's task is different. Whenever you type a key, this routine must set COUNT back to zero, since a struck key indicates that the PC is active. In addition, it must turn the screen on if it was off. If the screen was off, we simply have to MOVSW from STORAGE back into the screen buffer. That code looks like this:

```
INTERCEPT_KEYBOARD_INT  PROC    NEAR
        ASSUME  CS:CODE_SEG,DS:CODE_SEG,ES:SCREEN
        PUSHF                           ;Push all used registers.
        PUSH    ES
        PUSH    DS
        PUSH    SI
        PUSH    DI
        PUSH    CX
        PUSH    CS
        POP     DS
        MOV     COUNT,0                 ;Reset the count that turns off screen .
        CMP     SCREEN_OFF,0FFH         ;Screen off?
        JNE     JUMP
        MOV     CX,SCREEN               ;Screen is off, turn it on.
        MOV     ES,CX
        MOV     DI,SCREEN_OFFSET        ;ES:DI points at screen, DS:SI at
        LEA     SI,STORAGE              ; STORAGE.
        MOV     CX,2000                 ;Move 2000 words back to the screen.
        CLD                             ;Make sure DI and SI are incremented.
REP     MOVSW                           ;Move to screen.
        NOT     SCREEN_OFF              ;Reset SCREEN_OFF flag back to 0.
JUMP:   POP     CX                      ;Now jump to Keyboard Interrupt.
        POP     DI
        POP     SI
        POP     DS
```

```
        POP     ES
        POPF
        JMP     CS:KEYBOARD_INT
INTERCEPT_KEYBOARD_INT  ENDP
```

Finally, the SCREEN_OFF flag is reset with NOT SCREEN_OFF so we know not to restore the screen again until it needs it. That's both halves of our program, each of which run at different times, but still communicate through COUNT and SCREEN_OFF.

Screen Flicker

There is one more point to be made concerning screen-handling. If you simply put characters into the graphics card's screen buffer (B800:0000), screen flicker (or snow) will result. (There is no similar problem on the monchrome monitor.)

This can be avoided easily enough if we do what BIOS does. Before putting a character into the buffer, you must check the status port on the video controller. You should only put characters into the screen buffer when a screen retrace is beginning. This occurs when a particular signal goes low.

The graphics video controller's status port is at I/O address 03DAH, and the monochrome video controller port is at 03BAH. To load a variable STATUS_PORT with the correct I/O address for the video controller's status port, you can include code in your booster like that in the following example. Here we can use INT 10H, Service 15 to check what kind of monitor is being used:

```
BOOSTER         PROC     NEAR
                :
        MOV     AH,15
        INT     10H
        MOV     STATUS_PORT,03BAH
        TEST    AL,4
        JNZ     EXIT
        MOV     SCREEN_SEG_OFFSET,8000H
        MOV     STATUS_PORT,03DAH

EXIT:   MOV     DX,OFFSET LOAD_PAD
        INT     27H
BOOSTER         ENDP
        CODE_SEG         ENDS
        END     FIRST
```

To put characters onto the screen, you have to make sure the status signal has just gone low—to catch the signal's falling edge. To check this, we first check that it is low. When we are sure it is low, we wait for it to go high; as soon as it goes low again (the falling edge), we immediately put our character into the screen buffer. For example, if we were loading ASCII bytes from memory storage named PAD and using the attribute in ATTRIBUTE, this is how we would do it:

```
PUT_CHAR        PROC    NEAR    ;Puts one char on screen and advances position
        PUSH    DX
        MOV     AH,PAD[BX]      ;Get the char to be put onto the screen
        MOV     SI,2            ;Loop twice, once for char, once for attribute
        MOV     DX,STATUS_PORT  ;Get ready to read video controller status
P_WAIT_LOW:                     ;Start waiting for a new horizontal scan -
        IN      AL,DX           ;Make sure the video controller scan status
        TEST    AL,1            ;is low
        JNZ     P_WAIT_LOW
P_WAIT_HIGH:                    ;After port has gone low, it must go high
        IN      AL,DX           ;before it is safe to write directly to
        TEST    AL,1            ;the screen buffer in memory
        JZ      P_WAIT_HIGH
        MOV     ES:[DI],AH      ;Move to screen, one byte at a time
        MOV     AH,ATTRIBUTE    ;Load attribute byte for second pass
        INC     DI              ;Point to next screen postion
        DEC     SI              ;Decrement loop counter
        JNZ     P_WAIT_LOW      ;If not zero, do it one more time
        INC     BX              ;Point to next char in pad
        POP     DX
        RET                     ;Exeunt
PUT_CHAR        ENDP
```

The top loop, P_WAIT_LOW, makes sure the signal is low. The next loop, P_WAIT_HIGH, loops while the signal is high. Immediately after becoming low, the falling edge, we put our character into the buffer:

```
P_WAIT_LOW:                     ;Start waiting for a new horizontal scan -
        IN      AL,DX           ;Make sure the video controller scan status
        TEST    AL,1            ;is low
        JNZ     P_WAIT_LOW
P_WAIT_HIGH:                    ;After port has gone low, it must go high
        IN      AL,DX           ;before it is safe to write directly to
        TEST    AL,1            ;the screen buffer in memory
        JZ      P_WAIT_HIGH
      → MOV     ES:[DI],AH      ;Move to screen, one byte at a time
```

If snow on the screen is ever a problem when you are working with a graphics screen, you can use this simple technique to eliminate it. It will slow down your screen-handling abilities somewhat, but not noticeably unless you are working with the entire screen.

THE PROGRAM PHOTO.ASM

The program at the end of this chapter is PHOTO.ASM. PHOTO will give you more control over the screen. It is a memory-resident program that will store a screenful of data at the push of a key, and restore at the push of another key.

For instance, if you are assembling a program and have errors, you can store the screen by pressing a key, say ^N. When you edit the .ASM file to correct it, you can refer back to the errors by typing another key, say ^F, which flashes the screen with the errors back on the display.

In addition, PHOTO lets you load up to three screens from files. For instance, I have an ASCII table in a file named A.DAT. When PHOTO is run, it looks for the files A.DAT, B.DAT, and C.DAT. If you don't have them, there is no problem. If you do, however, these files are loaded in with PHOTO. When you press ^A, the contents of A.DAT (the ASCII table) is flashed on the screen for reference. When you press ^B, B.DAT appears—which might hold telephone numbers—even if you are running some other program. Each of these .DAT files cannot be more than 2,000 bytes (the size of the screen) in length; anything over 2,000 bytes is truncated.

After you've typed a trigger key and a new screen is flashed onto the display, typing any other key restores the screen to the way it was before the trigger key was typed.

Trigger Keys

These control keys, ^N, ^F, ^A, ^B, and ^C, are already programmed into PHOTO.ASM. If you find them inconvenient, you must supply your own scan and ASCII codes for the trigger keys you pick. To make this switch easier, the five scan and ASCII codes for these keys are stored together in the beginning of the program in a location named KEYS:

```
        COPY_RIGHT DB  '(C) S. HOLZNER 1985'  ;An Ascii signature
      → KEYS    DW    310EH,2106H,1E01H,3002H,2E03H ;A Sample: ^N,^F,^A,^B,^C
;       KEYS    DW    5 DUP(0)
```

If you want to choose different trigger keys, comment out the sample line and uncomment the next one, filling in your values.

How PHOTO.ASM Works

PHOTO.ASM handles the screen in much the same way that BLANK.ASM does. It simply treats the video buffer in memory as a set of 4,000 bytes that it can operate on by changing them at will. After it has intercepted a trigger key, it stores the screen in the same way BLANK does. Since it's already loaded in the files to display, or stored the screenful of data it is to restore, PHOTO only has to transfer these bytes into the video buffer (in the same way BLANK restores the screen).

PHOTO then waits until you type another character. As soon as you do, it uses another string operation to restore the screen to its original state and gives control back to you.

LISTING 5.4 PHOTO.ASM

```
INTERRUPTS      SEGMENT AT 0H   ;This is where the keyboard interrupt
        ORG     9H*4            ;holds the address of its service routine
KEYBOARD_INT    LABEL   WORD
INTERRUPTS      ENDS

SCREEN  SEGMENT AT 0B000H       ;A dummy segment to use as the
SCREEN  ENDS                    ;Extra Segment

ROM_BIOS_DATA   SEGMENT AT 40H  ;BIOS statuses held here, also keyboard buffer

        ORG     1AH
        HEAD DW      ?                  ;Unread chars go from Head to Tail
        TAIL DW      ?
        BUFFER       DW      16 DUP (?)         ;The buffer itself
        BUFFER_END   LABEL   WORD

ROM_BIOS_DATA   ENDS

CODE_SEG        SEGMENT
        ASSUME  CS:CODE_SEG
        ORG     100H            ;ORG = 100H to make this into a .COM file
FIRST:  JMP     LOAD_SNAPSHOT   ;First time through jump to initialize routine

        COPY_RIGHT DB  '(C) S. HOLZNER 1985'  ;An Ascii signature
        KEYS    DW   310EH,2106H,1E01H,3002H,2E03H ;A Sample: ^N,^F,^A,^B,^C
;       KEYS    DW   5 DUP(0)
        FLASHED    DB       0              ;Have we flashed a screenful? 1=yes
        SNAPSHOT_OFFSET      DW      0          ;Chooses 1st 250 bytes or 2nd
        SCREEN_SEG_OFFSET       DW      0       ;0 for mono, 8000H for graphics
        IO_CHAR         DW      ?               ;Holds addr of Put or Get_Char
        FILE_SIZE       DW      0               ;Read in this many bytes
        OLD_KEY_INT     LABEL   WORD
        OLD_KEYBOARD_INT        DD      ?       ;Location of old kbd interrupt
        FILE            DB  'A.DAT',0           ;Asciiz. Changed to B.Dat, etc .
        WS_FLAG         DB      0               ;← Set to 1 to strip WordStar
        SNAPSHOT             DB      10000 DUP (32) ;Storage for screens

SNAP    PROC    NEAR            ;The keyboard interrupt will now come here.
        ASSUME  CS:CODE_SEG
        PUSH    AX              ;Save the used registers for good form
        PUSH    BX
        PUSH    CX
        PUSH    DX
        PUSH    DI
        PUSH    SI
        PUSH    DS
        PUSH    ES
        PUSHF                   ;First, call old keyboard interrupt
        CALL    OLD_KEYBOARD_INT

        ASSUME  DS:ROM_BIOS_DATA        ;Examine the char just put in
        MOV     BX,ROM_BIOS_DATA
        MOV     DS,BX
        MOV     BX,TAIL                 ;Point to current tail
        CMP     BX,HEAD                 ;If at head, kbd int has deleted char
```

LISTING 5.4 CONTINUED

```
        JE      IN                      ;So leave
        SUB     BX,2                    ;Point to just read in character
        CMP     BX,OFFSET BUFFER        ;Did we undershoot buffer?
        JAE     NO_WRAP                 ;Nope
        MOV     BX,OFFSET BUFFER_END    ;Yes--move to buffer top
        SUB     BX,2                    ;Point to just read in character
NO_WRAP:MOV     DX,[BX]                 ;** Typed character in DX now **
        LEA     SI,KEYS                 ;Point to Keys for search
        CMP     FLASHED,1               ;Should we restore screen?
        JE      RESTORE                 ;Yes, jump there
        CMP     DX,CS:[SI]              ;Compare to first key (Store screen)
        JE      STORE                   ;So Store
        ADD     SI,2                    ;Point to next key
        CMP     DX,CS:[SI]              ;Second key -- should we flash screen?
        JE      FLASH                   ;Yes
        MOV     CX,3                    ;No -- check for .Dat keys (A.Dat,etc)
        MOV     SNAPSHOT_OFFSET,4000    ;Point to beginning of .Dats in memory
TEST:   ADD     SI,2                    ;Increment to next key
        CMP     DX,CS:[SI]              ;Is it right?
        JE      DATS                    ;Yes, flash a .Dat file on screen
        ADD     SNAPSHOT_OFFSET,2000    ;Point to next .Dat
        LOOP    TEST                    ;And go back until all three are done
        JMP     OUT                     ;No keys matched. Jump Out.
STORE:  MOV     TAIL,BX                 ;Delete character from buffer
        MOV     FLASHED,0               ;Switch Modes on Flashed
        MOV     SNAPSHOT_OFFSET,0       ;Point to screen storage part of pad
        LEA     AX,GET_CHAR             ;Make IO use Get_char so current screen
        MOV     IO_CHAR,AX              ;is stored
        CALL    IO                      ;Store Screen
IN:     JMP     OUT                     ;Done here, let's go.
FLASH:  MOV     TAIL,BX
        MOV     FLASHED,1             ;Switch Modes, next key will restore screen
        MOV     SNAPSHOT_OFFSET,2000    ;Point to screen storage part
        LEA     AX,GET_CHAR             ;Make IO use Get_char so current screen
        MOV     IO_CHAR,AX              ;is stored
        CALL    IO                      ;Store Screen
        MOV     SNAPSHOT_OFFSET,0       ;Use 1st 250 bytes of Snapshot memory
        LEA     AX,PUT_CHAR             ;Make IO use Put-Char so it does
        MOV     IO_CHAR,AX
        CALL    IO                      ;Put result on screen
        JMP     OUT                     ;Done here.
RESTORE:
        MOV     FLASHED,0               ;Restore screen from memory
        MOV     TAIL,BX                 ;Delete character from buffer
        MOV     SNAPSHOT_OFFSET,2000    ;Point to storage part of memory
        LEA     AX,PUT_CHAR             ;Make IO call Put_Char as it scans
        MOV     IO_CHAR,AX              ;over all locations in screen
        CALL    IO                      ;Restore screen
        JMP     OUT                     ;And leave

DATS:   MOV     TAIL,BX
        MOV     FLASHED,1             ;Switch Modes, next key will restore screen
        PUSH    SNAPSHOT_OFFSET         ;Save this while Offset set for storing
        MOV     SNAPSHOT_OFFSET,2000    ;Point to screen storage part
        LEA     AX,GET_CHAR             ;Make IO use Get_char so current screen
        MOV     IO_CHAR,AX              ;is stored
        CALL    IO                      ;Store Screen
        POP     SNAPSHOT_OFFSET         ;Restore pointer to stored .Dat
        LEA     AX,PUT_CHAR             ;Make IO use Put-Char so it does
        MOV     IO_CHAR,AX
```

LISTING 5.4 CONTINUED

```
        CALL    IO                          ;Put result on screen

OUT:    POP     ES                          ;Do the Pops of all registers.
        POP     DS
        POP     SI
        POP     DI
        POP     DX
        POP     CX
        POP     BX
        POP     AX
        IRET                        ;An interrupt needs an IRET
SNAP    ENDP

GET_CHAR        PROC    NEAR        ;Gets a char from screen and advances position
        PUSH    DX
        MOV     SI,2                ;Loop twice, once for char, once for attribute
G_WAIT_LOW:
        MOV     AH,ES:[DI]          ;Do the move from the screen, one byte at a time
        INC     DI                  ;Move to next screen location
        DEC     SI                  ;Decrement loop counter
        CMP     SI,0                ;Are we done?
        JE      LEAVE               ;Yes
        MOV     SNAPSHOT[BX],AH         ;No -- put char we got into snapshot
        JMP     G_WAIT_LOW          ;Do it again
LEAVE:  INC     BX                  ;Update location
        POP     DX
        RET
GET_CHAR        ENDP

PUT_CHAR        PROC    NEAR        ;Puts one char on screen and advances position
        PUSH    DX
        MOV     AH,SNAPSHOT[BX]         ;Get the char to be put onto the screen
        MOV     SI,2                ;Loop twice, once for char, once for attribute
        MOV     ES:[DI],AH          ;Move to screen, one byte at a time
        ADD     DI,2
        SUB     SI,2
        INC     BX                  ;Point to next char
        POP     DX
        RET                         ;Exeunt
PUT_CHAR        ENDP

IO      PROC    NEAR               ;This scans over all screen positions
        ASSUME  ES:SCREEN                   ;Use screen as extra segment
        MOV     BX,SCREEN
        MOV     ES,BX

        MOV     DI,SCREEN_SEG_OFFSET        ;DI will be pointer to screen postion
        MOV     BX,SNAPSHOT_OFFSET              ;BX will be location pointer
        MOV     CX,25                       ;There will be 10 lines
LINE_LOOP:
        MOV     DX,80                       ;And 25 spaces across
CHAR_LOOP:
        CALL    IO_CHAR                     ;Call Put-Char or Get-Char
        DEC     DX                          ;Decrement character loop counter
        JNZ     CHAR_LOOP                   ;If not zero, scan over next character
        LOOP    LINE_LOOP                   ;And now go back to do next line
        RET                                 ;Finished
IO      ENDP
```

LISTING 5.4 CONTINUED

```
READ_FILE       PROC    NEAR                ;Reads .Dats and formats in memory.
        PUSH    CX                          ;Save used registers
        PUSH    DX
        PUSH    DI
        ASSUME  DS:CODE_SEG,ES:CODE_SEG
        MOV     BX,AX                       ;Put passed file handle in BX
        MOV     CX,2000                     ;Ask for 2000 bytes (Tops)
        LEA     DX,DATA                     ;Point DS:DX at Data area at end
        MOV     AH,3FH                      ;Ask for reading service
        INT     21H                         ;And go get 'em
        MOV     CX,AX                       ;Store number of bytes read
        MOV     AH,3EH                      ;Now close file
        INT     21H
        CALL    WS                          ;Strip high bit if necessary
        LEA     SI,DATA                     ;Transfer from CS:[SI] to DS:[BX] now
        CMP     CX,2000                     ;Make sure on number of bytes read in.
        JBE     THE_LOOP
        MOV     CX,2000                     ;Format file into Snapshot area now
THE_LOOP:                                   ;Loop over character by character
        CMP     BYTE PTR [SI],9             ;Is it a tab?
        JNE     NOTAB                       ;Add 8 spaces for tabs
        ADD     DI,8
        INC     SI                          ;And point to next character
        JMP     CONT
NOTAB:  CMP     BYTE PTR [SI],13            ;Is it a carriage return?
        JNE     OK                          ;No, store the character
FILL:   INC     SI                          ;Found a <CR>. Fill to end of line
        DEC     CX                          ;Get rid of line feeds
        CMP     BYTE PTR [SI],13            ;Treat additional <CR>s as new lines
        JE      CR
        CMP     BYTE PTR [SI],' '           ;Bona Fide character?
        JB      FILL                        ;No, keep going past all linefeeds
CR:     CMP     CX,0                        ;Yes, start to fill to end of line here
        JLE     FIN                         ;Check on loop index
        INC     CX                          ;And readjust it from skipping lf.s
        MOV     AX,DI                       ;AH will check if we're at end of line
        SUB     AX,OFFSET SNAPSHOT+4000 ;Get distance into screen
        MOV     DL,80                       ;Divide by 80 to find columns
        DIV     DL
CHECK:  CMP     AH,79                       ;Remainder of 79?
        JA      CONT                        ;If more, have begun a new line.
ADD:    INC     DI                          ;Add a space by incrementing DI
        INC     AH                          ;And keep track by incrementing AH too .
        JMP     CHECK                       ;At edge of screen?
OK:     CMP     DI,OFFSET SNAP    ;Past end of storage area? (Many tabs and CRs)
        JAE     FIN                         ;Yes, don't move byte into it
        MOVSB                               ;No, safe to move byte from [SI] to [DI]
CONT:   LOOP    THE_LOOP                    ;And keep going for all bytes in file
FIN:    POP     DI
        POP     DX
        POP     CX
        RET                                 ;Exit here.
READ_FILE       ENDP

WS      PROC    NEAR                        ;This will strip high bits from the
        CMP     WS_FLAG,1                   ;  read-in file if WS_Flag = 1
        JNE     RETWS                       ;IF WS_Flag is not 1, exit
        PUSH    SI                          ;Store used registers
        PUSH    CX
```

LISTING 5.4 CONTINUED

```
        LEA     SI,DATA                 ;Point to read-in file
        MOV     CX,2000                 ;Do 2000 bytes
ALOOP:  AND     BYTE PTR CS:[SI],127    ;Strip top bit
        INC     SI                      ;Point to next one.
        LOOP    ALOOP                   ;And keep going
        POP     CX                      ;Pops
        POP     SI
RETWS:  RET                             ;And Exit.
WS      ENDP

LOAD_SNAPSHOT           PROC    NEAR    ;This procedure intializes everything
        ASSUME  DS:INTERRUPTS   ;The data segment will be the Interrupt area
        MOV     AX,INTERRUPTS
        MOV     DS,AX

        MOV     AX,KEYBOARD_INT         ;Get the old interrupt service routine
        MOV     OLD_KEY_INT,AX          ;address and put it into our location
        MOV     AX,KEYBOARD_INT[2]      ;OLD_KEYBOARD_INT so we can call it.
        MOV     OLD_KEY_INT[2],AX

        MOV     KEYBOARD_INT,OFFSET SNAP  ;Now load the address of our program
        MOV     KEYBOARD_INT[2],CS         ;routine into the keyboard interrupt

        MOV     AH,15                   ;Ask for service 15 of INT 10H
        INT     10H                     ;This tells us how display is set up
        TEST    AL,4                    ;Is it?
        JNZ     READ                    ;Yes - jump out
        MOV     SCREEN_SEG_OFFSET,8000H ;No - set up for graphics display
READ:   PUSH    CS                      ;Now read in A.Dat, B.Dat etc.
        POP     DS                      ;Set DS correctly
        MOV     CX,3                    ;Loop over three files
        LEA     DI,SNAPSHOT+4000        ;Store starting in this area
LOOP:   ASSUME  DS:CODE_SEG             ;Loop over files
        LEA     DX,FILE                 ;Point to file name
        MOV     AX,3D00H                ;Service 3DH, attribute 0 for file
        INT     21H                     ;Open file
        JC      EXIT                    ;If not found, exit
        CALL    READ_FILE               ;Pass file handle in AX to Read_File
        ADD     DI,2000                 ;Point to next storage area
        MOV     BX,DX                   ;Change A.Dat into B.Dat etc.
        INC     BYTE PTR CS:[BX]        ;A.DAT→B.DAT etc.
        LOOP    LOOP                    ;Keep going over all files.
EXIT:   MOV     DX,OFFSET LOAD_SNAPSHOT ;Set up everything but LOAD_SNAPSHOT to
        INT     27H                     ;stay and attach itself to DOS
LOAD_SNAPSHOT           ENDP
DATA:
        CODE_SEG        ENDS

        END     FIRST   ;END "FIRST" so 8088 will go to FIRST first.
```

Chapter 6
Disk Handling

INTRODUCTION

The IBM family uses disks as its primary storage medium. This primacy was not always unquestioned; in the beginning it looked as though the PC would store its data on cassette tape. In fact, however, there is very little support for the cassette outlet, although all standard PCs (not XTs or ATs) have them. These PCs can use the cassette port if you buy a five-dollar cable. The only BIOS support is a block write and read, and only BASIC has commands to read and write from tape (it only reads and writes BASIC programs).

Disks can vary in storage capacity from 160K (single-sided disks under DOS 1.1) to 20M (the AT hard disk). Even so, their general structure is the same. The four primary parts are the Boot Record, the File Allocation Table (FAT), the Directory, and the Data.

In Table 6.1 there is some information concerning disk(ette) formats, which we'll need later in the chapter.

Table 6.1 Disk Information Table

Disk	Cap.	FAT	Dir. Size	# Files	Sectors/Cluster	FAT Size
SS 8 Sec	160K	FF	4 Sectors	64	1	1 Sector
SS 9 Sec	180K	FC	4	64	1	1
DS 8 Sec	320K	FE	7	112	2	2
DS 9 Sec	360K	FD	7	112	2	2
High Dens.	1.2M	F9	14	224	1	7
XT Disk	10M	F8	32 (Max.)	512 (Max.)	8	8
AT Disk	20M	F8	32 (Max.)	512 (Max.)	4	40

(Cap. means capacity, and the byte in the column labeled FAT indicates the first, identifying, byte in the File Allocation Table.)

DISK ORGANIZATION

To understand how a disk works, it is necessary to examine all its parts. To do that, we will start with floppy disks and continue on to the hard disks which, logically, are very like floppies.

All disks are broken up into **tracks**, and there are 40 tracks on normal, double-density, floppies. Hard disks, made up of a number of parallel hard platters, use the concept of **cylinders**, which is really just a convenient idea grouping all the tracks at a certain radius on the platters together. Hard disks use cylinders to minimize disk head movement. The idea is to store data with a minimum of head movement by using up all the tracks at a certain radius first.

The 40 tracks of a floppy (track 0 is around the outside, track 39 near the hub) are split up into **sectors**. Sectors are an invariable 512 bytes under any DOS format (so far). Under DOS 1.1, there were 8 sectors per track, and under DOS 2+, there are 9. In fact, this was one of the major differences between DOS 1.1 and DOS 2.0 (the other was subdirectories). When we take a look at the diskette **table**, we'll see the actual byte that was changed from 8 to 9. Floppy disk capacity changed at the same time. Under DOS 1.1 and 8 sectors per track, a double-sided diskette could hold 40 × 8 × 2(sides) × 512 = 320K. Under DOS 2+, a double-sided diskette can hold 40 × 9 × 2(sides) × 512 = 360K.

Sectors on a Disk

The way a double-sided floppy is set up is this: the boot record is logical sector 0, the very first sector on the disk. The two pairs of sectors 1–2 and 3–4 each contain a copy of the **File Allocation Table**, one sector long under DOS 1.0 and 1.1, and two sectors long under DOS 2+ or 3+. Two copies are made of this table since it's so important, and they may be used to check one another. The directory occupies seven sectors under DOS 2+ and 3+, and fills logical sectors 5–11 on every double-sided, nine-sectored disk.

For those disks from which you can boot your PC, the file IBMBIO.COM, the disk part of BIOS, starts right after the directory. After IBMBIO.COM comes IBMDOS.COM, also expected to occupy this location on boot disks. After IBMDOS.COM come the actual data, cluster by cluster. This data, your files, are sliced up into clusters and stored carefully.

The Boot Record

The first sector on any floppy is the boot record. Even if you don't have the system files (IBMBIO.COM and IBMDOS.COM) on the diskette, so you can't boot with it, the boot record is still on that disk so it can give you the message: "Non-system disk or disk error."

When you boot your PC, the ROM BIOS programs try to read in the boot record of a floppy in drive A: (if it's not there it might check the hard disk if you have one). If the floppy is there, the boot record is read and control is given to it. It will try to read in the two programs IBMBIO.COM and IBMDOS.COM. These two programs are always in a specific place on the disk (right after the directory), which is why you have to put the "system" on the diskette at format time and cannot add it later unless you specifically left room.

Let's take a quick look at the boot record with DEBUG. Using the Load command, we can load the boot record into memory at DS:80. We will use drive 0 (A:), sector 0, and load a total of one sector like this:

```
-L80 0 0 1
```

And then Dump it:

```
-D80
08F7:0080  EB 2C 90 49 42 4D 20 20-32 2E 30 00 02 02 01 00   K,.IBM  2.0.....
08F7:0090  02 70 00 D0 02 7D 02 00-09 00 02 00 00 00 00 00   .p.P.}..........
08F7:00A0  0A DF 02 25 02 09 2A FF-50 F6 0F 02 CD 19 FA 33   ._.%..*.Pv..M.z3
08F7:00B0  C0 8E D0 BC 00 7C 8E D8-A3 7A 00 C7 06 78 00 21   ¦.P<.¦.X#z.G.x.!
08F7:00C0  7C FB CD 13 73 03 E9 95-00 0E 1F A0 10 7C 98 F7   ¦{M.s.i.... .¦.w
08F7:00D0  26 16 7C 03 06 1C 7C 03-06 0E 7C A3 03 7C A3 13   &.¦....¦...¦#.¦#.
08F7:00E0  7C B8 20 00 F7 26 11 7C-05 FF 01 BB 00 02 F7 F3   ¦8 .w&.¦...;..ws
08F7:00F0  01 06 13 7C E8 7E 00 72-B3 A1 13 7C A3 7E 7D B8   ...¦h~.r3!.¦#~}8
```

We can see "IBM 2.0", so we suspect that there is some kind of data here. We can look for a JMP to the real code, normal in a .COM file, with Unassemble:

```
-U80
08F7:0080 EB2C          JMP     00AE    ← Jump to 00AE
08F7:0082 90            NOP
08F7:0083 49            DEC     CX
                         :
                         :
```

And then Unassemble the code at 00AE:

```
-UAE
08F7:00AE FA            CLI
08F7:00AF 33C0          XOR     AX,AX
08F7:00B1 8ED0          MOV     SS,AX
08F7:00B3 BC007C        MOV     SP,7C00
08F7:00B6 8ED8          MOV     DS,AX
08F7:00B8 A37A00        MOV     [007A],AX
08F7:00BB C70678002l7C  MOV     WORD PTR [0078],7C21
08F7:00C1 FB            STI
08F7:00C2 CD13          INT     13
08F7:00C4 7303          JNB     00C9
```

```
08F7:00C6 E99500         JMP     015E
08F7:00C9 0E             PUSH    CS
08F7:00CA 1F             POP     DS
08F7:00CB A0107C         MOV     AL,[7C10]
```

You can see that among the very first things the boot record does is to use BIOS INT 13H, the disk interrupt, to start working with the disk.

In hard disks, the situation is a little different. There you can *partition* the disk as you want it, under different operating systems. The master boot record, at the very beginning of the disk, gives DOS information indicating how the disk is partitioned. From this information, the PC reads the DOS boot record from the beginning of the DOS partition. The rest of the partition is set up as any floppy might be (but is larger). We'll cover hard disk boot records and partitions shortly.

The File Allocation Table (FAT) and Clusters

Immediately after the boot record on diskettes comes the File Allocation Table. The way IBM chose to keep track of files on a diskette is intriguing. The sectors of a disk are grouped together in clusters, and it is these clusters that are really kept track of individually. This means that the minimum amount of space a file can occupy is a cluster. If you look in the directory listing to find the number of free bytes, you will see that the number is always some multiple of the cluster size. The number of sectors in a cluster varies from disk format to format. With single-sided disks, there is only one sector in a cluster (which doesn't seem like much of a cluster). With double-sided disks, there are two sectors in a cluster; the free space in a directory listing is always some multiple of 1K. High-density floppies are back to one sector/cluster, XTs have eight, and ATs have four. (See Table 6.1.)

Every cluster on a disk is accounted for. This means that there has to be a table somewhere on the disk with an entry for each cluster. This table is the File Allocation Table, or FAT. For each cluster on the disk, there is one location in the FAT.

Files can be broken up into pieces for disk storage, but the smallest size they can be broken into is one cluster. On a double-sided floppy, that's 1,024 bytes. If we had a file that was 1,025 bytes long, it would have to be stored in two clusters, even though the second one would be practically empty. In addition, the file's clusters do not have to come right after one another on the disk. Let's say your disk's file clusters looked like those in Figure 6.1A. If File 2 was deleted, they would look like those in Figure 6.1B. If we wrote File 4 to the disk now, the optimal use of disk space would be to use what is available. Even if File 4 is long, we could break it up into two pieces as shown in Figure 6.1C.

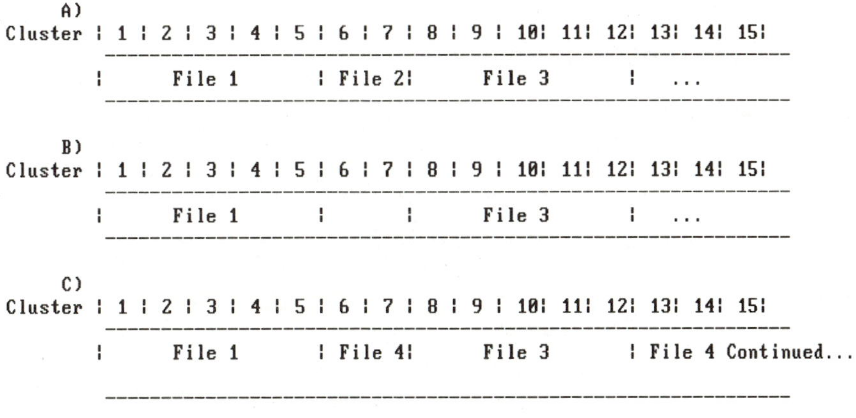

Figure 6.1A,B,C Files in the FAT.

In this way, the clusters that a file is stored in may be scattered all over the disk, matching what space is available. The FAT keeps track of them by the method of **chaining**.

HOW THE FAT WORKS

We can get a file's first cluster number from the file's directory entry (as we'll see below). After we read that cluster from the disk, we have to find the next cluster the file occupies. For this, we turn to the FAT. The number stored in the first cluster's FAT entry is the FAT entry of the file's *next* cluster on the disk. Stored in *that* location is the number of the next cluster used, and so on through the disk.

Usually, FAT entries are 12 bits long, but under DOS 3+ they were made 16 bits long on fixed disks. We will work through the more difficult 12-bit FAT here.

The first two FAT entries (0 and 1) are always filled with the three starter bytes FD FF FF on a double-sided nine-sector floppy (the most common format). You can always tell what type of disk you are dealing with by checking the first byte in the FAT. For each type of disk configuration this byte is different. (See the Disk Information Table under the column labeled FAT, for FAT Identification Byte.) If you use DOS INT 21H Service 1BH, DS:BX will point to the FAT identification byte in memory. The fact that the first three bytes are always used in the FAT leaves us with no loss in data space, since they would map the FAT itself anyway. Since each FAT entry is 12 bits long, these first three bytes make up two FAT entries. After these entries comes actual data storage.

Let's examine how DOS stores a file by assuming that we want to put a file that is 3,073 bytes long on the disk. If the FAT looks like the one in Figure 6.2A (starting with the first allowed entry number, that for cluster #2), then when DOS enters, it will scan up this line. It finds a 0 recorded for cluster 6, which means the cluster is available. It continues up the FAT, finding another 0 in entry 7. DOS allocates the first 1,024 bytes of the file to cluster 6, and indicates where the next cluster is to be found by placing a 7 in entry 6, as shown in Figure 6.2B.

A 6 is recorded also in the file's directory entry as the file's first cluster number. To read the file you read in cluster 6 first, and, seeing FAT entry 6 holds a 7, you read in cluster 7 next. DOS can allocate the first 3 K (3,072) bytes of the file by chaining it together as shown in Figure 6.2C (FF7 marks a bad cluster).

Since the file is 3,073 bytes long, though, there is still one awkward byte to keep track of, and DOS must allocate an entire cluster, 1,024 bytes, for it. This is the tradeoff it pays for a relatively small and compact FAT. If clusters were only 512 bytes long, the FAT would have to be twice as long. DOS reserves this last cluster by placing an end of file marker, FFF, in the FAT, telling any program chaining through the file that the chain is over. This FFF can be seen in Figure 6.2D. You might also notice that DOS has skipped over the bad cluster, marked with an FF7H, in cluster eight's entry.

The process looks simple, and it is conceptually, but the real FAT on disk is hardly as smooth as this abbreviated example might indicate.

When the switch was made to nine sectors a track, the FAT went from one to two sectors. Under DOS 2.0 and 2.10, therefore, there is enough room to give each cluster on a floppy its own word in the FAT, but IBM waited until DOS 3+ to use 16-bit FAT entries.

Twelve bits seems like an unusual choice, but it is actually quite economical. There are 300 plus clusters on a double-sided floppy. DOS couldn't point to them all with an eight-bit entry for each, since the largest number you can fit into eight bits is 255, less than it needs. With single-sided disks, IBM wanted to keep the FAT to a minimum of space, one sector on the disk; but since there are only 256 words in a sector, not each cluster could have its own word. Compromise gave each cluster 12 bits, that is, one and a half bytes. This means each FAT entry must be expressed as a three-digit hex number such as CCCH or FFFH.

THE REAL FAT

The 8088's method of storing 16-bit words by reversing the bytes, and the fact that each FAT entry is really 12 bits long, makes the real FAT quite a tangle. IBM provides a simple method of finding what's in the FAT for a given entry number, and that is all that is really important to us. This formula (the **FAT recipe**) is:

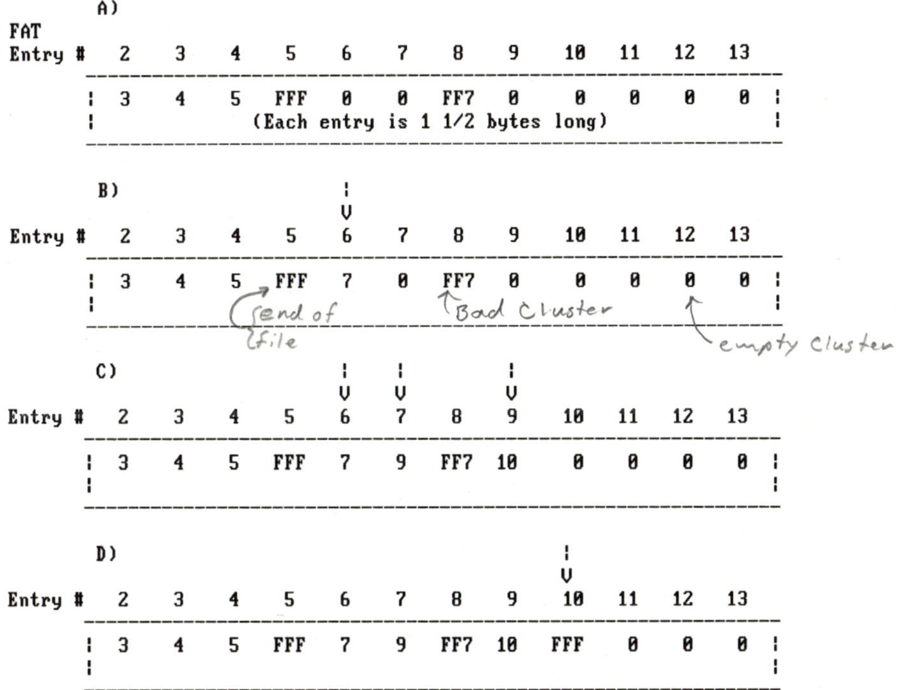

Figure 6.2A,B,C,D How DOS Stores Files.

1. If you have some cluster's number and want to read its FAT entry, multiply it by 1.5 (the number of bytes in each entry) and keep only the whole part of the result (in other words, find INT(3 × cluster number/2)).
2. The resulting number is your index into the FAT. Using the MOV instruction, move the word at that location in the FAT into a register (something like this: MOV AX,[BX]).
3. If your original cluster number was even, keep the low order 12 bits of the result, if it was odd, keep the higher 12 bits.

These 12 bits are the entry in the FAT for that cluster number.

For an appreciation of how much smoother this makes everything, let's take a look at the **real** File Allocation Table. For instance, if we have two 12-bit numbers, 123H and 456H, as the entries for clusters 4 and 5, Figure 6.3 shows how they would appear in the FAT.

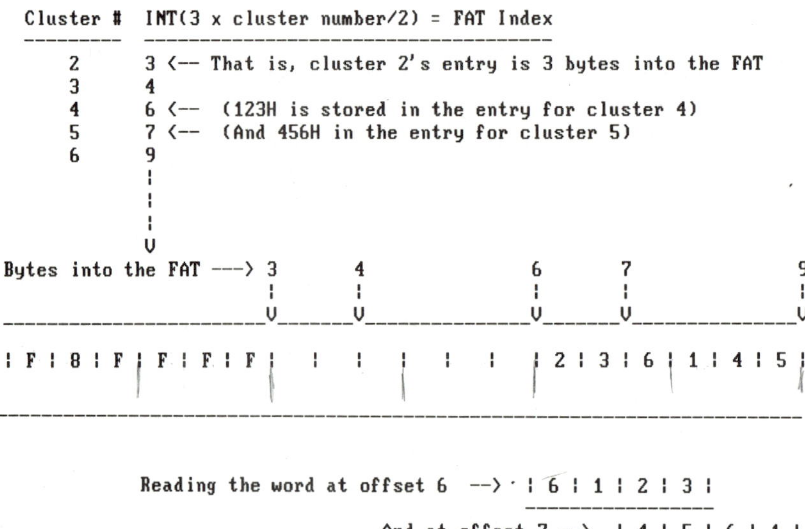

Figure 6.3 The Actual FAT.

If our numbers 123H and 456H are the entries for clusters 4 and 5, then to find them we have to read the words at locations 6 and 7 in the FAT. These two words, read into a register, are 6123H and 4561H. Using the rule above covering odd and even cluster numbers, we regain our original 123H and 456H. 123H and 456H were translated in the FAT into the almost unrecognizable bytes 23 61 45, mixing them thoroughly.

THE DIRECTORY

Right after the two copies of the FAT comes the disk directory. On a double-sided, nine-sector diskette, the directory fills logical sectors 5–11.

In Figure 6.4 you will find a copy of the directory entry for a file named BASEBALL.BAT. All directory entries are 32 bytes long. The first 8 bytes are given to the file's name, in our case, BASEBALL. The next three bytes, 8–10, are given to the file's extension, BAT. Byte 11 carries the file's attribute. Bytes 12–21 are reserved for use by DOS and are available for future expansion into new abilities.

The file's creation time, or the time it was last written to, is densely packed into bytes 22–25. The two bytes 22 and 23 store the creation time of day in a word formed like this:

$$\text{Time} = (\text{seconds}/2) + 2^{5} \times (\text{minutes}) + 2^{11} \times (\text{hours})$$

The date is stored in bytes 24–25 like this:

$$\text{Date} = (\text{days}) + 2^{5} \times (\text{months}) + 2^{9} \times (\text{year} - 1980)$$

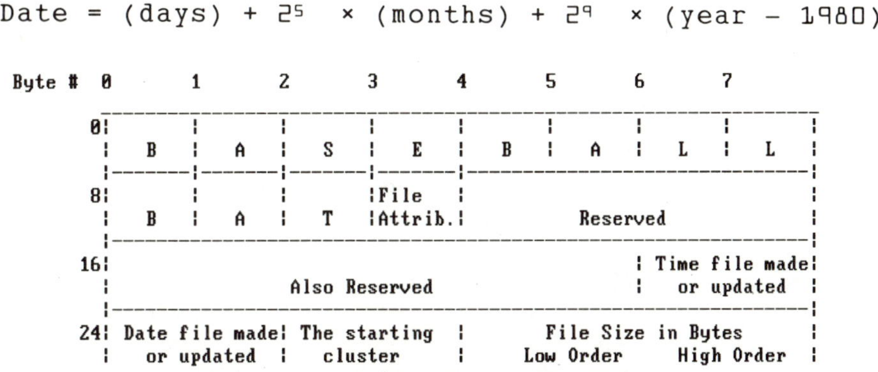

Figure 6.4 Baseball.Bat's Directory Entry.

Both of these words are stored, as usual, with the low byte first. Subtracting 1980 from the year is an economical thing to do since you can pack more bits into the space you have left.

The next six bytes make undeleting possible. Bytes 26–27 contain the starting cluster number of the file on the disk and the next four contain the file size. These bytes give you the number of the cluster where the very first 1K section of your file is stored.

The last four bytes, 28–31, are the file size in bytes. This is the only place DOS keeps accurate track of the file's size. As usual, these are stored low word, high word, and in each word the low byte comes first.

Using DEBUG, we can take a direct look at a file's directory entry. On a double-sided floppy, there are seven sectors of directory, so there are 7x512/32 = 112 directory entries possible.

```
-L100 0 5 1
-D100
08F7:0100  49 42 4D 42 49 4F 20 20-43 4F 4D 27 00 00 00 00   IBMBIO  COM'....
08F7:0110  00 00 00 00 00 00 00 60-54 07 02 00 80 12 00 00   .......'T.......
08F7:0120  49 42 4D 44 4F 53 20 20-43 4F 4D 27 00 00 00 00   IBMDOS  COM'....
08F7:0130  00 00 00 00 00 00 00 60-54 07 07 00 80 42 00 00   .......'T....B..
08F7:0140  43 4F 4D 4D 41 4E 44 20-43 4F 4D 20 00 00 00 00   COMMAND COM ....
08F7:0150  00 00 00 00 00 00 00 60-54 07 18 00 80 45 00 00   .......'T....E..
08F7:0160  44 4F 53 20 32 2D 31 30-20 20 20 08 00 00 00 00   DOS 2-10    ....
08F7:0170  00 00 00 00 00 00 47 72-4B 08 00 00 00 00 00 00   ......GrK.......
-Q
```

You can see that each directory entry takes up 32 bytes here. First comes the name, such as "IBMBIO COM" and then the attribute, 27 (Read-Only, Hidden, System, and the Archive Bit are all set at once). The last four bytes of IBMBIO.COM's entry are 80 12 00 00, and from that we get the size 0000 1280, or 4,736 bytes.

The Disk Data

After the directory, the actual data is stored. Each cluster of data is carefully mapped out in the FAT, and each file's name and length are stored in the directory. If this diskette is a boot diskette, the directory is followed immediately by the files IBMBIO.COM and IBMDOS.COM.

In this chapter, however, we are as concerned with how files work as with how the disk itself works. We want to find out how to manipulate individual sectors and clusters in assembly language. BIOS and DOS have different conventions for naming sectors. We will see that this comes in handy for hard disks—the DOS Services will treat the first available sector on the disk as the first one in the DOS partition, and the BIOS Services will treat it as the actual, physical first sector on the disk.

Logical Sectors and Tracks

Track 0, Sector 1 on a floppy holds the boot record. This is the way BIOS INT 13H requires you to specify a sector: track number, then the sector number in that track. DOS requires that you use **logical sectors** to use DOS INTs 25H and 26H.

Logical sectors start from 0 and run, on a double-sided, nine-sectored floppy, up to 2(sides) × 40(tracks) × 9(sectors) − 1 = 719. For some unfathomable reason, IBM did not start the BIOS sectoring at 0, but at 1. For that reason, logical sector 0 is Track 0, Head 0, Sector 1 in BIOS' terms (NOT Track 0, Head 0, Sector 0). Logical sector 1 is Track 0, Head 0, Sector 2. This continues until all the sectors in the current track and current head (that is, side) are used.

On a floppy, logical sector 8 is Track 0, Head 0, Sector 9. Logical Sector 9 is Track 0, Head 1, Sector 1—the head value changes before the track does. After we reach the end of track 0, head 1, we move on to track 1, head 0.

The boot record is therefore logical sector 0, and logical sectors 1–2 and 3–4 each contain copies of the FAT.

The Diskette Table

While we're discussing disk organization, it is worth taking some time to discuss the diskette table. The diskette table, also called the **diskette base table**, is a simple 11 bytes long; but, like much of the rest of the PC, it summarizes much. The diskette table holds the operating parameters for the diskette drives. There is a similar table for the fixed disks, but it is considerably more complex.

This table is stored in ROM at high memory. It is not unchangeable, however. IBM changed the diskette parameters from DOS version to version by storing the address of the diskette table in low memory, at 0000:0078H. Since this is in RAM, it can be readily changed. DOS does change this and establishes its own table in memory when it's read in, although the original table is still inside your PC in ROM.

The first two bytes are concerned with such quantities as step rate time and head load/unload times, constants that have to do with the time it takes for the diskette head to engage a track.

The third byte is, in practice, about the only hardware time that you can change without harm. It holds the time it takes the diskette motors to turn off after an operation (currently set to about two seconds).

Byte four tells you the number of bytes per sector. Only a few formats are allowed here, and programs actually do change this number since this is a way that copy protection can be done. DOS can only read in 512 byte sectors with the default diskette table it uses. Programs will typically store some different number of bytes, say 256, in a few crucial sectors. When DOS fails to copy them intact the whole program is disabled. The program itself can read in these sectors after modifying the diskette table.

Byte five lets DOS know how many sectors there are in each track. You'll find the major difference between DOS 1.1 and 2.0 right in this byte. When DOS switched from eight sectors per track to nine, increasing storage capacity by 9/8 (320 K to 360 K), this byte was the one that was changed from eight to nine.

The next three bytes are concerned with the layout of the sector on the disk, including such items as gap length and data lengths.

The ninth byte is the fill byte, that is, the byte used to fill newly formatted sectors on the disk. The PC uses F6H as the fill byte, so if you browse through your diskette with a program like DEBUG and find a sector of F6H's, it is an indication that that sector has never been used before.

Byte 10 is the head settle time; in other words, the time given for the diskette head to come to rest after it has shot into position over the track. This time has been growing smaller with successive versions of DOS, which is why diskette reads are faster. The original DOS version set this to about 25 milliseconds, but it's now about 15.

The last byte, byte 11, gives the diskette motor start and warm up time. This time was originally .5 seconds, but now is about .25 seconds.

HARD DISKS AND PARTITIONS

If you are going to work directly with FATs and directories, you still need to know one important item. A disk like the XT disk can be divided up into up to four partitions, and carry up to four completely different operating systems. How are you to know where to find just where something is in an absolute sense?

It turns out that in the DOS partition, everything is set up the same way as in floppy disks—the single-sector boot record comes first, then the FAT, then the directory. If you want to look at the directory sectors themselves, all you must do is to find the correct logical sectors on the disk and read them in using DOS INT 25H, or the Load command in DEBUG. (Check the Disk Information Table at the beginning of the chapter to learn how long the directory and FAT are on different disks.) Either of these two commands are smart enough to stick to the DOS partition on the disk, even when working at a very low, sector-by-sector level. Thus, Logical Sector 0 on a hard disk is still the boot record, and so on up.

On the other hand, there are times when the real structure of the disk becomes important. Since this is the case, we should concern ourselves with the real way the disk is set up. Here we use only INT 13H, the BIOS disk interrupt. With it you can specify cylinder number and head number at the most basic level.

Boot Records

Every hard disk starts, on the very first sector of the disk (Cylinder 0, Head 0, and Sector 1) with a boot record and **Partiton Table**. The boot record is not the same one you will find at the beginning of the DOS partition at all, since its primary task is to read in the correct boot record (the one in the 'bootable' parition) and give it control. Only one partition can be 'bootable' on the disk.

This all-disk boot record, as all boot records must, ends with the characteristic signature 55AAH. Right before that, at the very end of the boot record (offsets 1BEH to 1FDH), is where the partition table is kept. The partition table carries this information for each partition: whether it is a DOS partition or not, whether it is the one to boot from, where it starts (head, sector, and cylinder numbers), where it ends, and how many sectors come before it on the disk (that is, how far it is from the beginning, in sectors). Figure 6.5 shows how the partition table is set up (offsets are from the beginning of the 512-byte boot record):

```
000      Beginning of Boot Record
 :
 :                                       Head     Sector  Cylinder
                              ------------------------------------
1BE      Partition 1 starts at ¦ Boot  ¦        ¦        ¦        ¦
                              ------------------------------------
1C2      Partition 1 ends at   ¦  SYS  ¦        ¦        ¦        ¦
                              ------------------------------------
1C6      Partition 1 sect. start ¦              ¦                 ¦
                              ------------------------------------
1CA      Partition 1 No. Sectors ¦              ¦                 ¦
 :                            ------------------------------------
 :       Partition 2 starts at ¦ Boot  ¦        ¦        ¦        ¦
                              ------------------------------------
         Partition 2 ends at   ¦  SYS  ¦        ¦        ¦        ¦
                              ------------------------------------
         Partition 2 sect. start ¦              ¦                 ¦
                              ------------------------------------
         Partition 2 No. Sectors ¦              ¦                 ¦
                              ------------------------------------
         Partition 3 starts at ¦ Boot  ¦        ¦        ¦        ¦
                              ------------------------------------
         Partition 3 ends at   ¦  SYS  ¦        ¦        ¦        ¦
                              ------------------------------------
         Partition 3 sect. start ¦              ¦                 ¦
                              ------------------------------------
         Partition 3 No. Sectors ¦              ¦                 ¦
                              ------------------------------------
         Partition 4 starts at ¦  Boot ¦        ¦        ¦        ¦
                              ------------------------------------
         Partition 4 ends at   ¦   SYS ¦        ¦        ¦        ¦
 :                            ------------------------------------
 :       Partition 4 sect. start ¦              ¦                 ¦
                              ------------------------------------
1FA      Partition 4 No. Sectors ¦              ¦                 ¦
                              ------------------------------------
1FE      Boot Signature        ¦  55   ¦  AA    ¦
                              ------------------
```

Figure 6.5 A Partition Table.

Each partition is given 16 bytes. The boot field, always the first field in any partition's record, is 80H if you can boot from that partition, and 00 otherwise. Only one partition can have 80H as the first byte. The field labeled SYS above is a system label—1 if the operating system of that partition is DOS, 0 otherwise.

Only one byte has been supplied to store the cylinder number of the partition. Cylinder numbers, however, can go up to 1023 (see below). For this reason, the top two bits of the cylinder number are stored in the top two bits of the Sector field. Packing the bits this way is the PC's usual method of storing cylinder numbers. When we use INT 13H, we'll have to store the cylinder number in CH, and its top two bits in the top two bits of CL, which also holds the Sector number. Although this method is annoying, we have to get used to it.

Let's take a look at a boot record/partition table on an XT. Here we will write a DEBUG program to read in Head 0, Cylinder 0, Sector 1 of the hard disk. Keep in mind that if we used INT 25H and asked for logical sector 0, we would get the boot record of the DOS partition, not the boot record of the whole disk.

```
A>DEBUG
-A100
08FF:0100 MOV   AH,2            ← Request Sector Reading
08FF:0102 MOV   DL,80           ← Hard disk drive 1
08FF:0104 MOV   DH,0            ← Head 0
08FF:0106 MOV   CH,0            ← Cylinder 0
08FF:0108 MOV   CL,1            ← Sector 1
08FF:010A MOV   AL,1            ← Read 1 sector
08FF:010C MOV   BX,200          ← And put it at CS:200
08FF:010F INT   13
08FF:0111 INT   20
08FF:0113
-G111

AX=0000  BX=0200  CX=0001  DX=0080  SP=FFEE  BP=0000  SI=0000  DI=0000
DS=08FF  ES=08FF  SS=08FF  CS=08FF  IP=0111   NV UP EI NG NZ AC PE NC
08FF:0111 CD20          INT     20
```

After running this program, let's take a look at the end of the boot record for the partition table:

```
-D
08FF:0380  00 00 00 00 00 00 00 00-00 00 00 00 00 00 00 00   ................
08FF:0390  00 00 00 00 00 00 00 00-00 00 00 00 00 00 00 00   ................
08FF:03A0  00 00 00 00 00 00 00 00-00 00 00 00 00 00 00 00   ................
08FF:03B0  00 00 00 00 00 00 00 00-00 00 00 00 00 00 00 00   ................
08FF:03C0  00 00 00 00 00 00 00 00-00 00 00 00 00 00 00 00   ................
08FF:03D0  00 00 00 00 00 00 00 00-00 00 00 00 00 00 00 00   ................
08FF:03E0  00 00 00 00 00 00 00 00-00 00 00 00 00 00 80 00   ................
08FF:03F0  02 00 01 03 51 30 01 00-00 00 03 51 00 00 55 AA   ....Q0.....Q..U*
-Q
```

It turns out that on this disk there is only one partition, partition 4. The first byte of the partition record is at 08FF:03EE, and it is an 80H, so we can boot from this partition. The beginning of this partition is at Head 0, Sector 2, Cylinder 0; in other words, right after the disk boot record we've already read in. You can see that this DOS partition starts just one sector from the beginning, and that it takes up the whole disk. The SYS byte, here at 08FF:03F2, is one, so we know this is a DOS partition. We can tell that the DOS partition takes up the whole disk by looking at its end address, or by noting that it takes up 5103H (20739) sectors—10,618,368 bytes. (This number is stored starting at

08FF:03FA.) The last two bytes, as expected, are the boot record signature bytes, 55AAH.

One final point to notice is that whenever boot records are read in, they are always read in to location 0000:7C00, so if you need absolute addresses, you can plan accordingly.

We can make up a short program using the information in the disk boot record. For example, let's say that we wanted to find out whether a hard disk will boot up under DOS. This program, CHKBOOT.ASM is shown in Lisiting 6.1. It will check drive C: and print out either 'DOS Bootable' if the hard disk will boot itself with DOS or 'Not DOS Bootable' otherwise.

LISTING 6.1 CHKBOOT.ASM

```
CODE_SEG SEGMENT
         ASSUME CS:CODE_SEG,DS:CODE_SEG
         ORG     100H
ENTRY:   JMP     TEST

         NOT_MSG DB 'Not '
         MSG     DB 'DOS Bootable$'

TEST:    MOV     DL,80H
         MOV     DH,0
         MOV     CH,0
         MOV     CL,1
         MOV     AL,1
         MOV     AH,2
         MOV     BX,200H
         INT     13H
         MOV     BX,3EEH
         MOV     CX,4
         LEA     DX,NOT_MSG
LOOPER:  CMP     BYTE PTR [BX],80H
         JE      CHKDOS
         SUB     BX,16
         LOOP    LOOPER
         JMP     PRINT
CHKDOS:  CMP     BYTE PTR [BX+4],1
         JNE     PRINT
         LEA     DX,MSG
PRINT:   MOV     AH,9
         INT     21H
         INT     20H
CODE_SEG ENDS
         END     ENTRY
```

All CHKBOOT.ASM does is to read in the disk boot record and check the partition table. To read in the boot record, use INT 13H. Since this is the only practical way an assembly language programmer has of reaching absolute sectors, this interrupt is covered in detail later in the chapter.

SUBDIRECTORIES

Subdirectories on the PC were a great innovation, and in this section we are going to take a look at how they work. In particular, we're going to look at a subdirectory named A:\TEST, whose contents are BASICA.COM and PRINT.COM.

To get a look at TEST's directory entry, we first load in the directory sectors from disk A:. On a double-sided, nine-sector disk, the directory is seven sectors long, beginning at sector five. We can therefore load in the directory this way in DEBUG:

```
A>DEBUG
-L 100 0 5 7
```

As it happens, the entry for the subdirectory TEST is very near the beginning, as we can see with a quick dump of memory starting at CS:100:

```
-D100
08F7:0100  44 45 42 55 47 20 20 20-43 4F 4D 20 00 00 00 00   DEBUG   COM ....
08F7:0110  00 00 00 00 00 00 00 60-54 07 02 00 80 2E 00 00   .......'T.......
08F7:0120  45 44 4C 49 4E 20 20 20-43 4F 4D 20 00 00 00 00   EDLIN   COM ....
08F7:0130  00 00 00 00 00 00 00 60-54 07 0E 00 00 12 00 00   .......'T.......
08F7:0140  4D 4F 52 45 20 20 20 20-43 4F 4D 20 00 00 00 00   MORE    COM ....
08F7:0150  00 00 00 00 00 00 00 60-54 07 13 00 80 01 00 00   .......'T.......
08F7:0160  54 45 53 54 20 20 20 20-20 20 20 10 00 00 00 00   TEST        .....
08F7:0170  00 00 00 00 00 00 EA A5-74 0C 14 00 00 00 00 00   ......j%t........
```

Directly after the spaces (Hex 20) that fill out the filename is the file's attribute, 10H, which makes TEST a subdirectory. Before we can read in the file TEST to examine its contents, we have to give it a non-zero length (the length is stored in the last four bytes of the directory entry). To do that, we first turn it into a normal file (attribute 0).

We can change the attribute to 0 with an edit command. By counting spaces, you can see that the byte we want to edit is byte 11 (the twelfth byte) in the line beginning 08F7:0160; so we edit 08F7:016B, changing the attribute to 0:

```
-D100
08F7:0100  44 45 42 55 47 20 20 20-43 4F 4D 20 00 00 00 00   DEBUG   COM ....
08F7:0110  00 00 00 00 00 00 00 60-54 07 02 00 80 2E 00 00   .......'T.......
08F7:0120  45 44 4C 49 4E 20 20 20-43 4F 4D 20 00 00 00 00   EDLIN   COM ....
08F7:0130  00 00 00 00 00 00 00 60-54 07 0E 00 00 12 00 00   .......'T.......
08F7:0140  4D 4F 52 45 20 20 20 20-43 4F 4D 20 00 00 00 00   MORE    COM ....
```

```
08F7:0150  00 00 00 00 00 00 00 60-54 07 13 00 80 01 00 00   .......'T.......
08F7:0160  54 45 53 54 20 20 20 20-20 20 20 10 00 00 00 00   TEST       .....
08F7:0170  00 00 00 00 00 00 EA A5-74 0C 14 00 00 00 00 00   ......j%t.......
-E16B          ←
08F7:016B  10.00
```

Giving TEST a Length

Now we have to give our new file a length. We know that each directory entry uses 32 (20H) bytes, and that there are two files in this subdirectory—BASICA.COM and PRINT.COM. We also know that there are two other entries in any subdirectory, seen as the '.' and '..' entries when you type "DIR". That makes, we expect, four directory entries, so we will give the file TEST a length of 4 × 20H, or 80H. The file's length is kept in the last four bytes as low word, high word, so we choose the first of the four bytes to edit, 08F7:017C:

```
-D100
08F7:0100  44 45 42 55 47 20 20 20-43 4F 4D 20 00 00 00 00   DEBUG   COM ....
08F7:0110  00 00 00 00 00 00 00 60-54 07 02 00 80 2E 00 00   .......'T.......
08F7:0120  45 44 4C 49 4E 20 20 20-43 4F 4D 20 00 00 00 00   EDLIN   COM ....
08F7:0130  00 00 00 00 00 00 00 60-54 07 0E 00 00 12 00 00   .......'T.......
08F7:0140  4D 4F 52 45 20 20 20 20-43 4F 4D 20 00 00 00 00   MORE    COM ....
08F7:0150  00 00 00 00 00 00 00 60-54 07 13 00 80 01 00 00   .......'T.......
08F7:0160  54 45 53 54 20 20 20 20-20 20 20 10 00 00 00 00   TEST       .....
08F7:0170  00 00 00 00 00 00 EA A5-74 0C 14 00 80 00 00 00   ......j%t.......
-E16B
08F7:016B  10.00
-E17D          ←
08F7:017C  00.80
```

Let's take a final look before writing out this modified directory to the diskette:

```
-D100
08F7:0100  44 45 42 55 47 20 20 20-43 4F 4D 20 00 00 00 00   DEBUG   COM ....
08F7:0110  00 00 00 00 00 00 00 60-54 07 02 00 80 2E 00 00   .......'T.......
08F7:0120  45 44 4C 49 4E 20 20 20-43 4F 4D 20 00 00 00 00   EDLIN   COM ....
08F7:0130  00 00 00 00 00 00 00 60-54 07 0E 00 00 12 00 00   .......'T.......
08F7:0140  4D 4F 52 45 20 20 20 20-43 4F 4D 20 00 00 00 00   MORE    COM ....
08F7:0150  00 00 00 00 00 00 00 60-54 07 13 00 80 01 00 00   .......'T.......
08F7:0160  54 45 53 54 20 20 20 20-20 20 20 00 00 00 00 00   TEST       .....
08F7:0170  00 00 00 00 00 00 EA A5-74 0C 14 00 80 00 00 00   ......j%t.......
```

We have to make sure we write it in the correct sectors on the diskette. Since the Write command is the opposite of the Load command, we can use practically the same syntax to write:

```
-W 100 0 5 7
```

Examining TEST

Now TEST is just a file like any other file and we can load it into DEBUG with the Load command. First we set the name of the file we will be working on with the N or Name command, and then load TEST in:

```
-NTEST
-L
-D
08F7:0100  2E 20 20 20 20 20 20 20-20 20 20 10 00 00 00 00   .           .....
08F7:0110  00 00 00 00 00 00 EA A5-74 0C 14 00 00 00 00 00   ......j%t.......
08F7:0120  2E 2E 20 20 20 20 20 20-20 20 20 10 00 00 00 00   ..          .....
08F7:0130  00 00 00 00 00 00 EA A5-74 0C 00 00 00 00 00 00   ......j%t.......
08F7:0140  42 41 53 49 43 41 20 20-43 4F 4D 20 00 00 00 00   BASICA  COM ....
08F7:0150  00 00 00 00 00 00 00 60-54 07 15 00 00 66 00 00   .......'T....f..
08F7:0160  50 52 49 4E 54 20 20 20-43 4F 4D 20 00 00 00 00   PRINT   COM ....
08F7:0170  00 00 00 00 00 00 00 60-54 07 2F 00 00 12 00 00   .......'T./.....
```

Here is the inner workings of the subdirectory TEST. Most important is the starting cluster in the FAT. Since the FAT has an entry for all clusters on the disk, there is only one FAT on a diskette; there is no separate FAT for this subdirectory.

The file TEST reserves space in the FAT for the files it contains. Table 6.2 shows the starting cluster numbers for the various files.

Table 6.2 Starting Cluster Numbers

Filename	Starting Cluster
	14H
..	00
BASICA.COM	15H
PRINT.COM	2FH

What this means is: The entry marked ".." tells DOS what TEST's parent directory is. In this case the parent directory is the main directory, so it "begins" at 00 in the FAT. The entry marked "." is the space in the FAT for the file TEST itself, the one that holds the directory entries. Here we see that TEST begins at cluster 14H on the disk. If you look back to the original directory, you will see that the file preceding TEST in the directory is MORE.COM, a 384-byte file (180H). MORE.COM takes up only one cluster, and by looking at its directory entry, you can see that one cluster is cluster 13H.

TEST starts at cluster 14H, and that one cluster is enough to hold the four directory entries it contains. The first file in A:\TEST, BASICA.COM, is free to start right after TEST on the disk, so it starts at cluster 15H. BASICA.COM is about 26K long, or 26 (1AH) clusters, so the next file (PRINT.COM) can be stored starting 26K further down, at cluster 2FH.

That's how subdirectories work. Unless you really need to do all the work yourself (as is the case in undeleting files), it is better to use the DOS subdirectory services if you can.

Now that we've examined disk structure in some detail, we're able to take a look at what system services are offered. We will examine all that INT 13H has to offer us, since we now have the background to be able to use it. There is, after all, no reason to do all the work yourself if the system services will do it for you.

BIOS DISK SUPPORT

BIOS is the fundamental channel to the disks in the IBM PC. It offers the large disk I/O interrupt, INT 13H. Mostly, for our purposes, this interrupt is worthwhile because it will read and write sectors. But it will also format tracks, run diagnostics, or recalibrate a drive.

INT 13H works for both hard disks and floppy drives. To distinguish between the two, different drive numbers are used. For floppy-disk drives, the numbers 0–3 are allowable, and for hard disks, 80H–87H. In addition, floppy disks only support Services 0–5. Hard disks support the full range of INT 13H Services, 0–14H.

INT 13H Service 0—Reset Disk

Input	Output
AH=0	No Carry → AH=0, Success. Carry → AH=Error Code (See Service 1).

NOTE: If DL is greater than or equal to 80H, reset hard disk.

This is a hard reset to the disk controller. If you ever have reason to believe that the disks are in an unstable state, this will reset things to their boot status. If, for example, you are getting inordinate numbers of errors, you might try this service.

If there is an error in using this service, the carry flag will be set, and AH will have an error code. You can decode it using the Disk Error Code list given in the next service, Service 1.

INT 13H Service 1—Read Status of Last Operation

Input

AH=1

Output

Disk Error Codes:
AL=00 No Error.
AL=01 Bad Command passed to controller.
AL=02 Address Mark not found.
AL=03 Diskette is Write Protected.
AL=04 Sector not found.
AL=05 Reset failed.
AL=07 Drive parameters wrong.
AL=09 DMA across segment end.
AL=0BH Bad track flag seen.
AL=10H Bad error check seen.
AL=11H Data is error corrected.
AL=20H Controller failure.
AL=40H Seek operation has failed.
AL=80H No response from disk.
AL=0BBH Undefined error.
AL=0FFH Sense operation failed.

NOTE: Hard disk systems: DL<80H use diskette(s)
DL<80H use hard disk.

This service is valid for floppies and hard disks, and it checks status of the LAST disk operation done. If you have a hard disk in the system, you must select whether you want a report from the floppy controller or the hard disk controller by setting DL above or below 80H. The return comes in AL, and is set according to the list of Disk Error codes above. As you can see, the number of things that can go wrong with a system as complex as disks is large. The disks, after all, are the subsystem of the PC with the most moving parts.

INT 13H Service 2—Read Sectors into Memory

Input

AH=2
DL=Drive Number
DH=Head Number
CH=Cylinder or Track (Floppies) Number
CL=Sector Number
AL=Number of Sectors to Read (Floppies 1-8
Hard Disks 1-80H)
ES:BX=Address of buffer for reads and writes.

Output

No Carry→AH=0, Success.
Carry→AH=Disk Error Code. (See Service 1)

NOTE: For hard disks, Drive number in DL can range from 80H to 87H. See note below on packing cylinder numbers greater than 255.

Here's the way DOS or BIOS reads from the disk. You must supply the Drive number, Head number, Cylinder number, and Sector number. If you want to find the number of heads and tracks on a disk that you are working on, use INT 13H Service 8, which returns that information.

Reading from a Hard Disk

If we wanted to read from a 10M hard disk, for example, there are two platters, or four heads. There are 17 sectors per track. As mentioned, a cylinder is made up of all the tracks that can be reached with the heads in one position. A 10M hard disk has 306 tracks per surface, so there are 306 cylinders, for a total of 306 × 4(heads) = 1224 tracks. As always, there are 512 bytes per sector.

Only the CH register is available to hold the cylinder number; yet in hard disks, the cylinder number can be greater than 255. IBM allows values up to 1023 in an attempt to leave options open for the future. The problem that remains is packing 10 bits into eight, and, as we've mentioned, that is done is by storing only the bottom eight bits of the cylinder number in CH. The top two bits of the cylinder number go into the top two bits of CL (in addition to the sector number already there).

For example, to read Sector 16 (10H) of Cylinder 304 (130H), put the bottom eight bits of the cylinder number (30H) into CH. Then multiply the high byte of the cylinder number (01H) by 40H, and add it to the sector number in CL, 16 (10H). This leaves 30H in CH, and 40H + 0H = 50H in CL.

After you set the track/cylinder number, the sector number (starting with one on every track), and the head number, you can read in the sector(s) you want. With floppies you can read in up to eight sectors at once. With hard disks, up to 80H sectors.

If you don't have time or the motivation to figure out track, head, and sector numbers, and if you know what logical sector you want to read in, you are better off with DOS INTs 25H and 26H.

INT 13H Service 3—Write Sectors to Disk

Input

AH=3
DL=Drive number
DH=Head number
CH=Cylinder or track (floppies) number
CL=Sector Number
AL=Number of sectors to Write (Floppies 1–8
Hard Disks 1–80H)
ES:BX=Address of buffer for reads and writes.

Output

No Carry→AH=0, Success.
Carry→AH=Disk error code. (See Service 1)

NOTE: For hard disks, Drive number in DL can range from 80H to 87H.

This service has practically the same inputs and outputs as the last service, except this one writes to the disk. This interrupt, in the wrong hands, can do damage. It will write directly to the disk sector by sector (or even write multiple sectors), so there is a risk that you may overwrite sensitive data. Caution is always indicated here. With this service you can write a new directory onto any disk, or a new FAT. Sector-by-sector writing is very powerful. With this and the preceding service, you can tailor the disks any way you want to.

If there was an error, the carry flag will be set and AH will hold the error code. (See Disk Error Codes in Service 1.)

INT 13H Service 4—Verify Sectors

<u>Input</u>

AH=4
DL=Drive number
DH=Head number
CH=Cylinder or track (floppies) number
CL=Sector number
AL=Number of sectors
(Floppies 1–8
Hard Disks 1–80H)

<u>Output</u>

No Carry→AH=0, Success.
Carry→AH=Disk error code. (See Service 1)

NOTE: For hard disks, Drive number in DL can range from 80H to 87H.

This service simply checks the specified sectors on the disk(ette). Once you invoke this service, the sectors you want examined will be read. If there are any problems, the carry flag will be set and AH will carry the Disk Error Code. (See Service 1.) This is handy if you suspect bad spots on your disk.

INT 13H Services 5,6, and 7—Formatting

<u>Input</u>

AH=5,6 or 7
DH=Head Number
DL=Drive number (80H-87H only allowed for hard disks.)
CH=Cylinder or track (floppies) number

<u>Output</u>

No Carry→AH=0, Success.
Carry→AH=Disk error code. (See Service 1)

NOTE: For hard disks, Drive number in DL can range from 80H to 87H.

AH=5 Format desired track.
AH=6 Format desired track and set bad sector flags.
AH=7 Format the desired disk starting at indicated track.

This is the way DOS formats. If you want to format an entire disk, use Service 7. This service is essentially an internal service, since there are very few reasons you would ever want to format individual tracks (besides certain copy-protection schemes).

Please note that services beyond 5 will not work on floppies; only hard disks can offer all 15H services of INT 13H. If you request a service number greater than 5 and specify a floppy disk, you will get a "bad command" error (see the Disk Error table in Service 1).

INT 13H Service 8—Return Drive Parameters

Input	Output
AH=8	DL=Number of drives attached to controller.
DL>80H	DH=Maximum value for Head Number.
	CH=Maximum cylinder value.
	CL=Maximum value for sector number and high bits of cylinder number (see below).

This is an exceptionally handy tool to have if you want to work on hard disks. For example, say you want to undelete a file (recover an erased file); you have to know what type of disk you're working with, and what values it may have for various parameters.

The return is limited to CX and DX. These values are returned in the standard INT 13H manner. DH returns the maximum value for Head number. CH returns the maximum possible cylinder value. CL returns the maximum possible Sector value, and the top two bits of the cylinder number are again packed into CL. In addition, DL returns the number of drives attached to the hard disk controller.

INT 13H Service 9—Initialize Drive

INT 13H Service 9 just initializes the drives to the characteristics in the hard disk table, labeled FD_DISK in the BIOS listing. If you want to take a look, this table is pointed to by the address in the vector for INT 41H. When you start up your machine, BIOS takes care of this for you.

INT 13H Services 0AH and 0BH—Read and Write Long Sectors

Input	Output
AH=0AH (Read)	No Carry→AH=0, Success.
AH=0BH (Write)	Carry→AH=Disk Error Code.
DL=Drive number, 80H–87H allowed	(See Service 1)
DH=Head number.	
CH=Cylinder number.	
CL=Sector number.	
AL=Number of Sectors, 1–79H for long reads and writes.	
ES:BX=Address of buffer for reads and writes.	

Read and write Long give you the chance to use the error correcting bytes at the end of a sector, the ECC bytes. These bytes are new on hard disks, and are not available in floppies. To some extent, data can be corrected if it is read in and discovered to be incorrect by checking the four ECC bytes at the end of the sector.

This means that every read and write will be 512 + 4 = 516 bytes per sector, so you'll have to either supply or read that amount in the buffer at ES:BX. Also, you are restricted to working with a maximum of 79H sectors at a time when you work with long sectors.

INT 13H Service 0CH—Seek

Input	Output
AH=0CH	No Carry→AH=0, Success.
DH=Head number.	Carry→AH=Disk Error Code. (See Service 1)
DL=Drive number, 80H–87H allowed.	
CH=Cylinder number.	
CL=Sector Number.	

This hard disk service requires no buffer in memory. All it does is to see if it can successfully seek the indicated sector and set the carry flag if it cannot. If the carry flag is set, the AH register will hold the Disk Error Code. (See Service 1.)

INT 13H Service 0DH—Alternate Disk Reset

INT 13H Service 0DH is just another disk reset, as is INT 13H Service 0. The only difference seems to be that this one is exclusively for hard disks, while Service 0 can reset diskette drives, too.

INT 13H Services 0EH and 0FH—Read and Write Sector Buffer.

Input	Output
AH=0EH (Read)	No Carry→AH=0, Success.
AH=0FH (Write)	Carry→AH=Disk Error Code (See Service 1)
DL=Drive number, 80H–87H allowed.	
DH=Head number.	
CH=Cylinder number.	
CL=Sector number.	
ES:BX=Address of buffer for reads and writes.	

This service can be useful. For example, before formatting, IBM recommends that you write the sector buffer out. Writing to disk and reading from it is buffered in the PC, and with these services you can gain some control of that process. You can ask that the sector buffer be read time and time again into memory, for example. Repeated calls will generate the same dumping of the sector buffer into your ES:BX buffer.

INT 13H Service 10H—Test Drive Ready

This is an internal check that BIOS can make, testing whether or not a hard disk drive is ready.

INT 13H Service 11H—Recalibrate Hard Drive

Input	Output
AH=11H (Read)	No Carry→AH=0, Success.
	Carry→AH=Disk Error Code (See Service 1)
DL=Drive number, 80H–87H allowed.	

This service is used if it is suspected that the head assembly has lost its place. What it does is retract the heads fully and reset their extension parameters. From then on, it will be known how far the heads extend the disks with more accuracy. There is usually no reason for you to use this service—its use should be left to BIOS.

INT 13H Diagnostic Services

Input	Output
AH=12H (RAM Diagnostic)	No Carry→AH=0, Success.
AH=13H (Drive Diagnostic)	Carry→AH=Disk Error Code (See Service 1)
AH=14H (Controller Diagnostic)	
DL=Drive number, 80H–87H allowed.	

This, the last of INT 13H, indicates how complex hard disk drives are by comparison with floppies. These three services allow internal diagnostics to be run. If there is an error, the carry flag will be set and AH will carry the Disk Error Code. (See Service 1.)

AH=12H initiates a Controller RAM diagnostic, which checks all the internal memory of the system. AH=13H is a drive diagnostic, which tests the physical condition of the drive. AH=14H is a controller diagnostic, and the controller will perform a number of internal tests, returning an error if there was one.

DOS SERVICES

DOS provides services that we have not yet covered. In particular, DOS provides INTs 25H and 26H, Absolute Disk Read and Write, and a number of INT 21H services. We will cover the two interrupts 25H and 26H before finishing up with the INT 21H services.

INTs 25H/26H—Disk Read/Write

Input	Output
AL=Drive Number (0=A,1=B,etc).	No Carry→ Success.
CX=Number of Sectors.	Carry→AH=80H Disk didn't respond.
DX=First Logical Sector.	AH=40H Seek failed.
DS:BX=Buffer address.	AH=20H Controller failure.
	AH=10H Bad CRC error check.
	AH=08 DMA overrun.
	AH=04 Sector not found.
	AH=03 Write protect error.
	AH=02 Address Mark missing
	AH=00 Error unknown.

NOTE: The flags are left on the stack after this INT call because information is returned in the current flags. After you check the flags that were returned, make sure you do a POPF. Also, this INT destroys the contents of ALL registers.

DOS INT 25H reads from the disk and DOS INT 26H writes to the disk. The registers are set in the same fashion for each interrupt; the only difference is that in once case you are reading from the disk and in the other you are writing to it.

The only real difference here between DOS disk handling and BIOS disk handling is that BIOS requires track or cylinder number, head number, and so on, while the DOS Interrupts require that you use the logical sector number (as discussed earlier). All DOS really does is to calculate the head number, cylinder number, and so forth, and pass control directly to BIOS.

Even so, DOS INTs 25H and 26H do not even save the registers they use. You must assume that all registers have been changed. In addition, information is returned in the carry flag (that is, if there was an error, it will be set), so the flags that were originally set when the INT 25H call was made are left on the stack. After you check whether the carry flag has been set, pop the flags (POPF) to make sure the stack doesn't grow and grow. This can be catastrophic in an .EXE file as you outgrow the space allocated in the STACK segment, or in a .COM file when the stack grows back from the end of the segment and overwrites code or data.

These are interesting interrupts to intercept, since they return error codes. When DOS receives an error code from a disk operation, it retries the operation (up to five times) to eliminate the error. Since it covers up problems, you often do not get any advance warning that errors are piling up on one of your disks until it crashes. If you watch the errors yourself, you can get some advance warning.

INT 21H Service 0EH—Select Disk

Input

AH=0EH
DL=Drive Number
(DL=0→A
DL=1→B, etc).

This is the way DOS selects the default disk. Whenever you type B:, for example, this is the service that gets called. Usually, if you want to search for files or open them up, you can simply include their pathnames and use a file handle service. But sometimes nothing less than changing disks will do.

Note that Service 3BH is more comprehensive than this earlier DOS service, because Service 3BH allows you to change the current directory, including changing default disk drives. For that reason, Service 3BH is the preferred service.

INT 21H Service 19H—Find Current Disk

Input	Output
AH=19H	AL=Current Disk (0=A, 1=B, and so on.

This service is the counterpart of the previous one, and is handy if you want to find out where you are. All you must do is to call INT 21H with AH=19H, and AL will return the code of the current disk drive. In particular, if AL is 0, you are on the A: disk; if AH=1, the B: disk; and so on.

You might use this service if your program is directed to use a file on a certain disk and you don't know which disk you are already on.

INT 21H Services 1BH/1CH—FAT Information

Input	Output
AH=1BH (Use Default Drive) =1CH (Use Drive Specified in DL 0=Default, 1=A . . .).	DS:BX points to the "FAT Byte" DX=Number of Clusters. AL=Number of Sectors/Cluster. CX=Size of a Sector (512).

These services are often useful. In DOS 1.1, the entire FAT was kept in memory, and DS:BX would return pointing to the FAT. Starting with DOS 2+, however, this is no longer the case—only the "FAT Byte", the disk identification byte is pointed to by DS:BX. Once you know what this byte is, you know exactly what disk format you are expected to work with. Rather than restricting themselves to a particular disk format, professional programs will try to meet the user's needs.

In addition, the number of clusters on the disk is returned in DX, the number of sectors per cluster in AL, and the size of sectors in CX (so far, always 512). This information often comes in handy.

To get this information for the default drive, use Service 1BH. To specify the drive you want, use Service 1CH. We can take a quick look at Service 1CH with DEBUG. Here we have a double-sided, 9-sectored, floppy in Drive B:

```
-A100
08F7:0100 MOV   AH,1C    ←Select Service 1CH
08F7:0102 MOV   DL,2     ←And Look at Drive B:
08F7:0104 INT   21
08F7:0106 INT   20
08F7:0108
```

```
-G106

AX=1C02  BX=420E  CX=0200  DX=0162  SP=FFEE  BP=0000  SI=0000  DI=0000
DS=00E3  ES=08F7  SS=08F7  CS=08F7  IP=0106   NV UP DI PL NZ NA PO NC
08F7:0106 CD20          INT     20
```

DX holds the number of usable clusters (162H = 354). If we add to this one sector for the boot record, four sectors of FAT (since there are two copies), and seven sectors of directory, that is an additional 12 sectors or six clusters. This adds up to the total space on the disk—2 sides × 40 tracks × 9 sectors per track/2 sectors per cluster = 360K.

AL holds the number of sectors/cluster, two, and CX holds the size of a physical sector, 200H = 512. DS:BX, the location of the FAT byte, is 00E3:420E. If we dump that address, we find:

```
-D00E3:420E
00E3:420E  FD 00                                            }.
00E3:4210  56 42 E3 00 00 00 F6 F6-F6 F6 F6 F6 F6 F6 F6 F6  VBc...vvvvvvvvvv
00E3:4220  F6 F6 F6 F6 F6 F6 F6 F6-F6 F6 F6 F6 F6 F6 F6 F6  vvvvvvvvvvvvvvvv
00E3:4230  F6 F6 F6 F6 F6 F6 F6 F6-F6 F6 F6 F6 F6 F6 F6 F6  vvvvvvvvvvvvvvvv
00E3:4240  F6 F6 F6 F6 F6 F6 F6 F6-F6 F6 F6 F6 F6 F6 F6 F6  vvvvvvvvvvvvvvvv
00E3:4250  F6 F6 F6 F6 F6 F6 02 02-00 02 01 01 01 00 02 70  vvvvvv.........p
00E3:4260  00 0C 00 63 01 02 05 00-CC 03 70 00 FD FF FF FF  ...c....L.p.}...
00E3:4270  FF FF 00 00 F6 F6 F6 F6-F6 F6 F6 F6 F6 F6 F6 F6  ....vvvvvvvvvvvv
00E3:4280  F6 F6 F6 F6 F6 F6 F6 F6-F6 F6 F6 F6 F6           vvvvvvvvvvvvv
-Q
```

As expected, the first byte is 0FDH, the code for a double-sided, nine-sectored floppy.

INT 21H Service 36H—Get Free Disk Space

Input	Output
AH=36H	AX=0FFFH→Drive Number Invalid
DL=Drive Number (0=Default	AX=Number of Sectors/Cluster.
1=A . . .)	BX=Number of available Clusters.
	CX=Size of a Sector (512).
	DX=Number of Clusters.

This service returns just the same output as the last service, 1CH, except that instead of pointing at the FAT byte, BX holds the number of free clusters. Let's take a look at the same floppy we used in the last example with this service to find out how much space is available on it.

```
-A100
08F7:0100 MOV    AH,36    ←Select Service 36H
08F7:0102 MOV    DL,2     ←And look at Drive B: again.
08F7:0104 INT    21
```

```
08F7:0106 INT   20
08F7:0108
-G106

AX=0002  BX=00C0  CX=0200  DX=0162  SP=FFEE  BP=0000  SI=0000  DI=0000
DS=08F7  ES=08F7  SS=08F7  CS=08F7  IP=0106   NV UP DI PL NZ NA PO NC
08F7:0106 CD20          INT     20
-Q
```

This time, the registers come back with the same information as before, except for BX, which holds the number of free clusters. In this case, that is 0C0H. This means that there are 2 × 512 × 0C0H (192) = 196,608 free bytes on the disk, or 192K.

This is the service DOS uses when looking at a directory to tell you how many free bytes there are available. Since the smallest piece of the disk that is kept track of is the cluster, 1,024 bytes on this kind of floppy, the amount of disk space available will always be some multiple of 1,024 exactly.

If you are writing large amounts of data to a disk, it might be prudent to check how much space is left from time to time.

INT 21H Services 39H/3AH Create/Delete a Subdirectory

Input	Output
AH=39H (Create Subdirectory)	No Carry→ Success.
=3AH (Delete Subdirectory)	Carry→AH has error value.
DS:DX point to ASCIIZ string	AH=3 Path Not Found.
with directory name.	AH=5 Access Denied.

Service 39H is the service MKDIR uses. All you have to do to create a new subdirectory is to point DS:DX at a string like this:

```
SUB_DIR DB 'B:\TEST',0
           :
           :
LEA      DX,SUB_DIR
MOV      AH,39H
INT      21H
```

and a new subdirectory will be made. If there is some problem, an error will be returned.

This service creates a file with the subdirectory's name, and initializes it with entries for itself and its parent directories. Although it is hard to see the need for a program to create a subdirectory, you might want to write a comprehensive disk manager that serves as a DOS shell, or you might want an important program to have exclusive access to its own subdirectory.

Service 3AH is used by RMDIR to remove a subdirectory. Keep in mind that the subdirectory has to be empty before you can remove it (delete all files in it with Service 41H first). If you try to delete a subdirectory that is not empty, you will get error number 5.

INT 21H Service 3BH—Change Current Directory

Input	Output
AH=3BH	No Carry→ Success.
DS:DX point to ASCIIZ string with directory name.	Carry→AH has error value. AH=3 Path Not Found.

This service lets you change default directories, and it can be very useful when programs are searching for files. This is the same service used by the CD command. Since you can specify pathnames when you use file handles, it is often not necessary to change directories. On the other hand, if you are doing a lot of manipulation in a particular subdirectory, moving to that subdirectory means that you won't have to preface all file names with the subdirectory's pathname.

INT 21H Service 47H—Get Current Directory on Specified Drive

Input	Output
AH=47H	No Carry→ Success, ASCIIZ at DS:SI
DS:SI point to 64 byte buffer.	Carry→AH=15 Invalid Drive Specified.
DL=Drive Number.	

NOTE: Drive letter is NOT included in returned ASCIIZ string.

This completes the last of the disk services. Service 47H is very useful, telling you just where you are on the disk. It returns the name of the current default directory on a particular disk at a location pointed to by DS:SI.

To call this service, point DS:SI at a 64-byte free region, and put the drive number in DL. The ASCIIZ string that is returned at DS:SI lists the current directory, but it will NOT include a drive. For example, if you are on drive B:, in a subdirectory B:\JUST\CHECKING, this is the kind of return you will get:

```
-A100
08F7:0100 MOV   AH,47
08F7:0102 MOV   SI,80
08F7:0105 MOV   DL,2
08F7:0107 INT   21
08F7:0109 INT   20
08F7:010B
-G

Program terminated normally
```

```
-D80
08F7:0080  4A 55 53 54 5C 43 48 45-43 4B 49 4E 47 00 00 00   JUST\CHECKING...
08F7:0090  00 00 00 00 00 00 00 00-00 00 00 00 00 00 00 00   ................
08F7:00A0  00 00 00 00 00 00 00 00-00 00 00 00 00 00 00 00   ................
08F7:00B0  00 00 00 00 00 00 00 00-00 00 00 00 00 00 00 00   ................
08F7:00C0  00 00 00 00 00 00 00 00-00 00 00 00 00 00 00 00   ................
08F7:00D0  00 00 00 00 00 00 00 00-00 00 00 00 00 00 00 00   ................
08F7:00E0  00 00 00 00 00 00 00 00-00 00 00 00 00 00 00 00   ................
08F7:00F0  00 00 00 00 00 00 00 00-00 00 00 00 00 00 00 00   ................
-Q
```

The drive name, B:, is missing. If you are going to be using pathnames, you must supply the drive names yourself, unless you stick to the default drive.

CACHE.ASM

Now that we've worked through the full system services provided for assembly language programmers, it would be good to find a utility that makes it all work a little better. The program for Chapter 6 is CACHE, a disk caching program that will increase disk-access speed.

You can select the number of sectors that will be kept in cache. There is one line in CACHE.ASM, near the beginning of the program:

```
        ORG     100H              ;ORG = 100H to make this into a .COM file
FIRST:  JMP     LOAD_CACHE        ;First time through jump to initialize routine
        CPY_RGT DB      '(C)1985 S.Holzner'     ;A signature in bytes
  ;THIS IS THE ONLY PLACE YOU MUST SET THIS NUMBER. EACH SECTOR = 512 BYTES.
      → TBL_LEN DW      64 ;← # OF SECTORS TO STORE IN CACHE, MIN=24, MAX=124.
```

which you can change to the number of sectors you want to have stored. Keep in mind that each sector adds 512 bytes to the memory-resident code. The minimum number here is 24, the maximum is 124.

How CACHE.ASM Works

CACHE is like a virtual disk, but without the full memory requirements. What it does is to store the most frequently used sectors on a disk in memory by examining all the BIOS disk writes and reads. If a sector that is already in memory is to be read, it is read from memory, not the disk. If a sector is to be written, the sector in memory is updated along with the disk (making CACHE into what is called a **write-through** cache).

If the sector to be read is not in memory, it is read into memory and then given to the program that is reading it. This can speed up working with floppies significantly. When a new sector is read in, the stored sector that was read the longest time ago is overwritten— the standard algorithm for disk caches in larger machines.

DOS can set BUFFERs, which is similar to CACHE. Buffers are also write-through disk caches used in disk handling. On the other hand, these buffers are only used while a program is running—each time a program is invoked they start fresh. CACHE is more useful because it helps not only individual program to run faster, but also frequently run programs. For example, if you are programming, and continually edit, assemble, and run a program, CACHE will help speed this process up significantly, while requiring DOS to use a large number of buffers will not.

LISTING 6.2 CACHE.ASM

```
INTERRUPTS      SEGMENT AT 0H     ;This is where the disk interrupt
        ORG     13H*4             ;holds the address of its service routine
DISK_INT        LABEL   DWORD
DISK_INT_WORD   DW 2 DUP(0)
INTERRUPTS      ENDS

CODE_SEG        SEGMENT
        ASSUME  CS:CODE_SEG
        ORG     100H              ;ORG = 100H to make this into a .COM file
FIRST:  JMP     LOAD_CACHE        ;First time through jump to initialize routine

        CPY_RGT DB      '(C)1985 S.Holzner'     ;A signature in bytes
  ;THIS IS THE ONLY PLACE YOU MUST SET THIS NUMBER. EACH SECTOR = 512 BYTES.
        TBL_LEN DW      64 ;← # OF SECTORS TO STORE IN CACHE, MIN=24, MAX=124.
        TIME    DW      0               ;Time used to time-stamp each sector
        OLD_CX  DW      0       ;Stores original value of CX (CX is used often)
        LOW_TIM DW      0       ;Used in searching for least recently used sect.
        INT13H  LABEL DWORD
        INT13H_WORD DW 2 DUP(0)         ;Stores the original INT 13H address
        RET_ADR LABEL   DWORD  ;Playing games with the stack here to preserve
        RET_ADR_WORD    DW      2 DUP(0)            ;flags returned by Int 13H

DISK_CACHE      PROC    FAR     ;The Disk interrupt will now come here.
        ASSUME  CS:CODE_SEG
        CMP     AX,201H         ;Is this a read (AH=2) of 1 sector (AL=1)?
```

LISTING 6.2 CONTINUED

```
        JE      READ            ;Yes, jump to Read
        CMP     AH,3            ;No. Perchance a write or format?
        JB      OLD_INT         ;No, release control to old disk Int.
        JMP     WRITE           ;Yes, jump to Write
OLD_INT:PUSHF                   ;Pushf for Int 13H's final Iret
        CALL    INT13H          ;Call the Disk Int
        JMP     PAST            ;And jump past all usual Pops
READ:   PUSH    BX              ;Push just about every register ever heard of
        PUSH    CX
        PUSH    DX
        PUSH    DI
        PUSH    SI
        PUSH    DS
        PUSH    ES
        MOV     DI,BX           ;Int 13H gets data address as ES:BX, switch to ES:DI
        ASSUME  DS:CODE_SEG     ;Make sure all labels found correctly
        PUSH    CS              ;Move CS into DS by pushing CS, popping DS
        POP     DS
        MOV     OLD_CX,CX       ;Save original CX since we're about to use it
        CMP     DH,0            ;DH holds requested head -- head 0?
  JNE     NOT_FAT1              ;Nope, this can't be the first Fat sector
        CMP     CX,6            ;If this is the directory, check if we have a
        JE      FAT1            ; new disk.
        CMP     CX,2            ;Track 0 (CH)? Sector 2 (CL)?
        JNE     NOT_FAT1        ;If not, this sure isn't the FAT1
FAT1:   CALL    FIND_MATCH  ;DOS reads in this sector first to check disk format
        JCXZ    NONE            ;We'll use it for a check-sum. Do we have it
        MOV     BX,DI           ; stored yet? CX=0→no. If yes, restore BX
        MOV     CX,OLD_CX       ; and CX from original values
        PUSHF                   ;And now do the Pushf and call of Int13H to read
        CALL    INT13H          ; FAT1
        JC      ERR             ;If error, leave
        MOV     CX,256          ;No error, FAT1 was read, check our value
        CLD                     ;Make sure we increment.
REPE    CMPSW                   ; with CMPSW -- if no match, disk was changed
        JCXZ    BYE             ;Everything checks out, Bingo, exit.
        LEA     SI,TABLE        ;New Disk! Zero all the old disk's sectors
        MOV     CX,TBL_LEN      ;Loop over all entries, DL holds drive #
CLR:    CMP     DS:[SI+2],DL    ;Is this stored sector from the old disk?
        JNE     NO_CLR          ;Nope, don't clear this entry
        MOV     WORD PTR DS:[SI],0      ;Match, zero this entry, zero first word
NO_CLR: ADD     SI,518      ;Move on to next stored sector (512 bytes of stored
        LOOP    CLR         ; sector and 3 words of identification & time-stamp)
        JMP     BYE             ;Reset for new disk, let's leave
NONE:   CALL    STORE_SECTOR    ;Store FAT1 if there was no match to it
        JC      ERR             ;Error -- exit ungraciously
        JMP     BYE             ;No Error, Bye.
NOT_FAT1:                       ;The requested sector was not FAT1. Let's
        CALL    FIND_MATCH      ;get it. Or do we have it already?
        JCXZ    NO_MATCH        ;No, jump to No_Match, store sector
        MOV     CX,512          ;ES:DI and DS:SI already set up from Find_Match
        CLD                     ;Make sure we increment.
REP     MOVSB                   ;Move 512 bytes to requested memory area
        CMP     WORD PTR [BX+4],0FFFFH          ;Is this a a directory sector?
        JE      BYE             ;Yes, don't reset time (already highest poss.)
        INC     TIME            ;No, reset the time, this sector just accessed
        MOV     AX,TIME         ;Move time into Time word of sector's 3 words
        MOV     [BX+4],AX       ; of identification
```

LISTING 6.2 CONTINUED

```
        JMP     BYE             ;And leave.
NO_MATCH:
        CALL    STORE_SECTOR    ;Don't have this sector yet, get it.
        JC      ERR             ;If read failed, exit with error
BYE:    CLC                     ;The exit point. Clear carry flag, set AX=1
        MOV     AX,1            ; CY=0 → no error, AH=0 → error code = 0
ERR:    POP     ES              ;If error, preserve flags and AX with error code
        POP     DS              ;Pop all conceivable registers (except AX)
        POP     SI
        POP     DI
        POP     DX
        POP     CX              ;Now that the flags are set, we want to get th e
        POP     BX              ;old flags off the stack (put there by original
PAST:   POP     CS:RET_ADR_WORD ;Int call) To do that we save the return address
        POP     CS:RET_ADR_WORD[2]      ;first and then pop the flags harmlessly
        POP     CS:OLD_CX       ;into Old_CX, and then jump to RET_ADR.
        JMP     CS:RET_ADR      ;Done with read. Now let's consider write.
WRITE:  PUSH    BX              ;Push all registers, past and present
        PUSH    CX
        PUSH    DX
        PUSH    DI
        PUSH    SI
        PUSH    DS
        PUSH    ES
        PUSH    AX
        CMP     AX,301H         ;Is this a write of one sector?
        JNE     NOSAVE          ;No, don't save it in the sector bank
        PUSH    CS              ;Yep, set DS (for call to Int13H label) and
        POP     DS              ; write this sector out
        PUSHF
        CALL    INT13H
        JNC     SAVE        ;If there was an error we don't want to save sector
        POP     CS:OLD_CX       ;Save AH error code, Pop old AX into Old_CX
        JMP     ERR             ;And jump to an ignoble exit
SAVE:   MOV     OLD_CX,CX       ;We're going to save this sector.
        MOV     DI,BX           ;Set up DI for string move (to store written
        CALL    FIND_MATCH      ; sector. Do we have it in memory? (set SI)
        JCXZ    LEAVE           ;Nope, Leave (like above's Bye).
        XCHG    DI,SI           ;Exchange destination and source
        PUSH    ES              ;Set up DS:SI to point to where data written
        POP     DS              ; from. We'll then use a string move
        PUSH    CS              ;Set up ES so ES:DI points to sector bank
        POP     ES              ; SI was set by Find_Match, Xchg'd into DI
        MOV     CX,512          ;Get ready to move 512 bytes
        CLD                     ;Make sure we increment.
REP     MOVSB                   ;Here we go
LEAVE:  POP     AX              ;Here is the leave
        JMP     BYE             ;Which only pops AX and then jumps to Bye
NOSAVE: PUSH    CS              ;More than 1 sector written, don't save but
        POP     DS              ; do zero stored sectors that will be written
        MOV     AH,0            ;Use AX as loop index (AL=# of sectors to write)
TOP:    PUSH    CX              ;Save CX since destroyed by Find_Match
        CALL    FIND_MATCH      ;Do we have this one?
        JCXZ    NOPE            ;Nope if CX = 0
        MOV     WORD PTR [BX],0 ;There is a match, zero this sector
NOPE:   POP     CX              ;Restore CX, the sector index
        INC     CL              ;Move on to next one
        DEC     AX              ;Decrement loop index
        JNZ     TOP             ;And, unless that gives 0, go back again
POPS:   POP     AX              ;Pop 'em all, starting with AX
```

LISTING 6.2 CONTINUED

```
        POP     ES
        POP     DS
        POP     SI
        POP     DI
        POP     DX
        POP     CX
        POP     BX
        JMP     OLD_INT          ;And go back to OLD_INT for write.
DISK_CACHE      ENDP

FIND_MATCH      PROC    NEAR     ;This routine finds a sector in the sector bank
        PUSH    AX               ;And returns SI set to sector's entry, BX set
        LEA     SI,SECTORS       ; to the beginning of the 'table' -- the 3 words
        LEA     BX,TABLE         ;that precede all sectors. If there was no match
        MOV     AX,TBL_LEN       ; CX=0. When Int13H called, CH=trk #, CL=sec.#
        XCHG    AX,CX            ; DH=head #, DL=Drive #. Get Tbl_Len into CX
FIND:   CMP     DS:[BX],AX       ;Compare stored sector's original AX to current
        JNE     NO               ;If not, not.
        CMP     DS:[BX+2],DX     ;If so, check DX of stored sector with current
        JE      GOT_IT           ;Yes, there is a match, leave
NO:     ADD     BX,518           ;Point to next Table entry
        ADD     SI,518           ;And next sector too
        LOOP    FIND             ;Keep looping until there is a match
GOT_IT: POP     AX               ;If there is no match, CX will be left 0
        RET                      ;Return
FIND_MATCH      ENDP

STORE_SECTOR    PROC    NEAR     ;This routine, as it says, stores sectors
        MOV     BX,DI            ;Original BX (ES:BX was original data address)
        MOV     CX,OLD_CX        ; and CX restored (CX=trk#, Sector#)
        PUSHF                    ;Pushf for Int 13H's Iret and call it
        CALL    INT13H
        JNC     ALL_OK           ;If there was an exit, exit ignominiously
        JMP     FIN              ;If error, leave CY flag set, code in AH, exit
ALL_OK: PUSH    CX               ;No error, push used registers
        PUSH    BX               ; and find space for sector in sector bank
        PUSH    DX
        LEA     DI,SECTORS       ;Point to sector bank
        LEA     BX,TABLE         ; and Table
        MOV     CX,TBL_LEN       ; and get ready to loop over all of them to
CHK0:   CMP     WORD PTR DS:[BX],0      ;find if there is an unused sector
        JE      FOUND            ;If the first word is 0, use this sector
        ADD     DI,518           ;But this one isn't so update DI, SI and
        ADD     BX,518           ; loop again
        LOOP    CHK0
        MOV     LOW_TIM,0FFFEH   ;All sectors were filled, find least recently
        LEA     DI,SECTORS       ; used and write over that one
        LEA     SI,TABLE
        MOV     CX,TBL_LEN       ;Loop over all stored sectors
CHKTIM: MOV     DX,LOW_TIM       ;Compare stored sector to so-far low time
        CMP     [SI+4],DX
        JA      MORE_RECENT      ;If this one is more recent, don't use it
        MOV     AX,DI            ;This one is older than previous oldest
        MOV     BX,SI            ;Store sector bank address (DI) and table
        MOV     DX,[SI+4]        ; entry (now in SI)
        MOV     LOW_TIM,DX       ;And update the Low Time to this one
MORE_RECENT:
        ADD     DI,518           ;Move on to next stored sector
        ADD     SI,518           ;And next table entry
        LOOP    CHKTIM           ;Loop again until all covered
```

LISTING 6.2 CONTINUED

```
        MOV     DI,AX            ;Get Sector bank address of oldest into DI
FOUND:  POP     DX               ;Restore used registers
        POP     SI               ;Old BX (data read-to-address) → SI
        POP     CX
        MOV     [BX],CX          ;Store the new CX as the sector's first word
        MOV     [BX+2],DX        ;2nd word of Table is sector's DX
        INC     TIME             ;Now find the new time
        MOV     AX,TIME          ;Prepare to move it into 3rd word of Table
        CMP     DH,0             ;Is this directory or FAT? (time→FFFF)
        JNE     SIDE1            ;If head is not 0, check other head
        CMP     CX,9             ;Head zero, trk# 0, first sector? (directory)
        JLE     DIR              ;Yes, this is a piece we always want stored
        JMP     NOT_DIR          ;No, definitely not FAT or directory
SIDE1:  CMP     DH,1             ;Head 1?
        JNE     NOT_DIR          ;No, this is not File Alloc. Table or directory
        CMP     CX,2             ;Part of the top of the directory?
        JA      NOT_DIR          ;No, go to Not_Dir and set time
DIR:    MOV     AX,0FFFFH        ;Dir or FAT, set time high so always kept
NOT_DIR:MOV     [BX+4],AX        ;Not FAT or dir, store the incremented time
        PUSH    ES               ;And now get the data to fill the sector
        POP     DS               ;SI, DI already set. Now set ES and DS for
        PUSH    CS               ; string move.
        POP     ES
        MOV     CX,512           ;Move 512 bytes
        CLD                      ;Make sure we increment.
REP     MOVSB                    ;Right here
        CLC                      ;Clear the carry flag (no error)
FIN:    RET                      ;Error exit here (do not reset CY flag)
STORE_SECTOR    ENDP
TABLE:  DW      3 DUP(0)         ;Table and sector storage begins right here
SECTORS:                         ;First thing to write over is the following
                                 ; booster program.
LOAD_CACHE        PROC     NEAR  ;This procedure intializes everything
        LEA     BX,CLEAR
        ASSUME  DS:INTERRUPTS    ;The data segment will be the Interrupt area
        MOV     AX,INTERRUPTS
        MOV     DS,AX
        MOV     AX,DISK_INT_WORD         ;Get the old interrupt service routine
        MOV     INT13H_WORD,AX           ; address and put it into our location
        MOV     AX,DISK_INT_WORD[2]      ; INT13H so we can call it.
        MOV     INT13H_WORD[2],AX
        MOV     DISK_INT_WORD,OFFSET DISK_CACHE ;Now load the address of Cache
        MOV     DISK_INT_WORD[2],CS      ;routine into the Disk interrupt
        MOV     AX,TBL_LEN               ;The number of sectors to store in cache
        MOV     CX,518                   ;Multiply by 518 (3 words of id and 512
        MUL     CX                       ; bytes of sector data)
        MOV     CX,AX                    ;Also, zero all the bytes so that
ZERO:   MOV     BYTE PTR CS:[BX],0       ; Store_Sector will find 1st word a 0,
        INC     BX                       ; indicating virgin territory.
        LOOP    ZERO
        MOV     DX,OFFSET TABLE          ;To attach in memory, add # bytes to
        ADD     DX,AX                    ;store to Table's location and use
        INT     27H                      ; Int 27H
LOAD_CACHE        ENDP
CLEAR:
        CODE_SEG          ENDS
        END     FIRST            ;END ""FIRST'' so 8088 will go to FIRST first.
```

Chapter 7

Groups and Advanced Pseudo-OPS

INTRODUCTION

Until now, we have been working with *what* you have been programming, rather than *how*. If you have mastered the concepts up to this point, you understand much of what assembly language is all about on the PC, and you can do most of the things it is capable of doing.

On the other hand, when it comes time to develop major applications, the style we have developed is a little clumsy. In practice it is often difficult to confine a large program to a single .ASM file, for example. It is much better to divide the code between several such files. When you change the code in one, you won't have to assemble and link the entire program at once, but can link in already assembled sections without changing them.

Much of what we will examine in this chapter is what people think of when they think of advanced assembly language—macros, SALUT, libraries, and so forth. The advanced use of assembly language is whatever helps you program more effectively, and macros are as much a part of that as is knowledge about the disk system.

PRINTING OUT A TRIAL MESSAGE

In the coming pages, we will examine the various ways of performing a very mundane task: printing out the message "This is a test. This is ONLY a test." The number of ways this is possible are practically endless, but we will limit ourselves to the main variations.

Printing the Trial Message Directly

The first, simplest way to print out our trial message is simply to print it from the main body of the program, using INT 21H, Service 9. This is all we have to do:

```
CODE_SEG SEGMENT
         ASSUME CS:CODE_SEG,DS:CODE_SEG
         ORG      100H
ENTRY:   JMP      TEST

         MSG      DB 'This is a test. This is ONLY a test.$'

TEST:    LEA      DX,MSG
       → MOV      AH,9
       → INT      21H
         INT      20H
CODE_SEG ENDS
         END      ENTRY
```

This is the shortest way. All we've done is to make a little .COM file (all our examples will be .COM files in this chapter) that has an entry point at 100H and skips over the data area with JMP TEST. We don't even need a PROC or ENDP pseudo-OP, we can use labels instead. We could have used TEST PROC NEAR and TEST ENDP, but the final .COM file would have been identical, because PROC NEAR just serves to label a location, as TEST: does.

Near Labels

Labels can be either NEAR or FAR. A NEAR label is reached from inside the same segment, and a FAR label can be reached from outside. In other words, NEAR labels only use offsets and FAR labels use both segment and offset values. A NEAR label can be defined these ways:

```
TEST:
TEST     EQU      $
EXTRN    TEST:NEAR
TEST     LABEL    NEAR
TEST     PROC     NEAR
```

All of these are equivalent. TEST EQU $ takes a little explaining. The '$' character in an assembly language file stands for the current position of assembly in the file (in bytes). It is very much like the value IP, the instruction pointer, would have if the file was running. TEST EQU $ sets the name TEST to the current address in the file.

The statement EXTRN TEST:NEAR will be covered later. It tells the assembler that it won't find TEST defined in the current .ASM file, but that the label TEST is to be found in a file that will be linked together with this one. In the meantime, the assembler is directed to treat the label as a NEAR label, and to leave space for its address in assembled instructions. The linker will fill this address space in.

Far Labels

FAR labels can be defined this way:

```
EXTRN   TEST:FAR
TEST    LABEL   FAR
TEST    PROC    FAR
TEST    EQU FAR PTR $
```

These labels can all be JMPed to from another segment. The only one that takes a little explaining is TEST EQU FAR PTR $; all that we're doing there is overriding the usual offset-only value of $ with a PTR operator.

To make our example above into a working .COM file, all you have to do is MASM (or ASM) it, LINK it, and then run it through EXE2BIN.

SUBROUTINES

The next level is just to use a subroutine. In this case, we don't have the code to print out the message in the main part of the program; instead we wrap it up into a subroutine, PRINT_MSG. To send our message, we only need to call PRINT_MSG:

```
CODE_SEG SEGMENT
        ASSUME CS:CODE_SEG,DS:CODE_SEG
        ORG     100H
ENTRY:  JMP     TEST

        MSG     DB 'This is a test. This is ONLY a test.$'

TEST    PROC    NEAR
      → CALL    PRINT_MSG--------
        INT     20H             |
TEST    ENDP                    |
                                |
PRINT_MSG       PROC    NEAR    |
        LEA     DX,MSG  ←--------
        MOV     AH,9
        INT     21H
        RET
PRINT_MSG       ENDP

CODE_SEG ENDS
        END     ENTRY
```

When you call a NEAR subroutine, IP is pushed onto the stack and then filled with the address stored in the CALL instruction. When you call a FAR subroutine, first CS and then IP are pushed onto the stack, and then they are filled with the values stored in the CALL instruction. FAR subroutines can ONLY be used in .EXE files. The RET always found at the end of subroutines will pop either one word (NEAR) or two words (FAR), depending on how the PROC is defined. If you have written TEST PROC FAR, two words get popped. PROC and RET therefore make the whole process automatic.

You can also, as we have done, call an address that is stored in memory. For instance, a NEAR call may look like:

```
CALL WORD PTR [BX]
```

A FAR call like this:

```
CALL DWORD PTR [BX]
```

This kind of programming is often useful if you have a central "dispatching" section of the program, as DOS INT 21H does, that has to send control to various places depending on what is required. All it has to do is store a table of addresses and send control to them by calling them.

LINKING

The next way of printing out our message is to divide the work between two files and to link them together in the end. Here's an example:

```
File 1.

CODE_SEG SEGMENT PARA PUBLIC 'CODE'
         EXTRN   MSG:NEAR
         ASSUME CS:CODE_SEG,DS:CODE_SEG
         ORG     100H

TEST     PROC    NEAR
         LEA     DX,MSG
         MOV     AH,9
         INT     21H
         INT     20H
TEST     ENDP

CODE_SEG ENDS
         END     TEST

         File 2.

CODE_SEG SEGMENT BYTE PUBLIC 'CODE'
         PUBLIC  MSG
```

```
          ASSUME CS:CODE_SEG,DS:CODE_SEG

          MSG     DB 'This is a test. This is ONLY a test.$'

CODE_SEG ENDS
          END
```

This takes a little more thought. We are putting the main part of our code in File 1, and the message itself into File 2. When the assembler assembles File 1, it will find the line:

```
CODE_SEG SEGMENT PARA PUBLIC 'CODE'
          EXTRN   MSG:NEAR
          ASSUME CS:CODE_SEG,DS:CODE_SEG
          ORG     100H

TEST      PROC    NEAR
        → LEA     DX,MSG
          MOV     AH,9
          INT     21H
          INT     20H
TEST      ENDP
```

The EXTRN Pseudo-OP

On the other hand, there is no MSG in File 1 at all. This would generate an error unless we forestall the problem by letting the assembler know that it shouldn't expect to find MSG in this file with the EXTRN pseudo-OP:

```
CODE_SEG SEGMENT PARA PUBLIC 'CODE'
        → EXTRN   MSG:NEAR
          ASSUME CS:CODE_SEG,DS:CODE_SEG
          ORG     100H

TEST      PROC    NEAR
        → LEA     DX,MSG
          MOV     AH,9
          INT     21H
          INT     20H
TEST      ENDP
```

This EXTRN says that MSG will be found only at link time, and it will be a NEAR label. The assembler then assembles LEA DX,MSG, leaving a blank space in the command for the offset of MSG. If LINK does not subsequently find a label MSG in some other file, you will get an error message: UNRESOLVED EXTERNALS: MSG.

The PUBLIC Pseudo-OP

You must match all your EXTRNs with PUBLICs in other files. FILE2 looks like this:

```
CODE_SEG SEGMENT BYTE PUBLIC 'CODE'
     →  PUBLIC  MSG
        ASSUME CS:CODE_SEG,DS:CODE_SEG

        MSG     DB 'This is a test. This is ONLY a test.$'

CODE_SEG ENDS
        END
```

Notice in particular the line PUBLIC MSG. This line is to match the corresponding EXTRN MSG:NEAR in FILE1. Every time you have an EXTRN in one file, it must be matched by a PUBLIC pseudo-OP in another file. In this case, we are requesting the assembler to notice that MSG will be required by some other file. Any label can be made PUBLIC—labels in the code like TEST:, or procedures like TEST PROC FAR.

Unless you have a PUBLIC for each EXTRN, the linker will give you error messages for unresolved externals. Only if you declare a label PUBLIC will the label itself be retained so it can be matched to EXTRNs in other files. Otherwise, the label is lost and replaced by a number.

The Use of ORG

As in a normal .COM file, control will enter at 100H, so we have to make some provision for it. This can be done with the ORG 100H statement in File 1. Even though other parts of the final .COM file will come later, we are requiring that this part go at 100H.

In File 2 we don't need to supply any ORG statements, although we could have if we wished. For example, we could say ORG 200H and everything would have worked well, since the code generated by File 1 at ORG 100H ends long before 200H, where FILE2 would be loaded. In our example, FILE2 comes after the code in FILE1, but how far after? How does the linker know where to place FILE2 after FILE1 in the .COM file?

The assembler has certain rules about this process. For example, whenever the assembler assembles an .ASM file, it orders the segments alphabetically. In other words, DATA_SEG is put after CODE_SEG. This default setting of the assembler can be overridden by the /S switch, which directs the assembler not to sort the segments, but to leave them in the order encountered.

In our example here, we only have one segment in both files, CODE_SEG. Let's look at the SEGMENT declaration in both files 1 and 2 (also notice that the EXTRN in FILE1 is matched by the PUBLIC in FILE2):

```
File 1.

CODE_SEG SEGMENT PARA PUBLIC 'CODE' ←
         EXTRN    MSG:NEAR
         ASSUME CS:CODE_SEG,DS:CODE_SEG
         ORG      100H

TEST     PROC     NEAR
         LEA      DX,MSG
         MOV      AH,9
         INT      21H
         INT      20H
TEST     ENDP

CODE_SEG ENDS
         END      TEST

         File 2.

CODE_SEG SEGMENT BYTE PUBLIC 'CODE' ←
         PUBLIC   MSG
         ASSUME CS:CODE_SEG,DS:CODE_SEG

         MSG      DB 'This is a test. This is ONLY a test.$'

CODE_SEG ENDS
         END
```

Using SEGMENT PUBLIC

In the statement CODE_SEG SEGMENT PARA PUBLIC 'CODE', PUBLIC directs the linker to link any segments with the same name, CODE_SEG, consecutively. Since the linker encounters FILE1 first, it will go first and FILE2 will go second. In the statement, CODE_SEG is the segment's name, and PARA is its 'align-type', which indicates how it is loaded. PARA means that this segment must start on a 16-byte boundary. Other possible align types are BYTE (start anywhere), WORD (start on word boundary), or PAGE (start on 256-byte boundary—the last two Hex places of the address are 0). The first segment of a .COM file, like FILE1, should always begin on a 16-byte boundary, so we use PARA here.

PUBLIC indicates that all other segments with the same name should be loaded consecutively in the order they are encountered by the linker. In other words, since it sees FILE1 first, the code in FILE1 comes before the code in FILE2.

USING SEGMENT COMMON AND AT

There are other possibilities besides PUBLIC. You can also use COMMON, which means that all segments of the same name start at the same place, that is, they overlap (like COMMON in FORTRAN). You can use STACK, which means that the STACK segment for this module will be added to the STACK segment in other modules to give more stack space for the final .EXE file (.COM files don't need stacks). Or you can say AT XXXX—for example, AT 0000, as we have already done (we pointed to the Interrupt Vector Table with a statement like: INT_VECTORS SEGMENT AT 0000).

'CODE' is the **class type** of the segment we are defining. Class is used to group multiple segments together often beyond 64K boundaries, a capablility we won't use at all. The only time we will use class is when combining STACK segments. These segments should always have the same class, named STACK, like this: STACK SEGMENT PARA STACK 'STACK'. We could have omitted the class definition 'CODE' here altogether.

BYTE versus PARA

In FILE2, we still use PUBLIC, but we no longer use PARA. Instead, we use BYTE:

```
CODE_SEG SEGMENT BYTE PUBLIC 'CODE' ←
         PUBLIC  MSG
         ASSUME CS:CODE_SEG,DS:CODE_SEG

         MSG     DB 'This is a test. This is ONLY a test.$'

CODE_SEG ENDS
         END
```

This means that the linker will first load FILE1 on a paragraph boundary. When it encounters FILE2, it will put that code at the next byte right after the code from FILE1. The default, if you specify neither PARA nor BYTE, is PARA, in which case the code in FILE2 would start on the next paragraph boundary. This would make the final .COM file a little longer, but of course it would still work.

What happens when the two files are linked together is that the linker stores any references to external symbols. Since FILE1 references MSG in FILE2, and since MSG is loaded right after FILE1 in memory, the linker will put the appropriate address of MSG into the command that requires it in FILE1 (this command is LEA DX,MSG). Figure 7.1 shows the way it would look in memory.

```
|---------------------------------------|
|       ORG      100H                   |
|       LEA      DX,MSG                 |
|       MOV      AH,9                   |
|       INT      21H                    |
|       INT      20H                    |
|---------------------------------------|
|       MSG      'This is a test.$'     |
|---------------------------------------|
```

Figure 7.1 Successive Files in Memory.

Entry Points

Another point to be made here is that each .COM or .EXE file can have only one entry point—the address control is transferred to when the program is started. Here, though, we are linking multiple files together, so you must select the entry point yourself. In this case, we want to enter at 100H in FILE1 since FILE1 is the main program. For this reason, we put the statement:

```
CODE_SEG SEGMENT PARA PUBLIC 'CODE'
         EXTRN    MSG:NEAR
         ASSUME CS:CODE_SEG,DS:CODE_SEG
         ORG      100H

TEST     PROC     NEAR
         LEA      DX,MSG
         MOV      AH,9
         INT      21H
         INT      20H
TEST     ENDP

CODE_SEG ENDS
         END      TEST ←
```

at the end of FILE1. This defines an entry point that is stored in the .EXE file's header. At the end of FILE2, by contrast, there is no specified entry point:

```
CODE_SEG SEGMENT BYTE PUBLIC 'CODE'
        PUBLIC  MSG
        ASSUME CS:CODE_SEG,DS:CODE_SEG

        MSG     DB 'This is a test. This is ONLY a test.$'

CODE_SEG ENDS
        END ←
```

and this is the way it should be for all subsequent files linked in.

To LINK these two files together, this is the command we use:

```
LINK FILE1+FILE2
```

The LINK command works like this:

```
A>LINK FILE1+FILE2
IBM Personal Computer Linker
Version 2.20 (C)Copyright IBM Corp 1981, 1982, 1983, 1984

Run File [FILE1.EXE]: TEST.EXE
List File [NUL.MAP]:
Libraries [.LIB]:
```

We get the chance to specify the name of the .EXE file, and here we call it TEST.EXE (the default would have been FILE1.EXE, since FILE1 was the first file linked). In addition, we can specify the names of libraries to search. (We will see later in this chapter how to create our own libraries with the LIB.EXE program.) Now that TEST.EXE has been created, it can be run through EXE2BIN to produce TEST.COM. Once we run TEST.COM, MSG will be printed on the screen.

LINKED SUBROUTINES

All we've done so far is to link in MSG after the end of the code in FILE1. The next step is to link in an entire subroutine. For example, let's say we had a main procedure, named MAIN, which called a subroutine named SUB in another file. SUB, in turn, calls SUB_1, back in the first file, and SUB_1 prints the message. Here's how the two files, FILE1 and FILE2, look:

```
File 1.

CSEG    SEGMENT PARA PUBLIC 'CODE'
        PUBLIC  SUB_1
        EXTRN SUB:NEAR
        ASSUME CS:CSEG,DS:CSEG
        ORG     100H
ENTRY:  JMP     MAIN
MSG     DB         'This is a test. This is ONLY a test.$'

MAIN    PROC    NEAR
        CALL    SUB ←
        INT     20H
MAIN    ENDP

SUB_1   PROC NEAR
        LEA     DX,MSG
        MOV     AH,9
```

```
        INT     21H
        RET
SUB_1   ENDP

CSEG    ENDS
        END ENTRY

        File 2.

CSEG    SEGMENT BYTE PUBLIC 'CODE'
        ASSUME CS:CSEG,DS:CSEG
        EXTRN   SUB_1:NEAR
        PUBLIC  SUB

SUB     PROC    NEAR
        CALL    SUB_1 ←
        RET
SUB     ENDP

CSEG    ENDS
        END
```

Notice that in FILE1, SUB, a label like any other, is proclaimed EXTRN, and SUB_1, which is called from the other file, is proclaimed PUBLIC:

```
CSEG    SEGMENT PARA PUBLIC 'CODE'
        PUBLIC  SUB_1  ←
        EXTRN SUB:NEAR ←
        ASSUME CS:CSEG,DS:CSEG
```

In FILE2 we declare SUB_1 EXTRN and SUB PUBLIC (since MAIN will call it). Notice also that we use CSEG SEGMENT BYTE, not PARA, in FILE2 to avoid wasting space:

```
CSEG    SEGMENT BYTE PUBLIC 'CODE'
        ASSUME CS:CSEG,DS:CSEG
        EXTRN   SUB_1:NEAR ←
        PUBLIC  SUB        ←
```

When LINK encounters FILE2, it realizes that the segment there has the same name as the segment in FILE1—and they are both declared PUBLIC—so the code in FILE2 goes right after the code in FILE1. Because of the "BYTE" in CSEG SEGMENT BYTE PUBLIC 'CODE', the procedure SUB in FILE2 will go right after the end of SUB_1 from FILE1. It is not necessary to put things together so tightly here. If we had used PARA in FILE2, LINK would have filled the intervening space with zeroes, and the addresses would still have been filled in correctly later by LINK.

When the program is entered at 100H, control will jump to MAIN. MAIN calls SUB, now linked at the end of the program. SUB calls SUB_1, and SUB_1 does all the work.

Making a .COM File

To make one .COM file out of these two, we first MASM them independently:

```
MASM FILE1;
MASM FILE2;
```

then link:

```
LINK FILE1+FILE2;
```

and then convert to a .COM file with EXE2BIN. The final result can be run and print out MSG.

Using Data in FILE2

Note that although we were able to link in SUB from FILE2 this way, the MSG that is actually printed out is in FILE1. This is because if we had included the statement LEA DX,MSG in FILE2, we would have had trouble. If we include MSG in FILE2, we would have the result shown in Figure 7.2.

```
                    FILE1
!---------------------------------------!
!       ORG     100H                    !
!                                       !
!       CALL    SUB                     !
!               :                       !
!                                       !
!---------------------------------------!

                    FILE2
!---------------------------------------!
!       MSG     'This is a test.$'      !
!                                       !
!       SUB     PROC     NEAR           !
!               :                       !
!       LEA     DX,MSG                  !
!               :                       !
!---------------------------------------!
```

Figure 7.2 The Use of MSG.

When the assembler assembled FILE2, it would have seen LEA DX,MSG and stored the offset of MSG in the assembled command. Yet the offset it found was from the beginning of FILE2, not FILE1. (If MSG was in a different file, as in our example earlier, you could declare it EXTRN, and there would be no problem.) When the files are linked, FILE2 comes after FILE1, so the offset from the beginning of the segment will be wrong.

In other words, to use a command like LEA DX,MSG, or to reference any data in FILE2 with commands in FILE2, we need to know how far from the beginning of the program FILE2 will be. For this reason, groups were invented, and we will cover them right after covering Libraries.

LIBRARIES

After a time, you may find yourself with quite a collection of subroutines that you link together, and it may become difficult trying to remember just which subroutines are in which .OBJ files. At that point, it is advisable to make your own **library**, which can contain a number of assembled modules.

As you may recall, when you link files together, you can specify the names of libraries. The linker looks in these libraries only to find unresolved external references. If it finds the external symbol it is looking for in one of the libraries, the linker can link it in. Let's try this out by making a library out of FILE2.ASM from the above example:

```
        File 2.

CSEG    SEGMENT BYTE PUBLIC 'CODE'
        ASSUME CS:CSEG,DS:CSEG
        EXTRN   SUB_1:NEAR
        PUBLIC  SUB

SUB     PROC    NEAR
        CALL    SUB_1
        RET
SUB     ENDP

CSEG    ENDS
        END
```

Just to make this into a library and not just another .OBJ file, let's add a dummy module made from DUMMY.ASM to it:

```
CODE_SEG SEGMENT PARA PUBLIC 'CODE'
        PUBLIC   DUMMY
        ASSUME CS:CODE_SEG,DS:CODE_SEG

DUMMY   PROC    NEAR
        RET
DUMMY   ENDP

CODE_SEG ENDS
        END
```

First we assemble them:

```
A>MASM FILE2;
A>MASM DUMMY;
```

And then create our library, TEST.LIB. To make TEST.LIB, we will add FILE2.OBJ to DUMMY.OBJ:

```
A>LIB TEST.LIB FILE2+DUMMY;

IBM Personal Computer Library Manager
Version 1.00
(C)Copyright IBM Corp 1984
(C)Copyright Microsoft Corp 1984
```

This procedure produces our own library, TEST.LIB. To create a working .COM file, we LINK FILE1 with TEST.LIB:

```
A>LINK

IBM Personal Computer Linker
Version 2.20 (C)Copyright IBM Corp 1981, 1982, 1983, 1984

Object Modules [.OBJ]: FILE1
Run File [FILE1.EXE]:
List File [NUL.MAP]:
Libraries [.LIB]: TEST
Warning: No STACK segment

There was 1 error detected.
```

We get the usual STACK segment error since we are making a .COM file. All that remains is to run TEST.EXE file through EXE2BIN and to run TEST.COM. In this way, you can create libraries of all your most useful subroutines.

Library Commands

There are other ways of manipulating libraries. For example, the advanced user can add modules to a library, delete them, extract .OBJ files from them, or replace a module inside them with something newer. Although we won't go into detail here, here are the symbols that LIB expects you to use for the various operations:

```
Add      Delete      Extract      Replace      Del&Extract
 +         -            *           -+             -*
```

For example, let's say we have a large library named CONGRESS.LIB. To add a new .OBJ file, NEW.OBJ, to it, you could type:

```
A>LIB CONGRESS.LIB +NEW.OBJ;
```

To extract the module CHECK from CONGRESS.LIB and put it into CHECK.OBJ, we would type:

```
A>LIB CONGRESS.LIB *CHECK;
```

If OLD.OBJ was originally put into CONGRESS.LIB, we could delete it from CONGRESS.LIB this way:

```
A>LIB CONGRESS.LIB -OLD;
```

Keep in mind that if a subroutine in one of your .LIB files calls a subroutine in some other .LIB file, link the one with the call first. LINK won't know that it is supposed to include a particular module unless it is called. If it has already searched the correct library before you make the call, it won't be able to find the subroutine when you finally do call it.

GROUPS

We've been able to link in subroutines if they only contain code, but we can ask ourselves what would happen if we wanted to link a subroutine with data in like this:

```
MSG       DB        'This is a test. This is ONLY a test.$'
SEND_MSG PROC      NEAR
          LEA       DX,MSG
          MOV       AH,9
          INT       21H
          RET
SEND_MSG            ENDP
```

into the main program. In this case, MSG is stored in the same file that types it out.

As we have mentioned, the statement LEA DX,MSG will give us problems since it will be assembled to include the offset of MSG from the beginning of the file it is in, not the main file. To correct this problem, there are **groups**. All the GROUP pseudo-OP does is to collect a number of segments, even segments with different names, into one 64K or less area. When the files are linked together, the segments that belong to a particular group are all put inside that group in the order they were encountered by LINK.

The important thing about groups is that all the segments added together share a common segment address. You can load the segment registers in your program with this value instead of the value of the local segment. At link time, the linker sets all the offsets correctly. Here's how it looks:

```
        File 1.

CODE_GROUP       GROUP CODE_SEG ←
        EXTRN    SEND_MSG:NEAR
CODE_SEG SEGMENT
        ASSUME CS:CODE_GROUP,DS:CODE_GROUP ←
        ORG      100H

TEST    PROC     NEAR
        CALL     SEND_MSG
        INT      20H
TEST    ENDP

CODE_SEG ENDS
        END      TEST

        File 2.

CODE_GROUP       GROUP CSEG ←
CSEG    SEGMENT
        ASSUME   CS:CODE_GROUP,DS:CODE_GROUP ←
        PUBLIC   SEND_MSG

MSG     DB 'This is a test. This is ONLY a test.$'

SEND_MSG PROC    NEAR
        LEA      DX,MSG ←
        MOV      AH,9
        INT      21H
        RET
SEND_MSG         ENDP

CSEG    ENDS
        END
```

The only new parts (but don't forget about the PUBLICs and EXTRNs) are the statements:

```
CODE_GROUP       GROUP CSEG
        ASSUME   CS:CODE_GROUP,DS:CODE_GROUP
```

All we've done is to let the assembler know that the segment CSEG will go into CODE_GROUP. The ASSUMEs let the assembler know how the segment registers CS and DS will be set when the program is run. Now we are free to use CS and DS as if we were putting everything together in the same .ASM file.

You can reference the CODE_GROUP group with statements just as you had used for segments:

```
MOV     AX,CSEG   →  MOV     AX,CODE_GROUP
```

You can also use group names as segment overrides, like this:

```
MOV     AX,OFFSET CS:SEND_MSG  →  MOV     AX,OFFSET CODE_GROUP:SEND_MSG
```

When we use groups, we can reference data safely, such as this use in File 2 (where DS will be set to CODE_GROUP, so no segment override is needed):

```
File 2.

CODE_GROUP      GROUP CSEG ←
CSEG     SEGMENT
         ASSUME  CS:CODE_GROUP,DS:CODE_GROUP
         PUBLIC  SEND_MSG

MSG      DB 'This is a test. This is ONLY a test.$'

SEND_MSG PROC    NEAR
         LEA     DX,MSG ←
         MOV     AH,9
         INT     21H
         RET
SEND_MSG         ENDP

CSEG     ENDS
         END
```

We can even change these files so that we can reference MSG even if it is in File 1:

```
         File 1.

CODE_GROUP      GROUP CODE_SEG
         EXTRN   SEND_MSG:NEAR
         PUBLIC  MSG ←
CODE_SEG SEGMENT
         ASSUME CS:CODE_GROUP,DS:CODE_GROUP
         ORG     100H
ENTRY:   JMP     TEST
MSG      DB 'This is a test. This is ONLY a test.$' ←

TEST     PROC    NEAR
         CALL    SEND_MSG
         INT     20H
TEST     ENDP

CODE_SEG ENDS
         END     ENTRY

         File 2.

CODE_GROUP      GROUP CSEG
CSEG     SEGMENT
         ASSUME  CS:CODE_GROUP,DS:CODE_GROUP
         EXTRN   MSG:NEAR ←
```

```
          PUBLIC  SEND_MSG

SEND_MSG PROC     NEAR
          LEA     DX,MSG ←
          MOV     AH,9
          INT     21H
          RET
SEND_MSG          ENDP

CSEG      ENDS
          END
```

Keep in mind that an entry point is always needed in one (and only one) module, so we have an instruction END ENTRY at the end of File 1. At the end of File 2, there is no entry point instruction.

Groups and Different Segments

Groups can also collect different segments together; for example:

```
File 1.

CODE_GROUP        GROUP    SEG1,SEG2
SEG1      SEGMENT
          :
SEG1      ENDS

SEG2      SEGMENT
          :
SEG2      ENDS

          File 2.
CODE_GROUP        GROUP    SEG3
SEG3      SEGMENT
          :
SEG3      ENDS
```

When these files are linked together:

```
LINK FILE1+FILE2;
```

the segments will appear in the final code like this: SEG1,SEG2,SEG3. The group CODE_GROUP will let you keep your label offsets straight automatically. Using groups lets you freely use memory storage such as MOV NUMBER,5, in any module.

The only tricky part is making sure you always use the same group name—especially if you link your object modules into libraries. Also, keep in mind that even though groups will take care of the offsets for you at link time, you still have to declare labels EXTRN and PUBLIC if they are needed in another object module, since otherwise the assembler will give you errors.

MACROS

The methods we've covered so far have to do with linking. We have to turn now to a different subject that doesn't have to do with linking of files, but can get MSG printed out nonetheless. That subject is macros.

Macros seem to be an esoteric subject to many people, but in fact they are not esoteric at all. Macros can be short, and all they need are two pseudo-OPs, MACRO and ENDM. A macro is simply some lines of code, like this one:

```
PRINTOUT MACRO
         MOV      AH,9
         LEA      DX,MSG
         INT      21H
         ENDM
```

Whenever you use PRINTOUT as a command in your program, these three lines:

```
MOV      AH,9
LEA      DX,MSG
INT      21H
```

will be put into the code. In other words, the assembler expands (notice the macro definition comes before we use PRINTOUT):

```
PRINTOUT MACRO
         MOV      AH,9
         LEA      DX,MSG
         INT      21H
         ENDM

CODE_SEG SEGMENT
         ASSUME CS:CODE_SEG,DS:CODE_SEG
         ORG      100H
ENTRY:   PRINTOUT ←

         PRINTOUT ←

         INT      20H
CODE_SEG ENDS
         END      ENTRY
```

into this:

```
CODE_SEG SEGMENT
         ASSUME CS:CODE_SEG,DS:CODE_SEG
         ORG      100H
ENTRY:   MOV      AH,9
         LEA      DX,MSG
         INT      21H

         MOV      AH,9
         LEA      DX,MSG
         INT      21H

         INT      20H
CODE_SEG ENDS
         END      ENTRY
```

Here's how we could print out the message:

```
PRINTOUT MACRO
         MOV      AH,9
         LEA      DX,MSG
         INT      21H
         ENDM

CODE_SEG SEGMENT
         ASSUME CS:CODE_SEG,DS:CODE_SEG
         ORG      100H
ENTRY:   JMP      TEST

         MSG      DB 'This is a test. This is ONLY a test.$'

TEST:    PRINTOUT
         INT      20H
CODE_SEG ENDS
         END      ENTRY
```

After we assemble this and run it through LINK and EXE2BIN, we can DEBUG it. We expect to see the JMP at 100H, followed by the message 'This is a test. This is ONLY a test.$', and then the code MOV AH,9; LEA DX,[Address of MSG]; INT 21H; INT 20H. Here's what we find:

```
A>DEBUG TEST.COM
-R
AX=0000  BX=0000  CX=0032  DX=0000  SP=FFFE  BP=0000  SI=0000  DI=0000
DS=0905  ES=0905  SS=0905  CS=0905  IP=0100   NV UP DI PL NZ NA PO NC
0905:0100 EB26          JMP     0128  ← Here's the JMP over MSG.
-T

AX=0000  BX=0000  CX=0032  DX=0000  SP=FFFE  BP=0000  SI=0000  DI=0000
DS=0905  ES=0905  SS=0905  CS=0905  IP=0128   NV UP DI PL NZ NA PO NC
0905:0128 B409          MOV     AH,09 ← Here's the beginning of our program.
-U128 130
0905:0128 B409          MOV     AH,09
```

```
0905:012A 8D160301      LEA     DX,[0103]
0905:012E CD21          INT     21
0905:0130 CD20          INT     20
-Q
```

The assembler, as expected, expanded our macro into its component instructions. This use of a macro was simple. It might seem inefficient to include the full code for some task every time you want to do that task; after all, that is what subroutines are for. On the other hand, there are a number of times when you would have to duplicate instructions anyway. For example, if you have many subroutines, you might do a lot of PUSHing registers upon entry and POPping when you leave. You could define a macro PUSHA (named after the 80286 command it emulates):

```
PUSHA   MACRO
        PUSH    AX
        PUSH    CX
        PUSH    DX
        PUSH    BX
        PUSH    SP
        PUSH    BP
        PUSH    SI
        PUSH    DI
        ENDM
```

Followed at the end of each subroutine with POP:

```
POPA    MACRO
        POP     DI
        POP     SI
        POP     BP
        POP     SP
        POP     BX
        POP     DX
        POP     CX
        POP     AX
        ENDM
```

We could, for no particular reason, include PUSHA and POPA in the above example like this:

```
PRINTOUT MACRO
        MOV     AH,9
        LEA     DX,MSG
        INT     21H
        ENDM
PUSHA   MACRO
        PUSH    AX
        PUSH    CX
        PUSH    DX
        PUSH    BX
```

```
          PUSH     SP
          PUSH     BP
          PUSH     SI
          PUSH     DI
          ENDM

POPA      MACRO
          POP      DI
          POP      SI
          POP      BP
          POP      SP
          POP      BX
          POP      DX
          POP      CX
          POP      AX
          ENDM

CODE_SEG SEGMENT
          ASSUME CS:CODE_SEG,DS:CODE_SEG
          ORG      100H
ENTRY:    JMP      TEST

          MSG      DB 'This is a test. This is ONLY a test.$'

TEST:     PUSHA
          PRINTOUT
          POPA
          INT      20H
CODE_SEG ENDS
          END      ENTRY
```

Another such macro would be one that sets you up for INT 25H or 26H.

IF and ENDIF

Macros are also useful at assembly time. Here's a macro that will locate you the next multiple of 1K from the beginning of the code segment when you assemble. It also introduces us to the use of IF and ENDIF.

```
QUADPAGE   MACRO
     ....IF $ MOD 1024
     :   ORG $+1024-($ MOD 1024)
     :...ENDIF
         ENDM
```

Here the assembler evaluates $ MOD 1024 (keep in mind that $ is just like the current value of IP); if it is NOT zero, it performs the following commands until it sees ENDIF. If $ MOD 1024 IS 0, those commands are not performed.

If $ MOD 1024 is not zero, then ORG $+1024–($ MOD 1024) is put in the program as a command, and this sets the new origin to be some multiple of 1K into the code segment.

Assembler Math Pseudo-OPs

The assembler can do other arithmetic and logical operations besides MOD. For instance, it can do the operations shown in Table 7.1. (Please note: all quantities must be **immediate numbers** or already known to the assembler from an EQU.)

Table 7.1 Math Pseudo-OPs

Operation	Example
Multiplication	TEST EQU 5*1024
Integer Division	MOV AX,5/2 will assemble into MOV AX,2. The assembler manual says nothing about division, but MASM does perform it.
Addition	MOV BX,1010110B+10001101B
Subtraction	WREAD EQU 1200-983
Modulo	MOV BP,23 MOD 7
Shift Left, Shift Right	MOV CX,16 SHL 3
And	MOV DI, 0FF00H AND 11001100B
Or	ADD AX,0F0F0H OR 0AAAAH
Xor	SUB AX,0F0F0H XOR 0AAAAH
Not	MOV DX,NOT 0BBBBH

From the macro point of view, it is more important to know about conditional operators such as IF. The use of IF allows you to select what code goes into the final program—some code will be selected if the IF condition is true, for example, and some other code if the condition is false.

The conditions you can select include whether or not a symbol has been defined as EXTRN, whether or not some expression is 0 (such as $ MOD 1024), and what **pass** the assembler is in. This last concept is not one we will work with much in this book, but it is worth knowing that MASM and ASM are both two-pass assemblers. That is, code is always read twice. The first time through, the assembler calculates the relative offsets of labels from each other and stores them in a symbol table. The second time through, the actual code is generated. There are times when you want to do something in Pass 1, but not in Pass 2. If, however, you manipulate the code too much between passes, you will generate what is called a **phase error**, which means the assembler found different offsets for some label in the two different passes.

Table 7.2 contains the list of possible IFs and their conditions.

Table 7.2 IF Pseudo-OPs

Type of IF	Condition
IF X	True if X is NOT 0.
IFE X	True if X is 0.
IF1	True if the assembler is in Pass 1.
IF2	True if the assembler is in Pass 2.
IFDEF SYM	True if SYM has been defined.
IFNDEF SYM	True if SYM is undefined.
IFB ‹XXX›	True if XXX is blank—see below.
IFNB ‹XXX›	True if XXX is not blank—see below.
IFIDN ‹XXX›,‹YYY›	True if string XXX is the same as string YYY.
IFDIF ‹XXX›,‹YYY›	True if string XXX is different from string YYY.
ENDIF	EVERY IF must end with an ENDIF.
ELSE	An option to make IFs into Either-Or blocks.

The simplest type of IF works like the one we've already seen:

```
QUADPAGE   MACRO
    ....IF $ MOD 1024 ←
    :    ORG $+1024-($ MOD 1024)
    :...ENDIF
         ENDM
```

If the expression $ MOD 1024 is 0, then the following line(s) are executed. Notice the use of ENDIF at the end—ENDIF must follow all IF statements.

As you can see, there are many types of IFs. A number of these IFs are extremely useful when using macros. Since a macro is a set of commands that can be modified each time it is invoked by specifying parameters, it is sometimes desirable to know whether parameters have indeed been specified or whether they were left blank. For example, consider this macro in a file TEST.ASM, which uses the parameter OVERRIDE:

```
          DEFAULT MACRO   OVERRIDE
          IFNB <OVERRIDE>
          NUMBER DB OVERRIDE
          ELSE
          NUMBER  DB 255
          ENDIF
          ENDM

CODE_SEG SEGMENT
          ASSUME  CS:CODE_SEG,DS:CODE_SEG
          ORG     100H
ENTER:    JMP     SHORT TEST
```

```
        DEFAULT             ;Data Area ← Macro being used.
TEST:   INT      20H
CODE_SEG         ENDS
        END      ENTER
```

This is one way of including a default in your macros. Here DEFAULT is used in the data area of TEST.ASM to define a memory location NUMBER and initialize it. If we simply specify the macro's name, DEFAULT, the dummy OVERRIDE will be blank. Looking at our macro, this means that the IFNB will not be fufilled, so the ELSE condition will come into effect. Here the ELSE condition is NUMBER DB 255.

In other words, unless we specify some number when invoking DEFAULT, we will get NUMBER DB 255 in the code. You can examine the results of invoking a macro by looking at the listing file optionally generated when you use the assembler. Let's assemble TEST.ASM, the previous file, and look at what the use of DEFAULT in the data area has done. In this case, we ask for a .LST file, TEST.LST:

```
A>MASM TEST

IBM Personal Computer MACRO Assembler   Version 2.00
(C)Copyright IBM Corp 1981, 1984
(C)Copyright Microsoft Corp 1981, 1983, 1984

Object filename [TEST.OBJ]:
Source listing  [NUL.LST]: TEST.LST ←
Cross reference [NUL.CRF]:
49980 Bytes free

Warning Severe
Errors     Errors
0      0
```

Here's what the file TEST.LST looks like:

```
IBM Personal Computer MACRO Assembler   Version 2.00      Page      1-1
                                                 01-01-80

                                 DEFAULT MACRO   OVERRIDE
                                 IFNB <OVERRIDE>
                                 NUMBER DB OVERRIDE
                                 ELSE
                                 NUMBER  DB 255
                                 ENDIF
                                 ENDM
0000                   CODE_SEG  SEGMENT
                                 ASSUME  CS:CODE_SEG,DS:CODE_SEG
0100                             ORG     100H
0100  EB 01              ENTER:  JMP     SHORT TEST
                                 DEFAULT                        ←
```

```
0102  FF                        +            NUMBER  DB 255    ←
0103  CD 20             TEST:    INT      20H
0105                    CODE_SEG          ENDS
                                 END      ENTER
```

The expansion of every line of a macro in .LST files is always preceded by the + character you can see above. We can see that the macro DEFAULT has assembled into NUMBER DB 255.

If, by contrast, we have used DEFAULT 0 instead of just DEFAULT, we would have ended up with NUMBER DB 0 in the code. The utility of a statement like IFNB or IFB is evident.

Passing Parameters

The situation can be more complex. What if we had wanted to use DEFAULT, but we didn't have an immediate value (like 255 or 0) ready? In other words, what if we were using some counter, like VALUE in the example below, whose value was different at different points in the program? This is actually simple enough. We want to end up with a statement like NUMBER DB VALUE, and this is the way we can do it:

```
DEFAULT MACRO   OVERRIDE
IFNB <OVERRIDE>
NUMBER DB OVERRIDE
ELSE
NUMBER  DB 255
ENDIF
ENDM

VALUE    = 1
VALUE    = VALUE + 1

CODE_SEG SEGMENT
         ASSUME   CS:CODE_SEG,DS:CODE_SEG
         ORG      100H
ENTER:   JMP      SHORT TEST
         DEFAULT VALUE   ;Data Area ← Macro being used.
TEST:    INT      20H
CODE_SEG          ENDS
         END      ENTER
```

This same example could not have been done with EQU. If we had said VALUE EQU 1, then VALUE would have been 1 forever; its value cannot be changed. On the other hand, the = pseudo-OP allows reassignment, so the value of VALUE can be changed at different points throughout the program.

The example above assembles into the final command NUMBER DB VALUE; since VALUE equals two, this becomes NUMBER DB 2.

We could only use this DEFAULT macro once in the program. Using more than once would lead to multiple definitions of the label NUMBER, and consequently to errors.

Using % and &

What if, the first time, we wanted to define NUMBER1, the second time NUMBER2, and so forth? If we do things this way, we can use DEFAULT as often as we wish. This can be done with two new macro operators, % and &. Here's a fancy example, showing how this is accomplished:

```
DEFAULT MACRO   OVERRIDE
COUNTER=COUNTER+1
IFNB <OVERRIDE>
DEFINE  %COUNTER,OVERRIDE
ELSE
DEFINE  %COUNTER,255
ENDIF
ENDM

DEFINE  MACRO   NUM,VAL
NUMBER&NUM      DB VAL
ENDM

COUNTER = 0     ;← Initialize COUNTER to start with NUMBER1.

CODE_SEG SEGMENT
        ASSUME  CS:CODE_SEG,DS:CODE_SEG
        ORG     100H
ENTER:  JMP     SHORT TEST
        DEFAULT 0           ;Data Area ← Macro being used.
        DEFAULT             ;Data Area ← Macro being used.
TEST:   INT     20H
CODE_SEG        ENDS
        END     ENTER
```

What the % special operator does is to make sure that what is used is not the parameter name itself, such as COUNTER above, but the value that COUNTER represents. What & does is join a passed parameter together with text already in the macro. For example, look at the macro DEFINE:

```
DEFINE  MACRO   NUM,VAL
  NUMBER&NUM      DB VAL
  ENDM
```

What we want to generate is NUMBER1 as the label the first time this is used, NUMBER2 the next time, etc. If we had made DEFINE this way instead:

```
DEFINE   MACRO    NUM,VAL
  NUMBERNUM         DB VAL
  ENDM
```

the assembler would not see NUM at the tail end of "NUMBERNUM" at all, assuming it was merely one word. The correct way to merge NUMBER and the value represented by NUM is with &:

```
NUMBER&NUM        DB VAL
```

The assembler then fills in the parameter NUM as required.

On the other hand, when we call DEFINE from our first macro, DEFAULT, we want to pass the current value of COUNTER, which is incremented each time DEFAULT is used. We cannot, however, issue a command like:

```
DEFAULT COUNTER,255
```

since that will result in "COUNTER" being passed as a parameter, giving us:

```
NUMBERCOUNTER         DB 255
```

The correct thing is to pass COUNTER's value, not its name, and that is done with the % character:

```
DEFINE   %COUNTER,OVERRIDE
```

Take a moment to study this example since it is typical of the macros one runs into. Note also that we initialized COUNTER (with COUNTER=0) before incrementing it in DEFAULT. In this example, we are free to use DEFAULT more than once:

```
CODE_SEG SEGMENT
         ASSUME  CS:CODE_SEG,DS:CODE_SEG
         ORG     100H
ENTER:   JMP     SHORT TEST
         DEFAULT 0            ;Data Area ← Macro being used.
         DEFAULT              ;Data Area ← Macro being used.
TEST:    INT     20H
CODE_SEG         ENDS
         END     ENTER
```

The first use will result in NUMBER1 DB 0, and the second use will result in NUMBER2 DB 255. If you wish, you can practically define your own language simply using macros.

THE LOCAL PSEUDO-OP IN MACROS

There is another, and easier, way of making sure that you do not have multiple-definition problems when defining labels in macros, and that is the use of the LOCAL pseudo-OP. Whenever you use LOCAL, it *must* be the line immediately following the macro definition, like this:

```
CODE_GROUP          GROUP    CODE_SEG,DATA_SEG

PRINTOUT MACRO      MESSAGE
        LOCAL       MSG ←
DATA_SEG            SEGMENT BYTE PUBLIC 'DATA'
        MSG         DB MESSAGE,'$'
DATA_SEG ENDS
        MOV         AH,9
        LEA         DX,MSG
        INT         21H
        ENDM

CODE_SEG SEGMENT BYTE PUBLIC 'CODE'
        ASSUME CS:CODE_GROUP,DS:CODE_GROUP
        ORG         100H
ENTRY:  PRINTOUT 'This is a test. This is ONLY a test.'
        INT         20H
CODE_SEG ENDS
        END         ENTRY
```

In this case, we are defining MSG as LOCAL in the macro PRINTOUT. This means that whenever PRINTOUT is invoked, it will use a unique name for MSG, so we will not be redefining the label. LOCAL is almost always used when the macro needs internal labels, but not when these labels are to be referenced externally (such as NUMBER1 and NUMBER2 above).

MACRO LIBRARIES

Another fancy option is to include your macros in a Macro Library. This library, usually named with the extension .MAC, is read in at assembly time. We can convert our last macro example to use a macro library—TEST.MAC. Here is what is in the file TEST.MAC:

```
PRINTOUT MACRO      MESSAGE
        LOCAL       MSG
DATA_SEG            SEGMENT BYTE PUBLIC 'DATA'
        MSG         DB MESSAGE,'$'
```

```
DATA_SEG ENDS
        MOV     AH,9
        LEA     DX,MSG
        INT     21H
        ENDM
```

And this is what in the .ASM file:

```
CODE_GROUP      GROUP   CODE_SEG,DATA_SEG

INCLUDE TEST.MAC        ←

CODE_SEG SEGMENT BYTE PUBLIC 'CODE'
        ASSUME CS:CODE_GROUP,DS:CODE_GROUP
        ORG     100H
ENTRY:  PRINTOUT 'This is a test. This is ONLY a test.'
        PRINTOUT 'This is a test. This is ONLY a test.'
        INT     20H
CODE_SEG ENDS
        END     ENTRY
```

This assembly is done as usual—the macro(s) in TEST.MAC are simply put into the code at the position of the INCLUDE TEST.MAC statement. You can even include drive and pathnames with the INCLUDE command.

Other Macro Pseudo-OPs

The other macro pseudo-OPs available are these: EXITM, IRP, IRPC, PURGE, and REPT. They each deserve some attention.

The EXITM Pseudo-OP

The EXITM command can get you out of any macro—all it does is to place you after the ENDM command. This pseudo-OP is useful when you have loops (such as REPT will allow below) and want to exit on some condition. You can, for example, keep looping until an IF statement becomes true, and then execute an EXITM, as we'll see in an example when we examine REPT.

IRP and IRPC

The IRP and IRPC Pseudo-Ops can be very useful under some circumstances. IRP lets you repeat an operation a number of times, taking arguments from a list. For example, here's how you could use IRP:

```
IRP     NAME,<"This","is a","test.$">
DB      NAME
```

The angle brackets around the strings are required, but no angle brackets are required when defining the dummy, NAME in this case, that will be replaced with values. This example will be expanded into:

```
DB      "This"
DB      "is a"
DB      "test.$"
```

This in itself might not seem terribly useful, but consider that you can do the same for lists of numbers or even individual characters. IRPC is set up to take character by character from a string, and repeat a particular operation until the string is exhausted:

```
IRPC    VALUE,56789
DB      VALUE-3
```

This example generates:

```
DB      2
DB      3
DB      4
DB      5
DB      6
```

If we had enclosed 56789 in quotation marks, however, the entire string would have been treated as one argument, as in the previous example.

REPT

REPT is the pseudo-OP that loops in macros. You can give REPT a number and the loop will be performed that many times, unless you include an EXITM pseudo-OP as an exiting condition. You can use REPT to pad spaces in between parts of code so it ends on 256-byte boundaries, execute another macro a number of times, or even compare lists of parameters until a match is found.

Every REPT must end with an ENDM; if you are including REPT inside a macro (it need not be inside a macro, however), include an extra ENDM for the REPT part, as in the example below.

An Example Using Macro Pseudo-OPs

Here's an example using REPT, EXITM, and IF. This macro will pad space in your program with zeros, up to a maximum of 16 zeros. Once it reaches that limit, it will quit:

```
PAD      MACRO   NUMBER
COUNTER = 0      ;← Initialize COUNTER to start.
REPT     NUMBER
IF       COUNTER-16
DB       0
ELSE
EXITM
ENDIF
COUNTER=COUNTER+1
ENDM                       ;← Note: TWO ENDMs; one for REPT
ENDM                       ;← and one for MACRO.

CODE_SEG SEGMENT
         ASSUME  CS:CODE_SEG,DS:CODE_SEG
         ORG     100H
ENTRY:   JMP     SHORT TEST
         PAD     20
TEST:    INT     20H
CODE_SEG         ENDS
         END     ENTRY
```

We can look at the .LST file to see what happened. As we expected, there are 16 zeros, even though we invoked the macro with PAD 20:

```
IBM Personal Computer MACRO Assembler   Version 2.00      Page    1-1
                                         01-01-80

                              PAD      MACRO   NUMBER
                              COUNTER = 0     ;← Initialize COUNTER to start.
                              REPT     NUMBER
                              IF       COUNTER-16
                              DB       0
                              ELSE
                              EXITM
                              ENDIF
                              COUNTER=COUNTER+1
                              ENDM
                              ENDM

0000                 CODE_SEG SEGMENT
                        ASSUME  CS:CODE_SEG,DS:CODE_SEG
0100                    ORG     100H
0100  EB 10          ENTRY:  JMP      SHORT TEST
                             PAD      20
0102  00                      +             DB       0
0103  00                      +             DB       0
0104  00                      +             DB       0
0105  00                      +             DB       0
0106  00                      +             DB       0
0107  00                      +             DB       0
0108  00                      +             DB       0
0109  00                      +             DB       0
010A  00                      +             DB       0
010B  00                      +             DB       0
010C  00                      +             DB       0
010D  00                      +             DB       0
010E  00                      +             DB       0
010F  00                      +             DB       0
```

```
0110  00                    +           DB      0
0111  00                    +           DB      0
0112  CD 20         TEST:   INT     20H
0114                CODE_SEG        ENDS
                        END     ENTRY
```

PURGE

The last of the macro pseudo-OPs is PURGE. PURGE is very simple—its use eliminates a specified macro. For example, we could have said PURGE PAD above, and removed the definition of PAD from memory, allowing that space to be used for another macro definition. If you merely want to change the definition of a particular macro, however, you need not PURGE it first. Just redefining the macro will overwrite its definition. This brings us to our last macro topic: self-redefining macros.

SELF-REDEFINING MACROS

Despite an exotic-sounding name, self-redefining macros are actually quite easy to use, and they are quite common. You may have noticed that a major drawback with macros is that whenever invoked, they are expanded to their full length right there. If you have a number of commands that are more conveniently put into a subroutine, you probably wouldn't want to repeat them every time you wanted to use them; you would simply call the subroutine. With a normal macro, of course, you would get the full length (all the commands) right there in your program.

If, however, a macro itself contains a macro definition, the second macro is not defined until the first one—the one enclosing it—is run. That enclosed macro can have the same name, in fact. When that happens, the macro is redefined—the old definition is simply written over. In the example, the subroutine is PRINT. The first time the macro, OUTPUT, is run, it defines the subroutine PRINT and calls it. It also redefines itself so that from then on, OUTPUT just expands into CALL PRINT. Here's what it looks like:

```
        OUTPUT  MACRO
        JMP     SHORT OVER
MSG     DB      'This is a test. This is ONLY a test.$'
        PRINT   PROC    NEAR
        LEA     DX,MSG
        MOV     AH,9
        INT     21H
        RET
        PRINT   ENDP
OVER:   CALL    PRINT
```

```
        OUTPUT  MACRO    ;Macro being redefined.
        CALL    PRINT    ;Macro being redefined.
        ENDM             ;Macro being redefined.
        ENDM

CODE_SEG SEGMENT
        ASSUME  CS:CODE_SEG,DS:CODE_SEG
        ORG     100H
ENTRY:  OUTPUT
        OUTPUT
TEST:   INT     20H
CODE_SEG        ENDS
        END     ENTRY
```

Notice that we have a full macro definition inside OUTPUT, and that definition redefines OUTPUT:

```
OUTPUT  MACRO   ;Macro being redefined.
  CALL    PRINT   ;Macro being redefined.
  ENDM            ;Macro being redefined.
```

It is also worth noticing that, although we use labels in this macro (MSG and PRINT), we don't have to use LOCALs, since the macro that defines them is only used once.

In the example, OUTPUT is called twice. We can take a look at the resulting .LST file that this example produces:

```
IBM Personal Computer MACRO Assembler   Version 2.00      Page    1-1
                                                01-01-80

                           OUTPUT  MACRO
                           JMP     SHORT OVER
                     MSG   DB      'This is a test. This is ONLY a test.$'
                           PRINT   PROC    NEAR
                           LEA     DX,MSG
                           MOV     AH,9
                           INT     21H
                           RET
                           PRINT   ENDP
                     OVER: CALL    PRINT
                           OUTPUT  MACRO    ;Macro being redefined.
                           CALL    PRINT    ;Macro being redefined.
                           ENDM             ;Macro being redefined.
                           ENDM

0000                    CODE_SEG SEGMENT
                        ASSUME  CS:CODE_SEG,DS:CODE_SEG
0100                    ORG     100H
0100                    ENTRY:  OUTPUT
0100  EB 2E                  +          JMP     SHORT OVER
0102  54 68 69 73 20 69      +   MSG DB 'This is a test. This is ONLY a test.$'
0127                         +          PRINT   PROC    NEAR
0127  8D 16 0102 R           +          LEA     DX,MSG
012B  B4 09                  +          MOV     AH,9
012D  CD 21                  +          INT     21H
012F  C3                     +          RET
0130                         +          PRINT   ENDP
```

```
0130  E8 0127 R            +     OVER:    CALL     PRINT
                      OUTPUT
0133  E8 0127 R            +              CALL     PRINT   ←Redefined.
0136  CD 20          TEST:   INT      20H
0138                 CODE_SEG        ENDS
                           END      ENTRY
```

As we can see from the second invocation of OUTPUT, it has been redefined to a simple CALL PRINT.

This is as fancy as we'll get with macros. If you become proficient with them, you can practically make up your own language, but there is almost always a tradeoff to be made in speed and size. Still, if you are involved in long projects, macros help standardize code and make programming that much faster.

There is one other way that the IBM assembler helps you structure your code, and that is SALUT, the Structured Assembly Language Utility. Now that we've finished macros, SALUT is the last topic in this chapter.

SALUT

It may sometimes appear that assembly language is nothing more than long, tall, thin lines of terse commands, full of jumps and calls. Assembly language programs can become lengthy projects; unless they are well-documented, they can become very complex.

SALUT was an attempt to make assembly language programming more structured, but SALUT takes some time to learn and use correctly. SALUT is a preprocessor of assembly language code included with the IBM assembler. You pass it a file with the extension .SAL, and it produces one with the extension .ASM. For example, the command

```
SALUT ONLINE
```

will first copy ONLINE.SAL into ONLINE.BAK, and then create ONLINE.ASM for you. ONLINE.ASM can then be run through MASM and so on.

The way SALUT works is to use a number of commands like $IF and $ELSE for tests, rather than simple JEs or JGs. To set up a test, such as:

```
CMP      BX,AX
         JG       GREATER
                     :
                     :
GREATER:
```

you can type this in SALUT:

```
CMP      BX,AX
$IF      G
         :
         :
$ENDIF
```

Tests can be made with $IF. If you use $IF G, the following statements (until $ENDIF) will be executed if BX is greater than AX. This greater-than test, JG or JNG, is a signed compare. If you simply want to compare the magnitude of the 16-bit numbers in two registers (an unsigned compare) you would use JA or JB.

Let's imagine we want to make sure that the number in AX is greater than the number in BX. If BX › AX, we want to exchange them. It can be done this way in SALUT:

```
CODE_SEG SEGMENT
     ASSUME      CS:CODE_SEG,DS:CODE_SEG
     ORG       100H
ENTRY:  CMP      BX,AX
        $IF      G                    ;Signed compare.
        PUSH     BX
        PUSH     AX
        POP      BX
        POP      AX
        $ENDIF
TEST:   INT      20H
CODE_SEG ENDS
     END       ENTRY
```

When the comparison is done, all the PUSHes and POPs after $IF G are done if BX > AX, exchanging the two registers (the same thing could have been done using the XCHG command if we had wanted to). SALUT takes this .SAL file and converts it into a .ASM file:

```
A>SALUT TEST.SAL

A>TYPE TEST.ASM

CODE_SEG SEGMENT
     ASSUME      CS:CODE_SEG,DS:CODE_SEG
     ORG       100H
ENTRY:     CMP      BX,AX
;      $IF      G                   ;Signed compare.
     JNG $$IF1
         PUSH     BX
         PUSH     AX
```

```
            POP      BX
            POP      AX
;       $ENDIF
$$IF1:
TEST:        INT      20H
CODE_SEG ENDS
      END       ENTRY
```

$IF G became JNG $$IF1. This type of label, $$IF1, is the type of label SALUT inserts into the .ASM file. As you can see, the SALUT commands are retained but commented out. After CMP BX,AX, command jumps to $$IF1 if AX > BX, as it should. Notice also that SALUT indents blocks of instructions included in the same $IF to make reading the .ASM file easier.

$ELSE

Besides $IF and $ENDIF, there is also $ELSE, which has the same functional use as in the conditional pseudo-OPs we worked with earlier in the chapter. The two should not be confused, of course—IF is executed when the file is assembled, and $IF becomes code to be executed when the file is run. Here is an example using $ELSE. In this case, we check the denominator in a division command before executing it. If the denominator in BX is zero, an error would be caused by the instruction DIV BX, so we type out an error message rather than executing the command.

```
CODE_SEG SEGMENT
         ASSUME   CS:CODE_SEG,DS:CODE_SEG
         ORG      100H
ENTRY:   JMP      SHORT DIVCHK
         ERROR    DB 'Error!$'
DIVCHK:  CMP      BX,0
         $IF      NE
         DIV      BX
         $ELSE
         LEA      DX,ERROR
         MOV      AH,9
         INT      21H
         $ENDIF
TEST:    INT      20H
CODE_SEG ENDS
         END      ENTRY
```

Here we use CMP BX,0. If BX is not equal (NE) to zero, we execute the following commands; if it is equal to zero, we execute the $ELSE commands. The whole $IF $ELSE construction still ends with $ENDIF.

$DO and $ENDDO

You can also use loops in SALUT, with the $DO and $ENDDO pair. These loops can be translated into either jump commands or loop commands. Here is a program that searches for the first byte in a string that is NOT 255:

```
CODE_SEG SEGMENT
         ASSUME   CS:CODE_SEG,DS:CODE_SEG
         ORG      100H
ENTRY:   $DO                  ←
         INC      BX
         CMP      [BX],255
         $ENDDO   NE          ←
TEST:    INT      20H
CODE_SEG ENDS
         END      ENTRY
```

The condition for ending the loop is if the comparison CMP [BX],255 is not equal ($ENDDO NE). SALUT turns this .SAL file into this .ASM file:

```
CODE_SEG SEGMENT
         ASSUME   CS:CODE_SEG,DS:CODE_SEG
         ORG      100H
;NTRY:   $DO
ENTRY:
$$DO1:
              INC      BX
              CMP      [BX],255
;        $ENDDO   NE
         JE $$DO1
TEST:    INT      20H
CODE_SEG ENDS
         END      ENTRY
```

The $ENDDO NE has been converted into JE $$DO1. Once again, SALUT has let us do what we want to do and made it a little easier. Besides ending loops with JNE or a similar jump, you can end with the LOOP command (or any of the other loop commands, such as LOOPNZ or LOOPE).

In the following example, we loop up to 20 times, searching for the first non-255 element of some string. If that element is found, we leave the loop with the command $LEAVE. The CMP before the $LEAVE NE sets up the flags to be tested:

```
CODE_SEG SEGMENT
         ASSUME   CS:CODE_SEG,DS:CODE_SEG
         ORG      100H
ENTRY:   MOV      CX,20
```

```
        $DO
        INC      BX
        CMP      [BX],255
        $LEAVE   NE
        $ENDDO   LOOP
TEST:   INT      20H
CODE_SEG ENDS
        END      ENTRY
```

Here is how that .SAL file looks after SALUT is through:

```
CODE_SEG SEGMENT
        ASSUME   CS:CODE_SEG,DS:CODE_SEG
        ORG      100H
ENTRY:  MOV      CX,20
;       $DO
$$DO1:
            INC      BX
            CMP      [BX],255
;       $LEAVE   NE
        JNE $$EN1
;       $ENDDO   LOOP
        LOOP $$DO1
$$EN1:
TEST:   INT      20H
CODE_SEG ENDS
        END      ENTRY
```

If the $LEAVE condition is satisfied, then control jumps outside the loop, to a point just after the LOOP command.

SALUT Searches

So far in SALUT, we have examined the $IF, $ELSE, $ENDIF, $DO, and $ENDDO commands. SALUT can become more complex than that, however. In particular, SALUT lets you do what it calls a SEARCH. Whenever you have a loop with two exits, and the reason you exited the loop makes a difference, you can use a SEARCH. The problem with SEARCH is that it is no longer intuitive, as $IF and $DO have been. For every SEARCH, you need these commands:

```
$SEARCH
$EXITIF
$ORELSE
$ENDLOOP
$ENDSRCH
```

One such case where there are two exits from a loop, and it matters which one was taken, is with a command like REPE CMPSB. If you leave this loop because you found an unlike element, CX will not be zero. If, at the end of this loop, CX is zero, all the elements in the strings being compared matched.

A SEARCH Example

In the following example, we check through a buffer of characters (BUFFER) for the string of letters held in STRING. We do this by advancing through BUFFER, starting at each character in it and seeing if we can match the 16 characters of string in a row. If not, we move on through BUFFER until we get to its end.

This kind of example is perfect for a $SEARCH. However, unless you are very used to SALUT, it is much easier simply to code a $SEARCH using your own labels and jumps. In the end, SALUT makes the code in a $SEARCH easier to read for SALUT users, but commands like $EXITIF and $ORELSE don't make the code easier to the uninitiated. In particular, it is instructive to work through the comments of the example since they trace the flow of command. (In the same way, it is instructive to work through the SALUT flow charts in the Macro Assembler manual if you decide SALUT is for you.)

```
CODE_SEG SEGMENT
        COMMENT* This program looks for STRING in BUFFER. *
        ASSUME  CS:CODE_SEG,DS:CODE_SEG
        ORG     100H
ENTRY:  JMP     PROG
        STRING  DB   'Now is the time.'
        STR_LEN DW   16                   ;Length of STRING
        BUFFER  DB   'Now is NOT the time. Now is the time. Not now.'
        BUFFER_END LABEL WORD
        SUCCESS DB   'SUCCESS!$'
        FAILURE DB   'FAILURE!$'
PROG:   LEA     DI,BUFFER                ;Set up the pointers.
        LEA     SI,STRING

        $SEARCH
            MOV     CX,STR_LEN           ;Check if we can find whole string.
            REPE    CMPSB                ;Repeat WHILE Equal, 2 possible exits.
            CMP     CX,0                 ;CX=0 → Whole string was found.

        $EXITIF E                        ;If NE, go to $ORELSE. If E, Success!
            LEA     DX,SUCCESS           ; .. Success Block: string was found.
            MOV     AH,9                 ;  : After Success Block go to $ENDSRC H
            INT     21H                  ; .:

        $ORELSE                          ;$ORELSE: No success yet.
            INC     DI                   ;The code here is executed before
            LEA     SI,STRING            ; the $ENDLOOP test. We check here to
            CMP     DI,BUFFER_END        ; see if there's more BUFFER to examine.

        $ENDLOOP GE                      ;$ENDLOOP: Loop again? End if GE.
            LEA     DX,FAILURE           ; .. No more looping: Failure Block.
            MOV     AH,9                 ;  : After this go to $ENDSRCH.
            INT     21H                  ; .:
```

```
        $ENDSRCH

        INT     20H
CODE_SEG ENDS
        END     ENTRY
```

The $SEARCH permits you to break up your code nicely in a success block and a failure block, as the comments above signify. Here is the resulting .ASM file:

```
CODE_SEG SEGMENT
        COMMENT* This program looks for STRING in BUFFER. *
        ASSUME  CS:CODE_SEG,DS:CODE_SEG
        ORG     100H
ENTRY:  JMP     PROG
        STRING  DB   'Now is the time.'
        STR_LEN DW   16                 ;Length of STRING
        BUFFER  DB   'Now is NOT the time. Now is the time. Not now.'
        BUFFER_END LABEL WORD
        SUCCESS DB   'SUCCESS!$'
        FAILURE DB   'FAILURE!$'
PROG:   LEA     DI,BUFFER               ;Set up the pointers.
        LEA     SI,STRING

;       $SEARCH
$$DO1:
            MOV     CX,STR_LEN          ;Check if we can find whole string.
            REPE    CMPSB               ;Repeat WHILE Equal, 2 possible exits.
            CMP     CX,0                ;CX=0 → Whole string was found.

;       $EXITIF E                       ;If NE, go to $ORELSE. If E, Success!
        JNE $$IF1

            LEA     DX,SUCCESS          ; .. Success Block: string was found.
            MOV     AH,9                ;  : After Success Block go to $ENDSRCH
            INT     21H                 ; .:

;       $ORELSE                         ;$ORELSE: No success yet.
        JMP SHORT $$SR1
$$IF1:
            INC     DI                  ;The code here is executed before
            LEA     SI,STRING           ; the $ENDLOOP test. We check here to
            CMP     DI,BUFFER_END       ; see if there's more BUFFER to examine.

;       $ENDLOOP GE                     ;$ENDLOOP: Loop again? End if GE.
        JNGE $$DO1
            LEA     DX,FAILURE          ; .. No more looping: Failure Block.
            MOV     AH,9                ;  : After this go to $ENDSRCH.
            INT     21H                 ; .:

;       $ENDSRCH
$$SR1:

        INT     20H
CODE_SEG ENDS
        END     ENTRY
```

Finally, for comparison, here is the same .ASM file with labels added that make more sense:

```
PROG:   LEA     DI,BUFFER               ;Set up the pointers.
        LEA     SI,STRING
TOP_OF_LOOP:
            MOV     CX,STR_LEN          ;Check if we can find whole string.
            REPE    CMPSB               ;Repeat WHILE Equal, 2 possible exits.
            CMP     CX,0                ;CX=0 → Whole string was found.
        JNE NO_MATCH
            LEA     DX,SUCCESS          ; .. Success Block: string was found.
            MOV     AH,9                ;  : After Success Block go to $ENDSRCH
            INT     21H                 ; .:
        JMP SHORT EXIT
NO_MATCH:
            INC     DI                  ;The code here is executed before
            LEA     SI,STRING           ; the $ENDLOOP test. We check here to
            CMP     DI,BUFFER_END       ; see if there's more BUFFER to examine.
        JNGE TOP_OF_LOOP
            LEA     DX,FAILURE          ; .. No more looping: Failure Block.
            MOV     AH,9                ;  : After this go to $ENDSRCH.
            INT     21H                 ; .:
EXIT:
        INT     20H
```

It is a good idea to at least give SALUT a try. You may find that it fits your programming style and needs perfectly.

CONCLUSION

No single example program can encompass the number of methods we have covered in this chapter. Instead, it is recommended that you type in a few of the smaller examples and try something such as macro libraries or groups for yourself. Give it a try—they're often very useful.

Chapter 8

The 8087

INTRODUCTION

Starting with MASM release 2.0, the macro assembler can assemble more than 60 8087 commands. This is an immense improvement over the old days, when you had to include 8087 OP codes in your program explicitly.

The 8087 is the math-coprocessor designed and built to function with the 8088 that is already inside the IBM PC. The 8088 itself has only minimal math capability. For example, it can multiply up to results not larger than 32 bits, and divide numbers of up to only 32 bits by 16 bits, generating a 16-bit quotient and a 16-bit remainder. This type of division means that we cannot count on more than 16 bits of accuracy in the result, or four decimal places. In the modern world, four decimal places does not carry you far.

Furthermore, the 8088 can only handle integer arithmetic. If you want to work with floating point numbers, you have to write your own algorithms and implement them. In general, this is quite difficult. In addition, floating point simulations are usually very slow, and we want to do more on a computer anyway. It would be better if we could do sines and cosines, logs and natural logs, square roots and powers as well. It is for such a purpose that the 8087 was designed. It turns out that simulations on the 8088 are at least a factor of 100 times slower than the real thing on the 8087. And the 8087 is more accurate.

The internal accuracy of the 8087 is considerable. There are eight stack registers (it is a stack-oriented chip) in the 8087, and each one is 80 bits long (ten bytes). For integers, this means an accuracy up to 18 digits, and for floating point numbers an accuracy up to 16 digits. If your PC has an 8087 in it, you too can enjoy this type of accuracy.

GETTING STARTED

The assembler does not recognize 8087 commands immediately; instead, you must include the .8087 pseudo-OP in your .ASM files:

```
.8087
CODE_SEG         SEGMENT
ASSUME   CS:CODE_SEG,DS:CODE_SEG
ORG      100H
         :
```

or use the /R parameter:

```
A>MASM TEST; /R
```

to make sure the 8087 code is assembled. If neither of these commands is used, the assembler will give you syntax errors.

Using the .8087 pseudo-OP is preferred because including it in the .ASM file itself means it won't be forgotten when it comes time to assemble. A great boon to us is that DEBUG has also been written to Unassemble 8087 commands, so we can use it as before.

The assembler not only assembles 8087 commands, it also includes a WAIT command to the 8088 for each one (with the exception of one or two commands detailed later). This means that the 8088 will wait until the 8087 is done processing before proceeding. When we use DEBUG later on, we will see these WAITs.

ADDING INTEGERS

Let's begin immediately with one of the simplest of examples: adding two integers. In this example, we will add 3 and 1. Here's the code:

```
CODE_SEG SEGMENT
         ASSUME   CS:CODE_SEG,DS:CODE_SEG
         ORG      100H
ENTRY:   JMP      PROG
         OPERAND1 DW      3
         OPERAND2 DW      1
         RESULT   DW      0
PROG:    FILD     OPERAND1
         FIADD    OPERAND2
         FISTP    RESULT
         INT      20H
CODE_SEG ENDS
         END      ENTRY
```

Everything looks the same as usual until we get to the body of the program:

```
PROG:    FILD     OPERAND1
         FIADD    OPERAND2
         FISTP    RESULT
```

where the 8087 commands are. Every 8087 command begins with an F, as these do (and no 8088 commands begin with an F). The first command,

```
PROG:    FILD     OPERAND1          ←
         FIADD    OPERAND2
         FISTP    RESULT
```

tells the 8087 to load the integer number at OPERAND1 in memory onto the top of its stack. FILD is the integer load, as opposed to the floating point load, FLD. The next command,

```
PROG:    FILD     OPERAND1
         FIADD    OPERAND2          ←
         FISTP    RESULT
```

is the instruction for integer addition. Floating point addition, which we'll cover later, would use FADD. In this case, OPERAND2 is added to the value in the top of the 8087's stack. This is the result we want, so we store this number in memory, at the location RESULT:

```
PROG:    FILD     OPERAND1
         FIADD    OPERAND2
         FISTP    RESULT            ←
```

This command is an integer store—as opposed to FST, the floating point store—and pop command. The number on the top of the stack is stored and then the stack is popped, leaving it free for further operations.

Popping the stack is an important part of any program; if you do not, the stack will fill, and your calculations will not be done until you start to pop some numbers off. In this case we store the result in memory so we can take a look at it with DEBUG. For this example we will use the shortest integer format available, one-word integers. These are defined with DW:

```
OPERAND1 DW      3
OPERAND2 DW      1
RESULT   DW      0
```

This is only one of the six different available formats, and we'll cover the others soon. We can assemble this program since we've included the 8087 pseudo-OP:

```
CODE_SEG SEGMENT
.8087               ←
         ASSUME   CS:CODE_SEG,DS:CODE_SEG
         ORG      100H
ENTRY:   JMP      PROG
         OPERAND1 DW      3
                  :
                  :
```

All we need to do is to type MASM TEST;, link it with LINK TEST, and create TEST.COM with EXE2BIN TEST TEST.COM (and make sure our PC has an 8087 in it). This .COM file can be debugged this way:

```
A>DEBUG TEST.COM


-R
AX=0000  BX=0000  CX=001A  DX=0000  SP=FFFE  BP=0000  SI=0000  DI=0000
DS=090B  ES=090B  SS=090B  CS=090B  IP=0100   NV UP DI PL NZ NA PO NC
090B:0100 EB07          JMP     0109     ← Here's our first jump.
-T
AX=0000  BX=0000  CX=001A  DX=0000  SP=FFFE  BP=0000  SI=0000  DI=0000
DS=090B  ES=090B  SS=090B  CS=090B  IP=0109   NV UP DI PL NZ NA PO NC
090B:0109 9B            WAIT
```

Let's take a look at the rest of the program by unassembling it:

```
-U
090B:0109 9B            WAIT
090B:010A DF060301      FILD     WORD PTR [0103]
090B:010E 9B            WAIT
090B:010F DE060501      FIADD    WORD PTR [0105]
090B:0113 9B            WAIT
090B:0114 DF1E0701      FISTP    WORD PTR [0107]
090B:0118 CD20          INT      20
090B:011A 36            SS:
090B:011B 9C            PUSHF
090B:011C F6FF          IDIV     BH
090B:011E 76C2          JBE      00E2
090B:0120 9A9A003F0B    CALL     0B3F:009A
090B:0125 FF76C2        PUSH     [BP-3E]
090B:0128 E85ADE        CALL     DF85
```

As you can see, the assembler has added the required wait states for the 8088 while it waits for the 8087 to finish processing. From the above addresses, we see that OPERAND1 is at [103], OPERAND2 at [105], and RESULT at [107]. Let's take a look at them by dumping them:

```
-D103
090B:0103   03 00 01 00 00-00 9B DF 06 03 01 9B DE             ......._....^
090B:0110   06 05 01 9B DF 1E 07 01-CD 20 36 9C F6 FF 76 C2    ...._...M 6.v.vB
090B:0120   9A 9A 00 3F 0B FF 76 C2-E8 5A DE E8 CF E5 E9 CB    ...?..vBhZ^hOeiK
090B:0130   00 A1 9A F6 2B 06 98 F6-89 46 C2 A1 4E F6 3B 06    .!.v+..v.FB!Nv;.
090B:0140   98 F6 B9 00 00 72 01 41-3B 06 9A F6 BA 00 00 73    .v9..r.A;..v:..s
090B:0150   01 42 22 CA D1 E9 73 16-BF CA F6 BE C6 FE B9 11    .B"JQis.?Jv>F~9.
090B:0160   00 1E 07 FC F3 A5 9A 79-01 FE 09 E9 89 00 E8 1F    ...¦s%.y.~.i..h.
090B:0170   E1 D1 E8 72 03 E9 7F 00-A1 4E F6 3B 06 98 F6 73    aQhr.i..!Nv;..vs
090B:0180   18 89 46                                           ..F
```

The 3 and 1 in OPERAND1 and OPERAND2 are seen immediately. (Recall that the 8088 stores the low byte at a lower address so they appear as 03 00 01 00 instead of 00 03 00 01.) The place for RESULT holds 0. If we execute the entire program with a Go command, we'll load OPERAND1, add OPERAND2 to it, and then store the result in RESULT. Let's execute the program and dump the results:

```
-G118           ← Execute to the INT 20H instruction.
AX=0000  BX=0000  CX=001A  DX=0000  SP=FFFE  BP=0000  SI=0000 DI=0000
DS=090B ES=]090B  SS=090B  CS=090B  IP=0118   NV UP DI PL NZ NA PO NC
090B:0118 CD20          INT     20

-D103
```

And take a look at RESULT:

```
                          v
090B:0103   03 00 01 00 04-00 9B DF 06 03 01 9B DE             ......._....^
090B:0110   06 05 01 9B DF 1E 07 01-CD 20 36 9C F6 FF 76 C2    ...._...M 6.v.vB
090B:0120   9A 9A 00 3F 0B FF 76 C2-E8 5A DE E8 CF E5 E9 CB    ...?..vBhZ^hOeiK
090B:0130   00 A1 9A F6 2B 06 98 F6-89 46 C2 A1 4E F6 3B 06    .!.v+..v.FB!Nv;.
090B:0140   98 F6 B9 00 00 72 01 41-3B 06 9A F6 BA 00 00 73    .v9..r.A;..v:..s
090B:0150   01 42 22 CA D1 E9 73 16-BF CA F6 BE C6 FE B9 11    .B"JQis.?Jv>F~9.
090B:0160   00 1E 07 FC F3 A5 9A 79-01 FE 09 E9 89 00 E8 1F    ...¦s%.y.~.i..h.
090B:0170   E1 D1 E8 72 03 E9 7F 00-A1 4E F6 3B 06 98 F6 73    aQhr.i..!Nv;..vs
090B:0180   18 89 46                                           ..F
-Q
```

Now the location RESULT holds 4, as it should. Since the format of word integers is so simple, this is just about the easiest example we could choose. The next easiest example, of course, is subtraction.

SUBTRACTING INTEGERS

All we have to do here is to replace FIADD with the logical counterpart, FISUB:

```
CODE_SEG SEGMENT
.8087
         ASSUME   CS:CODE_SEG,DS:CODE_SEG
         ORG      100H
ENTRY:   JMP      PROG
         OPERAND1 DW      3
         OPERAND2 DW      1
         RESULT   DW      0
PROG:    FILD     OPERAND1
         FISUB    OPERAND2          ←
         FISTP    RESULT
         INT      20H
CODE_SEG ENDS
         END      ENTRY
```

From this we can make a .COM file and use DEBUG as before:

```
-R
AX=0000  BX=0000  CX=001A  DX=0000  SP=FFFE  BP=0000  SI=0000  DI=0000
DS=090B  ES=090B  SS=090B  CS=090B  IP=0100   NV UP DI PL NZ NA PO NC
090B:0100 EB07          JMP     0109
-T
AX=0000  BX=0000  CX=001A  DX=0000  SP=FFFE  BP=0000  SI=0000  DI=0000
DS=090B  ES=090B  SS=090B  CS=090B  IP=0109   NV UP DI PL NZ NA PO NC
090B:0109 9B            WAIT
-U
090B:0109 9B            WAIT
090B:010A DF060301      FILD    WORD PTR [0103]
090B:010E 9B            WAIT
090B:010F DE260501      FISUB   WORD PTR [0105]
090B:0113 9B            WAIT
090B:0114 DF1E0701      FISTP   WORD PTR [0107]
090B:0118 CD20          INT     20
090B:011A 6F            DB      6F
090B:011B 8B4606        MOV     AX,[BP+06]
090B:011E 257F00        AND     AX,007F
090B:0121 8B5E0A        MOV     BX,[BP+0A]
090B:0124 89470E        MOV     [BX+0E],AX
090B:0127 8166068OFF    AND     WORD PTR [BP+06],FF80
```

Here's how the data area looks before we run the program (note the 0 at [107]):

```
-D103
090B:0103  03 00 01 00 00-00 9B DF 06 03 01 9B DE            ........_....^
090B:0110  26 05 01 9B DF 1E 07 01-CD 20 6F 8B 46 06 25 7F   &..._...M o.F.%.
090B:0120  00 8B 5E 0A 89 47 0E 81-66 06 80 FF 8B 46 06 89   ..^..G..f....F..
090B:0130  47 0A 8B 46 08 89 47 0C-53 C4 46 06 06 50 B8 00   G..F..G.SDF..P8.
090B:0140  00 50 9A EB 03 C1 0C 89-5E 06 8C 46 08 8B 5E 0A   .P.k.A..^..F..^.
090B:0150  8B 47 02 89 46 F6 53 50-9A 06 00 43 09 06 53 8B   .G..FvSP...C..S.
090B:0160  5E F4 FF 77 04 9A 50 03-C1 0C 8B 5E 0A 89 47 06   ^t.w..P.A..^..G.
090B:0170  8B 76 0A 8B 7C 06 8B 4C-04 2B CF 8B 5E F6 8D 39   .v..|..L.+O.^v.9
090B:0180  B0 00 1E                                          0..
```

If we run the program we can find that 3−1 is indeed 2:

```
-G118

AX=0000  BX=0000  CX=001A  DX=0000  SP=FFFE  BP=0000  SI=0000  DI=0000
DS=090B  ES=090B  SS=090B  CS=090B  IP=0118   NV UP DI PL NZ NA PO NC
090B:0118 CD20          INT     20
```

```
-D103                             v
090B:0103   03 00 01 00 02-00 9B DF 06 03 01 9B DE              .......\_....^
090B:0110   26 05 01 9B DF 1E 07 01-CD 20 6F 8B 46 06 25 7F   &...\_...M o.F.%.
090B:0120   00 8B 5E 0A 89 47 0E 81-66 06 80 FF 8B 46 06 89   ..^..G..f....F..
090B:0130   47 0A 8B 46 08 89 47 0C-53 C4 46 06 06 50 B8 00   G..F..G.SDF..P8.
090B:0140   00 50 9A EB 03 C1 0C 89-5E 06 8C 46 08 8B 5E 0A   .P.k.A..^..F..^.
090B:0150   8B 47 02 89 46 F6 53 50-9A 06 00 43 09 06 53 8B   .G..FvSP...C..S.
090B:0160   5E F4 FF 77 04 9A 50 03-C1 0C 8B 5E 0A 89 47 06   ^t.w..P.A..^..G.
090B:0170   8B 76 0A 8B 7C 06 8B 4C-04 2B CF 8B 5E F6 8D 39   .v..|..L.+O.^v.9
090B:0180   B0 00 1E                                          0..
-Q
```

The last two examples here are multiplication and division.

MULTIPLYING AND DIVIDING INTEGERS

As might be expected from our previous programs, there are two corresponding commands for integer multiplication and division, FIMUL and FIDIV. We can multiply 3 by 2, for example, with this program:

```
CODE_SEG SEGMENT
.8087
         ASSUME   CS:CODE_SEG,DS:CODE_SEG
         ORG      100H
ENTRY:   JMP      PROG
         OPERAND1 DW      3
         OPERAND2 DW      2
         RESULT   DW      0
PROG:    FILD     OPERAND1
         FIMUL    OPERAND2          ←
         FISTP    RESULT
         INT      20H
CODE_SEG ENDS
         END      ENTRY
```

to find 6 deposited in RESULT.

What happens, though, when we try dividing 3 by 2 in integer arithmetic? For example, what if we did this:

```
CODE_SEG SEGMENT
.8087
         ASSUME  CS:CODE_SEG,DS:CODE_SEG
         ORG     100H
ENTRY:   JMP     PROG
         OPERAND1 DW      3
         OPERAND2 DW      2
         RESULT  DW       0
PROG:    FILD    OPERAND1
         FIDIV   OPERAND2          ←
         FISTP   RESULT
         INT     20H
CODE_SEG ENDS
         END     ENTRY
```

and then checked RESULT? We can create a .COM file from the above program, called FIDIV.COM, and DEBUG it:

```
-R
AX=0000  BX=0000  CX=001A  DX=0000  SP=FFFE  BP=0000  SI=0000  DI=0000
DS=090B  ES=090B  SS=090B  CS=090B  IP=0100   NV UP DI PL NZ NA PO NC
090B:0100 EB07          JMP     0109    ← Jump over the data.
-T

AX=0000  BX=0000  CX=001A  DX=0000  SP=FFFE  BP=0000  SI=0000  DI=0000
DS=090B  ES=090B  SS=090B  CS=090B  IP=0109   NV UP DI PL NZ NA PO NC
090B:0109 9B            WAIT
-U
090B:0109 9B            WAIT
090B:010A DF060301      FILD    WORD PTR [0103]
090B:010E 9B            WAIT
090B:010F DE360501      FIDIV   WORD PTR [0105]          ← Our division.
090B:0113 9B            WAIT
090B:0114 DF1E0701      FISTP   WORD PTR [0107]
090B:0118 CD20          INT     20
090B:011A 6F            DB      6F
090B:011B 8B4606        MOV     AX,[BP+06]
090B:011E 257F00        AND     AX,007F
090B:0121 8B5E0A        MOV     BX,[BP+0A]
090B:0124 89470E        MOV     [BX+0E],AX
090B:0127 816606B0FF    AND     WORD PTR [BP+06],FF80
```

Once again, we check to make sure RESULT at [107] is zero before starting:

```
-D103
090B:0103           03 00 02 00 00-00 9B DF 06 03 01 9B DE          ......._....^
090B:0110  36 05 01 9B DF 1E 07 01-CD 20 6F 8B 46 06 25 7F  6..._...M o.F.%.
090B:0120  00 8B 5E 0A 89 47 0E 81-66 06 80 FF 8B 46 06 89  ..^..G..f....F..
090B:0130  47 0A 8B 46 08 89 47 0C-53 C4 46 06 06 50 B8 00  G..F..G.SDF..P8.
090B:0140  00 50 9A EB 03 C1 0C 89-5E 06 8C 46 08 8B 5E 0A  .P.k.A..^..F..^.
```

```
090B:0150  8B 47 02 89 46 F6 53 50-9A 06 00 43 09 06 53 8B   .G..FvSP...C..S.
090B:0160  5E F4 FF 77 04 9A 50 03-C1 0C 8B 5E 0A 89 47 06   ^t.w..P.A..^..G.
090B:0170  8B 76 0A 8B 7C 06 8B 4C-04 2B CF 8B 5E F6 8D 39   .v..|..L.+O.^v.9
090B:0180  B0 00 1E                                           0..
```

and then run the program to check RESULT:

```
-G118
AX=0000  BX=0000  CX=001A  DX=0000  SP=FFFE  BP=0000  SI=0000  DI=0000
DS=090B  ES=090B  SS=090B  CS=090B  IP=0118   NV UP DI PL NZ NA PO NC
090B:0118 CD20          INT     20
-D103
090B:0103  03 00 02 00 02-00 9B DF 06 03 01 9B DE            ......._....^
090B:0110  36 05 01 9B DF 1E 07 01-CD 20 6F 8B 46 06 25 7F   6..._...M o.F.%.
090B:0120  00 8B 5E 0A 89 47 0E 81-66 06 80 FF 8B 46 06 89   ..^..G..f....F..
090B:0130  47 0A 8B 46 08 89 47 0C-53 C4 46 06 06 50 B8 00   G..F..G.SDF..P8.
090B:0140  00 50 9A EB 03 C1 0C 89-5E 06 8C 46 08 8B 5E 0A   .P.K.A..^..F..^.
090B:0150  8B 47 02 89 46 F6 53 50-9A 06 00 43 09 06 53 8B   .G..FvSP...C..S.
090B:0160  5E F4 FF 77 04 9A 50 03-C1 0C 8B 5E 0A 89 47 06   ^t.w..P.A..^..G.
090B:0170  8B 76 0A 8B 7C 06 8B 4C-04 2B CF 8B 5E F6 8D 39   .v..|..L.+O.^v.9
090B:0180  B0 00 1E                                           0..
-Q
```

Apparently, 3 divided by 2 appears to be 2. The cause for this is easy to find, however. In integer arithmetic, numbers are rounded off. When we load 3 with FILD, it is stored in the 8087 stack in **temporary real format**, a format that uses the full 80 bits the 8087 is capable of. Almost never, however, are all of these 80 bits seen outside the 8087. They are used for internal accuracy only. When we divided by 2, we got a result of 1.5, but FIDIV then rounds up any fractional answers by adding .5 to the result and then discarding the fractional part. This process is what gave us the 2 we finally see. Even if we had used FDIV, which would have given an answer of 1.5, FISTP rounds numbers off in just the same way before storing them—by adding .5 to the number in the stack top and then discarding the fractional part.

This raises the issue of how the 8087 stores numbers, and how we can convert from one format to another for output. In itself, this subject takes a little study.

8087 INTEGER FORMATS AND TWO'S COMPLEMENT NOTATION

We already know one format used by the 8087—word integers, defined with DW:

```
Bit #   15 14    0
        [  |      ]   One Word
```

These integers are stored in 16 bits. The left-most bit is used to store the integer's sign, so what is left to hold the number itself are the remaining 15 bits, giving a range of −32,768 to 32,767 (the range is unsymmetric because zero is counted as a positive number). These numbers are stored in just the same way as are the normal numbers the PC operates on. When they are negative, they are stored in what is called two's complement notation, which will be reviewed below.

The next size integer is the **short integer**, which is 32 bits long, and defined with DD:

```
SHORT_INT   DD   12345678
```

These integers can range from $-2x10^9$ to $2x10^9$. Here's how their bits are stored:

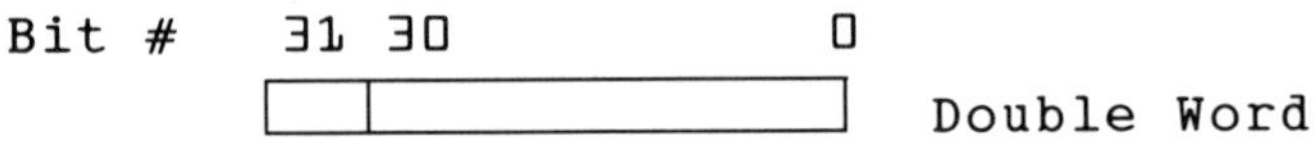

```
Bit #    31 30                 0
        |  |                   |    Double Word
```

The sign bit is held in bit 31, the leftmost bit, as usual.

Finally, if you really need **big integers**, there is the **long integer** format. This format is 64 bits, and can hold integers from -9×10^{18} to 9×10^{18}. If you need numbers larger than this, you must go to floating point notation. As it is, the 8087 can preserve 18 decimal places of accuracy with long integers. Long integers are defined with DQ, Define Quadword, since four words make up 64 bits:

```
LONG_INT DQ 123456789987654321
```

The bit pattern of Long Integers is as expected, with 63 bits (bits 0–62) of integer and one sign bit (bit 63):

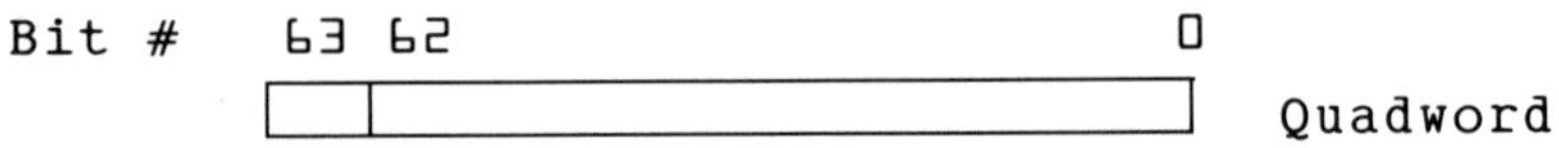

```
Bit #    63 62                            0
        |  |                              |    Quadword
```

We can imagine how to store positive numbers. For example, if we wanted to store 15, 0FH, in a word integer, here is how we'd do it:

```
000FH or 0000000000001111
```

When we want to store a negative number, however, the sign bit will be set, so the numbers 0000000000000000 to 0111111111111111 (0 to 7FFFH) are positive, and the numbers from 1111111111111111 to 1000000000000000 which represent the range from −1 to −8000H are negative.

NEGATIVE NUMBERS AND TWO'S COMPLEMENT NOTATION

It seems odd to have a number like 1111111111111111 (0FFFFH) equal to −1. If it were only up to the sign bit, we might expect that 1000000000000001 would be equal to −1. In fact, FFFFH is chosen so that the math will work. If we add −1 and 1, we expect to come up with 0. If we add 1 and 0FFFFH, we get:

```
 FFFFH
  +  1
------
10000H
```

in other words, 0 with a carry of 1. If we ignore the carry, as we do in signed integer calculations, we will end up with the correct answer of 0. Although we do ignore the carry, it is possible we might add two positive numbers such that the result exceeds the word's capacity for positive numbers. In this case, the top bit would be set, apparently leaving us with a negative number. For example, we might add 7FF9H + 3FH = 8038H, which has the top bit set. In this case, a new flag, the **Overflow Flag** is set, and we can check that in our calculations.

How do you find a number's two's complement? How, for example, can we find that −1 = 0FFFFH? There is a simple rule for it—simply flip all the bits in the number (with NOT) and add 1. This is exactly what NEG does.

We can see why this works if we flip the bits of 2 and try to find −2. By flipping the bits, we would get 1111111111111101; if we added that to 2, we would not end up with 0, but with a full house, 1111111111111111 (FFFFH). To make this FFFFH into 0 (and ignoring the carry), we have to add 1:

```
1111111111111101  ← NOT 2
+              10 ← 2
+               1
----------------
                0  (ignoring carry)
```

This means that −2 must be equal to 1111111111111101 + 1, or 1111111111111110 (FFFEH) as our formula predicts, since when we add 2 to it, we get 0:

```
1111111111111101  ]     = -2
+               1 ]
+              10
----------------
                0  (ignoring carry)
```

When you want to work with negative integers in either the 8088 or the 8087, this is the way to do it.

BINARY CODED DECIMAL

Another way of storing numbers in a format recognizable to the 8087 is in **Binary Coded Decimal** or BCD. BCD is particularly easy to work with for most people since it looks just like base 10 numbers. BCD numbers are 18 bytes long (defined with DT, Define Tenbytes) and the largest allowable digit is 9. Again, however, the leftmost bit, bit 79, is used for the sign. Unlike two's complement math, the only thing different about two numbers like 4 and −4 is the sign bit. If a BCD number is negative, the first byte is 80H; if positive, it is 0:

```
NUMBER   DT 00123456789999999999H
```

The only difference with BCD numbers is that you have to load them with FBLD instead of FILD, and store them in memory with FBSTP (store and pop) instead of FISTP. Here is a program that will give a result, in RESULT, of zero:

```
CODE_SEG SEGMENT
.8087
        ASSUME  CS:CODE_SEG,DS:CODE_SEG
        ORG     100H
ENTRY:  JMP     PROG
        OPERAND1 DT      00123456789999999999H
        OPERAND2 DT      80123456789999999999H   ;Note this is -1xOPERAND1.
        RESULT  DW      0
PROG:   FBLD    OPERAND1        ;Load the two BCD numbers.
        FBLD    OPERAND2
        FADD                    ;Add Stack top plus number below it.
        FISTP   RESULT          ;Store RESULT as an integer.
        INT     20H
CODE_SEG ENDS
        END     ENTRY
```

Finally, we will look at the last of the 8087 formats, floating point.

FLOATING POINT NUMBERS

Floating point calculations make up most of the work for the 8087. The format for such numbers, however, takes a little getting used to. If we have a number like 32.1, we know that we have $3x10^1$ plus $2x10^0$ and $1x10^{-1}$. On the other hand, the computer is a binary machine, so a number like 10.5 must be stored as 1×2^3 plus 1×2^1 plus 1×2^{-1} or 1010.1, where the point is a binary point. It is possible to store any number in binary that can be stored in decimal, it just takes more places. For instance, 0.75 can be broken down into 1/2 + 1/4, or $2^{-1} + 2^{-2}$, so .75 = .11B.

Normalized Format

The numbers stored in the 8087 are all "normalized," which means they appear with the binary point near the beginning; so 1010.1 would appear like this: 1.0101×2^3 . To expand this, just move the binary point three places to the right, giving us 1010.1 again. You can see that the first digit in any normalized binary number is always one. INTEL took advantage of that to make the leading 1 **implicit**. In other words, all that is stored of the **significand** is 0101. The exponent is still three—but to make matters even more complex, all exponents are stored after being added to some offset or **bias**.

For a short real, this bias is 7FH, or 127. For long reals, this number is 3FFH, or 1023. If our number is going to be stored as a short real, the exponent will be 3 + 127 = 130 = 82H. Finally, the first bit of any number is going to be the sign bit. Real numbers, like BCD numbers, are NOT stored in two's complement notation. If the sign bit is 1, the number is negative, if it is 0, the number is positive; that's the only distinction. The short real format looks like this:

```
Bit #   31 30     23 22                 0
          |_|_______|____________________|
           S  Exp.   Significand.
```

So 10.5 = 1010.1B will look like this:

```
                 Sign Bit
                    |
                    v
                  01000001001010000000000000000000
                   |_______| |____________________|
 [Exponent + Bias =   82H]       [Significand]
```

This can be made into Hex by grouping every four binary digits together:

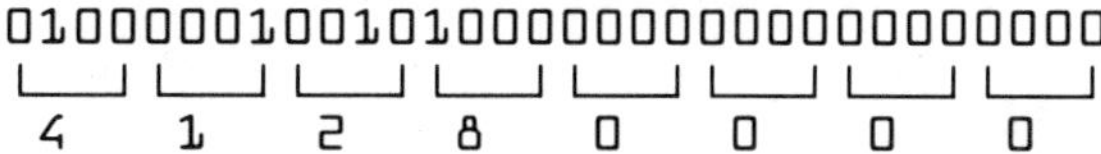

So 10.5 is stored as 41280000H. In fact, due to the the 8088's method of storing low bytes first inside a word and then low words first, 10.5 actually shows up in memory as 00 00 28 41.

This number seems very far from 10.5, and converting back to 10.5 for output can be quite difficult, here IBM gives us a hand. On the IBM assembler disk there is a library called IBMUTIL.LIB. This contains a number of programs to convert 8087 formats, and one of them converts to ASCII. We will use this library routine ourselves shortly. Before we do, though, let's make sure we review the format for long reals:

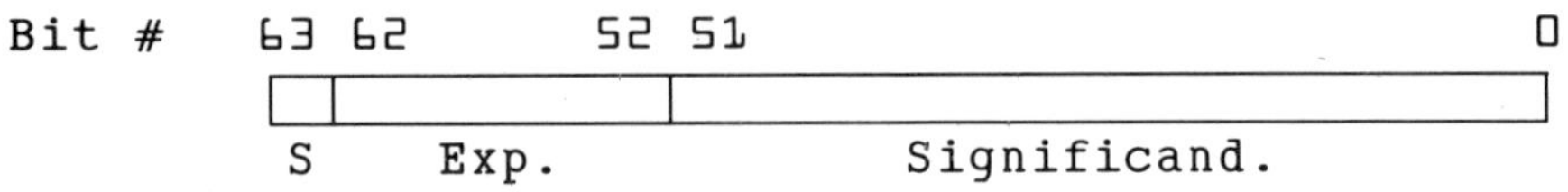

```
Bit #    63 62        52 51                                0
         ┌─┬──────────┬──────────────────────────────────┐
         └─┴──────────┴──────────────────────────────────┘
          S    Exp.                Significand.
```

Short reals have one sign bit, eight exponent bits, and 23 significand bits, for a total of 32 (define short reals with DD). Long reals have a sign bit, 11 bits of exponent (with a bias of 1023 (3FFH)) and 52 bits of significand, for a total of 64 bits (define long reals with DQ, Define Quadword).

Table 8.1 shows the values that each of the formats can hold.

Table 8.1 Ranges for the 8087 Formats

Format	Bits	Range
Word Integer	16	−32,768 to 32,767
Short Integer	32	-2×10^{9} to 2×10^{9}
Long Integer	64	-9×10^{18} to 9×10^{18}
BCD	80	−9...9 to 9...9 (18 nines)
Short Real	32	$8.43\times10-^{37}$ to 3.37×10^{38}
Long Real	64	$3.4\times10-^{4,932}$ to $1.2\times10^{4,932}$

IBMUTIL.LIB

To print out results from the 8087, IBM provided some assistance in the library IBMUTIL.LIB. In addition, there are programs you can link to that convert ASCII strings into floating point format. This conversion, ASCII to floating point, is done by the program $I8_INPUT. You can link this program into your own.

To use this and other IBMUTIL routines, you must enclose the data (ASCII strings and floating point numbers) in a segment named DATA, and put it into DGROUP, as shown below. Also shown is the segment MATHCODE, which must surround the call to $18_INPUT.

```
DATA     SEGMENT WORD PUBLIC 'DATA'
ASCIINUMBER DB 17 DUP(0)
DATA     ENDS
DGROUP   GROUP DATA

MATHCODE SEGMENT BYTE PUBLIC 'CODE'
EXTRN    $I8_INPUT
:
CALL     $I8_INPUT
: MATHCODE ENDS
```

You must expect all registers except the stack and segment registers to be destroyed. To convert from ASCII to numeric format, the input and output registers are listed in Table 8.2

Table 8.2 Input and Output for $IN_INPUT

Input

DS:SI	Address of ASCII characters to convert.
DS:DI	Address of 8 byte area for double precision.
AX	=0
BX	=Radix desired (1-36), integer only; =0 for floating point.
CX	Number of characters to read.

Output

DS:DI	8 byte result.	
AX	Low order part of 32 bit integer.	
BX	High order part of 32 bit integer.	
CL	Returned flags:	
	Bit Set in CL	Means
	0	Double Precsion Overflow.
	1	Explicit .,E,e,D,d was found.
	2	Explicit D or d was found.
	3	More than 7 digits in number.
	4	32 bit unsigned number invalid.
	5	32 bit signed number is invalid.
	6	No digits seen/number invalid.
	7	Decoded to an indefinite value.

Let's give this a try with some output. The output routine is $I8_OUTPUT, and it converts double-precision numbers into ASCII strings. Here's what you have to supply:

```
DS:SI            Address of double precision number.
```

And here are the outputs:

```
DS:DI             Address of string--17 bytes. The
                    first byte gives the string's length.
AX                =0 if number indefinite, 1 if number OK
BL                Sign character: '-' or blank.
DX                Base 10 exponent.
```

Let's divide 10.0 by 3.0 and print the result. Here's a program that allows us to do so, written in .EXE style. To use it, run this program through MASM and then link in IBMUTIL.LIB to create the executable .EXE file (do not use EXE2BIN to create the .COM file—just run the .EXE file):

LISTING 8.1 OUTPUT.ASM

```
.8087
DATA     SEGMENT WORD PUBLIC 'DATA'
         OP1      DQ 10.0
         OP2      DQ 3.0
DATA     ENDS
DGROUP   GROUP DATA

STACK    SEGMENT PARA    STACK    'STACK'
         DB       32 DUP('STACK')
STACK    ENDS

MATHCODE SEGMENT BYTE PUBLIC 'CODE'
         ASSUME   CS:MATHCODE,DS:DATA,SS:STACK
         EXTRN    $I8_OUTPUT:NEAR
ENTRY    PROC     FAR
         PUSH     DS
         XOR      AX,AX
         PUSH     AX
         MOV      AX,DATA
         MOV      DS,AX
         FLD      OP1
         FDIV     OP2
         FSTP     OP1
         LEA      SI,OP1
         CALL     $I8_OUTPUT
         XOR      CX,CX
         MOV      CL,BYTE PTR DS:[SI]
         MOV      AH,2
         MOV      DI,DX               ;SAVE EXPONENT IN DI
         MOV      DL,BL
         INT      21H
         MOV      DL,'.'
         INT      21H
 LOOPER: INC      SI
         MOV      DL,[SI]
         INT      21H
         LOOP     LOOPER
```

LISTING 8.1 CONTINUED

```
          MOV     DL,'E'
          INT     21H
          MOV     DL,'+'
          CMP     DI,0
          JG      EXPPOS
          NEG     DI
          MOV     DL,'-'
 EXPPOS:  INT     21H
          MOV     AX,DI
          AAM
          ADD     AX,3030H
          MOV     DL,AH
          MOV     CL,AL
          MOV     AH,2
          INT     21H
          MOV     DL,CL
          INT     21H
          RET
ENTRY     ENDP
MATHCODE ENDS
          END     ENTRY
```

We can create OUTPUT.EXE this way:

```
A>MASM
IBM Personal Computer MACRO Assembler   Version 2.00
(C)Copyright IBM Corp 1981, 1984
(C)Copyright Microsoft Corp 1981, 1983, 1984

Source filename [.ASM]: OUTPUT  ←
Object filename [OUTPUT.OBJ]:
Source listing  [NUL.LST]:
Cross reference [NUL.CRF]:
50092 Bytes free

Warning Severe
Errors  Errors
0       0
```

We could then link it, supposing IBMUTIL is on the B: drive:

```
IBM Personal Computer Linker
Version 2.20 (C)Copyright IBM Corp 1981, 1982, 1983, 1984

Object Modules [.OBJ]: OUTPUT   ←
Run File [OUTPUT.EXE]:
List File [NUL.MAP]:
Libraries [.LIB]: B:IBMUTIL     ←
```

Finally, we could run it, finding out that 10.0/3.0 is equal to:

```
A>OUTPUT
 .33333333333333333E+01
```

OUTPUT.ASM will only handle numbers with decimal exponents of two digits or less. Let's take a look at the way it works. The data is stored in the DATA segment, as required:

```
DATA     SEGMENT WORD PUBLIC 'DATA'
         OP1      DQ 10.0 ←
         OP2      DQ 3.0  ←
DATA     ENDS
DGROUP   GROUP DATA
```

There is also a STACK segment, since this file is intended to be a .EXE file. The code is kept in MATHCODE, also as required. The beginning starts off as a .EXE file should, preparing the stack for the return at the end:

```
MATHCODE SEGMENT BYTE PUBLIC 'CODE'
         ASSUME   CS:MATHCODE,DS:DATA,SS:STACK
         EXTRN    $I8_OUTPUT:NEAR
ENTRY    PROC     FAR      ←      (Prepare STACK for RET at end).
         PUSH     DS       ←
         XOR      AX,AX    ←
         PUSH     AX       ←
         MOV      AX,DATA  ←      (Set up DS).
         MOV      DS,AX    ←
         FLD      OP1
         FDIV     OP2
         FSTP     OP1
         LEA      SI,OP1
         CALL     $I8_OUTPUT
```

The division itself is easy enough. We just load OP1 (10.0) with FLD, divide with FLD OP2, store the number back in OP2, and pop the stack at the same time with FSTP:

```
MATHCODE SEGMENT BYTE PUBLIC 'CODE'
         ASSUME   CS:MATHCODE,DS:DATA,SS:STACK
         EXTRN    $I8_OUTPUT:NEAR
ENTRY    PROC     FAR
         PUSH     DS
         XOR      AX,AX
         PUSH     AX
         MOV      AX,DATA
         MOV      DS,AX
         FLD      OP1       ←
         FDIV     OP2       ←
         FSTP     OP1       ←
         LEA      SI,OP1
         CALL     $I8_OUTPUT
```

Finally, all we have to do is point DS:SI at OP2 and call our conversion program:

```
MATHCODE SEGMENT BYTE PUBLIC 'CODE'
         ASSUME  CS:MATHCODE,DS:DATA,SS:STACK
         EXTRN   $I8_OUTPUT:NEAR
ENTRY    PROC    FAR
         PUSH    DS
         XOR     AX,AX
         PUSH    AX
         MOV     AX,DATA
         MOV     DS,AX
         FLD     OP1
         FDIV    OP2
         FSTP    OP1
         LEA     SI,OP1            ←
         CALL    $I8_OUTPUT        ←
```

This call generates several outputs. We get the number of characters returned from the first byte in the string. This number we will save in CX so we can loop over the ASCII characters, typing them out. In addition, DX holds the base 10 exponent, and we save that number temporarily in DI. BX holds either a blank, ' ', if the number is positive, or '—' if negative, so we print that character first, with DOS Service 2. Right after that, we print a decimal point, since it will always go there:

```
MATHCODE SEGMENT BYTE PUBLIC 'CODE'
         ASSUME  CS:MATHCODE,DS:DATA,SS:STACK
         EXTRN   $I8_OUTPUT:NEAR
ENTRY    PROC    FAR
         PUSH    DS
         XOR     AX,AX
         PUSH    AX
         MOV     AX,DATA
         MOV     DS,AX
         FLD     OP1
         FDIV    OP2
         FSTP    OP1
         LEA     SI,OP1
         CALL    $I8_OUTPUT
         XOR     CX,CX                     ;(Zero CX).
         MOV     CL,BYTE PTR DS:[SI]
         MOV     AH,2
         MOV     DI,DX             ;SAVE EXPONENT IN DI
         MOV     DL,BL                     ;(Print sign).
         INT     21H
         MOV     DL,'.'
         INT     21H
LOOPER:  INC     SI
         MOV     DL,[SI]
         INT     21H
```

```
          LOOP     LOOPER
          MOV      DL,'E'
          INT      21H
          MOV      DL,'+'
          CMP      DI,0
          JG       EXPPOS
          NEG      DI
          MOV      DL,'-'
EXPPOS:   INT      21H
```

Next comes the short loop that prints the ASCII numbers in the returned string (i.e., 3333333333333333) out. This loop is named LOOPER. After LOOPER we have to print the 'E' for exponent and then the exponent's sign. If the exponent (stored in DI) is negative, we will make it positive (to print out in ASCII) and print a '–'. Otherwise, we will print out a '+':

```
MATHCODE SEGMENT BYTE PUBLIC 'CODE'
         ASSUME   CS:MATHCODE,DS:DATA,SS:STACK
         EXTRN    $I8_OUTPUT:NEAR
ENTRY    PROC     FAR
         PUSH     DS
         XOR      AX,AX
         PUSH     AX
         MOV      AX,DATA
         MOV      DS,AX
         FLD      OP1
         FDIV     OP2
         FSTP     OP1
         LEA      SI,OP1
         CALL     $I8_OUTPUT
         XOR      CX,CX
         MOV      CL,BYTE PTR DS:[SI]
         MOV      AH,2
         MOV      DI,DX              ;SAVE EXPONENT IN DI
         MOV      DL,BL
         INT      21H
         MOV      DL,'.'
         INT      21H
LOOPER:  INC      SI
         MOV      DL,[SI]
         INT      21H
         LOOP     LOOPER
         MOV      DL,'E'                ;(Print the 'E').
         INT      21H
         MOV      DL,'+'
         CMP      DI,0                  ;(Exponent negative?)
         JG       EXPPOS
         NEG      DI
         MOV      DL,'-'
EXPPOS:  INT      21H                   ;(Print exponent's sign).
```

The only thing that remains is to print out the exponent's magnitude. This number is stored in DI. To convert this number to base ten ASCII output is usually a little tedious. You must successively divide by ten and examine the remainders. These numbers are the base 10 digits you must print, but they come out in reverse order. The usual method is to push the remainder on the stack, divide by ten, push the remainder on the stack, divide by ten, and so on until there is nothing left. Then you pop them off, one at a time, add ASCII '0' to them, and print them. If we limit ourselves to two-digit exponents, we can do the same thing much more easily.

Using AAM

The 8088 can also do BCD arithmetic. It has a set of commands to adjust the results of adding BCD numbers, subtracting them, dividing, and multiplying. These commands are applied to make the result of the math operation come out correctly when done on Binary Coded Decimal numbers. One of these commands, ASCII Adjust for Multiplication, is very useful here, since it will convert the number in AX into BCD. Let's say AX holds 63H. After the AAM command, this number is converted to its decimal equivalent, 99, which means AH holds 9 and AL holds 9. All that is left is to add ASCII '0' to both AH and AL, and to print them out:

LISTING 8.2 8087 OUTPUT PROGRAM

```
MATHCODE SEGMENT BYTE PUBLIC 'CODE'
        ASSUME  CS:MATHCODE,DS:DATA,SS:STACK
        EXTRN   $I8_OUTPUT:NEAR
ENTRY   PROC    FAR
        PUSH    DS
        XOR     AX,AX
        PUSH    AX
        MOV     AX,DATA
        MOV     DS,AX
        FLD     OP1
        FDIV    OP2
        FSTP    OP1
        LEA     SI,OP1
        CALL    $I8_OUTPUT
        XOR     CX,CX
        MOV     CL,BYTE PTR DS:[SI]
        MOV     AH,2
        MOV     DI,DX               ;SAVE EXPONENT IN DI
        MOV     DL,BL
        INT     21H
        MOV     DL,'.'
        INT     21H
LOOPER: INC     SI
        MOV     DL,[SI]
        INT     21H
        LOOP    LOOPER
```

LISTING 8.2 CONTINUED

```
         MOV      DL,'E'
         INT      21H
         MOV      DL,'+'
         CMP      DI,0
         JG       EXPPOS
         NEG      DI
         MOV      DL,'-'
 EXPPOS: INT      21H
         MOV      AX,DI             ← (Exponent stored in DI).
         AAM                        ←
         ADD      AX,3030H          ←Add '0' to AH and AL.
         MOV      DL,AH             ←
         MOV      CL,AL             ←
         MOV      AH,2              ←
         INT      21H               ←
         MOV      DL,CL             ←
         INT      21H               ←
         RET
 ENTRY   ENDP
 MATHCODE ENDS
         END      ENTRY
```

This program can, of course, be adapted to print out exponents of any size that double precision is capable of providing.

8087 INSTRUCTIONS

For reference, we will list and discuss the most frequently used 8087 commands. These commands all begin with F, and if any command you see begins with F, it is safe to assume it is an 8087 command, because no 8088 commands do. The *Macro Assembler Reference Manual* also lists these commands (without the accompanying commentary) and all the others available in Version 2.0 of the assembler as well.

Immediately after the name of the command, we will show what the command does with a line like:

$2^{ST} - 1 \rightarrow ST$ (0.<=ST<=.5)

This means that the stack (ST) is replaced by the value $2^{ST} - 1$, but that the value in ST has to be between 0 and .5.

F2XM1—2* Minus One

How It Works:

$2^{ST} - 1 \rightarrow ST \qquad (0.<=ST<=.5)$

Many 8087 commands have hard to remember mnemonics—this one certainly does; two to the X minus one. This command sounds exceptionally useful until you find out that the power you raise two to must be in the interval of 0. to .5. Nevertheless, if you are willing to work with square roots and multiplications, you can fabricate any power of two this way.

The abbreviation ST always stands for the stack top, ST(1) as the number on the stack below it, all the way down to ST(7). Don't forget that it is your responsibilty to keep the stack from getting completely filled and therefore, jammed.

This instruction takes no arguments; and it uses only the stack top. Some formulae you might want to keep in mind while using this instruction include:

$$10^{ST} = 2^{ST} \times LOG_2\ 10$$
$$e^{ST} = 2^{ST} \times LOG_2\ e$$
$$Y^{ST} = 2^{ST} \times LOG_2\ Y$$

With these formulae, you can find 10ST, e^{ST}, and Y^{ST} from 2ST. There are special instructions to load LOG^2 e (FLDL2E) and to load LOG^2 10 (FLDL2T). These commands simply load their respective values into ST.

FADD—Addition

How It Works:

```
ST + ST(1) → ST          (Default)
ST + ST(n) → ST
ST(n) + ST → ST(n)
ST + Short_Real → ST
ST + Long_Real → ST
```

We have already seen this command at work; it simply adds two floating point numbers. If there are no arguments, the 8087 adds ST and ST(1) together, loads this new number into ST(1), and then pops the 8087 stack, leaving the result in ST.

If you use an argument like:

```
FADD     LONG_REAL
```

then LONG_REAL is added to ST, and the answer is left in ST. On the other hand, you can use commands like:

```
FADD ST,ST(3)
```

in which case ST(3) will be added to ST, and the result will be left in ST. Similarly, the command:

```
FADD ST(3),ST
```

will add ST to ST(3), and will leave the result in ST(3), NOT ST.
The integer version of this command is FIADD.

FBLD—Load BCD Number

How It Works:

```
BCD Number → ST
```

FBLD is for loading BCD numbers, and we have already seen this instruction in action. Its use is quite simple, provided you have stored the BCD number correctly (with DT, Define Tenbytes):

```
FBLD     BCD_NUMBER
```

The counterpart of this instruction is the one that follows, FBSTP.

FBSTP—Store BCD Number

How It Works:

```
ST → BCD Number in memory, Pop Stack
```

This accomplishes the reverse of FBLD, and also pops the stack. FBSTP stores a number in BCD format. If you wanted to convert from, say, integer to BCD, you could load the integer with FILD and store it with FBSTP. This command also keeps the stack trim by popping it.

FCLEX—Clear Exceptions

How It Works:

```
Clear Exception Flags
```

The 8087 has a set of flags like the 8088, and those flags will be covered in the following section on errors. The flags are stored in the 8087's status word. In order to check them, you have to store the status word in memory. The important part for IBM PC users is that these flags do not automatically reset. They stay set so that they can propagate through a whole calculation, and you can check any accumulated errors at the end if you wish. FCLEX clears these flags and sets them back to zero. If you intend to use error checking, you should start off any calculation with FCLEX.

FCOM—Comparison

How It Works:

```
Compare Number with ST
```

This is the first of the 8087's comparison instructions. FCOM is used with real numbers—short or long reals. To use it (the comparison to ST is implicit), just issue a command like:

```
FCOM      LONG_REAL_NUMBER
```

The results of this comparison are stored in the 8087's status word. The condition bits in the status word are of interest here. You can store the status word with the command FSTSW. The two bits C0 and C3 will be returned as shown in Table 8.3 after the comparison.

Table 8.3 Instruction FCOM MEM_OP

Result	C3	C0
ST > MEM_OP	0	0
ST < MEM_OP	0	1
ST = MEM_OP	1	0
Undeterminable	1	1

C0 is bit 8 of the status word, and C3 is bit 14. We can use this information immediately in a little test program to check the relative sizes of two memory values, A and B.

Here we will use the pseudo-Op RECORD to split our status word up into bit-by-bit fields. We define a dummy RECORD, M, and give names to all the bits in it. When we then use the command TEST ST8087,MASK C3, the assembler will substitute the correct Hex number for MASK C3. As we'll see later, C3 is bit 14, and the assembler will generate a "mask," which has bit 14 set. Here's how the program looks:

```
CODE_SEG SEGMENT
.8087
         ASSUME  CS:CODE_SEG,DS:CODE_SEG
         ORG     100H
ENTRY:   JMP     PROG
         A       DQ 10.0
         B       DQ 5.0
         ST8087  DW  0
         M RECORD BY:1,C3:1,TOP:3,C2:1,C1:1,C0:1,IT:1,X:1,P:1,U:1,O:1,Z:1,D:1,I :1
PROG:    FINIT
         FLD     A
         FCOMP   B
         FSTSW   ST8087
         MOV     DL,'A'
         MOV     AH,2
         INT     21H
         ;C3=0  C0=0 → A>B
         ;C3=0  C0=1 → A<B
         ;C3=1  C0=0 → A=B
         TEST    ST8087,MASK C3
         JZ      NOTEQ
         MOV     DL,'='
         JMP     SHORT PRINT
NOTEQ:   TEST    ST8087,MASK C0
         JNZ     LESS
         MOV     DL,'>'
         JMP     SHORT PRINT
LESS:    MOV     DL,'<'
PRINT:   MOV     AH,2
         INT     21H
         MOV     DL,'B'
         INT     21H
         FCLEX
         INT     20H
CODE_SEG ENDS
         END     ENTRY
```

We start off with a data area, as usual. Here we make A and B into double precision real numbers (long reals) by using DQ. We will store the status word in the word we have labeled ST8087. The dummy record M is divided up by bit, and each bit is given a name. These names will become clearer later when we work through the status word systematically; the only ones we are interested in here are C3 and C0.

The reason the bit names are so short is that a RECORD must be completely defined on one line. Notice also that the field TOP, which tells you which of the eight 8087 registers is the stack top currently, is three bits long so that it can hold numbers up to eight:

```
CODE_SEG SEGMENT
.8087
         ASSUME  CS:CODE_SEG,DS:CODE_SEG
         ORG     100H
ENTRY:   JMP     PROG
       → A       DQ 10.0
       → B       DQ 5.0
       → ST8087  DW  0
       → M RECORD BY:1,C3:1,TOP:3,C2:1,C1:1,C0:1,IT:1,X:1,P:1,U:1,O:1,Z:1,D:1,I:1
PROG:    FINIT
```

The first command used here is the useful command FINIT, which initializes the 8087 and clears the stack. We then load A and compare it to B with FCOMP. Immediately afterward, we store the status word in ST8087. In preparing to type out the answer (either A>B, A<B, or A=B), first type out "A" here:

```
CODE_SEG SEGMENT
.8087
        ASSUME  CS:CODE_SEG,DS:CODE_SEG
        ORG     100H
ENTRY:  JMP     PROG
        A       DQ 10.0
        B       DQ 5.0
        ST8087  DW  0
        M RECORD BY:1,C3:1,TOP:3,C2:1,C1:1,C0:1,IT:1,X:1,P:1,U:1,O:1,Z:1,D:1,I:1
PROG:   FINIT
        FLD     A                   ;Load A
        FCOMP   B                   ;Compare to B
        FSTSW   ST8087              ;Store the status word in memory.
        MOV     DL,'A'              ;Print out "A"
        MOV     AH,2
        INT     21H
```

Next check C3 and C0. If C3=1, then A=B. If C0=1, then A<B. Here's the way it is coded to type out either "=", "<", or ">", followed by "B":

```
CODE_SEG SEGMENT
.8087
        ASSUME  CS:CODE_SEG,DS:CODE_SEG
        ORG     100H
ENTRY:  JMP     PROG
        A       DQ 10.0
        B       DQ 5.0
        ST8087  DW  0
        M RECORD BY:1,C3:1,TOP:3,C2:1,C1:1,C0:1,IT:1,X:1,P:1,U:1,O:1,Z:1,D:1,I:1
PROG:   FINIT
        FLD     A
        FCOMP   B
        FSTSW   ST8087
        MOV     DL,'A'
        MOV     AH,2
        INT     21H
        ;C3=0   C0=0 → A>B
        ;C3=0   C0=1 → A<B
        ;C3=1   C0=0 → A=B
      → TEST    ST8087,MASK C3
        JZ      NOTEQ               ;C3 NOT set → jump.
      → MOV     DL,'='
        JMP     SHORT PRINT
NOTEQ:  TEST    ST8087,MASK C0  ←
        JNZ     LESS                ;C0 set → jump.
      → MOV     DL,'>'
        JMP     SHORT PRINT
LESS:   MOV     DL,'<'          ←
PRINT:  MOV     AH,2
        INT     21H
        MOV     DL,'B'
        INT     21H
```

```
        FCLEX
        INT     20H
CODE_SEG ENDS
        END     ENTRY
```

The integer version of FCOM is FICOM.

FDIV—Division

How It Works:

```
ST(1)/ST → ST(1)
ST/Short_Real → ST
ST/Long_Real → ST
ST/ST(n) → ST
```

We have seen FDIV before. This is the floating point divide command. If you use it without labels:

```
FDIV
```

it will divide ST(1) by ST and store the result in ST. If you use a Long or Short Real,

```
FDIV Long_Real
```

then ST will be divided by the real number and the result left in ST. Finally, if you use

```
FDIV ST,ST(n)
```

then ST will be loaded with ST(n)/ST.

The integer version of FDIV is FIDIV.

FILD—Load Integers

How It Works:

```
Word_Integer → ST
Short_Integer → ST
Long_Integer → ST
```

FILD is the way you can load integers into ST. Since the only format that the 8088 and the 8087 have in common is the word integer format (16 bits and two's complement sign), this command is quite popular. The corresponding command to store integers is FIST. If you have done calculations with the 8087 and now wish to manipulate the results with the 8088, FIST is often quite useful.

FINIT—Initialize 8087

How It Works:

```
Initializes 8087
```

This command is especially useful. It initializes and resets the 8087. If the stack has become full or if (for any other reason) you want to start from scratch, you can use FINIT. The timing between the 8087 and the 8088 is preserved. If, on the other hand, you suspect that the 8088 and 8087 are no longer communicating well (i.e., each is waiting for the other to finish), you might use FNINIT, which executes an immediate FINIT, instead of first waiting until the 8087 signals that it is free.

FIST—Store Integer

How It Works:

```
ST → Word_Integer
ST → Short_Integer
```

FIST, as we have said, provides a way of downloading 8087 results in a manner readable by the 8088. You can do whatever you want with floating point numbers and then, finally, load the final answer into memory with FIST, and you can then use it in the 8088.

FISTP—Store Integer and Pop Stack

How It Works:

```
ST → Word_Integer
ST → Short_Integer
ST → Long_Integer
```

FISTP has all the advantages of FIST, and two more. FISTP also pops the stack and keeps it from growing too large. It can also store numbers in the Long_Integer format (64 bits—use DQ), while FIST cannot. As with FIST, you can do all your floating point calculations first and then store them in integer format so they can be read by the 8088 CPU.

FLD—Load Real

How It Works:

```
Short_Real → ST
Long_Real → ST
Temp_Real → ST
```

FLD is the usual way of loading floating point numbers into ST. With it you can load short or long reals, as well as the temporary real format (80 bits) used internally in the 8087. The format is simply this:

```
FLD SHORT_REAL
```

as we have already seen. This is the way that the 8087 operates; you have to load its stack before you can really use it. Of course, all numbers that are loaded this way must be stored in the correct floating point format. To use this format you can do one of three things: you can let the assembler do the work by including constants in your .ASM file:

```
LONG_INT DQ 3.14159
```

you can do the dirty work yourself, or you can let the 8087 do the work. You can load integers and store numbers in floating point format. Keep track of the number of FLDs you have executed to make sure the stack does not grow uncontrollably.

FMUL—Multiply

How It Works:

```
ST(1) × ST → ST
Short_Real × ST → ST
Long_Real × ST → ST
ST × ST(n) → ST
ST × ST(n) → ST(n)
```

FMUL is the 8087's all-purpose real number multiplication instruction. With it you can multiply ST(1) and ST, pop the stack, and move the result from ST(1) into ST:

```
FMUL
```

or you can load a real number into ST with FLD and multiply it by some real number stored in memory:

```
FMUL SHORT_INTEGER
FMUL LONG_INTEGER
```

FMUL can also multiply different stack elements. For example,

```
FMUL ST, ST(7)
```

multiplies ST by ST(7) and leaves the result in ST. The other way around,

```
FMUL ST(7),ST
```

multiplies ST(7) by ST and leaves the results in ST(7).
The integer version of FMUL is FIMUL.

FNCLEX—Clear Exceptions No Wait

How It Works:

```
Clear Exceptions Without Waiting.
```

This is the version of FCLEX that does not wait until the 8087 signals that it is free. Usually, there is no advantage to using FNCLEX instead of FCLEX. If, however, you write what is called an **exception handler**—analogous to interrupt handlers in the PC—then you have to issue this command before returning to the interrupted calculation. We will not deal with exception handlers in this book.

FNSTSW—Store Status No Wait

How It Works:

```
Store Status Word Without Waiting.
```

This is another command that does not wait until the 8087 signals it is free before operating. The use for this command is usually to examine the busy bit (bit 15) of the status word to see when the 8087 is no longer busy. Typically, loops are put into code checking this bit until it becomes zero, at which time the 8087 is free.
This command is used like this:

```
FNSTSW  WORD_LENGTH_OP
```

FPATAN—Arc Tangent

How It Works:

```
Stack is Popped and ARCTAN(ST(1)/ST) → ST  (0<ST(1)<ST<+Infinity)
```

FPATAN is the command for partial arc tangent. This instruction takes no arguments. All you must do is supply it with the ratio Y/X, where X = ST, and Y is ST(1). To load Y, you can use FLD; another FLD for X will push Y into ST(1) and put X into ST. The resulting angle is left in ST and can be stored in memory with FSTP.

FPTAN—Tangent

How It Works:

```
TAN(ST) → Y/X   Y → ST(1)  X → ST
                           [Rest of the stack gets pushed]
```

FPTAN is the 8087's partial tangent command. With this command, you can also calculate sines and cosines, given the right trigonometric identities. When you call FPTAN, the value of ST must be 0 < ST < Pi/4. Instead of simply delivering a floating point answer, FPTAN gives you a ratio Y/X (Y in ST(1) and X in ST). This makes it easier to calculate other trigonometric values. If you want one number, you should divide Y by X with FDIV.

FSQRT—Square Root

How It Works:

```
Sqrt(ST) → ST
```

This instruction just gives you the square root of ST. In order not to give an undefined answer, ST must be positive. Finding square roots with the 8087 is actually a fast process, taking about the same time as division. Needless to say, emulating this command with the 8088 is a time-consuming and frustrating process.

FSTSW—Store Status

How It Works:

```
Status Word → Memory
```

This is a very common instruction used when you are doing error checking. The status word, as you'll see in the next section, defines the current state of the 8087 and includes the error flags. This command is preferred over the No-Wait version of the same thing, FNSTSW. FNSTSW is used almost exclusively in tight loops that check when the 8087 is not busy by checking the busy bit in the status word. We will make more use of the status word later.

FSUB—Subtraction

How It Works:

```
ST(1)-ST → ST
ST-Short_Real → ST
ST-Long_Real → ST
ST(n)-ST → ST
ST-ST(n) → ST
```

FSUB is the 8087's real subtraction command. It is advisable after any FSUB to check the status word for errors. The forms FSUB can take include those shown in Table 8.4.

Table 8.4 FSUB Formats

Command	Result
FSUB	(ST(1) − ST → ST(1))
FSUB SHORT_REAL	(ST − Short_Real → ST)
FSUB LONG_REAL	(ST − Long_Real → ST)
FSUB ST,ST(3)	(ST − ST(3) → ST)
FSUB ST(7),ST	(ST(7) − ST → ST(7))

The integer version of this command is FISUB.

FYL2X—Y × Log X_2

How It Works:

```
ST(1) × Log2 (ST) → ST
                    (Rest of stack gets popped)
                    0 < X
```

FYL2X is one of the two instructions in the 8087 that can calculate Log_2 values (the other is FYL2XP1). Nowhere do the 8087 mnemonics make less apparent sense—what FYL2X means is Y × Log_2 X. This immediate multiplication is useful, since you can find logs in other bases with the identity:

```
Logn X  = [1/Log2 n] × Log2 X
```

This is the 8087's method of raising numbers to powers—you must take the number's log first, multiply by the appropriate power, and then take the anti-log by exponentiating (using F2XM1).

FYL2XP1—Y × Log_2 (X+1)

How It Works:

```
ST(1) × Log2 (ST+1) → ST
                                        (Rest of stack gets popped.)
X < 0
```

This instruction is virtually identical with FYL2X, except that it adds one to X, which makes the accuracy higher when X is near one. On the other hand, X cannot be too close to one; it has to be in the range:

```
0 < |X| < (1-1/Sqrt(2)) = .2929
```

FYL2XP1, like FYL2X, takes no operands, assuming the use of ST(1) and ST.

FYL2XP1 concludes our survey of the most frequently used 8087 instructions. There are more to be found in the *Macro Assembler Reference Manual*. If you have questions about any of these instructions, the reference manual is a good place to turn to.

ERRORS AND ERROR CHECKING

No math-related computer discussion would be complete without a discussion of errors. Just as we can check the carry flag in the 8088, so there are provisions in the 8087 for error checking. Unless you know beforehand just what your input will be, you should check for errors.

The register that holds the 8087's error flags and status flags is called the Status Word. This word can be stored in memory with FSTSW like this: FSTSW MEM_WORD.

The status word is divided into status bits and exception flags (error flags). The top byte is diagrammed in Figure 8.1.

The topmost bit, bit 15, is the busy bit. If this bit is 1, the 8087 is busy executing some command. If this bit is 0, the 8087 is idle. If you use FSTSW, this bit should always be 0 since this instruction waits until the 8087 is free before executing. On the other hand, the no-wait form of this instruction,

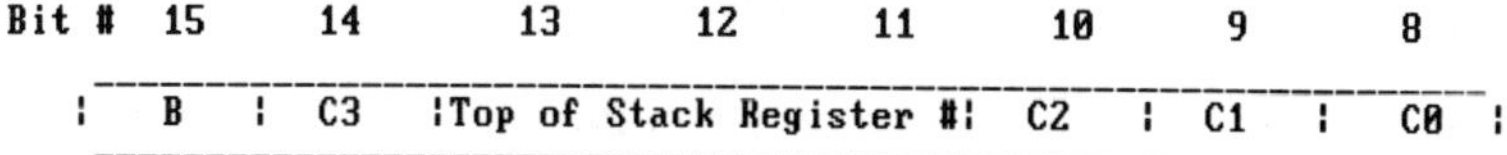

Figure 8.1 Status Word Top Byte.

FNSTSW, does not wait until the 8087 is free, and you can check on the 8087 at any time with it. The four **condition codes**, C3–C0, are used to hold the results of compares, as we saw with FCOM. If we used the instruction FCOM MEM_OP, here is the way the condition codes C3–C0 would be set:

```
00_0      ST > MEM_OP
00_1      ST < MEM_OP
10_0      ST = MEM_OP
```

Note that C1 is NOT set for compare instructions.

The 8087 also has an examine command, FXAM, which will set C3–C0 depending on the contents of ST. This instruction is often very useful. The results of FXAM are shown in Table 8.5

Table 8.5 FXAM Results

C3–C0	Error
0000	Valid, > 0, Unnormalized
0001	Invalid, > 0, Zero Exponent
0010	Valid, < 0, Unnormalized
0011	Invalid, < 0, Zero Exponent
0100	Valid, > 0, Normalized
0101	Positive Infinity
0110	Valid, < 0, Normalized
0111	Negative Infinity
1000	Positive Zero
1001	Empty
1010	Negative Zero
1011	Empty
1100	Invalid, > 0, Zero Exponent
1101	Empty
1110	Invalid, < 0, Zero Exponent
1111	Empty

A normalized number is one that fits into the normal format of 8087 reals—biased exponent and implicit leading one. If, though, a number is very small, it would have leading zeros (not ones) once the smallest exponent for that format has been used. In that case, the number is no longer normalized, but the 8087 can still operate on it.

The three bits labeled Top of Stack Register # hold the number (0–7) of the register that is the current top of stack (ST). You can watch this number to make sure you know where you are in the stack and that it does not overflow.

The bottom eight bits of the status word look like Figure 8.2.

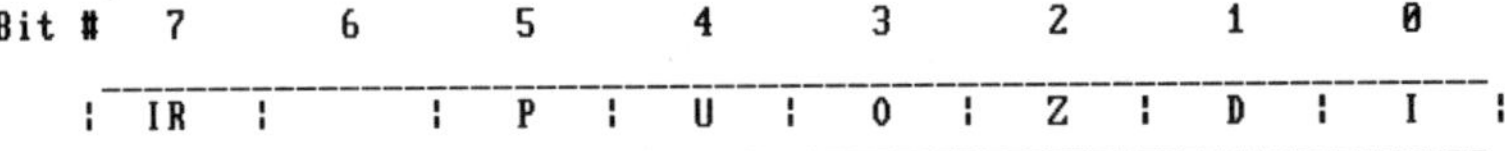

Figure 8.2 Status Word Bottom Byte.

The IR bit indicates whether or not an Interrupt Request is pending from the 8087 to the 8088. We will not deal with 8087 interrupts here.

The six flags—P, U, O, Z, D, and I—indicate exceptions and can be checked after every math operation. Until these flags are cleared with FCLEX or FINIT, however, they stay set once they are set. This means that error flags can propagate through an entire calculation, even an involved one, and can be checked at the end.

If the exception occurred, the corresponding bit is one. Otherwise, the bit is 0. The flags are shown in Table 8.6.

Table 8.6 Exception Flags

Bit Set	Error
P	**Precision**. Some precision has been lost in working with the current operand.
U	**Underflow**. The number's exponent is too small to be represented in the requested format. In other words, the result is non-zero but too small to fit in the format asked for.
O	**Overflow**. The other extreme: the number is too large to fit into the requested format.
Z	A divide by zero occurred.
D	**Denormalization**. At least one of the operands used was denormalized, e.g.: it has the smallest possible exponent, but a non-zero significand.
I	**Invalid operation**. Some invalid operations include stack over- and underflow, dividing zero by zero, taking the negative square root of a number.

Using Error Checking

We can put this knowledge to work at once. In the example, we will perform two divisions—one a valid division and one a division by zero. Each time we will check the status word to examine the exception flags. Here's the way the program looks:

```
CODE_SEG SEGMENT
.8087
        ASSUME   CS:CODE_SEG,DS:CODE_SEG
        ORG      100H
ENTRY:  JMP      PROG
        OP1      DQ 10.0
        OP2      DQ 5.0
        OP3      DQ 0.0
        NOPROB   DB 'No '
        PROB     DB 'Divide by Zero',13,10,'$'
        ST8087   DW  0
        SW RECORD B:1,C3:1,TOP:3,C2:1,C1:1,C0:1,IT:1,X:1,P:1,U:1,O:1,Z:1,D:1,I:1
PROG:   FINIT
        FLD      OP1
        FDIV     OP2
        MOV      AH,9
        LEA      DX,NOPROB
        FSTSW    ST8087
        TEST     ST8087,MASK Z
        JZ       OK1
        LEA      DX,PROB
OK1:    INT      21H
        FCLEX
        FINIT
        FLD      OP1
        FDIV     OP3
        MOV      AH,9
        LEA      DX,NOPROB
        FSTSW    ST8087
        TEST     ST8087,MASK Z
        JZ       OK2
        LEA      DX,PROB
OK2:    INT      21H
        INT      20H
CODE_SEG ENDS
        END      ENTRY
```

To define the bit-by-bit flags in the status word, we use a Record pseudo-OP. As we saw earlier, the definition of a record has to fit on one line (132 characters), so we make the abbreviation of each flag rather terse. Here's how the status word is stored in memory:

```
ODE_SEG SEGMENT
.8087
        ASSUME   CS:CODE_SEG,DS:CODE_SEG
        ORG      100H
ENTRY:  JMP      PROG
        OP1      DQ 10.0
        OP2      DQ 5.0
        OP3      DQ 0.0
```

```
  NOPROB   DB 'No '
  PROB     DB 'Divide by Zero',13,10,'$'
→ ST8087   DW  0
→ SW RECORD B:1,C3:1,TOP:3,C2:1,C1:1,C0:1,IT:1,X:1,P:1,U:1,O:1,Z:1,D:1,I:1
```

By defining some dummy Record SW, we have given names to each bit, and the assembler will recognize these names when we use them again. To check the Zero bit, for instance, we use the 8088 command TEST, along with the pseudo-OP MASK Z. The assembler knows where in the word-long operand the Z bit is supposed to be from our Record definition. It will make a "mask" for us that can be ANDed to another number. For example, if the Z bit was the third bit place, the mask would be: 0000000000000100, or 0004. Here's how we use MASK Z:

```
PROG:     FINIT
          FLD      OP1
          FDIV     OP2
          MOV      AH,9
          LEA      DX,NOPROB
          FSTSW    ST8087
        → TEST     ST8087,MASK Z
          JZ       OK1
          LEA      DX,PROB
OK1:      INT      21H
```

In the program, we take the operand OP1 and first divide it by OP2. We then reload OP1 and divide it by OP3:

```
CODE_SEG SEGMENT
.8087
         ASSUME  CS:CODE_SEG,DS:CODE_SEG
         ORG     100H
ENTRY:   JMP     PROG
       → OP1     DQ 10.0
       → OP2     DQ 5.0
       → OP3     DQ 0.0
         NOPROB  DB 'No '
         PROB    DB 'Divide by Zero',13,10,'$'
         ST8087  DW  0
         SW RECORD B:1,C3:1,TOP:3,C2:1,C1:1,C0:1,IT:1,X:1,P:1,U:1,O:1,Z:1,D:1,I:1
```

In this case, the first division is 10.0 divided by 5.0, which will not lead to a division by zero. The second division, 10.0 divided by 0.0, however, will. In order to do these divisions, we start off with a FINIT to reset the 8087 and clear all exception flags. We then load OP1 into ST with FLD and divide by OP2:

```
CODE_SEG SEGMENT
.8087
         ASSUME  CS:CODE_SEG,DS:CODE_SEG
         ORG     100H
ENTRY:   JMP     PROG
         OP1     DQ 10.0
         OP2     DQ 5.0
```

```
        OP3      DQ 0.0
        NOPROB   DB 'No '
        PROB     DB 'Divide by Zero',13,10,'$'
        ST8087   DW  0
        SW RECORD B:1,C3:1,TOP:3,C2:1,C1:1,C0:1,IT:1,X:1,P:1,U:1,O:1,Z:1,D:1,I:1
PROG:   FINIT          ←
        FLD      OP1   ←
        FDIV     OP2   ←
```

We have to check the status word to make sure there was no divide by zero error. We will print out the results with the string printing function, Service 9 of INT 21H, so we start by optimistically loading DX with the address of the no-error message, NOPROB:

```
CODE_SEG SEGMENT
.8087
        ASSUME   CS:CODE_SEG,DS:CODE_SEG
        ORG      100H
ENTRY:  JMP      PROG
        OP1      DQ 10.0
        OP2      DQ 5.0
        OP3      DQ 0.0
      → NOPROB   DB 'No '
      → PROB     DB 'Divide by Zero',13,10,'$'
        ST8087   DW  0
        SW RECORD B:1,C3:1,TOP:3,C2:1,C1:1,C0:1,IT:1,X:1,P:1,U:1,O:1,Z:1,D:1,I:1
PROG:   FINIT
        FLD      OP1
        FDIV     OP2
      → MOV      AH,9
      → LEA      DX,NOPROB
        FSTSW    ST8087
        TEST     ST8087,MASK Z
        JZ       OK1
        LEA      DX,PROB
OK1:    INT      21H
```

To check if there really was no error, store the status word in a memory location we have set aside, ST8087, with the command FSTSW ST8087. We can check to see if the zero-divide bit was set with TEST ST8087, MASK Z:

```
CODE_SEG SEGMENT
.8087
        ASSUME   CS:CODE_SEG,DS:CODE_SEG
        ORG      100H
ENTRY:  JMP      PROG
        OP1      DQ 10.0
        OP2      DQ 5.0
        OP3      DQ 0.0
        NOPROB   DB 'No '
        PROB     DB 'Divide by Zero',13,10,'$'
      → ST8087   DW  0
      → SW RECORD B:1,C3:1,TOP:3,C2:1,C1:1,C0:1,IT:1,X:1,P:1,U:1,O:1,Z:1,D:1,I:1
PROG:   FINIT
        FLD      OP1
        FDIV     OP2
        MOV      AH,9
        LEA      DX,NOPROB
      → FSTSW    ST8087
```

```
        → TEST     ST8087,MASK Z
          JZ       OK1
          LEA      DX,PROB
OK1:      INT      21H
```

If the results of this TEST were zero, the zero-bit flag was not set (we ANDed zero with the MASK Z). In that case we want to print out the default message. Otherwise, of course, there has been an error, so we must load the address of PROB, the error message, into DX. We print out the results with INT 21H:

```
CODE_SEG SEGMENT
.8087
          ASSUME   CS:CODE_SEG,DS:CODE_SEG
          ORG      100H
ENTRY:    JMP      PROG
          OP1      DQ 10.0
          OP2      DQ 5.0
          OP3      DQ 0.0
          NOPROB   DB 'No '
          PROB     DB 'Divide by Zero',13,10,'$'
          ST8087   DW  0
          SW RECORD B:1,C3:1,TOP:3,C2:1,C1:1,C0:1,IT:1,X:1,P:1,U:1,O:1,Z:1,D:1,I:1
PROG:     FINIT
          FLD      OP1
          FDIV     OP2
          MOV      AH,9
          LEA      DX,NOPROB
          FSTSW    ST8087
        → TEST     ST8087,MASK Z
        → JZ       OK1
        → LEA      DX,PROB
OK1:      INT      21H
```

The second half of the program is the same. After using FCLEX, then FINIT to be sure, we divide OP1 by OP3 and print out the result in the same way:

```
CODE_SEG SEGMENT
.8087
          ASSUME   CS:CODE_SEG,DS:CODE_SEG
          ORG      100H
ENTRY:    JMP      PROG
          OP1      DQ 10.0
          OP2      DQ 5.0
          OP3      DQ 0.0
          NOPROB   DB 'No '
          PROB     DB 'Divide by Zero',13,10,'$'
          ST8087   DW  0
          SW RECORD B:1,C3:1,TOP:3,C2:1,C1:1,C0:1,IT:1,X:1,P:1,U:1,O:1,Z:1,D:1,I:1
PROG:     FINIT
          FLD      OP1
          FDIV     OP2
          MOV      AH,9
          LEA      DX,NOPROB
          FSTSW    ST8087
          TEST     ST8087,MASK Z
          JZ       OK1
          LEA      DX,PROB
OK1:      INT      21H
        → FCLEX
        → FINIT
```

```
        → FLD     OP1
        → FDIV    OP3
          MOV     AH,9
          LEA     DX,NOPROB
          FSTSW   ST8087
          TEST    ST8087,MASK Z
          JZ      OK2
          LEA     DX,PROB
OK2:      INT     21H
          INT     20H
CODE_SEG ENDS
          END     ENTRY
```

This second case is the one that does yield an error. In general, error checking on the 8087 is not difficult, thanks to the status word.

Now that we've worked our way from doing things correctly to doing them incorrectly, this finishes our discussion of the 8087.

LOCATE.ASM

Since we cannot assume that all, or even most, of the people that read this book have 8087s in their PCs, we will not provide a long 8087 example. A long 8087 example, such as matrix multiplication, typically has only a few 8087 commands anyway; the majority of the program simply sets the data up by using the 8088 and makes sure what the 8087 is doing is correct.

Instead, this example program, the last in the book, will tie together some of the skills we've picked up in previous chapters and provide a program of real utility. LOCATE.COM is a program that will find strings for you by searching through whole subdirectories at a time. For example, imagine we wanted to find the string SEGMENT in our current subdirectory. All we need to type is:

```
LOCATE SEGMENT
```

and we'll get a return something like:

```
FOUND IN TEST.ASM:
7    DATA    SEGMENT WORD PUBLIC 'DATA'

FOUND IN TEST.ASM:
A    STACK   SEGMENT PARA    STACK   'ST

FOUND IN TEST.ASM:
MATHCODE SEGMENT BYTE PUBLIC 'CODE'
```

where LOCATE types out a number of bytes surrounding the string to give you the context.

LOCATE is case-sensitive. If you want to find the string "LoOk OuT!", you have to ask LOCATE to locate "LoOk OuT!", not anything else. (It is pretty easy to change LOCATE and make it case-insensitive, however.)

Also, LOCATE can check other subdirectories for you. If you have a file named PATH.DAT in your main area on the disk, LOCATE will read additional paths from it and search those, as well as the current subdirectory. PATH.DAT should only have pathnames and carriage return-line feeds in it—including a <cr> <lf> after the last pathname. Here's an example:

```
\LEVEL1
B:
C:\DEEP\DEEPER\DEEPEST
```

LOCATE searches the current subdirectory, say A:\SUB, first, and then it checks in the main area of the current disk, A:\, for PATH.DAT. Since we've put one there, LOCATE reads it in and starts the search all over again, beginning with A:\LEVEL1, then searching B:\, and ending up with C:\DEEP\DEEPER\DEEPEST.

How LOCATE Works

LOCATE simply starts by searching through the current subdirectory file by file. It uses the DOS interrupts to find file names, open files; it reads them in, and then closes them. A simple search algorithm searches for the first letter in the string throughout the file. Once it is found, a string comparison from that point on is done between the string and the characters in the file. If the full string matches, LOCATE has scored a hit, and the context surrounding the string is typed out.

After exhausting the current subdirectory, LOCATE opens PATH.DAT in the main directory, if it's there, and performs the same process over again using those pathnames as prefixes to the files it will search through.

LISTING 8.3 LOCATE.ASM

```
CODE_SEG        SEGMENT
        ASSUME  CS:CODE_SEG,DS:CODE_SEG,ES:CODE_SEG
        ORG     100H                    ;Start off right for a .Com file
ENTRY:  JMP     LOCATE                  ;Skip over Data area

        COPY_RIGHT DB '(C)1985 S.Holzner'       ;Author's Mark
        FOUND_MSG DB 13,10,13,10,'FOUND IN $'   ;Like it says
        LEN  DW 1                               ;The file length (low word)
        PATH_LEN        DW 0                    ;Length of Path.Dat
        NUMBER  DW 0                            ;Number of bytes read from file
        EXTRA_PATHS     DB 0                    ;=1 if we open & use Path.Dat
        OLD_BX  DW 0                            ;Save pointer to path at CS:DBH
        OLD_SI  DW 0                            ;Save SI as pointer also
```

LISTING 8.3 CONTINUED

```
        START_FLAG      DB 0                    ;For searches in PAth.Dat
        PATH_DAT        DB "\PATH.DAT",0        ;Asciiz string of Path.Dat

LOCATE  PROC    NEAR            ;Here we go

        MOV     DX,0B0H         ;Move Disk Transfer Area to CS:0B0H
        MOV     AH,1AH          ; Matched file information goes there
        INT     21H

        MOV     DI,5CH          ;Use CS:5CH to put '*.*'0 at for search
        CALL    PUT             ; in current directory
        MOV     DX,5CH          ;Point to '*.*'0 for search
        MOV     AH,4EH          ; and find first matching file
        INT     21H             ;Match now at DTA, 0B0H
LOOP:                           ;Loop over matches now
        MOV     BX,0CAH         ;Get file length, came from match
        MOV     DX,[BX]
        MOV     LEN,DX          ;Store in Len
        CMP     DX,60*1024      ;Don't write over stack, allow < 64K files
        JB      NOT_BIG         ;Range extender (Find > 127 bytes ahead)
        JMP     FIND
NOT_BIG:CMP     DX,0            ;Was this a 0 length file (disk dir or label)?
        JA      FILE_OK         ;No, go on and read it
        JMP     FIND            ;Yes, find next file and skip this one
FILE_OK:CALL    READ_FILE       ;Get the file into memory
        MOV     CX,NUMBER       ;Prepare to loop over all read bytes
        MOV     DI,OFFSET PATHS+300     ;File starts at Offset Paths+300
SEARCH:                                 ;Use Repne Scasb & DI to search for the
        MOV     BX,82H          ;first letter of the string, which is at CS:82H
        MOV     AL,BYTE PTR [BX]        ;Load into AL for Repne Scasb
REPNE   SCASB                           ;Find first letter
        JCXZ    FIND            ;If out of file to search, find next file
        MOV     BX,80H          ;How many chars in string? Get from CS:80H
        XOR     DX,DX           ;Set DX to zero
        MOV     DL,[BX]         ;Get # of chars in string
        DEC     DX              ;Get rid of space typed after 'Locate'
        MOV     SI,83H          ;Search from second typed letter (1st matched)
CPLOOP: DEC     DX              ;Loop counter
        CMPS    BYTE PTR [DI],[SI]      ;See how far we get until no match
        JZ      CPLOOP
        DEC     DI              ;At end, reset DI (Scasb increments 1 too much )
        CMP     DX,0            ;If DX is not zero, all letters did not match
        JA      SEARCH          ;If not a match, go back and get next one
        LEA     DX,FOUND_MSG    ;FILE HAS BEEN FOUND, say so.
        MOV     AH,9            ;Request string search
        INT     21H
        MOV     AH,2            ;Now to print filename. Without Path.Dat, at
        MOV     BX,0DBH         ; CS:CEH, with Path.Dat at CS:DBH
        CMP     EXTRA_PATHS,1   ; Using Path.Dat yet?
        JE      PRINT           ;Yes, print
        MOV     BX,0CEH         ;No, reset BX to point to CS:CEH
PRINT:  MOV     DL,[BX]         ;Print out the filename until 0 found
        CMP     DL,0            ;Is it 0?
        JE      MORE            ;If yes,print out sample at More:
        INT     21H             ;Print filename character
        INC     BX              ;Point to next character
        JMP     PRINT           ;Go back relentlessly until done
MORE:   PUSH    DI              ;Save DI,BX,CX
        PUSH    BX
```

LISTING 8.3 CONTINUED

```
        PUSH    CX
        MOV     CX,40           ;Prepare to type out total of 40 characters
        MOV     AH,2            ;With Int 21H service 2
        MOV     DL,':'          ;But first, add ':' to filename
        INT     21H             ;And a carriage return linefeed
        MOV     DL,13
        INT     21H
        MOV     DL,10
        INT     21H
        SUB     DI,20           ;DI points to end of found string, move back
        MOV     BX,OFFSET PATHS+300     ;Beginning of file
        CMP     DI,BX           ;If before beginning, start at beginning
        JA      GO
        MOV     DI,BX
GO:     ADD     BX,LEN          ;Now BX=end of file (to check if we're past it)
SHOW:   MOV     DL,[DI]         ;Get character from file
        INC     DI              ;And point to next one
        CMP     DI,BX           ;Past end?
        JA      SHOWS_OVER      ;Yes, jump out, look for next match
        CMP     DL,30           ;Unprintable character?
        JA      POK             ;No, OK
        MOV     DL,' '          ;Yes, make it a space
POK:    INT     21H             ;Print Character
        LOOP    SHOW            ;And return for the next one
SHOWS_OVER:                     ;End of printout
        POP     CX              ;Restore the registers used above
        POP     BX
        POP     DI
        JMP     SEARCH          ;Return to search more of the file
FIND:   CALL    FIND_FILE       ;This file done, find next match
        CMP     AL,18           ;AL=18 → no match
        JE      OUT             ;And so we leave
        JMP     LOOP            ;If match found, go back once again
OUT:    INT     20H             ;End of Main Program
LOCATE   ENDP

PUT     PROC    NEAR                    ;This little gem puts a '*.*'0
        MOV     BYTE PTR [DI],'*'       ;Wherever you want it, just send
        MOV     BYTE PTR [DI+1],'.'     ;It a value in DI. '*.*'0 used as
        MOV     BYTE PTR [DI+2],'*'     ;Universal wildcard in searches
        MOV     BYTE PTR [DI+3],0
        RET
PUT     ENDP

WS      PROC    NEAR                    ;Strip the bits for WordStar
        CMP     CX,0                    ;If there is a length of 0, e.g.
        JE      FIN                     ;Directory entries, etc. do nothing.
WSLOOP: AND BYTE PTR [BX],127           ;Set top bit to zero
        INC     BX                      ;Point to next unsuspecting byte
        LOOP    WSLOOP                  ;And get it too.
FIN:    RET                             ;To use, send this program BX and CX
WS      ENDP

FIND_FILE       PROC    NEAR    ;The file finder
        MOV     AH,4FH          ;Try service 4FH, find next match, first
        INT     21
        CMP     AL,18           ;AL = 18 → no match
        JE      CHECK           ;Range extender.
        JMP     NEW
```

LISTING 8.3 CONTINUED

```
CHECK:  CMP     EXTRA_PATHS,1   ;Have we used path.Dat?
        JE      NEXT_PATH       ;Yes, get next path, this one used up
        INC     EXTRA_PATHS     ;No, set it to 1
        MOV     AX,3D00H        ;Request file opening for Path.Dat
        LEA     DX,PATH_DAT     ;Point to '\PATH.DAT'0
        INT     21H
        JNC     READ            ;If there was a carry, Path.Dat not found
DONE:   MOV     AL,18           ;And so we exit with AL=18
        JMP     END
READ:   MOV     CX,300          ;Assume the max length for Path.Dat, 300.
        MOV     BX,AX           ;Move found file handle into BX for read
        MOV     AH,3FH          ;Set up for file read
        LEA     DX,PATHS        ;Put the file at location Paths (at end)
        INT     21H             ;Read in the file
        ADD     AX,OFFSET PATHS         ;Full offset of end of Path.Dat
        MOV     PATH_LEN,AX     ;Get Path.Dat end point for loop
        MOV     AH,3EH          ;Now close the file
        INT     21H             ;Close file
        MOV     OLD_SI,OFFSET PATHS     ;Save for future path-readings
        MOV     CX,300                  ;Get ready to Un-WordStar
        MOV     BX,OFFSET PATHS         ;300 bytes at location Paths
        CALL    WS                      ;Strip high bit for WS
NEXT_PATH:              ;Come here to find next path to search for files
        MOV     SI,OLD_SI               ;Point to start of next path
        MOV     DI,5CH  ;Move will be to CS:5CH for '\path\*.*0' file find
        MOV     BX,0DBH ;Also to CS:DBH; will assemble full path & filename
        MOV     START_FLAG,0    ;Start the path search
CHAR:   CMP     SI,PATH_LEN     ;Past end of possible path names?
        JGE     DONE            ;Yes, we're done. Leave with AL=18
        CMP     BYTE PTR [SI],30        ;Carriage return or linefeed?
        JB      NEXT                    ;Yes, get next char
        MOV     START_FLAG,1            ;First char, stop skipping chars
        MOV     AL,[SI]                 ;Get char from Path.Dat
        MOV     [BX],AL                 ;Move char to DBH
        INC     BX                      ;And increment to next location there
        MOVSB                           ;Also move to 5CH area
        JMP     CHAR                    ;And go back for more
NEXT:   CMP     START_FLAG,1    ;Bad char, have we been reading a real pathname?
        JE      PDONE           ;Yes, Have reached the end of it.
        INC     SI              ;No, keep skipping chars to find pathname
        JMP     CHAR
PDONE:  MOV     OLD_SI,SI       ;Save SI for the next path.
        MOV     BYTE PTR [DI],'\'       ;Add '\' to both paths
        MOV     BYTE PTR [BX],'\'
        INC     BX                      ;Move BX on for next time
        MOV     OLD_BX,BX               ;And save it.
        INC     DI                      ;Move to next location at 5CH and
        CALL    PUT                     ;Put '*.*'0 there to find all files.
        MOV     DX,5CH                  ;Start the search for all files in
        MOV     AH,4EH                  ; the new path.
        MOV     CX,0                    ;Set the file attribute to 0
        INT     21H
        CMP     AL,18                   ;Did we find any new files in new path?
        JE      NEXT_PATH               ;No, get the next path.
NEW:    CMP     EXTRA_PATHS,1           ;Yes,Move found filename to DBH area to
        JNE     END                     ; read it in-only if DBH area is active
        MOV     BX,OLD_BX               ; (i.e. Extra_Paths=). Restore BX
        MOV     SI,0CDH                 ;And point to found filename in DTA
CLOOP:  INC     SI                      ;Next letter from found filename
```

LISTING 8.3 CONTINUED

```
        MOV     AH,[SI]                   ;Move it to the DBH area so we can read
        MOV     [BX],AH                   ; in the file (needs pathname\filename)
        INC     BX                        ;Next character in 5CH area.
        CMP     BYTE PTR [SI],0           ;Is this the last character?
        JNE     CLOOP                     ;Nope, get next one
END:    RET                               ;After path & filename assembled, return
FIND_FILE       ENDP

READ_FILE       PROC    NEAR    ;Looks for filename at CEH or DBH & reads it
        PUSH    AX              ;Push everything to save it.
        PUSH    BX
        PUSH    CX
        PUSH    DX
        MOV     DX,0DBH         ;Try the DBH area
        CMP     EXTRA_PATHS,1             ;Has it been used?
        JE      OK              ;Yes
        MOV     DX,0CEH  ;No, not using paths yet, use filename only, at CEH OK:
        MOV     AX,3D00H        ;Prepare for file reading
        INT     21H             ;And do so.
        MOV     BX,AX           ;Move file handle into BX to read
        MOV     DX,OFFSET PATHS+300       ;Read into data area at Paths+300 bytes
        MOV     CX,LEN                    ;Read the full file's length in bytes
        MOV     AH,3FH                    ;Read it in at last
        INT     21H
        MOV     NUMBER,AX                 ;# bytes actually got.
        MOV     AH,3EH                    ;Close file
        INT     21H
        MOV     BX,OFFSET PATHS+300       ;Clean up the WordStar high bit.
        MOV     CX,LEN                    ;For the full file
        CALL    WS                        ;Strip high bit for ws
        POP     DX                        ;Pop everything and return
        POP     CX
        POP     BX
        POP     AX
        RET                               ;Fin of Read_File
READ_FILE       ENDP
PATHS:                                    ;Here's the end of program marker

CODE_SEG        ENDS
        END     ENTRY                     ;End 'Entry' so DOS starts at 'Entry'
```

Appendix A
BIOS and DOS Reference

This appendix is intended for use as a reference. We will work through all the interrupts the PC has, from 0 to FF, making this one of the most complete references available. Now that you know about programming, it is essential to know what the system offers you. The only thing we won't cover in detail are the additions to DOS in DOS 3+, since extended error checking can get long-winded (there are some 88 extended error codes). If you find any of the descriptions of the DOS 3+ additions interesting, you can find a full description in the DOS *Technical Reference Manual*.

If we have discussed an Interrupt or an Interrupt Service before, the appropriate chapter reference is given, and the Input and Output registers are listed. Otherwise, each interrupt is given some discussion here.

BIOS INTERRUPTS

First we'll cover the BIOS Interrupts, then work on through the DOS ones.

Interrupt 0—Divide by 0

This is the first of the BIOS interrupts—BIOS uses interrupts 0 to 1FH, and DOS continues from 20H upward. Interrupt 0 is the divide by zero routine; if the 8088 executes a divide by zero, then this interrupt is called. It prints out its message, "Divide Overflow", and usually stops program execution.

If you work in program development, you may see Interrupt 0 for another reason. Since this address is at the bottom of memory (0000:0000), you might get a "Divide Overflow" message if your stack has been destroyed. In other words, if SS and SP are set to 0000:0000, you'll get this message, and it is almost a sure sign of stack problems.

Interrupt 1—Single Step

No one, except a debugger, uses this interrupt. It is used to single step through code, with a call to this interrupt between executed instructions.

Interrupt 2—Non-Maskable Interrupt (NMI)

This is a hardware interrupt. This interrupt cannot be blocked off by using STI and CLI; it always gets executed when called. If the parity-checking memory in your PC detects an error, this interrupt puts the message "PARITY CHECK 2" on the screen.

Interrupt 3—Breakpoint

This is another debugger interrupt. DEBUG uses this interrupt with the Go command. If you want to execute all the code up to a particular address and then stop, DEBUG will insert an INT 3 into the code at that point and then give control to the program. When the INT 3 is reached, DEBUG can take control again.

Interrupt 4—Overflow

This is similar to INT 0. If there is an overflow condition, this interrupt is called. Usually, though, no action is called for, and BIOS simply returns.

Interrupt 5—Print Screen

This interrupt was chosen by BIOS to print the screen out. If you use the PrtSc key on the keyboard, this is the interrupt that gets called. Needless to say, your program can also issue an INT 5 by just including that instruction in the program. There are no arguments to be passed.

Interrupts 6 and 7—Reserved

Interrupts 6 and 7 are reserved for future BIOS use. You can, of course, write interrupt-handlers for them yourself, but you have to make sure no future version of BIOS uses them.

Interrupt 8—Time of Day

This is another hardware interrupt. This interrupt is called to update the PC's internal time of day (stored in the BIOS data area) 18.2 times a second. If the date needs to be changed, this interrupt will handle that, too.

This interrupt calls INT 1CH as well. If you want to intercept the timer and do something 18.2 times a second, it is recommended you intercept INT 1CH instead of this one.

Interrupt 9—Keyboard

This is an interrupt we are familiar with. Whenever you touch a key on the keyboard, an INT 9 is generated. The waiting keystroke is read in from the keyboard's port, processed, and placed into the keyboard buffer if required.

If you want to make your own keyboard utility, this is the interrupt to intercept. Since INT 9 does a lot of work in deciphering which key was struck, it is recommended that you let it read in the key from the keyboard, process it, then you can read what was typed from the keyboard buffer.

Interrupt 0AH—Reserved

This interrupt is another reserved interrupt for later BIOS use.

Interrupts 0BH–0FH

These interrupts point to the BIOS routine D_EOI, which is BIOS' End of Interrupt routine. All this routine does is to reset the interrupt handler at port 20H and return.

INT 10H Service 0—Set Screen Mode

Input	Output	
AH=0	Screen Set to:	
AL=0	40 × 25 B&W	Graphics Screen
1	40 × 25 Color	Graphics Screen
2	80 × 25 B&W	Graphics Screen
3	80 × 25 Color	Graphics Screen
4	320 × 200 Color	Graphics Screen
5	320 × 200 B&W	Graphics Screen
6	640 × 200 Color	Graphics Screen
7	80 × 25 Monochrome (Monochrome Screen)	

See Chapter 5.

INT 10H Service 1—Set Cursor Type

Input	Output
AH=1 CH = Cursor Start Line CL = Cursor End Line	New Cursor

See Chapter 5.

INT 10H Service 2—Set Cursor Position

Input	Output
DH,DL = Row, Column BH = Page Number AH=2	Cursor position changed.

NOTE: DH,DL = 0,0 = Upper Left

See Chapter 5.

INT 10H Service 3—Find Cursor Position

Input	Output
BH=Page Number AH=3	DH,DL=Row, Column of Cursor. CH,CL=Cursor Mode currently Set.

See Chapter 5.

INT 10H Service 4—Read Light Pen Position

Input	Output
AH=4	AH=0→Light pen switch not down. AL=1→DH,DL=Row, Column of light pen position CH Raster line (Vertical) 0–199 BX Pixel column (Horizontal) 0–319,639

See Chapter 5.

INT 10H Service 5—Set Active Display Page

Input	Output
AL=0–7 (Screen modes 0,1) 0–3 (Screen modes 2,3) AH=5	Active page changed.

Different Pages Available in Alphanumeric Modes Only (Graphics Adapters). See Chapter 5.

INT 10H Service 6—Scroll Active Page Up

Input

AL=#Lines blanked at bottom (0→Blank whole area).
CH,CL=Upper Left Row,Column of area to scroll.
DH,DL=Lower Right Row,Column of area to scroll.
BH=Attribute used on blank line.
AH=6

See Chapter 5.

INT 10H Service 7—Scroll Active Page Down

Input

AL=#Lines blanked at bottom (0→Blank whole area).
CH,CL=Upper Left Row,Column of area to scroll.
DH,DL=Lower Right Row,Column of area to scroll.
BH=Attribute used on blank line.
AH=7

See Chapter 5.

INT 10H Service 8—Read Attribute and Character at Cursor Position

Input	Output
BH = Page Number AH=8	AL=Character read (ASCII). AH=Attribute of character (Alphanumerics only).

See Chapter 5.

INT 10H Service 9—Write Attribute and Character at Cursor Position

Input

BH=Page Number
BL→Alpha Modes=Attribute
    Graphics Modes=Color
CX=Count of characters to write
AL=IBM ASCII code.
AH=9

Output

Character written on screen at Cursor Position.

See Chapter 5.

INT 10H Service 10—Write Character ONLY at Cursor Position

Input

BH=Page Number
CX=Count of characters to write
AL=IBM ASCII code.
AH=0AH

Output

Character written on screen at Cursor Position.

See Chapter 5.

INT 10H Service 11—Set Color Palette

Input

BH=Palette Color ID
BL BH=0→BL=Background Color
   BH=1→BL=Palette Number
        (0=Green/Red/Yellow)
        (1=Cyan/Magenta/White)
AH=11

You can set border colors in 640 × 200 mode. See Chapters 4 and 5.

INT 10H Service 12—Write Dot

Input

DX=Row Number (0–199) [0,0] is upper left.
CX=Column Number (0–319,639)
AL=Color Value (0–3)
AH=12

If bit 7 of AL is 1, the color value is XORed with the current value of the dot. See Chapter 5.

INT 10H Service 13—Read Dot

Input	Output
DX=Row Number (0–199) CX=Column Number (0–319,639) AH=13 [0,0] is upper left.	AL=Color Value (0–3)

If bit 7 of AL is 1, the color value is XORed with the current value of the dot. See Chapter 5.

INT 10H Service 14—Teletype Write to Active Page

Input

AL=IBM ASCII code.
BL=Foreground Color
(Graphics mode).
AH=14

See Chapter 5.

INT 10H Service 15—Return Video State

Input	Output
AH=15	AH=Number of alphanumeric columns on screen. AL=Current mode (See INT 10H Service 0). BH=Active display page.

See Chapter 5.

INT 11H—Equipment Determination

Input	Output
	Bits of AX 15,14 = Number of Printers 13 = Not used 12 = Game Adapter attached 11,10,9 = Number of RS232 cards installed. 8 = Unused. 7,6 = Number of Diskette drives. (00→1;01→2;10→3;11→4 If Bit 0 = 1) 5,4 = Video Mode (00 Unused, 01=40×25 Color Card 10=80×25 Color Card, 11=80×25 Monochrome) 3,2 = Motherboard RAM (00=16K,01=32K,10=48K,11=64K) 1 = Not used. 0 = 1 if there are diskette drives attached.

This is a handy Interrupt, and it will tell you to some extent just how the PC you are working with is configured. One serious omission is that no information concerning the coprocessor, the 8087, is returned.

INT 12H—Determine Memory Size

Input	Output
	AX=Number of Contiguous 1K Memory Blocks.

This Interrupt checks the size of installed memory as represented by the internal DIP switches. For example, if you have 256K on the motherboard, INT 12H will leave 100H = 256 for 256K in AX.

INT 13H—Service 0 Reset Disk

Input	Output
AH=0	No Carry → AH=0, Success. Carry → AH=Error Code (See Service 1).

Hard disk systems: DL=80H→reset diskette(s) DL=81H→reset hard disk. See Chapter 6.

INT 13H Service 1—Read Status of Last Operation

Input	Output	
AH=1	Disk Error Codes:	
	AL=00	No Error.
	AL=01	Bad Command passed to controller.
	AL=02	Address Mark not found.
	AL=03	Diskette is Write Protected.
	AL=04	Sector not found.
	AL=05	Reset failed.
	AL=07	Drive parameters wrong.
	AL=09	DMA across segment end.
	AL=0BH	Bad track flag seen.
	AL=10H	Bad error check seen.
	AL=11H	Data is error corrected.
	AL=20H	Controller failure.
	AL=40H	Seek operation has failed.
	AL=80H	No response from disk.
	AL=0BBH	Undefined error.
	AL=0FFH	Sense operation failed.

Hard disk systems: DL<80H→use diskette(s) DL>80H→use hard disk. Errors 05, 07, 11H, 0BBH, 0FFH only valid for hard disks, Error 03 only valid for floppies. See Chapter 6.

INT 13H Service 2—Read Sectors into Memory

Input

AH=2
DL=Drive Number
DH=Head Number
CH=Cylinder or Track (Floppies) Number
CL=Sector Number
AL=Number of Sectors to Read (Floppies 1–8
Hard Disks 1–80H
Hard Disks Read/Write Long 1–79H).
ES:BX=Address of buffer for reads and writes.

Output

No Carry→AH=0, Success.
Carry→AH=Disk Error Code. (See Service 1)

For hard disks, Drive number in DL can range from 80H to 87H. See Chapter 6 on packing cylinder numbers greater than 255.

INT 13H Service 3—Write Sectors to Disk

Input	Output
AH=3	No Carry→AH=0, Success.
DL=Drive Number	Carry→AH=Disk Error Code. (See Service 1)
DH=Head Number	
CH=Cylinder or Track (Floppies) Number	
CL=Sector Number	
AL=Number of Sectors to Write (Floppies 1–8	
Hard Disks 1–80H	
Hard Disks Read/Write Long 1–79H).	
ES:BX=Address of buffer for reads and writes.	

For hard disks, Drive number in DL can range from 80H to 87H. See Chapter 6.

INT 13H Service 4—Verify Sectors

Input	Output
AH=4	No Carry→AH=0, Success.
DL=Drive Number	Carry→AH=Disk Error Code. (See Service 1)
DH=Head Number	
CH=Cylinder or Track (Floppies) Number	
CL=Sector Number	
AL=Number of Sectors	
(Floppies 1–8	
Hard Disks 1–80H	
Hard Disks Read/Write Long 1–79H).	

For hard disks, Drive number in DL can range from 80H to 87H. See Chapter 6.

INT 13H Services 5,6, and 7—Formatting

Input	Output
AH=5,6 or 7	No Carry→AH=0, Success.
DH=Head Number	Carry→AH=Disk Error Code. (See Service 1)
DL=Drive Number (80H–87H only allowed for hard disks.)	
CH=Cylinder or Track (Floppies) Number	
For hard disks, Drive number in DL can range from 80H to 87H.	

AH=5 Format desired track.
AH=6 Format desired track and set bad sector flags.
AH=7 Format the desired disk starting at indicated track.

Service 5 is *only* supported by floppies. Services 6 and 7 work only on Hard disks. See Chapter 6.

INT 13H Service 8—Return Drive Parameters

Input	Output
AH=8	DL=Number of drives attached to controller.
DL>80H	DH=Maximum value for Head Number.
	CH=Maximum cylinder value.
	CL=Maximum value for sector number and high bits of cylinder number (See Chapter 6).

This Service Works *only* on Hard Disks. See Chapter 6.

INT 13H Service 9—Initialize Drive

This is a service used internally by BIOS to initialize the drive, and point INT 41H to the drive's parameter block. See Chapter 6.

INT 13H Services 0AH and 0BH—Read and Write Long Sectors

Input	Output
AH=0AH (Read)	No Carry→AH=0, Success.
AH=0BH (Write)	Carry→AH=Disk Error Code. (See Service 1)
DL=Drive Number (80H–87H allowed)	
DH=Head Number.	
CH=Cylinder Number.	
CL=Sector Number.	
AL=Number of Sectors (1–79H for long reads and writes).	
ES:BX=Address of buffer for reads and writes.	

These services work *only* on hard disks. See Chapter 6.

INT 13H Service 0CH—Seek

Input	Output
AH=0CH DH=Head Number. DL=Drive Number (80H–87H allowed) CH=Cylinder Number. CL=Sector Number.	No Carry→AH=0, Success. Carry→AH=Disk Error Code. (See Service 1)

This service works *only* on hard disks. See Chapter 6.

INT 13H Service 0DH—Alternate Disk Reset

This is an alternate disk reset, used only for hard disk drives. You can still use Service 0 to reset disks as well. See Chapter 6.

INT 13H Services 0EH and 0FH—Read and Write Sector Buffer

Input	Output
AH=0EH (Read) AH=0FH (Write) DL=Drive Number (80H–87H allowed) DH=Head Number. CH=Cylinder Number. CL=Sector Number. ES:BX=Address of buffer for reads and writes.	No Carry→AH=0, Success. Carry→AH=Disk Error Code (See Service 1)

These services work *only* on hard disks. See Chapter 6.

INT 13H Service 10H—Test Drive Ready

This service is an internal one, testing whether or not a hard disk drive is ready. See Chapter 6.

INT 13H Service 11H—Recalibrate Hard Drive

Input	Output
AH=11H (Read)	No Carry→AH=0, Success.
	Carry→AH=Disk Error Code (See Service 1)
DL=Drive Number (80H–87H allowed)	

This service works only on hard disks. See Chapter 6.

INT 13H—Diagnostic Services

Input	Output
AH=12H (RAM Diagnostic)	No Carry→AH=0, Success.
AH=13H (Drive Diagnostic)	Carry→AH=Disk Error Code (See Service 1)
AH=14H (Controller Diagnostic)	
DL=Drive Number (80H–87H allowed)	

These services work only on hard disks. See Chapter 6.

INT 14H, AH=0—Initialize RS232 Port

Input

AH=0
Bits of AL:

0,1	Word Length. 01→7 Bits, 11→8 Bits.
2	Stop Bits. 0→1, 1→2 stop bits.
3,4	Parity. 00→None, 01→Odd, 11→Even.
5,6,7	Baud Rate. 000→110
	001→150
	010→300
	011→600
	100→1200
	101→2400
	110→4800
	111→9600

This service sets up the RS232 port, and configures it for one of the eight baud rates possible. Please note that you must have an RS232 card before you can use this service.

INT 14H, AH=1—Send Character

Input	Output
AH=1 AL=Character to send.	If Bit 7 of AH is set, failure. If Bit 7 is not set, bits 0–6 hold status (see INT 14H, AH=3).

With this service you can send data over the serial port. Load the character to send in AL and call INT 14H with AH=1. If the send was a success, Bit 7 of AH will be 0 on return, and the other bits (0–6) will hold the current status of the line. These statuses are listed in the description of INT 14H Service 3.

INT 14H, AH=2—Receive Character

Input	Output
AH=2	AL=Character Received. AH=0, success. Otherwise, AH holds an error code (see INT 14H, AH=3).

This service lets you read a character from the RS232 port. If there was an error, AH holds the error code (see the error and status table in the next Service, INT 14H, Service 3).

INT 14H, AH=3—Return Status

Input	Output
AH=3	AH Bits Set: 7→Time Out. 6→Shift Register Empty. 5→Holding Register Empty. 4→Break detected. 3→Framing Error. 2→Parity Error. 1→Overrun Error. 0→Data Ready. AL Bits Set: 7→Received Line Signal Detect. 6→Ring Indicator. 5→Data Set Ready. 4→Clear to Send. 3→Delta Receive Line Signal Detect.

INT 14H, AH=3 continued

Input	Output
	2→Trailing Edge Ring Detector. 1→Delta Data Set Ready. 0→Delta Clear to Send.

With this service you can read the RS232 port's status. AH and AL will return with values coded as shown.

INT 15H Cassette—I/O

Input	Output
AH=0 → Turn Cassette Motor On. AH=1 → Turn Cassette Motor Off. AH=2 → Read one or more 256 byte blocks. Store data at ES:BX. CX=Count of Bytes to read. AH=3 → Write one or more 256-byte blocks from ES:BX. Count of bytes to write in CX.	DX=Number of bytes actually read. Carry flag set if error. If Carry, AH=01→CRC Error. =02→Data transitions lost. =04→No Data Found.

This is the only support given to the PC's cassette interface in BIOS. Cassettes are rarely used, but they can provide large amounts of storage. A typical cassette can store a megabyte or so of data. On the other hand, unless your cassette player is of high quality, you will almost certainly get errors. This method of data storage is not recommended unless you store everything twice.

INT 16H Service 0—Read Key from Keyboard

Input	Output
AH = 0	AH=Scan Code AL=ASCII code

See Chapter 3.

INT 16H Service 1—Check if Key Ready to be Read

Input	Output
AH = 1	Zero Flag=1 → Buffer Empty Zero Flag=0 → AH=Scan Code AL=ASCII Code

See Chapter 3.

INT 16H, Service 2—Find Keyboard Status

Input	Output
AH = 2	AL=Keyboard Status byte.

See Chapter 3.

INT 17H Service 0—Print Character in AL

Input	Output
AH=0 AL=Character to be printed. DX=Printer Number (0,1,2)	AH=1→ Printer Time Out.

This is the way BIOS communicates with your printer. To print one character, place it in AL, set AH to zero, and issue an INT 17H instruction. DX must be set to the printer number you wish to print on; these numbers range from 0–2, and correspond to ascending printer cards. If you only have one printer, choose zero.

INT 17H Service 1—Initialize Printer Port

Input	Output
AH=1 DX=Printer Number (0,1,2)	AH=Printer Status Bits Set of AH: 7→Printer Not Busy. 6→Acknowledge. 5→Out of Paper. 4→Selected. 3→I/O Error. 2→Unused. 1→Also Unused. 0→Time Out.

This service does a reset of the printer and prepares it for output. On return, AH holds the printer's status, as listed above. For example, if you initialize a printer, you will typically get a return of AH=10H, which has bit 4, Selected, set. If you select a printer you do not have (like selecting printer 2 when you only have one printer), you will get Time Out for status.

INT 17H Service 2—Read Printer Status into AH

Input	Output
AH=2 DX=Printer Number (0,1,2)	AH Set to Status Byte as in INT 17H, AH=1.

This service lets you check on your printer if you think there is something wrong.

INT 18H—Resident BASIC

This interrupt starts up ROM resident BASIC. If you do not have a disk in your PC to boot it with, this interrupt gets called. You can try calling this with DEBUG—it is startling to see BASIC take over.

INT 19H—Bootstrap

This interrupt loads the bootstrap record in from disk, if there is one. If not, INT 18H gets executed (ROM BASIC).

INT 1AH Service 0—Read Time of Day

Input	Output
AH=0	CX=High Word of Timer Count. DX=Low Word of Timer Count. AL=0 If Timer has not passed 24 hours since last read.

This is one way to find out what time it is. The PC's counter increments at a rate of 65,536 counts per hour, or about 18.204 per second. If the timer is set correctly, you can decipher this count to find the time of day.

INT 1AH Service 1—Set Time of Day

<u>Input</u>

AH=1
CX=High Word of Timer Count.
DX=Low Word of Timer Count.

This is the previous service's natural counterpart. Here you can set the time to whatever you wish. Note that since it takes 65,536 counts to make one hour, CX will simply be the hour of the day.

INT 1BH—Keyboard Break Address

This interrupt vector doesn't hold the address of an interrupt; instead, it holds the address that control will be transferred to it your program is broken with a ^Break. You might want to write and install your own ^Break handler. That can easily be done by redirecting this interrupt vector.

INT 1CH—Timer Tick Interrupt

This interrupt functions much like INT 8 since it gets called 18.2 times a second. In fact, it is called by INT 8. Originally, INT 1CH points only to an IRET command, although you can redirect it wherever you wish.

INT 1DH—Video Parameter Tables

This interrupt vector points to the address of the parameter tables that the 6845 video controller uses. These tables set things like the power-on number of columns and others.

INT 1EH—Diskette Parameters

Interrupt vector 1EH is similar to INT 1DH in that it points to a table of parameters. In this case, though, the parameters are for the power-on diskette parameters, not the video parameters. This is the Diskette Base Table.

INT 1FH—Graphics Character Definitions

This is an interesting interrupt by any standard. Like the previous interrupts, INT 1FH is not really an interrupt at all, but the address of a table in memory. This address lets you define the the top 128 ASCII characters in high-resolution graphics mode (graphics screens only). For high-resolution graphics this is actually pretty easy. Each character is given its own eight by eight grid of dots on the screen in which it is defined. (This gives it just enough dots so that 80 characters can fit comfortably into one row across the screen and 25 up and down.) Each **pixel** (which means picture element), or dot, can be either on or off on the screen, just as a bit can be either 1 or 0. Computerwise, then, our character becomes eight rows of eight bits each. Eight bits naturally becomes one byte, and so our character becomes eight bytes, one on top of the other. To turn a dot in some row of some character on, just make its matching position in that byte a 1. The table is therefore nothing more than 128 characters, one after the other, with eight bytes each or 1,024 bytes complete.

DOS INTERRUPTS

Interrupt 1FH is the last BIOS Interrupt, and DOS starts with INT 20H.

INT 20H—Terminate

This instruction we know very well. At the end of programs, INT 20H gives control back to DOS and terminates our program.

Interrupt 21H

Interrupt 21H is the DOS service interrupt. To call one of these services, load AH with the service number, and the other registers as shown.

INT 21H Service 0—Program Terminate

Input

AH = 0

This service call is exactly the same as INT 20H; and all it does is to end your program and return control to DOS.

INT 21H Service 1—Keyboard Input

Input	Output
AH = 1	AL = ASCII code of struck key Does Echo on screen

Checks for ^C or ^Break. See Chapter 3.

INT 21H Service 2—Character Output on Screen

Input

DL=IBM ASCII character.
AH=2

See Chapter 5.

INT 21H Service 3—Standard Auxiliary Device Input

Input	Output
AH=3	Character in AL

This service reads a character from the standard auxiliary device. Auxiliary input from the asynchronous communications adapter is read and returned in AL.

INT 21H Service 4—Standard Auxiliary Device Output

Input

AH=4
DL=Character to output.

This service outputs a byte to the asynchronous communications adapter. The byte is passed to this service in DL.

INT 21H Service 5—Printer Output

Input

AH=5
DL=Character to output.

This service outputs a byte to the standard printer device. As with Service 4, the byte to be written to the printer is passed in DL. You could also use INT 17H for this purpose.

INT 21H Service 6—Console I/O

Input		Output
AH = 6		
DL = FF	→	AL holds character if one ready
DL < FF	→	Type ASCII code in DL out
		Does NOT Echo on screen

Does not check for ^C or ^Break. See Chapter 3.

INT 21H Service 7—Console Input Without Echo

Input	Output
AH = 7	AL = ASCII code of struck key
	NO Echo on screen.

Does not check for ^C or ^Break. See Chapter 3.

INT 21H Service 8—Console Input Without Echo with ^C Check

Input	Output
AH = 8	AL = ASCII code of struck key.
	Does NOT echo the typed key.

Checks for ^C or ^Break. See Chapter 3.

INT 21H Service 9—String Print

Input

DS:DX point to a string that ends in '$'.
AH=9

See Chapter 5.

INT 21H Service A—String Input

Input	Output
AH = 0AH	Buffer at DS:DX filled.
[DS:DX]=Length of buffer	Echo the typed keys.

Checks for ^C or ^Break. See Chapter 3.

INT 21H Service 0BH—Check Input Status

Input	Output
AH = 0BH	AL = FF → Character ready.
	AL = 00 → Nothing to read in.

^Break is checked for. See Chapter 3.

INT 21H Service 0CH—Clear Buffer and Invoke Service

Input	Output
AH = 0CH	Standard Output from the selected Service.
AL = Keyboard Function #	

^Break is checked for. See Chapter 3.

INT 21H Service 0DH—Disk Reset

Input

AH=0DH

See Chapter 6.

INT 21H Service 0EH—Select Disk

Input

AH=0EH
DL=Drive Number
(DL=0→A
DL=1→B
and so on).

See Chapter 6.

INT 21H Service 0FH—Open Pre-Existing File

Input

DS:DX points to an FCB.
AH=0FH

Output

AL=0 → Success
AL=FF → Failure

See Chapter 4.

INT 21H Service 10H—Close File

Input

DS:DX points to an FCB.
AH=10H

Output

AL=0 → Success
AL=FF → Failure

See Chapter 4.

INT 21H Service 11H—Search for First Matching File

Input

DS:DX points to an unopened FCB
AH=11H

Output

AL=FF → Failure
AL=0 → Success
DTA holds FCB for match.

See Chapter 4.

INT 21H Service 12H—Search for Next Matching File

Input	Output
DS:DX points to an unopened FCB	AL=FF → Failure
AH=12H	AL=0 → Success
	DTA holds FCB for match.

Use this Service after Service 11H. See Chapter 4.

INT 21H Service 13H—Deletes Files

Input	Output
DS:DX points to an unopened FCB	AL=FF → Failure
AH=13H	AL=0 → Success

See Chapter 4.

INT 21H Service 14H—Sequential Read

Input	Output
DS:DX points to an opened FCB.	Requested Record put in DTA.
AH=14H	AL=0 Success.
Current Block and Record Set in FCB.	=1 End of File, no data in record.
	=2 DTA Segment too small for record.
	=3 End of File; record padded with 0

Record address incremented. See Chapter 4.

INT 21H Service 15H—Sequential Write

Input	Output
DS:DX points to an opened FCB.	One record read from DTA and written.
AH=15H	AL=0 Success.
Current Block & Record Set in FCB.	=1 Disk full.
	=2 DTA Segment too small for record.
	Record Address Incremented.

See Chapter 4.

INT 21H Service 16H—Create File

Input	Output
DS:DX points to an unopened FCB. AH=16H	AL=0 Success. =FF Directory Full.

See Chapter 4.

INT 21H Service 17H—Rename File

Input	Output
DS:DX points to a MODIFIED FCB. AH=17H	AL=0 Success. =FF Failure.

Modified FCB → Second file name starts six bytes after the end of the first file name, at DS:DX+11H. See Chapter 4.

INT 21H Service 18H—Internal to DOS

This service is used internally by DOS.

INT 21H Service 19H—Find Current Disk

Input	Output
AH=19H	AL=Current Disk (0=A, 1=B, and so on).

See Chapter 6.

INT 21H Service 1AH—Set the DTA Location

Input	Output
DS:DX points to new DTA address. AH=1AH	None.

See Chapter 6.

INT 21H Service 1BH—FAT Information for Default Drive

Input	Output
AH=1BH	DS:BX points to the "FAT Byte" DX=Number of Clusters. AL=Number of Sectors/Cluster. CX=Size of a Sector (512).

See Chapter 6.

INT 21H Service 1CH—FAT Information for Specified Drive

Input	Output
AH=1CH DL=Drive Number (0=Default 1=A...)	DS:BX points to the "FAT Byte" DX=Number of Clusters. AL=Number of Sectors/Cluster. CX=Size of a Sector (512).

See Chapter 6.

INT 21H Services 1DH–20H—Internal to DOS

These services, 1DH to 20H, are also used internally by DOS only.

INT 21H Service 21H—Random Read

Input	Output
DS:DX points to an opened FCB. Set FCB's Random Record field at DS:DX+33 and DS:DX+35 AH=21H	AL=00 Success. =01 end of file, no more data. =02 not enough space in DTA segment =03 end of file, partial record padded with 0s.

See Chapter 4.

INT 21H Service 22H—Random Write

Input

DS:DX points to an opened FCB.
Set FCB's Random Record field
at DS:DX+33 and DS:DX+35
AH=21H

Output

AL=00 Success.
=01 Disk is full.
=02 not enough space in DTA
segment.

See Chapter 4.

INT 21H Service 23H—File Size

Input

DS:DX points to an unopened FCB.
AH=23H

Output

AL=00 Success.
=FF No file found that matched FCB.
Random Record Field set to file length
in records, rounded up.

See Chapter 4.

INT 21H Service 24H—Set Random Record Field

Input

DS:DX points to an opened FCB.
AH=24H

Output

Random Record Field set to match
Current Record and Current Block.

See Chapter 4.

INT 21H Service 25H—Set Interrupt Vector

Input

AH=25H
AL = Interrupt Number
DS:DX = New Address

This is DOS's recommended way of intercepting interrupts. To intercept an interrupt, simply fill DS:DX with the new address it should point to and AL with the interrupt type. You can find the interrupt vector's original contents with Service 35H.

INT 21H Service 26H—Create a New Program Segment

This is the old version of this call. For DOS 2+, you should use Service 4BH.

INT 21H Service 27H—Random Block Read

Input

DS:DX points to an opened FCB.
Set FCB's Random Record field
at DS:DX+33 and DS:DX+35
AH=27H

Output

AL=00 Success.
=01 end of file, no more data.
=02 not enough space in DTA segment.
=03 end of file, partial record padded with 0s.
CX=Number of records read.
Random Record Fields set to access next record.

See Chapter 4.

INT 21H Service 28H—Random Block Write

Input

DS:DX points to an opened FCB.
Set FCB's Random Record field
at DS:DX+33 and DS:DX+35
CX=number of records to write.
AH=28H

Output

AL=00 Success.
=01 Disk is full.
=02 not enough space in DTA segment.
Random Record Fields set to access next record.

CX=0 → file set to the size indicated by the Random Record field. See Chapter 4.

INT 21H Service 29H—Parse Filename

Input

DS:SI = Command line to parse.
ES:DI = Address to put FCB at.
AL = Bit 0=1 → Leading separators are scanned off command line.
Bit 1=1 → Drive ID in final FCB will be changed ONLY if a drive was specified.

Output

DS:SI = 1st character after filename.
ES:DI = Valid FCB

INT 21H Service 29H continued

Input

Bit 2=1 → Filename in FCB changed
ONLY if command line includes filename.
Bit 3=1 → Filename extension in FCB
will be changed ONLY if command line
contains a filename extension.
AH=29H

If the command line does not contain a valid filename, ES:[DI+1] will be a blank. This service is a useful one for processing file names from input. All you must do is to supply the address of a command line, and Service 29H will scan it for a file name something like: A:BASEBALL.BAT. If it finds a file name, the service will place an unopened FCB for the file at address ES:DI.

INT 21H Service 2AH—Get Date

Input	Output
AH=2AH	CX = Year − 1980 DH = Month (1=January, etc.) DL = Day of the month.

This is a handy service for finding the date, assuming it was set correctly. All you need do is to load AH with 2AH and you will get the return listed above.

INT 21H Service 2BH—Set Date

Input	Output
CX = Year − 1980 DH = Month (1=January, etc.) DL = Day of the month. AH=2BH	AL = 0 Success. AL = FF Date not valid.

This service is the counterpart of 2BH, and makes setting the date easier than doing it yourself.

INT 21H Service 2CH—Get Time

Input	Output
AH=2CH	CH = Hours (0–23) Cl = Minutes (0–59) DH = Seconds (0–59) DL = Hundredths of seconds (0–99)

Service 2CH lets you find the time without having to calculate it yourself from the time counter in memory.

INT 21H Service 2DH—Set Time

Input	Output
AH=2DH	AL = 0 Success.
CH = Hours (0–23)	AL = FF Time is Invalid.
CL = Minutes (0–59)	
DH = Seconds (0–59)	
DL = Hundredths of seconds (0–99)	

This service is the counterpart of 2CH, and it makes it easy to set the time, in the format shown above.

INT 21H Service 2EH—Set or Reset Verify Switch

Input

AH=2EH
DL=0
AL=1 → Turn Verify On.
  =0 → Turn Verify Off.

This function call turns verification for disk writing on or off. Disk errors are very unusual, but there are times when it doesn't hurt to make sure.

INT 21H Service 2FH—Get Current DTA

Input	Output
AH=2FH	ES:BX = Current DTA address.

This service is often useful if you want to change the DTA's location, but want to restore it later. It's also useful for keeping track of the DTA if you change it frequently.

INT 21H Service 30H—Get DOS Version Number

Input	Output
AH=30H	AL=Major Version Number (3 in DOS 3.1) AH=Minor Version Number BX=0 CX=0

If AL returns 0, you are working with a version of DOS before 2.0. If you are planning to use advanced features, or even pathnames, it pays to check the DOS version to make sure it will support what you want.

INT 21H Service 31H—Terminate Process and Keep Resident

Input

AH=31H
AL=Binary Exit Code
DX=Size of memory request in paragraphs.

Exit code can be read by a parent program with Service 4DH. It can also be tested by ERRORLEVEL commands in batch files. This is a new method preferred to INT 27H in the newer versions of DOS. The reason this method is preferable is because it can return an exit code (in AL) to a parent process. See Service 4DH.

INT 21H Service 32H—Internal to DOS

This service is only used internally in DOS.

INT 21H Service 33H—Control Break Check

Input	Output
AH=33H	
AL=0 → Check state of ^Break Checking.	DL=0 → Off. DL=1 → On.
=1 → Set the state of ^Break Checking. (DL=0→ Turn it Off. DL=1→ Turn it On.)	

When Control Break checking is on, DOS checks to see if a ^Break is pending each time a DOS service is called. Otherwise, you may wait a long time for your ^Break to be honored. This service lets you turn checking on and off at will.

INT 21H Service 34H—Internal to DOS

This service is only used internally in DOS.

INT 21H Service 35H—Get Interrupt Vector

Input	Output
AH=35H AL=Interrupt Number	ES:BX = Interrupt's Vector.

This call matches Service 25H, which sets vectors. In advanced machines, the interrupt table need not start at 0000:0000, so the recommended method of intercepting an interrupt is to use this service and Service 25H to do the work for you.

INT 21H Service 36H—Get Free Disk Space

Input	Output
AH=36H DL=Drive Number (0=Default 1=A...)	AX=0FFFH→Drive Number Invalid AX=Number of Sectors/Cluster. BX=Number of available Clusters. CX=Size of a Sector (512). DX=Number of Clusters.

See Chapter 6.

INT 21H Service 37H—Internal to DOS

This service is used only internally in DOS.

INT 21H Service 38H—Returns Country Dependent Information

Input

AH=38H
DS:DX = address of 32-byte block.
AL=0

Output

Filled in 32-byte block (see below)

The 32-byte block looks like this:

2 Bytes DATE/TIME Format.
1 byte of currency symbol (ASCII)
1 byte set to 0.
1 byte thousands separator (ASCII)
1 byte set to 0.
1 byte decimal separator (ASCII)
1 byte set to 0.
24 bytes used internally.

The DATE/TIME format has these values:

0 = USA (H:M:S M/D/Y)
1 = EUROPE (H:M:S D/M/Y)
2 = JAPAN (H:M:S D:M:Y)

In DOS 3+ you can set, as well as read, these values. If you're writing international software, this service will tell you what protocol you should use for times, dates, currencies, and other facts.

INT 21H Service 39H—Create a Subdirectory

Input

AH=39H
DS:DX point to ASCIIZ string
with directory name.

Output

No Carry→ Success.
Carry→AH has error value.
AH=3 Path Not Found.
AH=5 Access Denied.

See Chapter 6.

INT 21H Service 3AH—Delete a Subdirectory

Input

AH=3AH
DS:DX point to ASCIIZ string with directory name.

See Chapter 6.

Output

No Carry→ Success.
Carry→AH has error value.
AH=3 Path Not Found.
AH=5 Access Denied or Subdirectory not empty.

INT 21H Service 3BH—Change Current Directory

Input

AH=3BH
DS:DX point to ASCIIZ string with directory name.
See Chapter 6.

Output

No Carry→ Success.
Carry→AH has error value.
AH=3 Path Not Found.

INT 21H Service 3CH—Create a File

Input

DS:DX points to ASCIIZ filename.
CX=Attribute of File.
AH=3CH

See Chapter 4.

Output

No Carry →AX=File Handle.
Carry → AL=3 Path not found.
=4 Too many files open.
=5 Dir full, or previous Read-Only file exists.

INT 21H Service 3DH—Open a File

Input

DS:DX points to ASCIIZ filename.
AL=Access Code.
AH=3DH V
[Access Codes:
AL=0 File Opened for Reading.
AL=1 File Opened for Writing.
AL=2 File Opened for Reading and Writing.]

See Chapter 4.

Output

No Carry → AX=File Handle.
Carry → AL=Error Code
(Check Error Table).

INT 21H Service 3EH—Close a File Handle

Input

BX holds a valid File Handle.
AH=3EH

Output

Carry → AL=6 → Invalid handle.

See Chapter 4.

INT 21H Service 3FH—Read from File or Device

Input

DS:DX = Data Buffer Address.
CX=Number of bytes to read.
BX=File Handle.
AH=3FH

Output

No Carry→ AX=Number of bytes read.
Carry→ AL=5 Access Denied.
AL=6 Invalid Handle.

See Chapter 4.

INT 21H Service 40H—Write to File or Device

Input

DS:DX = Data Buffer Address.
CX=Number of bytes to write.
BX=File Handle.
AH=40H

Output

No Carry→ AX=Number of bytes written.
Carry→ AL=5 Access Denied.
AL=6 Invalid Handle.

Full disk is NOT considered an error. Check the number of bytes you wanted to write (CX) against the number actually written (returned in AX). If they do not match, the disk is probably full. See Chapters 4 and 5.

INT 21H Service 41H—Delete a File

Input	Output
DS:DX = ASCIIZ filename.	No Carry→ Success.
AH=41H	Carry→ AL=2 File Not Found.
	AL=5 Access Denied.

No wildcards allowed in filename. See Chapter 4.

INT 21H Service 42H—Move Read/Write Pointer

Input	Output
BX=File Handle	No Carry→DX:AX=New Location of Pointer.
CX:DX=Desired offset.	Carry→AL=1 Illegal Function Number.
AL=Method Value	AL=6 Invalid Handle.
AH=42H V	

Method Values (AL):
- AL=0 Read/Write Pointer moved to CX:DX from the start of the file.
- AL=1 Pointer incremented CX:DX bytes.
- AL=2 Pointer moved to end-of-file plus offset (CX:DX).

See Chapter 4.

INT 21H Service 43H—Change File's Attribute

Input	Output
DS:DX = ASCIIZ Filestring.	No Carry→Success.
AL=1→ File attrib. changed. CX holds new attribute.	Carry→AL=2 File Not Found.
AL=0→ File's current attribute returned in CX.	AL=3 Path Not Found.
AH=43H	AL=5 Access Denied.
	If AL was 0, CX returns the attribute.

See Chapter 4.

INT 21H Service 44H—I/O Control

This service is a very complex one. You can read about it in the *DOS Technical Reference Manual*, but it is beyond the scope of this book. It is used for I/O Control (IOCTL) when you set up and define your own devices. With IOCTL you can request I/O and get input or output status.

INT 21H Service 45H—Duplicate a File Handle

Input	Output
BX=File Handle to duplicate. AH=45H	No Carry→AX=New, duplicated Handle. Carry→AL=4 Too many files open. AL=6 Invalid Handle.

See Chapter 4.

INT 21H Service 46H—Force Duplication of a File Handle

Input	Output
BX=File Handle to duplicate. CX=Second File Handle. AH=46H	No Carry→Handles refer to same "stream" Carry→AL=6 Invalid Handle.

See Chapter 4.

INT 21H Service 47H—Get Current Directory on Specified Drive

Input	Output
AH=47H DS:SI point to 64-byte buffer. DL=Drive Number.	No Carry→ Success, ASCIIZ at DS:SI Carry→AH=15 Invalid Drive Specified.

Drive letter is NOT included in returned ASCIIZ string. See Chapter 6.

INT 21H Service 48H—Allocate Memory

Input	Output
AH=48H BX=Number of paragraphs requested	No Carry→AX:0000 memory block address. Carry→AL=7 Memory control blocks destroyed. AL=8 Insufficient Memory, BX contains maximum allowable request.

This is the first of the DOS memory allocation services. When you load a .COM file, all of memory is given to it. But when you load a .EXE file, this is not necessarily the case. Nor is it the case if the .COM file itself loads another program and runs it.

The way a program can request more memory is with this service. All you need to do is to put the requested number of paragraphs (each 16 bytes long) into BX and call Service 48H. If there was an error, check AL. If it holds an eight, BX contains the largest number of paragraphs you can request. The usual procedure is to load BX with a large number to begin with, find out how many blocks you can actually request (in BX), and then issue a second call for that amount.

INT 21H Service 49H—Free Allocated Memory

Input	Output
AH=49H	No Carry → Success.
ES=Segment of block being freed	Carry → AL=7 Memory Control Blocks Destroyed. =9 Incorrect Memory Block Address.

You must use this service to free memory that was allocated by Service 48H. In addition, a program that will load and run another program must first free the memory in which it is to load the second program.

In general, it is not a good idea for memory-resident programs to use these memory allocation services, since you may free memory belonging to another program, and DOS will most likely crash.

INT 21H Service 4AH—SETBLOCK

Input	Output
AH=4AH	No Carry → Success.
ES=Segment of block to modify.	Carry → AL = 7 Memory Control Blocks Destroyed. = 8 Insufficient Memory; BX holds maximum possible request.
BX=Requested size in paragraphs.	= 9 Invalid Memory Block Address.

With this service you can shrink or expand memory blocks. A program might wish to temporarily give some memory to another program, for example. Again, if you are expanding, you can call this service with a huge request and find out what is possible to request.

INT 21H Service 4BH—Load or Execute a Program (EXEC)

Input

AH=4BH
DS:DX=ASCIIZ string with drive, pathname, filename.
ES:BX=Parameter Block Address (see below)
AL=0 → Load and execute the program
AL=3 → Load but create no PSP, don't run. (Overlay)

Output

No Carry →Success
Carry:
AL=1 Invalid Function Number
AL=2 File Not Found on Disk
AL=5 Access Denied
AL=8 Insufficient Memory for requested operation.
AL=10 Invalid Environment.
AL=11 Invalid Format.

Parameter Block for AL = 0:

Segment Address of environment to pass. (Word)
Address of command to put at PSP+80H (DWord)
Address of default FCB to put at PSP+5CH (DWord)
Address of 2nd default FCB to put at PSP+6CH (DWord)

Parameter Block for AL = 3:

Segment Address to load file at (Word).
Relocation Factor for image (Word).

This is a unique service call. With it you can load another program and run it, or load a program and not run it. (For overlays, part of your code stays on disk if it all can't fit in memory and can be read in later.) The environment is a set of strings indicating something about the operating environment of the PC. For example, if you set Verify on, a string VERIFY=ON will be found there. The default environment segment address is found at offset 2CH in your PSP; if you don't wish to change the environment, you can pass that value. The same thing happens—the subprogram "inherits" the parent's environment—if you leave this value zero.

Before loading another program into memory, however, you must free some memory for it with Service call 4AH. If you load another program in and run it, control returns to the instruction after INT 21H in the parent program when the subprogram is done.

INT 21H Service 4CH—Exit

Input

AH=4CH
AL=Binary return code.

This is the way to end your program if you want to communicate with a calling program. The binary return code in AL can be checked by the batch commands IF and ERRORLEVEL. In addition, a program that was loaded and run can send a return code to the parent program if it uses the next service, INT 21H Service 4DH.

INT 21H Service 4DH—Get Return Code of Subprocess

Input	Output
AH=4DH	AL=Binary return code from subprocess AH=0 If subprocess ended normally. 1 If subprocess ended with a ^Break. 2 If it ended with a critical device error. 3 If it ended with Service 31H.

With this service you can communicate with a subprocess. The binary return code loaded into AL in the last service, Service 4CH, can be retrieved with this call. In addition, AH tells you how the subprocess ended—normally, with a ^Break, with a critical device error, or with Service 31H.

INT 21H Service 4EH—Find First Matching File

Input	Output
DS:DX→ASCIIZ filestring. CX=Attribute to match. AH=4EH	Carry→AL=2 No Match Found. AL=18 No More Files. No Carry→DTA filled as follows: 21 Bytes reserved. 1 Byte Found Attribute. 2 Bytes File's Time. 2 Bytes File's Date. 2 Bytes Low Word of Size.

INT 21H Service 4EH continued

Input

Output

2 Bytes High Word of Size.
13 Bytes Name and Extension of found file in ASCIIZ form (NO pathname).

See Chapter 4.

INT 21H Service 4FH—Find Next Matching File

Input

Use Service 4EH BEFORE 4FH.
AH=4FH

Output

Carry→AL=18 No More Files.
No Carry→DTA filled as follows:
21 Bytes reserved.
1 Byte Found Attribute.
2 Bytes File's Time.
2 Bytes File's Date.
2 Bytes Low Word of Size.
2 Bytes High Word of Size.
13 Bytes Name and Extension of found file in ASCIIZ form (NO pathname).

See Chapter 4.

INT 21H Services 50H–53H Internal to DOS

These services are used only internally in DOS.

INT 21H Service 54H—Get Verify State

Input	Output
AH=54H	AL=0→ Verify is OFF. 1→ Verify is ON.

Service 54H checks whether disk writes are being verified or not. If Verify is on, AL will return 1; if it is off, it will return 0. Verify can be turned off and on with Service 2EH.

INT 21H Service 55H—Internal to DOS

This service is used only internally in DOS.

INT 21H Service 56H—Rename File

Input	Output
DS:DX=ASCIIZ filestring to be renamed.	No Carry→Success.
ES:DI=ASCIIZ filestring that holds the new name.	Carry→ AL=3 Path Not Found.
AH=56H	AL=5 Access Denied.
	AL=17 Not Same Device.

File CANNOT be renamed to another drive. See Chapter 4.

INT 21H Service 57H—Get or Set a File's Date and Time

Input	Output
BX=File Handle.	No Carry:
AL=0→Get Date & Time	CX returns time.
	DX returns date.
AL=1→Set Time to CX.	File's date and time set.
Set Date to DX.	
	Carry→AL=1 Invalid Function Number.
	6 Invalid Handle.

The time and date of a file are stored like this:

Time = 2,048×Hours + 32×Minutes + Seconds/2
Date = 512×(Year−1980) + 32×Month + Day

See Chapter 4.

INT 21H Service 58H—Internal to DOS

Service 58H is used only internally in DOS.

INT 21H Service 59H—Get Extended Error (DOS 3+)

This service is called when there has been an error—when a DOS service has set the carry flag, or AL returns 0FFH. In these cases, this service can return an extended error code, tell you where the error was physically (Locus), and suggest corrective action.

INT 21H Service 5AH—Create Unique File (DOS 3+)

Service 5AH will create a temporary file with a unique name. It returns a string with the file's name.

INT 21H Service 5BH—Create a New File (DOS 3+)

This service simply creates a new file, as does Service 3CH, except that Service 5BH will not create the new file if the same file name already exists.

INT 21H Service 5CH—Lock and Unlock Access to a File (DOS 3+)

When a file is shared, you can lock a certain number of bytes, or a byte range in a file with this service.

INT 21H Service 5E00H—Get Machine Name (DOS 3.10)

For the remainder of the DOS services, you must load the full word, here 5E00, into AX. This allows DOS to distinguish between, say, Services 5E00 and 5E02. This service, 5E00, returns with an ASCIIZ string filled with the computer's name—a 15-character string that can be set in PC networks.

INT 21H Service 5E02—Set Printer Setup (DOS 3.10)

This service is another network service, and makes it easy for a number of people to use the same printer by each sending it their own setup parameters.

INT 21H Service 5E03—Get Printer Setup (DOS 3.10)

This is the counterpart of the last service. Service 5E03 returns the setup parameters of a particular printer in the Network.

INT 21H Service 5F02—Get Redirection List Entry (DOS 3.10)

Service 5F02 monitors the data redirection that was done by the following service, 5F03.

INT 21H Service 5F03—Redirect Device (DOS 3.10)

This service defines the current directories and redirects printer output in a PC Network.

INT 21H Service 5F04H—Cancel Redirection (DOS 3.10)

Service 5F04 simply cancels a previously defined redirection of data.

INT 21H Service 62H—Get PSP (DOS 3+)

Since you can lose your way easily in a big network, this service returns the segment address of the PSP of the currently executing process.

ADDRESS VECTORS

The next three interrupt vectors actually hold important addresses instead of pointing to executable routines.

INT 22H—Terminate Address

This interrupt vector stores the address to which control will be transferred when your program is done. In general, you should let the DOS functions use this terminate address and not call it yourself.

INT 23H—Control Break Exit Address

This vector stores the address to which control will be transferred when you type ^Break. If you want to, you can write and install your own ^Break handler. This kind of handler can be ended with an IRET instruction, as usual.

INT 24H—Critical Error Handler

This vector holds the address to which control will be transferred if there is a critical error, such as trying to read from an empty diskette drive. You can intercept this error handler too and install your own handler. If the top bit of AH=0, the error was a disk error, otherwise this bit will be 1. Error codes can be found in the lower four bits of DI, set up like this:

0 = Diskette is write protected.
1 = Unknown Unit.
2 = The requested drive is not ready.
3 = Unknown command.
4 = Cyclic Redundancy Check error in the data.
5 = Bad request structure length.
6 = Seek Error.
7 = Media Type Unknown.
8 = Sector not found.
9 = The printer is out of paper.
A = Write Fault.
B = Read Fault.
C = General Failure.

If you just execute an IRET, DOS will take an action based on the contents of AL. If AL=0, the error will be ignored. If AL=1, the operation will be retried. If AL=2, the program will be terminated through INT 23H.

INT 25H—Absolute Disk Read

Input	Output
AL=Drive Number.	No Carry→ Success.
CX=Number of Sectors to Read.	Carry→AH=80H Disk didn't respond.
DX=First Logical Sector.	AH=40H Seek failed.
DS:BX=Buffer address.	AH=20H Controller failure.
	AH=10H Bad CRC error check.
	AH=08 DMA overrun.
	AH=04 Sector not found.
	AH=03 Write protect error.
	AH=02 Address Mark missing.
	AH=00 Error unknown.

Flags are left on stack after this INT call because information is returned in current flags. After you check the flags that were returned, make sure you do a POPF. Also, this INT destroys the contents of ALL registers. See Chapter 6.

INT 26H—Absolute Disk Write

Input

AL=Drive Number.
CX=Number of Sectors to Write.
DX=First Logical Sector.
DS:BX=Buffer address.

Output

No Carry→ Success.
Carry→AH=80H Disk didn't respond.
AH=40H Seek failed.
AH=20H Controller failure.
AH=10H Bad CRC error check.
AH=08 DMA overrun.
AH=04 Sector not found.
AH=03 Write protect error.
AH=02 Address Mark missing.
AH=00 Error unknown.

Flags are left on stack after this INT call because information is returned in current flags. After you check the flags that were returned, make sure you do a POPF. Also, this INT destroys the contents of ALL registers. See Chapter 6.

INT 27H—Terminate and Stay Resident

This is the interrupt used to make code memory-resident, one that we have seen before. You can make .COM files resident, but not .EXE files. If you need more space than 64K (the maximum for a .COM file), you can use INT 21H Service 31H.

To use this interrupt, simply set DS:DX to the address at which programs may be loaded in the future. That is, set DS:DX to the end of the program you want to keep in memory and add 1 to DX.

INTs 28H–2EH—Internal to DOS

These interrupts, 28H–2EH, are used by DOS only.

INT 2FH—Multiplex Interrupt

This interrupt sets up communication between two processes and can create queues. In practice, the use of this Interrupt is quite complex and beyond the scope of this book.

INT 30H–3FH—DOS Reserved

These interrupts are reserved for future DOS use.

INT 40H–5FH—Reserved

These interrupts are simply listed as reserved for future use.

INT 60H–67H—Reserved for User Software

Interrupts 60H–67H have been put aside for the user. Application programs may make use of these without fear of overlapping DOS or BIOS.

INTs 68H–7FH—Not Used

Interrupts 68H to 7FH are not used by any IBM software.

INTs 80H–85H—Reserved by BASIC

These are the interrupts BASIC uses.

INTs 86H–F0H—Used by BASIC Interpreter

When interpreted BASIC is running, it uses these interrupts for its own internal use.

INTs F1H-FFH—Not Used

These interrupts, the last in the machine, are not used.

That's it: We've accounted for every interrupt in the machine.

Appendix B

Device Drivers and IOCTL

INTRODUCTION

If you were very clever with hardware, you could build your own peripherals to the PC. For example, you might build your own (non-standard) diskette drive, or your own printer—even a laser printer. The question you would be faced with then is connecting it up to your computer so that the PC could run standard, commercial programs and still use your devices, even though the programs use DOS interrupts.

This used to be quite difficult, but possible, by intercepting interrupts and so on. Now IBM has made it much easier to connect a device using DOS itself by utilizing **Device Drivers**.

WHAT IS A DEVICE DRIVER?

A device driver handles the interface between the PC and the device you want to attach. What this means in the case of a disk drive, for example, is that DOS is able to treat your disk drive as it would one of its own. By requesting information from the device driver, DOS can find out how many sectors you are using on a track, whether you are using the standard IBM format (FAT followed by directory and so on), or whether you've changed a disk.

Block and Character Devices

There are two kinds of devices: block and character devices. Block devices are devices that work in blocks of data, in particular, disk drives. These types of devices are not given names, only letters. The first such device DOS loads from device drivers will be A, the next B, and so on.

Character devices, the other type, can have names. Typical character devices are CON, AUX, and PRN. If you put in a device driver, you can redefine any of these devices from the default simply by giving your devices these names (in the name field of the device header).

The Device Header

Device drivers are .EXE files that have a specific device driver header. To install a device driver named MYDISK, put the line DEVICE=MYDISK in your CONFIG.SYS file to be read at boot time. DOS will read in the file and examine the device header in it. Such a header looks like this in the beginning of the .EXE file:

DWORD	Pointer to next device header.
WORD	Attribute Word.
WORD	Pointer to strategy routine in this .EXE file.
WORD	Pointer to interrupt rountine in this .EXE file.
8 BYTES	Name or Unit field.

Pointer to Next Device Header

The first two words are an address (offset, segment) of the location of the next device driver header in this .EXE file. The last device driver header should have a −1 in this field so that DOS can chain all the devices together. If this is the only device in this .EXE file, use a −1 here.

The Attribute Word

The attribute word tells the PC something about your device: Whether it is a block or character device, whether it supports IBM format, or whether it should be treated as the standard input or output device. There is a breakdown of this word in Table B.1.

As you will see at the end of this appendix, if this device supports I/O control—IOCTL (DOS Service 44H)—you can do such things as change baud rate and so forth with this interrupt.

If a block device uses an IBM format, a FAT with a FAT byte, standard directory structure and so on, it should set bit 13 to zero. If this bit is zero, DOS will later send a request to the device driver to build a BIOS Parameter Block (BPB) for it, so that the BIOS calls will function. This parameter block (reviewed later) includes such information as the number of FATs, the number of root directory entries and so on.

Table B.1 The Attribute Word

Bit	Meaning
15	1 This device is a character device. 0 This device is a block device.
14	1 Supports the I/O control Int, IOCTL (DOS Service 44H) 0 Does NOT support IOCTL.
13	1 For block devices only: Non-IBM format. 0 For block devices only: IBM format.
11	1 Has removable media. 0 Does not support removable media.
10–4	Reserved.
3	1 This device is the clock device. 0 This device is NOT the clock device.
2	1 This device is the NUL device. 0 This device is NOT the NUL device.
1	1 This device is the standard output device. 0 This device is NOT the standard output device.
0	1 This device is the standard input device. 0 This device is NOT the standard input device.

If the device can handle "removable media" (diskettes or disk cartridges) the driver should set bit 11 in the device header to 1. In this case, DOS will be aware of the fact that you may have changed diskettes, and the new diskette may not even be the same format as the last one (for example, double-sided instead of single-sided). Whenever it needs to check if the disk has been changed, therefore, it reads in the first FAT sector and compares it to the old version.

Pointer to Strategy and Interrupt Routines in the .EXE file

The next word in the device header is the pointer to the strategy routine. This pointer is only a word long, so the strategy routine must start in the same segment as the device header itself. What is a strategy routine? Device drivers are broken up into two parts: one that queues and sets things up for requests (the strategy routine), and one that actually executes the request (the interrupt routine).

The way DOS asks the device to do something is with a device request. DOS calls the strategy routine first, and at that time ES:BX holds the address of the request header. The strategy routine stores the address of the request header on a queue. Immediately after the strategy routine returns, the interrupt routine is called (without parameters) so that the request can be fulfilled. The interrupt routine reads the request header address from the queue and performs the request. We will examine the structure of various requests shortly.

Name or Unit Field

Character devices can have names (CON, AUX, PRN, etc.), but block devices can only be "mapped" to drive letters: A, B, C, up to Z. For instance, if you want to install your device as the printer, give it the name PRN (left-hand justified and padded with spaces), making it the standard printer. To use it, you can then send data to the printer, or the device's handle (in this case, 4 is the handle for the standard printer). The standard devices all have handles already assigned: standard input device is 0, standard output is 1, standard error device is 2, standard AUX device (for serial data) is 3, and the standard printer is 4.

Block devices have unit numbers: drive A is unit 1, drive B is unit 2 and so on. DOS itself fills in the unit number here for block devices after you have filled its "INIT" request, so you don't put any name for the block device in this field at all. To reach this drive, you have to specify the correct drive number when using a system interrupt.

THE REQUEST HEADER

All requests have the same header. The device driver learns what it is supposed to do—initialize, I/O, etc—by the command code in the request header. Here is the request header's format:

BYTE	Length of request header and data to follow.
BYTE	Block devices: Unit Code.
BYTE	Command code—tells the device what to do.
WORD	Status (returned by device)
8 BYTES	Reserved.
: :	Additional data as needed for the specific request.

Length of Request Header and Data to Follow

This byte is self-explanatory. It tells the device driver how long the request header and data are together so that, if necessary, the device driver can copy it for its own use.

Block Devices: Unit Code

Block devices can have several subunits. This means that one device driver can be responsible for several disk drives. The number of drives the driver addresses is returned to DOS when DOS initializes the driver (with an INIT request). The "subunit" (drive number) that this request is for is stored in this byte.

Command Code

The one-byte command code tells the driver what the device is supposed to do. In Table B.2 are some values for the command code; we will not cover all possible command codes in this discussion (they are all listed in the *DOS Technical Reference Manual*).

Table B.2 Command Codes

Value	Meaning
0	INIT—initialize the device.
1	Media Check for Block devices (Has the disk been changed?)
2	Make a BPB—BIOS Parameter Block—so the BIOS calls will work.
3	IOCTL Input (See below).
4	Input—do a read.
8	Output—write data.
9	Output with verify.
12	IOCTL Output (See below).

Status Word

The status word is returned by the device to DOS. Bit 15 of this word is set if there was an error of some type in performing the request. If there was an error, the bottom byte of this word holds the error code so that DOS will know what's going on. Some error codes are shown in Table B.3.

Table B.3 Error Codes

Code	Meaning
00	Write Protect Attempt.
02	Device Not Ready.
04	CRC Error.
06	Seek Error.
08	Sector Not Found.
09	Printer out of Paper.
0C	General Failure.
0F	Invalid Disk Change.

From the type of error returned, DOS can treat your device like any normal device and inform the user that there has been an error of a specific type. This is a powerful utility—DOS is treating your disk drive as it would any IBM-standard drive.

Bit 9 in the status word is the busy bit. If a request was made and the device is busy, it can set this bit. Bit 8 is the "done" bit. If it is set to 1, the operation requested by this request header was completed successfully.

The Rest of the Request Header

The next 8 bytes of the request header are reserved for DOS's use. At the end, the request header is followed by the data that is needed to fill the request. For example, if the request header is requesting an I/O operation, one of the data items that will follow the request header is the address of the data buffer to be used.

USING REQUESTS

Let's work through a number of requests to see what they look like. Here is what the device driver for an Init looks like:

13 BYTE	Request header
BYTE	Number of units (Set by block devices only).
DWORD	End of memory-resident code.
DWORD	Pointer to BPB (BIOS parameter block).
BYTE	Drive number (DOS 3+).

When the device is first installed, DOS sends an INIT request. The device driver performs whatever initialization is needed in the device, and then sets a number of bytes in the request area. In particular, it sets the number of units (drives) it is responsible for if it is a block device, the location of the top of the code it wants to keep memory-resident so that initialization code can be cut off after use, the status word in the request header, and a pointer to an appropriate BIOS Parameter Block.

The BPB looks like this:

WORD	Bytes per sector.
BYTE	Sectors per cluster.
WORD	Number of reserved sectors (for partitioning).
BYTE	Number of FATs.
WORD	Number of root directory entries.
WORD	Total number of sectors in this device.
BYTE	Media descriptor (see below).
WORD	FAT length in sectors.

The media descriptor byte always has bits 3–7 set to 1, and bit 2 is set to 1 if the medium is removable. Bit 1 is set if the medium is 8 sector, and bit 0 is set if the medium is two-sided.

Under DOS 3+, DOS will fill in the drive letter of the first drive in the last field of the request.

I/O Requests

For I/O, the request looks like this:

13 BYTE	Request header
BYTE	Media descriptor byte
DWORD	Transfer address—the location of the buffer.
WORD	Number of bytes or sectors.
WORD	Starting sector number.
DWORD	DOS 3+: Pointer to volume identification if error code 0FH is returned.

The command code in the request header tells the device whether input or output is required. For block devices, I/O is specified in sectors, for character devices, in bytes. The number of bytes or sectors requested is found from the word above, and the device is responsible for setting that word to the number of actual bytes or sectors read or written.

The location of the buffer, or data transfer address, is given in the request as well, as is the starting sector number. (Although this has no meaning for character devices.) After the device is finished, it must set the status word in the request header.

If your device specifies (in the device header) that it can support IOCTL control, some of the I/O requests it receives may actually be IOCTL requests. For example, if the command code specifies an IOCTL read or IOCTL write, then DS:DX is pointing to a number of bytes that should be read from or written to the device's control channel. These bytes can be in your own format, as long as your device understands them. Any time your program wants to change the baud rate of a device, it can send along a control string to the device in this manner.

IOCTL—INT 21H SERVICE 44H

If your device can support it, you can control it through the use of DOS INT 21H, Service 44H, I/O control or IOCTL. With IOCTL, you can change the nature of the I/O undertaken by the device. For example, you can do resets or set parity bits. This service sends information to the device that is not for I/O, but rather controls the I/O that does occur.

As mentioned, IOCTL is used to send control strings that the device can interpret to its "control channel." Here is the way the registers are set for an IOCTL call:

Register	Value
AH	44H
DS:DX	Data Buffer
CX	Byte Count (To be read or written).
BX	File or Device Handle.
BL	Drive Number.
AL	Function Value.

Here are some possible function values:

AL	Meaning
0	Get Device information and return it in DX.
1	Set Device information from DX.
2	Read CX bytes from DS:DX into device control channel.
3	Write CX bytes from device control channel into buffer at DS:DX.
4	Use drive number in BL and execute function 2.
5	Use drive number in BL and execute function 3.

If your program, using IOCTL, requests Function 0 of a device that you have installed with a device driver, DOS can take the information about the device from the device header and code it in the DX register. This coded information includes such information as whether or not this device is the clock, null, or console output device, and whether or not this device can process control strings under functions 2 and 3. DOS knows whether or not the device can process control strings by examining bit 14 of the attribute byte in the device header. If the answer is yes, then your program can send control strings to the device by using IOCTL. When the strategy routine receives this request, it knows that the string waiting at address DS:DX is a control string, and not just normal data by checking the command code in the request header. Command code 3 means that CX bytes should be read from the buffer at DS:DX and written to the control channel, and command code 12 means that CX bytes should be written to the buffer from the control channel. This way, you can communicate with your device.

For character devices, you should use device handles and Functions 2 and 3 to control your device; for block devices, which are mapped to drive letters, use Functions 4 and 5, which specify drive numbers in BL.

Appendix C
About the Diskette

INTRODUCTION

This diskette contains both the .ASM and .COM versions of all the end-of-chapter examples in *Advanced Assembly Language for the IBM PC*. In the order they appear in both the book and on the diskette, these programs are: LOCK, UNLOCK, KEEPER, DIREX, PHOTO, CACHE, and LOCATE. In general, the use of these programs is kept straightforward, making the programs easy to use. Here is an overview of each program.

LOCK AND UNLOCK

This pair of programs lets you encrypt files with medium security (a determined specialist was able to break the code in about 28 hours of steady effort). To use them to lock a file named FILE.EXT, just type "LOCK FILE.EXT FILE.SBL", where FILE.SBL will be the scrambled version of the file. If you do not supply a second file name, LOCK will name the file FILE.LOC.

LOCK will ask you to type a pass-phrase. Once you do, the file will be encoded from a key made from the ASCII characters in the phrase. To decode the file, type "UNLOCK FILE.SBL FILE.EXT", and FILE.EXT will be regenerated. Be sure you type the SAME pass-phrase.

It is possible to double the security by encoding an already-encoded file a second time, but make sure to use the pass-phrases in reverse order of application.

KEEPER

KEEPER stores your DOS commands and lets you recall them. As KEEPER.ASM is set up on the diskette, it uses ^N as a trigger key. To install KEEPER, just run KEEPER.COM. If you want to recall some previous DOS command, type a ^N. A reverse-video window will appear on the screen with the last eight DOS commands. Using the cursor keys, you can make the command you want to recall blink. When you type another ^N, the command is re-entered at DOS level and the window disappears. If you don't want to choose any of the available commands, leave the blinking cursor on the bottom line and type ^N. No DOS command will be entered.

If you want to use a trigger key other than ^N, enter the scan and ASCII codes of your trigger key into KEEPER.ASM in the one location indicated and reassemble KEEPER.

DIREX

This utility is a directory manager. It has seven commands, which appear on the bottom of the screen for reference. The rest of the screen is filled with the file names of the current subdirectory. To use DIREX, move the reverse-video cursor that highlights file names around the screen with the cursor keys. You can select a number of files and perform an operation on them en masse (protecting, deleting, copying, etc.). To mark a file for further work, move the cursor to their name and press the space bar. The file name will stay highlighted when you move the cursor away. This file has now been marked. To unmark a file, move the cursor to its name and press the space bar again.

After you have marked the files, you can delete them all at once with the D command, protect them as read-only with P, unprotect them with U, or copy them to a new path with C. When you press C, DIREX asks you for the path name the files are to be copied to (e.g., B: or C:\ARCHIVE). You can work on the files in any subdirectory by using the N, or new directory command. When you press N, DIREX will ask you for a new path name to make the default. To quit, use Q.

PHOTO

This utility is a small screen manager. It is a memory-resident program that allows you to capture screens for later use, or to recall a few select screens that you have created yourself. For example, if you are assembling a file and there are some errors, you can save the screen (with ^N as PHOTO.COM is set up), edit the file, and then, while still in your editor, recall the screenful of errors with another key (^F as PHOTO.COM is set up). Once the recalled screen is displayed, touching any key restores the screen to its original condition (i.e., before you pushed ^N).

You can also install up to three of your own screens in memory, to be recalled with other control characters (^A, ^B, and ^C as PHOTO.COM is set up). When PHOTO.COM is run, it searches for the three files A.DAT, B.DAT, and C.DAT, in that order. Each file should be exactly 2,000 bytes long. If they are not there, PHOTO will still run without problem. If, however, they are there, they are loaded into memory to be recalled at will.

On this diskette is a sample file, A.DAT, with a screenful of ASCII codes that can be recalled at any time (by pressing ^A). To install your own trigger keys, simply enter the correct scan and ASCII codes as marked in PHOTO.ASM and reassemble the program.

CACHE

This program is a write-through disk cache system. It stores the most frequently used sectors in memory. The next time these sectors are read by some program, CACHE supplies them from memory instead of reading them from the disk. It is a "write-through" cache because as sectors get written, their copies in memory are updated as well.

This system is different from the buffers DOS uses, since the buffers are flushed when a program exits. With CACHE, you can go through the edit, assemble, and link cycle many times and save time each time you do since CACHE always stays in memory.

As CACHE.COM is set up, it will store up to 64 sectors in memory. You can change this by changing the one marked location in CACHE.ASM (the minimum is 24 and the maximum is 124).

LOCATE

LOCATE tries to find character strings in files. If you type "LOCATE This is a test.", LOCATE will try to find the character string in all the files in the current subdirectory. If a match is made (LOCATE is case-sensitive), the name of the file and the line in which the match was found are both printed out.

Besides searching the current subdirectory, you can have LOCATE search other directories as you require. To do this, place a file named PATH.DAT in the main directory of the current disk. In this file, place the names of the other paths you want LOCATE to search. Terminate each path name, even the last one, with a ‹cr› ‹lf›. Here is a sample PATH.DAT:

```
A:
\ARCHIVE
\RECORDS
```

LOCATE will read in PATH.DAT and search all the files in those paths for the specified string as well.

Index

D

E

F

G

H

I

J

K

L

M

N

O

P

R

S

About the Author

Steven Holzner earned his BS degree at MIT and recently completed a Ph.D. at Cornell, where he is a lecturer in physics. He has travelled to over 30 countries, lived for a year each in Hong Kong and Hawaii, and spends summers in Austria. He is a contributing editor for *PC Magazine* and part owner in a 100-acre estate in New York State.